Practical Business Process Modeling and Analysis

Design and optimize business processes incrementally for AI transformation using BPMN

Jim Sinur

Zbigniew Misiak

BJ Biernatowski

‹packt›

Practical Business Process Modeling and Analysis

Portfolio Director: Pavan Ramchandani

Program Manager: Divij Kotian

Content Engineer: Rounak Kulkarni

Technical Editor: Vidhisha Patidar

Copy Editor: Safis Editing

Proofreader: Rounak Kulkarni

Indexer: Pratik Shirodkar

Production Designer: Vijay Kamble

Relationship Lead: Alok Dhuri

Growth Lead: Nivedita Singh

First published: August 2025

Production reference: 1310725

Published by Packt Publishing Ltd.

Grosvenor House

11 St Paul's Square

Birmingham

B3 1RB, UK.

ISBN 978-1-80512-674-4

www.packtpub.com

This book is dedicated to my parents, who taught me values that have helped me throughout my life.

– Jim Sinur

I dedicate this book to Kasia (my wife) and Ewa (my daughter). Life with you is a gift from God!

– Zbigniew Misiak

I dedicate this book to my parents—thank you for your unwavering love and inspiring strength; my wife—you are my steadfast rock and loving anchor; and my children—may you lead with kindness and humanity in a world of autonomous machines.

– BJ Biernatowski

Foreword

We are living in an era where AI and digitalization are redefining the rules of the business game. Automation is no longer optional; it is a strategic necessity. Yet, as Bill Gates wisely pointed out: "*The first rule of any technology used in a business is that automation applied to an efficient operation will magnify the efficiency. The second is that automation applied to an inefficient operation will magnify the inefficiency*." In this context, business process modeling and analysis have become essential pillars for successful digital transformation.

This book, *Practical Business Process Modeling and Analysis*, arrives at a critical moment. Zbigniew Misiak, BJ Biernatowski, and Jim Sinur bring together a unique blend of practical experience, deep technical knowledge, and strategic vision. Zbigniew, widely known for his work as a BPM trainer and advocate through platforms such as BPM Tips and Udemy, has helped thousands of professionals understand the language and value of BPMN. BJ, in turn, enriches this perspective with his hands-on experience in major enterprise implementations and his direct involvement with platforms such as Microsoft Power Platform, K2, and Pega. Finally, Jim, one of the most influential voices in digital transformation and intelligent automation, provides the conceptual framework that binds the entire narrative together.

This is not merely a technical manual or academic guide—it is a roadmap, grounded in real-world use cases, best practices, and lessons learned from diverse business environments. The authors go beyond the "what" and "how" to also explain the "why," enabling you to tailor the content to your specific transformation challenges.

In a world where tools such as RPA, Make, Power Automate, and AI-based GPTs empower the automation of small workflows, it is vital not to bypass the process improvement phase prior to automation. Modeling a process flow in BPMN allows us to visualize the workflow, uncover redundancies and inefficiencies, identify areas for improvement, and decide which activities are suitable for automation through RPA or AI.

Throughout its chapters, you will find clear answers to some of the most pressing questions faced during any process improvement or redesign initiative: How can we identify the processes with the greatest impact? What level of detail is appropriate in our models? How do we build a sustainable process architecture? What role do modern tools such as low-code platforms, process mining, and AI play?

Having worked for more than two decades to promote and professionalize the BPM discipline across Ibero-America and Europe, I can confidently state that this book is an indispensable resource, both for those new to the world of process analysis and for seasoned professionals looking to stay abreast of the latest trends. More importantly, it offers an integrated vision that bridges technique and strategy, modeling and execution, theory, and practice.

If you are a professional involved in your organization's digital transformation—be it as an analyst, process architect, change leader, or citizen developer—this book will be your trusted guide. It will help you structure your initiatives, avoid costly mistakes, and lay the groundwork for a sustainable and agile future.

Thank you, Zbigniew, BJ, and Jim, for delivering a work that educates, inspires, and empowers. And thank you, the reader, for taking on the commitment to transform not just your processes, but the way your organization delivers value.

Pedro Robledo

Regional Director – ABPMP International

Contributors

About the authors

Jim Sinur is an independent thought leader in applying **digital business platforms (DBPs)**, **customer experience/journeys (CEJM)**, **business process management (BPM)**, **automation (RPA)**, low-code, advanced data management, and decision management at the edge applied to business outcomes. His research and areas of personal experience focus on automation and customer excellence, intelligent business processes, business modeling, business process management technologies, process collaboration for knowledge workers, process intelligence/optimization, data management, AI, IoT, and leveraging business applications in processes. Jim is also one of the authors of *BPM: The Next Wave*.

I want to thank all the customers and vendors I have had the pleasure of interacting with during my tenure at Gartner. Solving business processes and customer experience challenges together was a privilege.

Zbigniew Misiak is a BPM consultant with over 15 years of experience. He is currently employed at BOC Group as a senior consultant and helps customers introduce BPM as a management method and ADONIS as a process management tool. He is also a member of several Object Management Group Task Forces and the BPMN Model Interchange Working Group. Zbigniew is also a BPM trainer, both at BOC and on Udemy, where his courses about process modeling with BPMN help thousands of students worldwide. He runs a blog called *BPM Tips*.

I would like to thank my wife, Kasia, and daughter, Ewa, for their support, motivation, and feedback for the chapters I wrote.

BJ and Jim, writing this book with you was an honor! Thank you! A huge shoutout to Pedro for the Foreword.

Special thanks to the people who helped shape this book by reading my chapters and providing valuable contributions: Tony Benedict, Roger Burlton, Denis Gagné, Harald Kühn, Madison Lundquist, Serge Schiltz, Filip Stachecki, Roger Tregear, and Roland Woldt. Thank you very much for finding errors, suggesting improvements, answering my questions, and sharing your expertise!

This book is a summary of what I learned about process management and modeling as a consultant, trainer, and blogger.

I am very grateful for all the discussions and conversations about processes with my colleagues from BOC Group, BPMN MIWG, the team updating the OCEB exam, customers, students, and people participating in posts on my blog, as well as the readers. Also, this book owes a lot to people who reviewed my previous book about process modeling, written in Polish.

Finally, big thanks to the Packt team!

BJ Biernatowski is a digital transformation leader specializing in AI-driven process optimization, intelligent automation, and global operations. He has spearheaded large-scale initiatives at Microsoft, Amazon, UnitedHealth Group, and Nordstrom, consistently delivering measurable impact. His expertise spans process modeling, AI-assisted decision-making, and integrating emerging technologies across complex ecosystems.

Passionate about blending strategy with innovation, BJ designs scalable systems that accelerate agility and long-term competitiveness. He co-authored this book to empower practitioners with next-gen process models that drive sustainable transformation.

This book is what I wish I'd had 20 years ago, when I unexpectedly began my BPM journey. It's the product of hard-won insights, long hours, and a whole lot of growth. I'm deeply grateful to our content engineers, Rounak Kulkarni and Nithya Sadanandan, and to the entire Packt team for their steady support throughout the publishing process. A heartfelt thank you to my exceptional co-authors, Jim and Zbigniew, for your expertise, generosity, and meaningful contributions, and to Pedro for the wonderful Foreword. It's been an honor to work alongside you. To Mark Smith, Wayne Padcayan, Jay Olvey, Matt Jennings, Kristine MacRae, Igor Jericevich, and Joy Mookerji: your guidance and editorial insight have helped shape not only this book, but my thinking as a professional. I've been inspired by your accomplishments. My journey has been shaped by grit and growth, and I've come to believe in the power of perseverance. The strength to keep going, even when the path isn't clear. Each person's route is unique, but I hope that this book helps you move forward with clarity and purpose.

About the reviewers

Wayne Padcayan is a senior enterprise business and process architect and consultant with over 20 years of experience. In his current role, he helps companies align technology with their business strategy, process, and culture.

Mark Smith is a **Chief Development Officer** (CDO) at Cloud Lighthouse and crafts trustworthy AI strategies that scale. For 20 years, he has guided enterprises through technology waves, spotting gaps before they become roadblocks and translating big ideas into executable roadmaps. His focus today is singular: to de-risk and accelerate generative AI adoption in highly regulated environments.

Other contributors

We extend our heartfelt gratitude to the thought leaders and expert practitioners whose invaluable insights, time, and expertise have influenced the direction and impact of this project. Their generous contributions have been instrumental to our progress, and we sincerely appreciate their ongoing support:

- Betty-Jo Almond (https://www.linkedin.com/in/betty-jo-almond-414b2115b/)
- Tony Benedict (https://www.linkedin.com/in/tbenedict/)
- Roger Burlton (https://www.linkedin.com/in/roger-burlton-298164/)
- Denis Gagné (https://www.linkedin.com/in/denisgagne/)
- Matt Jennings (https://www.linkedin.com/in/matthewpjennings/)
- Igor Jericevich (https://www.linkedin.com/in/igorjeri/)
- Harald Kühn (https://www.linkedin.com/in/haraldkuehn/)
- Madison Lundquist (https://www.linkedin.com/in/madisonlundquist/)
- Kristine MacRae (https://www.linkedin.com/in/kristinemacrae/)
- Marie-Claude Milot (https://www.linkedin.com/in/marie-claude-milot-1387293/)
- Joy Mookerji (https://www.linkedin.com/in/joy-mookerji-97231a1/)
- Jay Olvey (https://www.linkedin.com/in/jay-olvey/)
- Serge Schiltz (https://www.linkedin.com/in/schiltzs/)
- Jaideep Sethiya (https://www.linkedin.com/in/jaideepjdsethiya/)
- Filip Stachecki (https://www.linkedin.com/in/fstachecki/)
- Roger Tregear (https://www.linkedin.com/in/rogertregear/)
- Roland Woldt (https://www.linkedin.com/in/rolandwoldt/)

Table of Contents

2

Pillars of a Successful Digital Transformation   45

3

The Wheel of BPM Driving Your Competitive Advantage   77

4

Long-Term Trends and the Impact on Your Job   125

5

Business Process 101   149

9

Advanced BPMN   293

10

Measuring the Business Value of Process Transformation   333

11

A Few Final Thoughts   369

Index   381

Other Books You May Enjoy   392

Preface

In a business landscape defined by relentless speed and digital complexity, the ability to model and analyze processes isn't optional; it's essential. *Practical Business Process Modeling and Analysis* distills the foundational knowledge every aspiring change agent needs to navigate transformation with confidence and clarity. Drawing on decades of global experience advising Fortune 500 companies, the authors provide practical insights that help you sidestep costly mistakes and bolster sponsor credibility while protecting your career trajectory.

With the pace of business change in 2025 accelerating beyond most organizations' capacity to respond, leaders face a growing mismatch between strategic ambition and executional readiness. Economic pressures demand agility, human dynamics complicate transformation, and the rise of AI-powered low-code tools introduces opportunities and risks that can reshape entire business units. CFOs and CTOs are racing to digitize—but success depends on more than technology. It requires people who understand how to analyze, model, and evolve business processes in real time.

Yet, while businesses can easily source developers, Six Sigma experts, and project managers, few professionals possess the hybrid skill set needed to incubate and support long-term digital programs. Why? Because the ecosystem of process analysis tools evolved in silos, remained under-recognized by mainstream media, and was under-taught in business schools, with notable exceptions such as Widener University (Chester, Pennsylvania, USA), the Warsaw School of Economics (Warsaw, Poland), and UNIR (La Rioja, Spain). Even rigorous programs at the Technical University of Eindhoven (Eindhoven, Netherlands) and QUT (Brisbane, Australia) offer depth but rarely prepare professionals to contribute as agile change agents on day one.

This book was written to fill that gap.

We speak to business professionals—not as theorists, but as practitioners who understand that transformation lives in nuance, speed, and systems thinking. Whether you become a software vendor, join a consulting firm, enroll in an academic program, self-educate online, or convince your boss to invest in training, you'll face trade-offs: vendor partiality, theoretical overload, or practical shallow dives. The truth is, there's no perfect path into this domain—but there is a pragmatic one.

We offer a blended approach that synthesizes strategic insight with hands-on experience. You'll learn how to deconstruct process artwork into executable logic, demystify modeling notations such as **Business Process Model and Notation (BPMN)**, and communicate the benefits of visualization without corporate jargon. You'll hear from global experts, including Jim Sinur, a leading voice in digital business, and see how shadow business architects are driving real change, often without formal credentials.

By the end of this book, you'll understand the actual value of business and process architecture, have learned how to build transformation credibility, and have unlocked ways to contribute meaningfully to your company's future. Whether you spend three days in a workshop in Boston, London, Hyderabad, or Warsaw or journey through these chapters, you'll emerge ready to act.

Who this book is for

This book is for business professionals, decision-makers, and participants in a digital change initiative leading to the digitization of your company's critical business processes. Basic skills with the Microsoft Office suite are required.

What this book covers

Chapter 1, Winning at Digital Transformation with Process Modeling, offers a strategic deep dive into process modeling as a cornerstone of **digital transformation (DTX)**. It explores how modeling not only enhances process efficiency but also serves as a planning and auditing tool that evolves alongside emerging business needs. With insights from **business process management (BPM)** pioneer Jim Sinur, it guides readers through the types, benefits, and future trajectory of process modeling, especially its growing synergy with AI, analytics, and adaptive technologies. Overall, the chapter sets the stage for understanding how visual modeling supports intelligent, goal-driven, and resilient enterprise systems.

Chapter 2, Pillars of a Successful Digital Transformation, uncovers the strategic foundations of DTX, emphasizing that success hinges not on technology alone, but on adaptable processes, empowered teams, and a clear vision. Through candid reflection and practical frameworks, it introduces seven transformation pillars, from scalable COEs to change management, that align technology with business goals. By exploring diverse triggers for change and common pitfalls, it guides decision-makers in crafting resilient, purpose-driven strategies for long-term impact.

Chapter 3, The Wheel of BPM Driving Your Competitive Advantage, introduces the "wheel of BPM" as a strategic framework for launching and sustaining BPM transformations. It explores how BPM drives enterprise-wide digital change by empowering internal teams, aligning with strategic goals, and fostering a culture of continuous improvement. By examining inflection points, governance models, and real-world case studies, it equips readers with actionable guidance to build resilient, scalable, and people-centric transformation programs—anchored not in software alone, but in thoughtful planning, cross-functional collaboration, and long-term vision.

Chapter 4, Long-Term Trends and the Impact on Your Job, examines the profound impact of long-term DTX trends on careers, workplace dynamics, and learning strategies. As technology evolves exponentially, professionals must adapt through continuous learning and skill evolution. The author highlights BPM as a cornerstone for building resilient organizations, encouraging a vendor-independent approach that prioritizes agility and strategic alignment. Central to this transformation is a learning mindset. The chapter introduces a practical framework consisting of curiosity, exploration, feedback, and reflection. By weaving together strategic insight, technical foundations, and accessible learning paths, this chapter sets the tone for a more inclusive, adaptable, and intelligently automated workplace.

Chapter 5, Business Process 101, introduces BPM as a key driver of organizational value creation. It advocates for a holistic, ecosystem-based view of processes, beyond simple task sequences, to include governance, dependencies, and strategic alignment. Readers are guided through the essentials of process modeling: its scenarios, tools, and audiences. From basic frameworks such as SIPOC and IGOE to modeling states (*as is* versus *to be*) and use cases (improvement, automation, and documentation), the chapter empowers professionals to design effective, readable, and purposeful models. It also explores modeling roles, sources of process knowledge, and modeling tools from diagramming apps to enterprise-grade suites. Ultimately, the chapter lays the groundwork for process thinking, offering a practical, adaptable roadmap to visualize, communicate, and improve processes across modern organizations.

Chapter 6, Establishing Process Architecture, introduces the concept of process architecture as a strategic blueprint for understanding, managing, and improving organizational processes. It explains how interconnected processes form value chains and why a simple list or set of diagrams isn't enough. By categorizing processes (management, core, and support) and establishing hierarchical models, organizations gain clarity on how work flows, who owns what, and how changes impact the broader system. It showcases both standardized approaches (such as APQC's PCF) and custom-built architectures, emphasizing stakeholder alignment, strategy integration, and visual navigation. The chapter also highlights how enriched process attributes—goals, KPIs, IT systems, and risks—empower smarter decision-making for optimization, automation, and transformation. Ultimately, process architecture emerges as a critical foundation for achieving maturity in BPM and enabling agile, cross-functional collaboration across the enterprise.

Chapter 7, Process Modeling Notations, traces the evolution of process modeling notations, highlighting the strengths and limitations of various approaches: from early ASME flowcharts to complex frameworks such as IDEF, LOVEM, UML, and EPC. It positions BPMN as the convergence of decades of modeling innovations, offering a standardized visual language for diverse stakeholders. Readers learn how BPMN balances simplicity with expressive power, supports automation through XML-based data exchange, and integrates key elements such as tasks, events, gateways, pools, and data objects. By unpacking BPMN's roots and its design philosophy, the chapter equips readers to interpret models with confidence, communicate across disciplines, and lay a foundation for intelligent process management in the digital age.

Chapter 8, BPMN – What You Need to Know, demystifies BPMN, making it accessible and practical for professionals seeking clarity in process design and communication. It introduces the key components of BPMN diagrams, including events, activities, gateways, swimlanes, artifacts, and data objects. With real-world examples such as complaint-handling processes, readers learn how to interpret and construct BPMN visuals, differentiate modeling styles, and avoid common pitfalls through best practices and anti-patterns. The chapter emphasizes BPMN's power not just as a modeling tool but as a medium for collaboration, automation, and thoughtful process improvement. Whether you're mapping simple sequences or complex conditional flows, this chapter lays the groundwork for intelligent, readable, and impactful process diagrams.

Chapter 9, Advanced BPMN, provides an overview of more advanced BPMN concepts that are helpful for technical modeling. It introduces the concept of handling various situations with events and shows in practice how and when to use additional types of events, tasks, sub-processes, and gateways. Finally, it also shows how BPMN can be extended with other standards or with attributes supporting common business scenarios. It also briefly covers standards such as **Decision Model and Notation (DMN)** and **Case Management Model and Notation (CMMN)**, which may be useful, for example, for process automation.

Chapter 10, Measuring the Business Value of Process Transformation, offers a comprehensive guide to measuring business value in process transformation. It underscores that digital initiatives only succeed when value is clearly demonstrated—through improved efficiency, reduced costs, empowered teams, and tangible ROI. Readers will learn how to build business cases using structured frameworks such as **Business Value Assessment (BVA)**, Balanced Scorecard, Lean, Six Sigma, and analyst-driven methodologies such as Forrester TEI. Packed with real-world case studies and examples, from citizen developer wins at Nordstrom to AI-driven logistics, the chapter equips professionals to quantify benefits across financial, operational, customer, and employee dimensions. It introduces tools to forecast value early, manage risks, and align transformation efforts with strategic objectives.

Chapter 11, A Few Final Thoughts, distills the book's insights into one cohesive guide for driving value through BPM. It revisits the core principles, such as modeling for clarity, enabling collaboration, and supporting DTX, and extends them into future-ready practices. Readers are encouraged to build process architectures, embrace standards such as BPMN, and measure outcomes through strategic KPIs. More than just a recap, the chapter charts your next steps: advancing skills in BPM; exploring adjacent domains, such as Lean, Six Sigma, and AI automation; and engaging with professional communities. It highlights the rising importance of process-centric thinking in an AI-driven workplace and offers practical advice for sustaining BPM programs—from governance and playbooks to tools and talent strategy.

To get the most out of this book

Resources related to the book are updated in this book's dedicated GitHub repository: `https://github.com/PacktPublishing/Practical-Business-Process-Modeling-and-Analysis`.

To familiarize yourself with the common terms and their definitions related to this topic, refer to the *Glossary* in the book's GitHub repository.

Conventions used

> **Tips or important notes**
> Appear like this.

Get in touch

Feedback from our readers is always welcome.

General feedback: If you have questions about any aspect of this book, email us at customercare@packtpub.com and mention the book title in the subject of your message.

Errata: Although we have taken every care to ensure the accuracy of our content, mistakes do happen. If you have found a mistake in this book, we would be grateful if you would report this to us. Please visit www.packtpub.com/support/errata and fill in the form.

Piracy: If you come across any illegal copies of our works in any form on the internet, we would be grateful if you would provide us with the location address or website name. Please contact us at copyright@packt.com with a link to the material.

If you are interested in becoming an author: If there is a topic that you have expertise in and you are interested in either writing or contributing to a book, please visit authors.packtpub.com.

Share Your Thoughts

Once you've read *Practical Business Process Modeling and Analysis*, we'd love to hear your thoughts! Scan the QR code below to go straight to the Amazon review page for this book and share your feedback.

https://packt.link/r/1805126741

Your review is important to us and the tech community and will help us make sure we're delivering excellent quality content.

Your Book Comes with Exclusive Perks – Here's How to Unlock Them

Unlock this book's exclusive benefits now

UNLOCK NOW

Scan this QR code or go to `packtpub.com/unlock`, then search this book by name. Ensure it's the correct edition.

Note: Have your purchase invoice ready before you start.

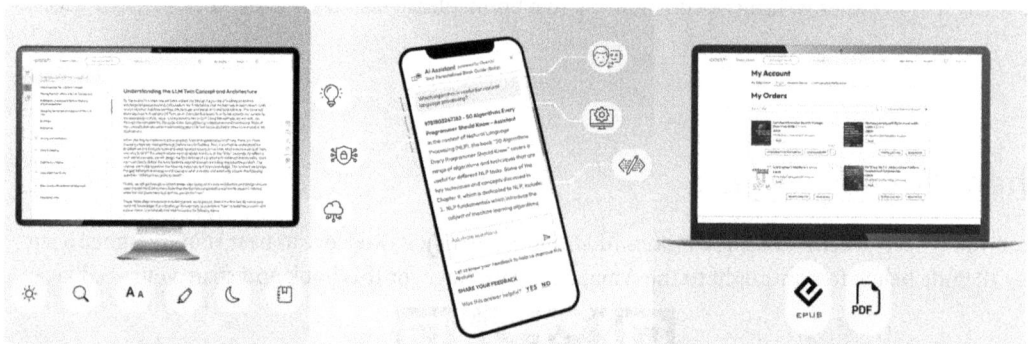

Enhanced reading experience with our next-gen reader:

- **Multi-device progress sync**: Learn from any device with seamless progress sync.

- **Highlighting and notetaking**: Turn your reading into lasting knowledge.

- **Bookmarking**: Revisit your most important learnings anytime.

- **Dark mode**: Focus with minimal eye strain by switching to dark or sepia mode.

Learn smarter using our AI assistant (Beta):

- **Summarize it**: Summarize key sections or an entire chapter.

- **AI code explainers**: In the next-gen Packt Reader, click the **Explain** button above each code block for AI-powered code explanations.

> **Note:**
> *The AI assistant is part of the next-gen Packt Reader and is still in beta.*

Learn anytime, anywhere:

Access your content offline with DRM-free PDF and ePub versions—compatible with your favorite e-readers.

Unlock your Book's Exclusive Benefits

Your copy of this book comes with the following exclusive benefits:

- Next-gen Packt Reader

- AI assistant (beta)

- DRM-free PDF/ePub downloads

Use the following guide to unlock them if you haven't already. The process takes just a few minutes and needs to be done only once.

How to unlock these benefits in three easy steps

Step 1

Have your purchase invoice for this book ready, as you'll need it in *Step 3*. If you received a physical invoice, scan it on your phone and have it ready as either a PDF, JPG, or PNG.

For more help on finding your invoice, visit `https://www.packtpub.com/unlock-benefits/help`.

> **Note**
> Did you buy this book directly from Packt? You don't need an invoice. After completing *Step 2*, you can jump straight to your exclusive content.

Step 2

Scan this QR code or go to `packtpub.com/unlock`.

On the page that opens (which will look similar to *Figure 0.1* if you're on desktop), search for this book by name. Make sure you select the correct edition.

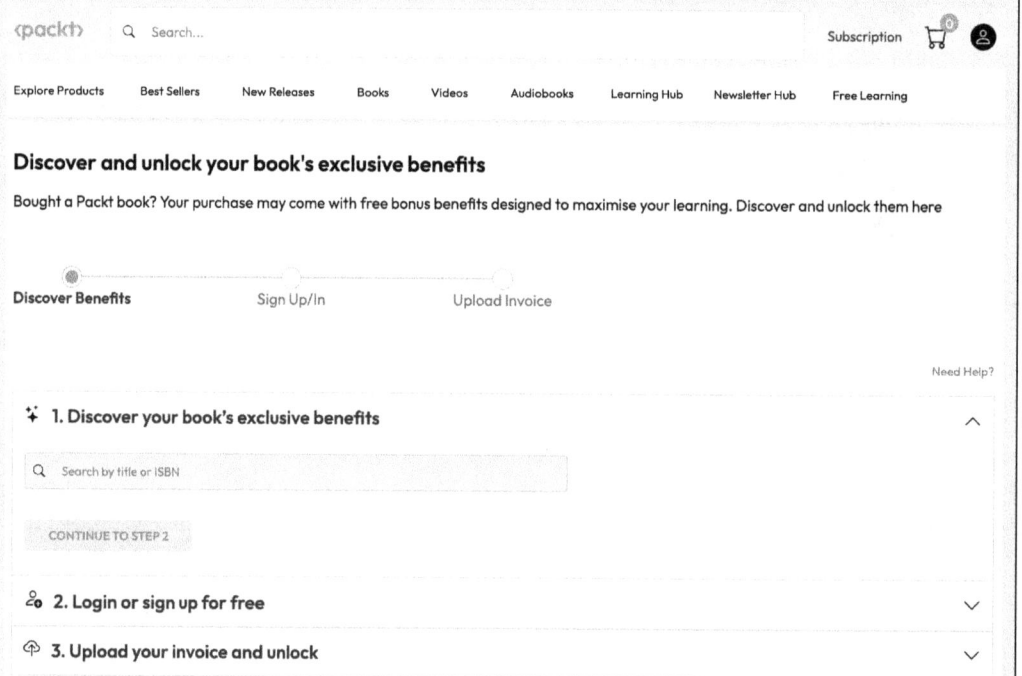

<packt>   🔍 Search...   Subscription 🛒⁰ 👤

Explore Products   Best Sellers   New Releases   Books   Videos   Audiobooks   Learning Hub   Newsletter Hub   Free Learning

Discover and unlock your book's exclusive benefits

Bought a Packt book? Your purchase may come with free bonus benefits designed to maximise your learning. Discover and unlock them here

Discover Benefits   Sign Up/In   Upload Invoice

Need Help?

✦ 1. Discover your book's exclusive benefits   ∧

🔍 Search by title or ISBN

CONTINUE TO STEP 2

👥 2. Login or sign up for free   ∨

☁ 3. Upload your invoice and unlock   ∨

Figure 0.1: Packt landing page for unlocking the book on desktop

Step 3

Sign in to your Packt account or create a new one for free. Once you're logged in, upload your invoice. It can be in PDF, PNG, or JPG format and must be no larger than 10 MB. Follow the rest of the instructions on the screen to complete the process.

Need help?

If you get stuck and need help, visit `https://www.packtpub.com/unlock-benefits/help` for a detailed FAQ on how to find your invoices and more. The following QR code will take you to the help page directly:

> **Note**
>
> If you are still facing issues, reach out to `customercare@packt.com`.

1

Winning at Digital Transformation with Process Modeling

Process modeling is more than plotting out process steps in advance of creating an automated standard operation process that meets current business needs. Process modeling is used throughout the life cycle of both standard and emergent processes designed to respond to change in an emergent/blossoming fashion. A standard process example is that of underwriting risk that can adapt to changing business conditions and stakeholder needs or demands.

In this chapter, you will learn the names of different processes, the different types of active processes today, and the future of processes as they adapt to changing conditions. This is particularly true of the impact of AI and its contribution to process intelligence. The shift in process behavior will put an emphasis on process modeling as a process auditing capability as well as a processing planning tool. The reader will be able to understand and leverage process modeling better than ever before.

The following topics are covered in this chapter:

- Is process modeling the key to real digital transformation?
- How does process modeling contribute to digital transformation?
- Types of process modeling today with usage guidelines
- What is the future of process modeling in the context of other modeling disciplines?
- What is the future of process modeling in the context of AI assistance?

> **Note**
>
> This chapter is authored by Jim Sinur. The chapter starts with the basics, projecting from the current value to the future value of processes and the process models that represent businesses. Jim brings significant credibility as a recognized process expert who has implemented processes and programming solutions.

Is process modeling the key to real digital transformation?

Digital transformation touches many aspects of an organization, including customer interaction, internal operations, management tactics, and the ability to adapt to changing business conditions. There are many on-ramps that organizations can take to achieve digital direction and velocity; however, processes are often the primary place for organizations to start or extend their digital efforts. Processes are heavily involved with the efficiency and effectiveness of customer interactions and operational excellence and effectiveness. It is not hard to understand the effectiveness of extraordinary processes as there are examples of successful businesses that leverage processes.

Amazon is an excellent example of an organization that delivers extraordinary processes that please its customers while optimizing internal operations with the help of tons of automation. Those processes are rife with digital technology that augments human interactions with excellent transparency and a pronounced lack of friction for customers and employees. With built-in feedback loops and the ability to audit the progression of goods for customers, employees/contractors, and management, Amazon continues to leverage its processes for profitability and satisfaction. This is no accident, rather the planned leverage of processes being used as a primary competitive advantage.

There are many known case studies in every industry in which agile processes are powered by combined business analytics and process modeling. While there is a rapid shift to include AI in these efforts, there are plenty of successful processes already without AI. Later in this chapter, we will talk about the impact of AI on processes. Typically, process models represent processes and the sequences and branches taken to attain the completion of a set of process goals. These models are static or dynamic visualizations of how a process progresses to a set of goals or outcomes. Processes are often created, crafted, and improved as human designers visually plot out the common happy paths of process progression and the exception paths before they are built. The visualization represented by the process models is often the critical content over which business professionals design their new or modified processes. Every decision and action step is plotted out, leveraging the highly visual process model.

Business professionals often use business analytics to support the process model-building efforts. Once crafted, the business professional may delegate the composition or building of the modeled process to other technical professionals who can sort out the technical supports necessary for each decision or step/sub-step in the model using either existing components, newly crafted components, or new wrappers for legacy systems/components. The process model then adds more value as a communication device across jobs with diverse skill sets. The process model becomes the "Rosetta Stone" across job functions by communicating the intent and context of the process and process steps. The value of a process model is in plotting out the steps in advance of creating an automated operational process that meets current and future business needs. Clever processes have options for anticipated change, making them even more valuable.

Process models also are helpful once a process is built and operating in place, even if it is a legacy system. Process models can be combined with data and process mining technologies to represent what has happened during past executions of business events/transactions. It gives business professionals a visual means to understand what happened over selected periods. In some cases, animation can be added to help visualize trends and obvious process bottlenecks. The real power of business and process improvement is often unlocked by combining business analytics on the process instance data to highlight opportunities to tweak processes for better throughput, better average timing of process instances/cases, and trapped exceptions with no hope of resolution. Visualization combined with descriptive, prescriptive, or predictive analytics is powerful for better business outcomes over time. In some cases, changes can be pretested to watch changes in outcomes before the actual changes are completed, by leveraging useful approaches such as simulations or digital twins.

To conclude, if processes are involved in your organization's interactions or operations, they will be critical to digital transformation efforts. If processes are present, a process model for visualization to humans is a must to communicate its intent and possible paths to business outcomes.

How does process modeling contribute to digital transformation?

Processes are everywhere in an organization; therefore, the process models are essential for digital transformation to progress. While only 20–30% of the most high-volume processes of an organization are automated in some way, there are ample opportunities for digital transformation. The easy step is to look at those processes, but sometimes the most essential and costly processes are outside the normal high-volume processes and looking for automation opportunities. For organizations to execute flawlessly, all processes are candidates for digital attention. Organizations can also benefit by finding procedural processes that can prevent risk, compete for skills more effectively, and stay compliant in a changing business environment. Finding these golden nuggets will require some digging. See *Figure 1.1* for the common names for processes typically found in organizations. Industry groups and competitive benchmarks can point to the kinds of processes to transform over and above the typical high-volume processes.

Common Names for Processes

- Actor, Step, Action
- Precedence
- Process Flows
- Workflows
- Activity Sets or Steps
- Case Collaboration
- Customer Journeys
- Best Practices
- Straight Through Processes
- Business Process Management (BPM)

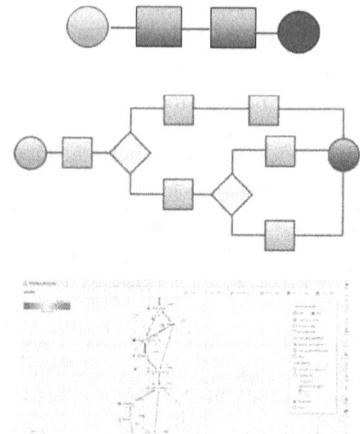

Figure 1.1 – Common names for processes

Often, organizations improve typical high-volume core processes by improving the customer experience and start to converge highly automated and internally focused processes to include the goals of the customer, making these processes more outside-in, AKA customer-centric over time. Most often, systems concentrate on internal organizational goals that are aimed at efficiency only. The primary goal of many organizational processes revolves around the cost and speed of transactional completion in a compliant manner, but not necessarily in favor of customer goals. Digital transformation is an opportunity to balance customer goals with internal organizational goals focusing primarily on profit. See Figure 1.2 for ideas on closing the gap between the customer experience and business processes. Many organizations believe they do not inflict pain on their customers when interacting with their core processes. These organizations need to classify the pain they cause and what characteristics cause the pain for customers. See *Figure 1.3* for an example customer pain index.

Close the Gap Between Customer Journeys & Business Processes

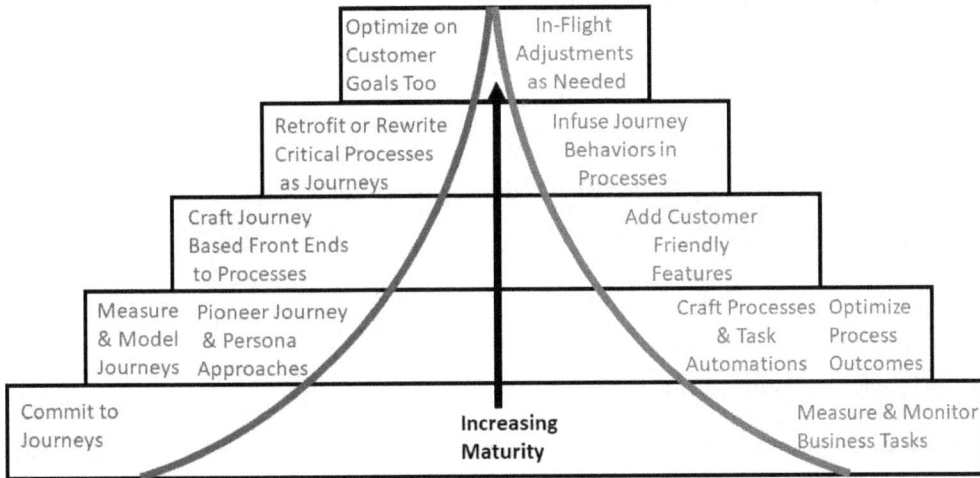

Optimize on Customer Goals Too	In-Flight Adjustments as Needed		
Retrofit or Rewrite Critical Processes as Journeys	Infuse Journey Behaviors in Processes		
Craft Journey Based Front Ends to Processes	Add Customer Friendly Features		
Measure & Model Journeys	Pioneer Journey & Persona Approaches	Craft Processes & Task Automations	Optimize Process Outcomes
Commit to Journeys	**Increasing Maturity**	Measure & Monitor Business Tasks	

Figure 1.2 – Close the gap between customer journeys and business processes

Many organizations believe they do not inflict pain on their customers when interacting with their core processes. These organizations need to classify the pain they cause and what characteristics cause that pain for customers. See *Figure 1.3* for an example customer pain index:

Journeys and Processes Inflict Pain in Most Organizations

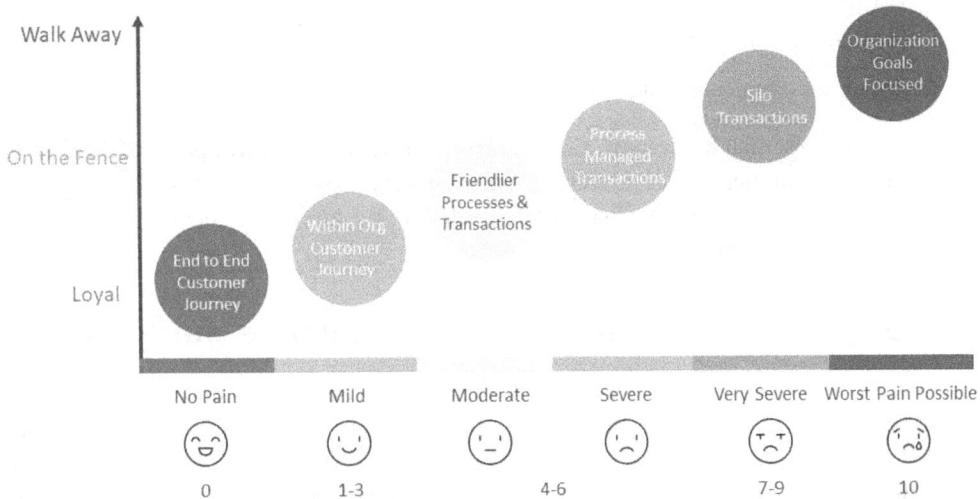

					Organization Goals Focused
Walk Away				Silo Transactions	
			Process Managed Transactions		
On the Fence		Friendlier Processes & Transactions			
	Within Org Customer Journey				
	End to End Customer Journey				
Loyal					

No Pain	Mild	Moderate	Severe	Very Severe	Worst Pain Possible
😄	🙂	😐	🙁	😣	😖
0	1-3	4-6	7-9		10

Figure 1.3 – Customer pain index

More than likely, there is an opportunity for more automation in those core processes. *Emerging digital technologies* combined with traditional technologies used in a new way or in different contexts hold potential benefits for organizations and their constituents. Examples under the watchful umbrella of modern cybersecurity include the following:

- AI / generative / decisioning / learning

- Analytics / poly analytics / mining

- **Business Process Management (BPM)** / development / automation

- Collaboration / content

- Business application / models / templates / components

- Cloud / integration / data fabrics / blockchain data

- IoT / edge hardware / digital twins

Making the existing processes friendlier and more intelligent is an excellent first step. Consider adding more robust assistance/intelligence to the participants (AKA resources) involved in process completion. *Typical process resources* include the following in the context of location and state:

- Managers

- Knowledge workers

- Skilled workers

- APIs, data meshes, and data and knowledge sources

- System components, bots, and algorithms

- Sensors, chips, controllers, and edge firmware

- Robots, drones, cameras, and so on

No matter the process that an organization chooses, a process model will point the way to the improvement opportunities for digital transformation efforts, especially when combined with AI, business analytics, process/data mining, and non-self-serving surveys of customers, employees, partners, contractors, and communities.

Types of process modeling today with usage guidelines

There may be a debate on whether to model or just jump into coding or composition and fail fast. We suggest modeling is a great way to plan more critical or complex processes. Today there are many options for developing processes and applications. There is great debate about modeling representation and even the need to model in the first place. Before we get into the representation issues, let's think about the reasons to model in the first place. We know tremendous pressure exists to get to code quickly to show results. There are better ways to compose code, link APIs, and leverage low-code approaches that might lead one away from models. After all, models generally don't execute directly, or do they? Though models might not seem to get to code as quickly, they help code the right solution to meet the needs. There are three great *reasons* to create a visual model, and they are as follows.

Visualize the connections between processes and resources

Management, customers, partners, and employees often think they understand the operational efforts needed to complete work, but they don't. Indeed, there is not a common understanding of operational processes and applications in all the contexts and views held by the collective participants. Creating an agreed-upon visual representation gives a solid construct for explanation to all managers and participants. Combining the different views and perspectives into a whole model makes a shared understanding of the likely outcome. The model identifies all the participant's roles, decisions, actions, and results.

Gain a common understanding of the current situation

Often, there are processes, data, events, and patterns belonging to each participant in an application or process that may have been created by their organizational position, role, or specialty. By better understanding the moving parts and how they contribute to business outcomes, existing processes and applications work better without needing to change the base process or application. If changes are being considered, the current state models can enable better approaches or remind developers or participants of crucial constraints.

Create a consensus on a future solution

Gaining consensus on a set of target processes and applications is essential in all transformations, especially in digital transformations. Creating a group of participants to define a new way forward and enabling them with models allows for faster progress. Models can be used to verify whether the new solution is correct from several perspectives outside the core design group. Also, it allows management to understand the sticking points in significant changes and engage participants early in the change process.

Often, organizations pick one of these approaches to start the modeling efforts and realize they need the other two to figure out the transformation efforts, including scope, skills, available resources, partners, technologies, and a reasonable schedule. It is crucial to determine what levels of pioneering and risk the transformation efforts will allow within the organization's culture in charge of the digital efforts.

Three different *process styles* require different process modeling approaches, each concentrating on representing how work is managed toward a business, process, or technical outcome. In more complex situations that deliver high-value outcomes, more than one style may be used. See the process styles in *Figure 1.4* for a visual representation of each style.

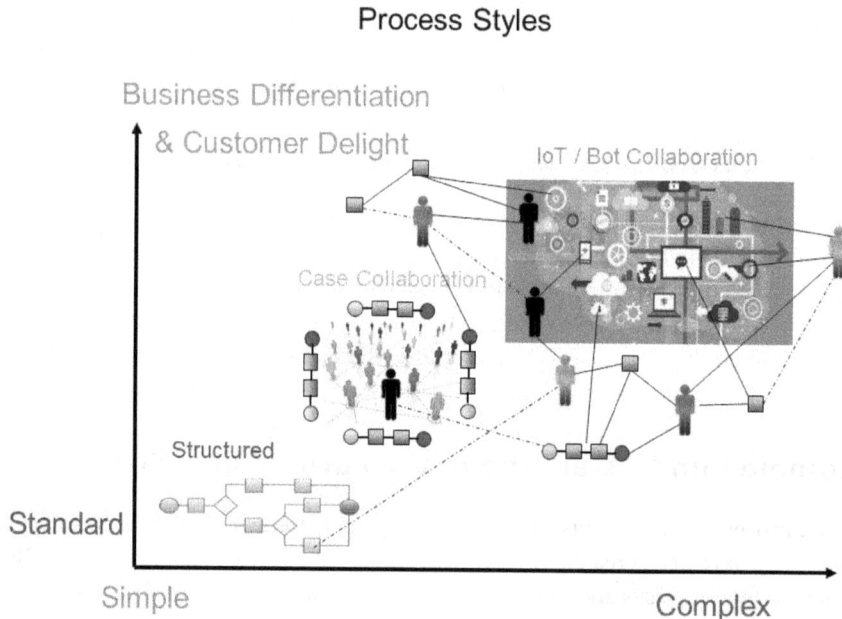

Figure 1.4 – Process styles

An explanation of each style is enumerated as follows.

Structured processes

While multiple process sub-styles exist in this category, they all start with planning a process and identifying almost all the paths and exceptions. Then a *process that is relatively static* and brittle is put into place. These can be whole processes or process snippets, meaning partial cohesive pieces of processes that are bound steps for specific results. Structured processes work best for standard and straightforward outcomes. Still, they can be expanded to take advantage of BPM and rule agility to make them less static and more adaptable to new business requirements and exceptions. Some organizations build extensive and comprehensive structured processes that become hard to test and maintain. The relationship between bots and these processes is more around the bots serving the process than vice versa. The extensive process brain controls it all.

Case collaboration

More dynamic processes start showing up in case management, where the goals and milestones are static, but the paths to these goals can vary. It is accurate *for knowledge-intensive work*, where one person does not understand how to solve or complete an individual case. Case collaboration can get even more agile and dynamic when the goals and milestones can change. This calls for adaptive case management. Bots can be used in a couple of scenarios to start. One is that a bot could contain automated personal assistants in the cloud that could grok large amounts of information from data lakes or produce deep analytic efforts on behalf of the knowledge worker. In this situation, the structured part of the process becomes a minor part of the overall process and evolves to snippets of process sequences or bots/personal assistants. This way, you could swap out AI agents or people at the direction of management. It introduces more complexity, but the case brain will control events and patterns fired from bots for potential decisions and actions.

IoT bot collaboration

Imagine a network of collaborating bots and IoT devices working together to decide what the next step should be and firing off another structured process, a case, or a set of bots to *meet dynamic goals* set by a managing agent. Of course, these agent collaborations and actions would have to be bound by constraints to avoid violating governance policies or rules. It is a very dynamic approach where the brains of the operation are no longer a central control process or case in charge. In this case, goals and constraints with contexts now lead the way. Real-world examples are emerging every day. One such use case is automatically feeding farm fields with water and fertilizer for bigger yields. See `https://jimsinur.blogspot.com/2013/07/smart-farm-operations-processes.html` for a case study.

There are three significant reasons for modeling processes. The most common is understanding the current processes, which will likely include process/data mining techniques and technologies as it automates part of the understanding of the current processes more scientifically. The next most common reason is to create a future process model that will most likely use visual modeling tools and get more detailed throughout the phases of progress. In complex or wide-scoped processes that coordinate many resources, a model of the connections and the boundaries the process crosses is also essential. Often, significant efforts will employ all three. Three styles of processes are also employed to achieve unique business outcomes. It is essential to understand all three, but the point of control that the processes need will point to a particular style or combination.

What is the future of process modeling in the context of other modeling disciplines?

Process models do not exist in a vacuum; they interact with other essential factors in both human and automated digital solutions. While process flows, decisions, cases, data, and result visualizations are often modeled well in many organizations, more models are needed as more intelligent dynamics are applied to digital solutions. Process models have served processes and business results well to date, but organizations need much more to model. The importance of semiotic representations of process components can't be overstated. However, digital solutions demand more modeling types over time. So far, we have identified another six underserved areas that have not been dealt with to date, represented in *Figure 1.5* as other necessary models.

Process Models in the Context of Other Models

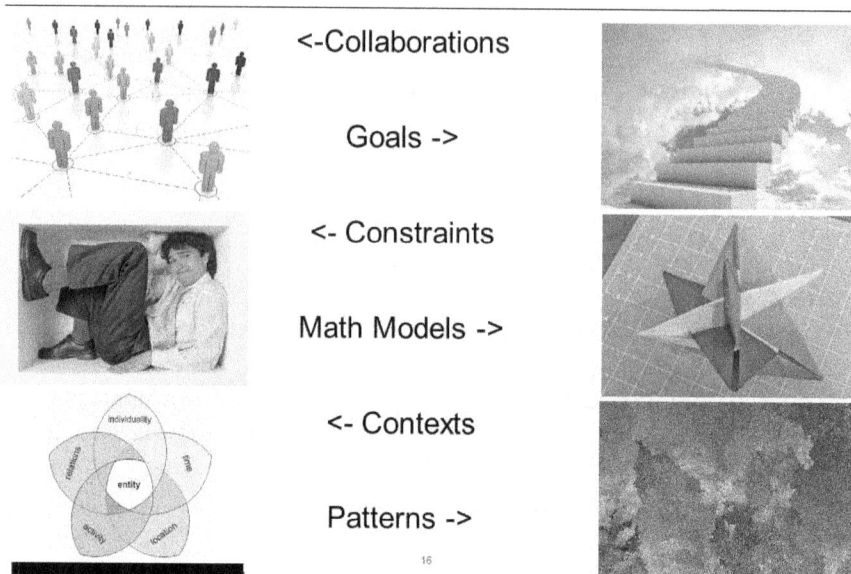

<-Collaborations

Goals ->

<- Constraints

Math Models ->

<- Contexts

Patterns ->

Figure 1.5 – Necessary other models

In the following sections, we enumerate areas that processes must deal with as larger scopes and more complexity are introduced to the process world.

Collaborations

There are few accepted representations of approaches to collaboration patterns, though we have seen some attempts to represent social interactions captured during social mining and analytics. It may take a while for this area to produce some common patterns of representation, and longer still to have a standard representation that spans vendors that support the human interaction needed to complete business outcomes or manage improvement or change efforts.

Goals

While there are a couple of great examples of goal models and goal interactions from a few brave vendors, no accepted modeling approach is universally embraced today. A few organizations have sensed the turn from flow-directed processes toward goal-driven processes. In processes that can self-determine direction and the next best action, the need for goals is essential.

Constraints

As processes become less structured and emergent, constraints will become more critical in the process governance and control arena. I have not seen any significant representation of boundary constraints showing a process surrounded by these protection mechanisms. Constraints and goals are necessary to allow for the inclusion of unsupervised AI in attaining business outcomes.

Math models

While there are some models for singular analytic approaches (such as PMML for predictive analytics), there is no known modeling method for the multiple interacting analytics that one can find in the intelligent processes that exist today, much less the inclusion of various types of AI behavior.

Contexts

As processes become more proactive in sensing active patterns and scenarios, there will be a need to represent the contexts that processes participate in and are interested in participating in to attain their outcomes or goals. These contexts will be inspected for advantages, threats, and learning experiences. Processes beyond internal and external organizational, industry, or geographic boundaries must be sensitive to meaning within different contexts.

Patterns

Today organizations seem more interested in events to react to than patterns of interest. This will change over time, but there is no accepted way to represent patterns today. Patterns of interest will eventually need semiotic representations, along with a classification scheme.

While we might all agree that modeling processes, decisions, goals, or data has significant benefits, there are disagreements on the modeling methods, standards, and the most important object to model. Let's examine the areas of friction in and around modeling. We have identified five areas of friction, but I imagine more issues lurking below the surface like there is only data or rules.

Process modeling trade-offs

Even within the process modeling domain itself, without consideration of other companion modeling assists, process modeling has some difficultbalances that need to be addressed, as outlined in the following sections.

Model the logical or the physical

A common argument often revolves around modeling the target logical model instead of the physical implementation model as it represents the pure need and would include things such as operational manuals skipped by the implementer. The implementation folks usually argue that the logical future model does not essentially reflect reality, and synchronizing both is impossible. Some organizations use the logical model as a specification and throw the logical model away as soon as the physical model emerges. Those who believe in rapid innovation favor creating the implementation quickly and failing fast. We prefer a rough logical model that includes operations manuals and iterates to completion.

Model to the standards or not

Many folks believe in modeling standards and say that standard modeling makes training, communicating, and attracting instant contributors from outside the organization easier. There is also a benefit from moving models around from one vendor to another without nasty conversions when switching to another platform already in use inside the organization, or even a new one. Some say that standards are difficult to work with and miss critical nuances that make a difference. Why use clunky standards when they just slow things down? While we prefer the ease of development over standards, we are tempted to iterate rather than model to perfection. There is a balance to be struck here.

Model cases over processes

There is a brewing argument that **Case Management Model and Notation (CMMN)** is very close to **Business Process Model and Notation (BPMN)** and could be easily be extended to support cases. We would agree if BPMN included goal modeling because cases work to milestone goals, and flow can take a back seat.

Model decisions over processes

There is also a growing debate about whether processes embed decisions or whether decisions are on top, as they determine the tasks to perform. We think you need both for very complex processes, and they should work together, but **Decision Model and Notation (DMN)** is the new kid on the block and doesn't get the respect it deserves.

Model goals over processes

The odd man out is goal modeling, as processes and decisions used to be rigid and unchanging. As both decisions and rules become more fluid, goal modeling makes more sense. The goals remain, and the goal target could change, but the path of decisions and process tasks can vary greatly. Goal and constraint modeling should get more attention than it does.

Modeling is excellent, but it can create religious wars when vendors try to make their approach and notation the center of the process world. Whatever models you embrace, make the decision at the beginning of the project and stick to your selection unless it needs significant adjustment. This is unlikely as fluid processes/cases are usually known about upfront, and approaches can be selected to support them. We strongly suggest that process models be selected to represent any real-world activity for process mining that will help improve any current/existing processes, as process visualization is great for business and technical professionals to understand activity in context. Process models are also handy for describing future states for stable and static processes or process snippets. It's only when the problems become more emergent or change volatility becomes excessive.

What is the future of process modeling in the context of AI assistance?

The value AI brings to process modeling will depend on how AI affects the actual processes modeled and whether the process model represents future designs or a representation of actual execution, in-flight or after the fact, when combined with process/data mining. We have identified three overlapping phases of AI's impact on processes:

- The first phase will be the augmentation of existing resources involved with the process completion/execution
- The second phase will replace specific resources or steps in the context of a process with AI-heavy process snippets, IoT devices, or bots, AKA agents
- The third phase is where AI becomes the controlling manager of processes, from a dynamic assembly of process components and execution of processes to monitoring process outcomes for adjustment in real time

The journey to smarter, more intelligent processes will likely be an evolution starting with smarter actions considered in changing contexts. As intelligent processes become more efficient at handling change, they will need to stay that way by recognizing patterns of threat and opportunity. Once intelligent processes see potential changes, they will likely make decisions in an unsupervised fashion within guidelines provided by the organization.

The resulting leverage of AI and analytics creates intelligent processes. AI will not be instantly included, but gradually adopted throughout a journey guided by the needs of processes built to support varied business outcomes. We have illustrated the *journey to smarter processes* in *Figure 1.6*, where processes not only service actions but also sense/recognize emergent patterns to support dynamic and informed business decisions to gain optimized business benefits.

Journey to Smarter Processes

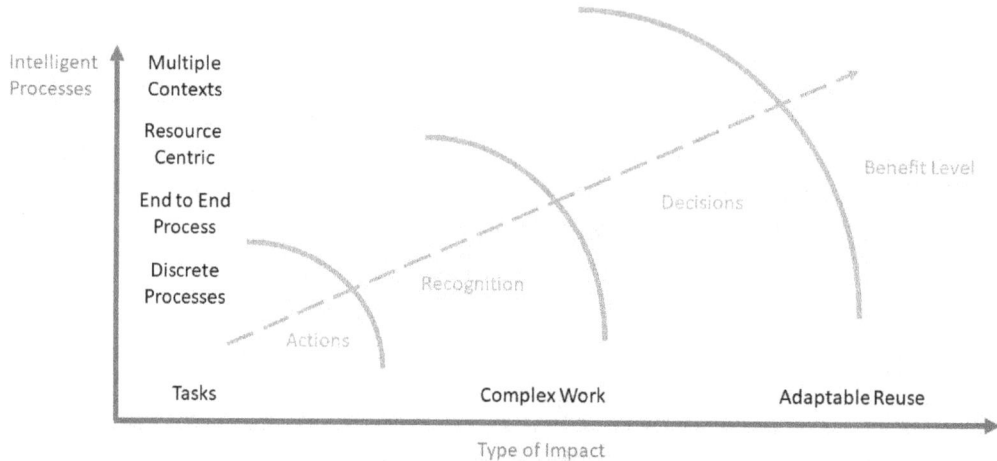

Figure 1.6 – Journey to smarter processes

Intelligent/smart processes show their IQ by the kind of work they include and the scope of impact they support. Standard processes/process snippets mainly support action steps for discrete tasks, typically with simple branching decisions to support static goals. These are depicted in the lower-left corner of *Figure 1.6*. The next level of intelligence is usually attained by including end-to-end processes and their actions or by recognizing patterns or events that might impact the process. As the complexity of the work increases, so does the number of resources along with the intelligence of the resources. The demand for intelligence takes off when the scope of processes crosses organizational and industry lines, often requiring more complex decisions that balance conflicting goals from various constituents. Often the next level of smart capacities is required by an emergent set of complex decisions that stem from dynamic change, requiring on-the-fly optimization. It implies the adaptable reuse of process snippets and bots that an intelligent AI-loaded bot might control. At some point in the evolution, processes change the point of control from flow directed to goal directed.

Flow directed versus goal directed

Some feel that there should never be any sequence of steps in a process. Others state that there would be chaos in processes without sequence, and people would be confused. It raises the question, *"Should processes be flow or goal-directed?"* The appeal of goal-directed processes is that the process emerges as it seeks its set of goals at any point in time. As the goal changes, the process automatically adjusts to meet the new set of goals and the weights for those goals. It is perfect for emerging processes where the flow or portions of a flow emerge as the time and target move.

We see significant portions of goal-directed processes in **Adaptive Case Management** and late-bound processes. The problem with this approach is that sometimes, actions are not understood until visualized after the fact. The appeal of flow-directed processes is that better practices can be selected and followed based on conditions that are known at the time. People like flow-directed processes because they can visually study, understand, and improve flows by adding new paths and exceptions while maintaining control. The problem is that it takes time to do all this in a time-to-market fashion, and control is exercised centrally, something that the world is moving away from because of the increased speed of change combined with increased complexity.

We think the days of extensive, centrally controlled, flow-directed processes are drawing to a close, but this doesn't eliminate the need for sequencing. We think the overall process should be goal directed and somewhat decentralized (with authority pushed to the edge by intelligent resources such as people, agents, bots, and things). However, there will still be snippets of sequences that will be utilized. Eventually, all resources will bid for work, and the sequence-based process will wane significantly, but we are not convinced the sequence will completely disappear. Large and rigid processes are becoming a bit of a dinosaur. The world is changing from flow-directed to goal-directed processes and distributed intelligence, and we must learn new skills and habits to manage emerging work. The minimum required is to let flows freely flow within constraint boundaries and audit the results after the fact to check whether new constraints are required.

Phases of AI in intelligent processes

There are three distinct phases that organizations will have to consider, but they could overlap in their application in any process. These phases are as follows.

AI and process phase 1

Processes often coordinate, leverage, and consume resources. These resources comprise humans, systems/components, data sources, and machines. Humans can range from low-level workers to highly skilled professionals that are rare and highly paid. Systems range from simple one-function components to work-focused process snippets to complex, highly functional legacy systems. Data can range from detailed, single-source base data to highly refined informational sources available from a data mesh in the cloud leveraging various kinds of content/formats. Machines range from single-function chips to complex devices guided by processes.

All these resources can be lifted to a higher level by adding smart capacities. Resources can learn through the assistance of AI/machine learning and pattern recognition. Resources can be augmented with *smart actions* to create better and faster. Generative AI resources can also be assisted through cognitive suggestions for decisioning. All these resources exercise supervised AI to make themselves smarter and faster. It used to be that humans were needed for creativity, but now generative AI can minimally generate a great starting spot, and finished deliverables at best. See *Figure 1.7* for examples of how resources combined with processes can assist in attaining business outcomes over and above the everyday actions that processes do for organizations. Often, higher-skilled and more expensive resources can be freed up as the work trickles down to lower-skilled resources augmented with AI.

Smart Processes Go Beyond Actions

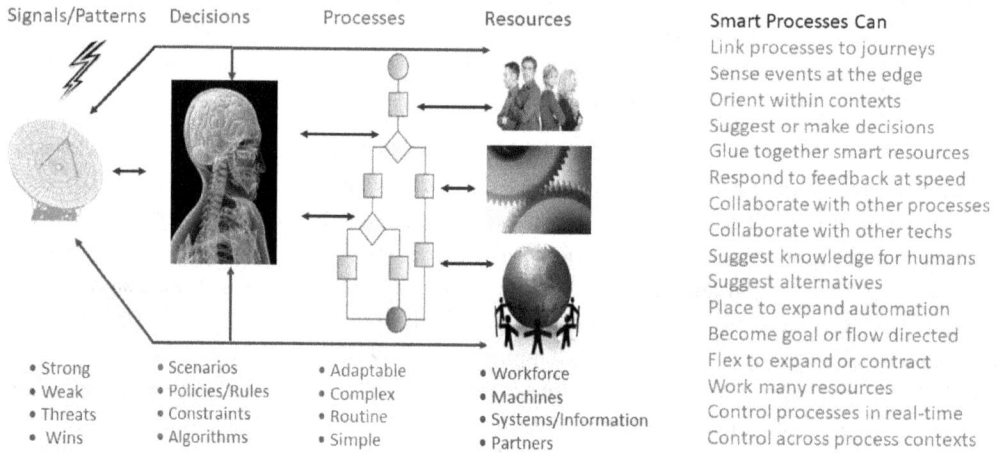

Figure 1.7 – Smart processes

AI and process phase 2

This second phase is more about displacing higher-paid and time-constrained resources with always-on resources and consistent bots and snippets. This will probably reduce the number of humans necessary for process/work completion. Where danger and timeliness are present in the solution, the more likely it is that AI automation will displace workers. In addition, where consistent precision is required, the AI bots are hard to beat. Where judgment and empathy are required, the human touch is essential. This calls for a semi-supervised AI where processes and humans interact to check the results of the AI in current processes or after the fact. Process control still resides with processes and humans are assisted by visual supports such as process models and dynamic real-time dashboards.

AI and process phase 3

This is where AI becomes the decider and controller for processes, displacing process management functions. It is almost entirely unsupervised except for the presence of goals and guardrails (constraints). The goals are needed to make sure that desirable business results are pursued. The constraints are needed to keep AI compliant with the global and local legal frameworks in force at any time. Management will be focused on creating great goals and safe guidelines. Here, AI is making lots of decisions in real time, not only for speed and cost but to stay on course in emergent problem domains. AI will create the process paths dynamically, control the bots bidding to complete tasks, and give permissions to services. Process models will likely be developed after the fact and combined with analytics and AI of their own. Explainability is the goal for AI and processes here.

Collaboration between processes and bots

As AI bots get smarter, they will replace certain decisions and actions in the process, but they will still collaborate. Processes will concentrate on sequential actions and likely become smaller snippets of what was an overall process of the past. Over time, this collaboration and sharing of decisions and work will become more fluid.

AI will be essential to link and assist businesses in gleaning higher levels of change agility while increasing business profitability and satisfying constituents' goals. See *Figure 1.8* for the goals businesses are looking to achieve with processes. We can see the role of more intelligent processes created, assembled, and managed by AI.

Processes & Bots Can Direct Intelligence Applied to Outcomes

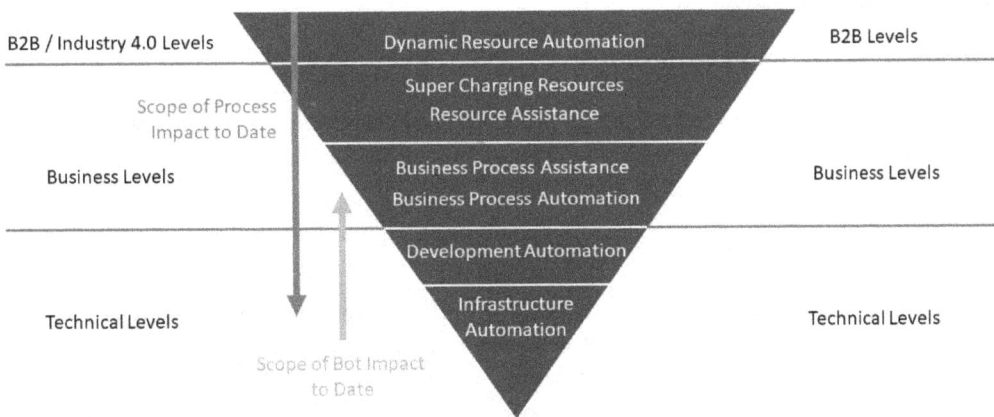

Figure 1.8 – Desired process goals

Process models as a critical representation of work progress will still be needed, but the role will likely change after the fact for at least the transparency of AI decisions and actions. AI is hard to audit, as are processes that employ AI. Process models, decision models, and other audit trails will aid businesses in trackability, bias, and privacy issues. As AI drives us into new laws and legal interactions, you can bet that after the fact, models will play a role. It can be assumed that process-modeling skills will be essential.

What's in it for my employer?

Businesses need business models to keep their operations profitable and optimized in a changing world. It matters not whether process models are used in design or audit mode; key behaviors and improvement opportunities can be discerned by analyzing process instances. Constituents are serviced by extraordinary processes and the models that represent them. Simply ask customers or employees about the impact of a good or bad process.

What's in it for me and my career?

Understanding process models and their impact on various aspects of a business is an essential skill and will grow in importance during the creation and management of all operational, tactical, and strategic processes.

Creating visual/conceptual representations of an action journey

Visualizations communicate better than most content and are great for collaborating across skill sets and organizational boundaries.

Enhancing the customer experience

Extraordinary processes create loyal customers, and flawed processes chase customers away. In today's world of change and lack of tolerance for poor interactions, tremendous and friendly processes help all constituents exude repeatable business and loyalty.

Delivering a balanced set of outcomes

Extraordinary processes represented by process models not only deliver on the organizational goals of profitability but strike the balance of including customer goals and outcomes while pleasing employees who can walk to organizations with better processes.

Summary

As you just read, the nature of processes will change over time. They will be involved in a dynamic dance of supporting changing goals within governance guidelines and constraints. Process modeling will be the explainable part of intelligent processes in the future. Until then, process models will be used to audit and optimize processes. Process models are a common communication vehicle for process planning and process auditing, whether the process is structured or dynamic; therefore, they are very valuable to organizations. Individuals will have to pick up modeling skills as visual communication becomes a key driver for future digital progress.

Unlock this book's exclusive benefits now

Scan this QR code or go to `packtpub.com/unlock`, then search this book by name.

Note: Keep your purchase invoice ready before you start.

2
Pillars of a Successful Digital Transformation

In the first chapter of our book, Jim Sinur made a case for the continuous importance of process and process modeling in consideration of how the blend of different work styles has historically driven enterprise optimization. These include structured processes, case-based collaboration, and IoT/bot collaboration – all of which are contributing to a shift from centralized operations to a more distributed, edge-based paradigm. Jim sees rapid advances in AI changing the role of business processes, taking companies from optimized and centrally controlled by "the brain" work organizations toward adaptive, goal-oriented, and fully distributed architectures.

We can expect to see major shifts in companies' technology landscapes as pervasive AI takes over responsibility for decision-making, control, and negotiations on how to best accomplish business goals and get work done between bots and humans. With wave after wave of technological progress sending shocks to operations via prototypes, new project releases, change management programs, and the continuous advancement of intelligent processes in work historically performed by us professionals, one may wonder how to avoid losing the human in the process. Being part of a digitization program without the right grounding/framework can create unpleasant and unintended consequences for workforces across all industries and geographies. Human brains operate best in routine environments, yet the frequency of change hitting us from multiple directions causes chaos, competing priorities, and difficulties adapting to quickly changing realities brought forth by **Digital Transformation (DTX)** agendas. To add to these challenges, DTX within a company may mean different things to different audiences based on people's roles in the organization, making it harder to communicate across teams.

This chapter discusses how to organize work around workstreams that will support major pillars of your company's DTX. Regardless of how and when DTX efforts start, most work streams will end up revolving around such pillars, bringing much-desired order to unruly seas of change.

In this chapter, we will cover the following topics:

- Introduction and overview of DTX

- What are the key pillars supporting digital transformations?

- How do digital transformations start?

  - Top-down

  - Grassroot

  - Legacy modernization

  - Triggered by an acquisition or merger

- How to craft a vision for digital change for your business group

- How to plan for the future

> **Note**
> This chapter is authored by BJ Biernatowski.

Introduction and overview of DTX

Several books have been written on DTX by a few highly recognized analysts, software architects, CEOs, and consultants. Over the last 15 years, as I've been studying the subject of process-led digital transformation, I have realized that the topic is vast, very quickly changing, and rife with business agendas of companies who aspire to own DTX, ultimately crowning themselves as your go-to source for everything DTX-related. These agendas manifest themselves through e-books, podcasts, and various *marchitecture* (marketing and architecture) materials, printed on glossy slides and funded by marketing budgets.

The challenge of learning about DTX from software vendors lies in the concern over "vendor lock-in." This refers to the perception that companies are compelled to adopt a vision of DTX that aligns more closely with the software vendor's perspective, rather than pursuing a path that aligns with their own strategic goals for digitizing and optimizing their operational processes.

This is not to say that you cannot learn about DTX by perusing these marketecture white papers or books. The challenge with such materials is their need for objectivity and the view of DTX defined by companies ultimately seeking to reach a leading market position by selling their view of what the transformation should look like for your business, unit, or that process you are maintaining single-handedly. The other challenge is the amount of time it would take to sift the truth from aspirations or half-truths, perhaps even truths reached on projects that were overinvested in or redone multiple times.

When Packt approached me to craft the vision for this book, I thought quite a bit about how to make this position different from all the titles I've read in the past. The following principles defined our approach to this project:

- Best practices and topics summarized in the book were gained by first-person participation in process transformation programs utilizing technologies and platforms from different vendors who've been in this space for many years. While this book highlights a few software products, we consciously try to separate creative and critical thinking from the toolset and any technology. The reason for this is that tools and technologies are continually expanding the definition of DTX without any clear boundaries. It's essential to understand and master some critical concepts before testing even the most advanced tools. There's an adage shared by a transformation consultant during a project: "*A fool with the best tool is still a fool,*" This still holds true for low code, AI, and DTX platforms such as **Intelligent Business Process Management Systems (iBPMS)**. An updated version of this adage states, "*And now, thanks to AI and low code, you can make foolish decisions even faster.*"

- This book covers various topics that can be applied to **Digital Change (DtC)** programs led by teams from different technical backgrounds. When we refer to DtC programs, we mean the operational, tactical, and incremental improvements that contribute to the overall DTX journey. For us, DTX represents an evolution, and the path to this North Star involves implementing incremental DtC initiatives.

- While your results may vary from those described in the book, there is no hard requirement that you experiment and utilize software products mentioned in the book. While we may bring up many arguments on why the tools we recommend would offer you the best bang for your buck with the best possible outcome, you are welcome to apply these concepts using your favorite process tools, and we won't hold that against you. Your mileage may vary though.

- Our book is written by practitioners for practitioners. Each author gained experience with the topics mentioned in the book through many years of practical work with demanding clients from medium to large Fortune 500 companies. Such work involved extensive air travel, long commutes, too many restaurant meals, working 14-hour days, personal and family sacrifices, and sometimes working through the night to fix that pesky issue blocking the project. When it comes to DTX, the stakes are usually very high as these programs often respond to existential threats facing businesses. Betting on technology can often be associated with betting on your reputation.

- Many topics addressed in this book exist as separate posts, documents, and templates generated through project teams, or consulting knowledge and frameworks kept close to the chest, as companies tend to protect the intellectual property that drives revenue. We intended to demystify and simplify some of these topics for you, understanding the value of your hard-earned dollars spent on this book. I like hanging out in bookstores and libraries, reviewing different positions related to DTX. You'd be surprised to find out that there are not that many practical positions out there, and many people literally learn about these topics by experimentation or watching webinars. There are glimpses of hope as some business schools are starting to see demand for college-level courses that cover these topics; however, they usually come with a hefty price tag and a long-term commitment required to complete the degree. When you are placed or asked to lead a transformation project, you don't have time for a two-year MBA degree, even in the online edition.

- Writing a book about DTX for a global audience aspiring to or in the midst of transforming a business with analysis and process modeling requires experience gained on many types of projects. The collective expertise of authors involves working with global US and European companies. We are aware of many innovative projects taking place in Latin America, the Middle East, Africa, and Asia. While the cultural aspect of work may be slightly different in those regions, applying our strategies to teams that practice diversity and empathy should result in similar results.

- Each author brings unique expertise to this publication. The coalescence of our experience and, at times, conflicting opinions should present you with an objective view of the topic, highlighting angles of topics where uniform truths may not exist. We hope that you will take our experience as you trailblaze the path of your company transformation. We give you the maps and instruments, hoping that you will set the course on your own.

- We decided not to use artificial examples and simplifications such as a pizza or coffee-making business process. The leave approval process is also not covered. While there are cases when such examples serve a purpose, work in an enterprise tends to be a lot more complex, and we'd hate to waste your time sharing our knowledge on simplistic examples. Our compilation of examples is pulled directly from projects we were part of.

- Business analysis and process modeling skills are gained on projects with different business objectives. I recognize the vastness of this continuum and the fact that many great people are doing a lot of very innovative work. We don't claim to know it all – we intend to share with you what we've learned throughout our journey, from thought leaders and mentors who shaped our thinking. Throughout our careers, we've been lucky to work with many top-notch teams and software vendors who are really pushing the boundaries of DTX.

- The practice of business and process analysis itself is going through a transformation driven by the need for fast-paced adaptability taking place within the inside of the company. Just like the world of software development has been revolutionized through the empowerment of citizen developers driving low-code solutions, so is the world of business and process architecture. No business owner these days has enough time to wait for the assignment of an architect to help define their business process landscape. The job of an architect is becoming one of a mentor, as the needs for business and process analysis emerge everywhere on a daily basis. We propose recognizing this wave of skillset democratization that runs parallel with and trails what, in the world of software development, is known as *shadow IT*. We welcome others to help us define the proper name for these citizen architects – change agents who are leading the redesigning and rearchitecting of business processes without the involvement of centralized enterprise architecture or management consultant teams specializing in selling implementation contracts.

- The global reach of this publication prompted us to designate 5% of book advances and royalties to the American Red Cross. We live on separate continents in three different geographies characterized by different climates. Despite being separated by about 5,880 miles (or 9,464 km), we've experienced and are worried about rising global temperatures and their impact on daily lives. Through a network of donors, volunteers, and employees, the American Red Cross shares a global mission of preventing and relieving suffering in areas impacted by climate change. We can teach you how to accelerate DTX for your employers from the comfort of your living room. The Red Cross' work is based on countless hours of volunteers who help other people get out of dire situations they never thought were possible. Get involved, learn about their work, donate, and volunteer. There are no quick and easy fixes to problems the Red Cross works on, and we felt it was important to elevate the importance of their work and the sacrifices of their volunteers. One day, we all may find ourselves in the path of a wildfire, hoping the Red Cross will be there to offer its help.

- We'd like to thank the multiple technical reviewers for their input on this book. Your deep experience and guidance are greatly appreciated.

- We will consider ourselves successful with this book if your abilities to initiate, plan for, and execute DtC programs improve substantially. We have tons of skin in the game.

With this quick introduction to the whys behind this project, let's focus a little bit on the book's topic to highlight the content we plan to cover in subsequent chapters.

The book you are reading is intended for decision-makers, stakeholders, or participants in business change projects that are part of a broader DTX.

Multiple takes on DTX

Before we start discussing different triggers of process-led **Digital Change** (**DtC**) programs, let's spend a little bit of time discussing what DTX is and what it is not. This should help us then frame DtC in the context of the broader DTX.

As of 2025, there are a couple of definitions of DTX worth noting. We will start by looking at **McKinsey & Company's**:

"Digital Transformation is the rewiring of an organization, with the goal of creating value by continuously deploying tech at scale."

Capgemini defines DTX as *"the use of technology to radically improve performance or reach of enterprises. The act of adopting and integrating technology into all aspects of business creating a foundational shift that enables sustainable innovation and creative growth for an organization."*

Cognizant sees DTX as *"the act of adopting and integrating technology into all aspects of business, creating a foundational shift that enables sustainable innovation and creative growth for an organization. It includes cultural changes, internal resource considerations, and product development that supports improved, technology-powered user experience."*

According to **Forrester**: *"Digital Transformation is the process of using digital assets to improve customer outcomes and operational agility. It is not just about applying technology to existing processes or experiences but reimagining a different business model that places technology at its core. Digital transformation is essential for businesses to survive and thrive in a changing industry landscape, and it requires digital maturity, agility, lean and fast execution."*

Per **Gartner,** *"digital transformation is a term used to describe the use of digital technologies to fundamentally change an organization's business model. It involves the integration of digital technology into all areas of a business resulting in fundamental changes to how businesses operate and the delivery of value to customers."*

IDC considers DTX as *"the application of 3rd Platform technologies such as cloud, mobile, big data, and social, coupled with organizational, operational, and business model innovation to create new ways of operating and growing businesses."*

For MIT, *"digital transformation is the use of technology to radically improve performance or reach of enterprises. It involves integrating digital technologies and solutions into all areas of a company and is not only technological but also cultural in nature. DTX changes the conditions under which business is done, the ways that change the expectations of customers, partners and employees. Digital capability empowers organizations to enhance existing processes and products and improve or even create new business models."*

Harvard Business Review sees DTX as *"a process that involves the use of digital technologies to create new or modify existing business processes, culture and customer experiences. It can involve IT modernization, digital optimization, or the invention of new digital business models."*

BPMInstitute.org defines DTX *"as the process of integrating technology throughout and across an organization to fundamentally change the way it operates internally and presents its products or services externally."*

Microsoft defines DTX as *"bringing together people, data and processes to transform your company and create value for your business needs. It's a business innovation fueled by the explosion of the cloud, AI, and the Internet of Things (IoT), providing organizations with new ways to understand, manage, and transform their business. It's also the process of using new technologies and business workflows to optimize, automate, and otherwise modernize an organization's business operations. Updating technological tools and approaches in this way helps organizations to improve internal processes, increase efficiency, and function with a greater level of flexibility and agility."*

If you've been curious enough to read through the multiple preceding definitions, it's hard not to notice that the rubber band applied to DTX is vast. The term's meaning also varies based on the type of organization defining it. Consulting and analyst companies try to stay generic; with their global reach offering services and frameworks, some software vendors bring all technological pieces into the mix pretty quickly.

However, even the most prominent and focused tech vendors expand their definitions of DTX over time as their technical capabilities offered to the market evolve. Personally, I like the HBR, BPM Institute, and Microsoft definitions the most, although what I am still missing in each one of them is the term *strategic adaptability*. What I've learned in the past is that many companies pursue DTX to accelerate the pace of internal change cascading through internal operations in response to quickly changing market conditions, new legislation, or external market pressures. Such an ability to evolve quickly can be extremely valuable in the marketplace, quoting Darwin: *"those who survive are the ones who most accurately perceive their environment and successfully adapt to it."*

Thus, DTX can be a vast topic, and even just having a conversation with anyone at your company about it can be pretty challenging, as different people in your organization may have different views of DTX. They can all be right, interestingly enough. The classic fable by John G. Saxe, originating in India, explains the concept of the limitations of perception.

Figure 2.1 – "The Blind Men and the Elephant" fable by John Godfrey Saxe (1816-1887)

Here's an excerpt from the fable/poem:

It was six men of Indostan

To learning much inclined,

Who went to see the Elephant

(Though all of them were blind),

That each by observation

Might satisfy his mind.

"God bless me! but the Elephant

Is very like a WALL!"

"This wonder of an Elephant

Is very like a SPEAR!"

"I see," quoth he, "the Elephant

Is very like a SNAKE!"

"'Tis clear enough the Elephant

Is very like a TREE!"

This marvel of an Elephant

Is very like a FAN!"

"I see," quoth he, "the Elephant

Is very like a ROPE!"

And so these men of Indostan

Disputed loud and long,

Each in his own opinion

Exceeding stiff and strong,

Though each was partly in the right,

And all were in the wrong!

DTX as an evolution versus revolution

To be more precise, DTX is one of those constantly evolving concepts that's changing as the software industry introduces new technical capabilities, allowing you to digitize and automate additional types of work that historically might have been out of reach. So, the metaphorical elephant from John Godfrey Saxe's fable, over time, can transform into a woolly mammoth or even a titanosaur, the largest dinosaur that ever roamed Earth. How many blind men would it take to describe what a titanosaur is as the DTX scope continues to grow over time, in 2-3 years? I think you will get the point – discussing DtC is a lot easier than tackling the whole topic of DTX.

Figure 2.2 – The scope of DTX is constantly growing

Besides its massive scale, what's essential to observe is that DTX is also a metaphor describing the digitized operations of our companies. It's hard to find one definition that represents a multi-dimensional concept that ultimately represents our business overlayed into the digital domain. Suppose DTX was a painting; it would most likely be portrayed as a fractal image or multiple fractal images constantly evolving in a 3D fashion, with some planes changing so fast that the human eye cannot observe the change, and some places changing very slowly. The following figures represent the cross-section of business, process, and data architectures that spin up multiple customer journeys supporting value chains inside our company:

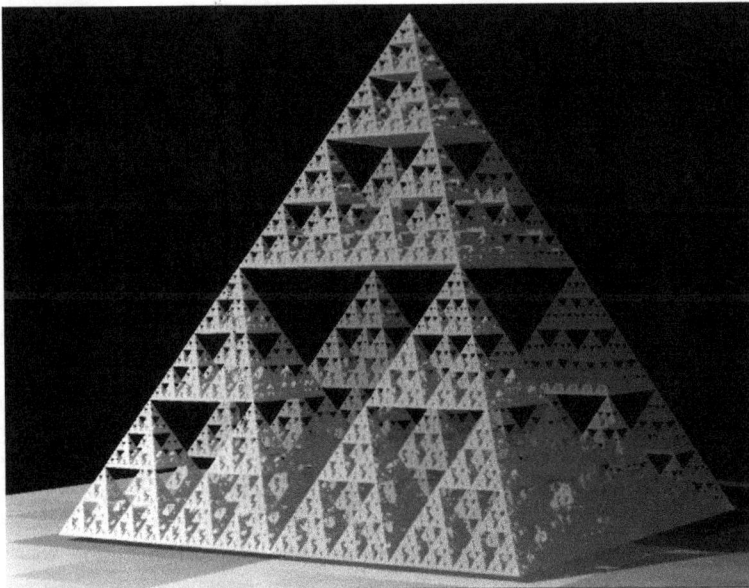

Figure 2.3 – Visual representation of digitally transformed company A

Figure 2.4 – Visual representation of digitally transformed company B

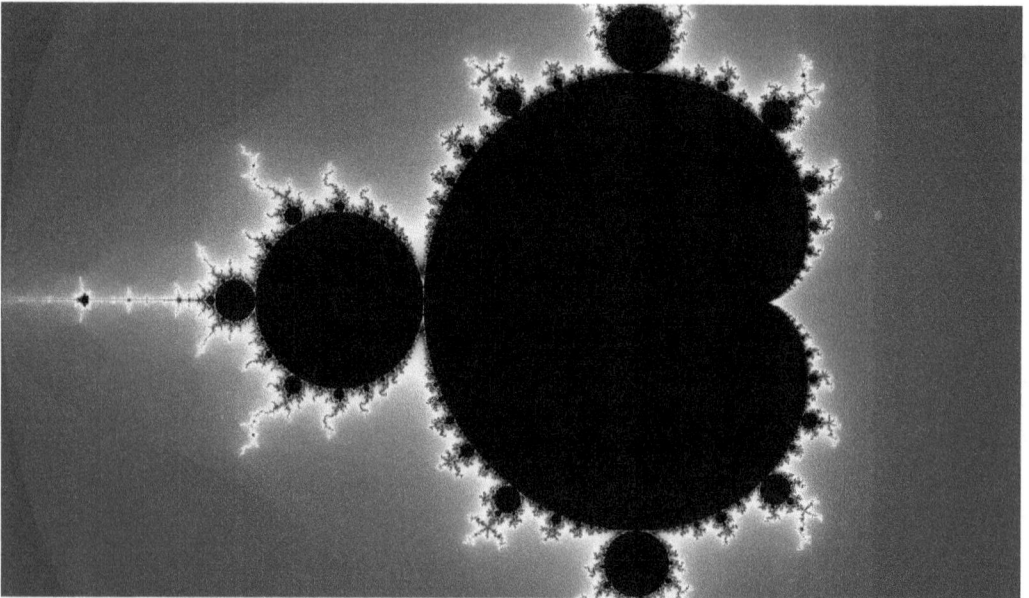

Figure 2.5 – Visual representation of digitally transformed company C

Think about this: our metaphors advance as technological progress advances; what does not change and stays constant is the definition of the business process. Many architects use the analogy of LEGO structures to represent business architecture. I have an issue with such a metaphor because this model assumes that networks of interconnected processes do not change or do not flex. If LEGO blocks were made from materials that twist, change shape, or stretch like slime, we'd add another dimension to this representation of our business. Another challenge I see is that LEGO blocks, once molded into a "house," are a house. A business can process online orders one day, yet another day, its infrastructure may be used to deliver drugs to a country's population, completely changing the business model and its purpose (and all design assumptions). What Amazon did during the COVID pandemic with the distribution of vaccines in the US is the best example of strategic adaptability at a massive scale.

The massive scale and architectural and technical complexities of DTX are why we are focusing our book on managing DtC, with a laser focus on process-led transformations, a smaller but significant slice of the whole DTX pie. Small does not mean unimportant or insignificant.

I've seen many small-scale projects that grew into programs over the years with the mission of completely changing the operations of the entire company. I was also part of large projects with lofty goals and armies of consultants that never grew outside one business unit. I have some theories about this phenomenon, and we will discuss those when we get into the **Business Value Assessments** (**BVAs**) and measuring ROI later in the book.

The other issue with definitions of DTX that jumps at me immediately concerns using the term business process. Pay attention to the following phrases:

- Bring together "process" to transform

- Use business workflows to optimize, automate, and modernize

- The use of digital technologies to create new or modify existing business processes

- Digital capability empowers organizations to not only enhance existing processes and products but also improve or even create new business models

- Apply technology to existing processes

    And this one…

- The rewiring of an organization

Learning from such definitions while working with teams involved in DTX efforts, I wondered if the authors crafting them had lived through at least one project or a program. Use digital technology to create new business processes, enhance existing processes, and apply technology to existing processes – sure, that makes a lot of sense. How about the rewiring of an organization? Has anyone ever tried to rewire the whole company while on a project? Yes, these slogans would sound great when having a quick hallway discussion with the CTO or a CFO. After reading tons of so-called definitions, I concluded that, many times, authors' intention was not to define; their intention was to sell – to sell digital technologies or supporting services to modernize business operations into a rewired version of your organization that would magically appear from the abyss of your company's legacy IT infrastructures like a phoenix. Throw more technology at your business problems, and your business problems will magically go away by "deploying tech at scale." Another challenge with these definitions is that they don't align with existing concepts from the business, process, and enterprise architecture domains used and practiced by influential professionals shaping DTX in many enterprises. To quote Jay Olvey, strategic business and process director and architect: *"The challenge in today's companies is not the lack of tech; it's the lack of know-how of how to implement tech platforms in support of strategic company goals. It's also the lack of a shared vision and performance metric alignment, along with communication and collaboration as well."*

From the technical point of view, Microsoft's definitions are most accurate, although I have an issue with the term workflow used in this context. It feels that the author of Microsoft 365's explanation meant to say use business workstreams, not workflows. Workflows are instances of automated business processes executing activities and tasks within workflow orchestration engines, whether low-code, iBPMS platforms, or CRM systems. I reserve the right to be wrong in this case, given that I worked for Microsoft.

Learning about advanced concepts from a variety of definitions can be challenging because universal truths don't exist in the world of business. To say it differently, going after universal truths requires a lot of critical thinking and questioning of both authors' intentions and the analysis of the timing of when such definitions were introduced to the market.

As far as the "rewiring" of existing business processes goes, one of the most common challenges in the modern medium to large-sized enterprise is that many business processes are not well defined or undergo a cycle of continuous change that happens very quickly. These process-based operations are executed by teams utilizing a multitude of platforms and IT systems, but to risk repeating myself, many of these business processes are poorly designed, may not even be defined, or they exist as multiple variants, duplicated in various systems of records and Excel spreadsheets serving as workarounds. Poor process design leads to suboptimal execution, which is where this book should come to the rescue.

Another elephant in the room worth mentioning: the majority of businesspeople in the modern enterprise, when asked about the definition of a business process, will stumble a little but most of the time will be able to explain in somewhat logical terms that a business process is a repeatable collection of steps a company uses to accomplish a goal with event-driven, end-to-end, and customer-oriented characteristics. Some will also add that a process is a standardized method the company or team uses to perform routine activities, and that they are critical to keeping your business on track and organized. BPM Institute's definition is logical and easy to grasp. In subsequent chapters, we will dive deep into these definitions and build upon them to understand more advanced process concepts.

The same person, when asked, may also bring an example of a business process they interact with daily, such as procure to pay, new employee onboarding, order processing, or customer onboarding. Things get tricky when you ask someone to capture the definition of their work. Sometimes it's the notation; sometimes it's the tooling; and sometimes it's the fact that the knowledge about our work expressed through swim lanes is spread out across many teams, people, and time zones. Sometimes, different people have different definitions of the work they are performing, and at times, policies and procedures are not adequately documented. Many times, we are only operating in the realm of the happy path, sweeping alternate scenarios and exceptions under the rug. Things get pretty complicated when we talk about business processes driving knowledge work, either emerging, ad hoc, or decision-intensive.

So why should you care about all of this? If the answer is not yet apparent, let's blame our definitions of DTX for this lack of clarity. Undertaking an effort to transform the operations of our business units digitally without the necessary clarity will only cause unnecessary "execution drag" on the project team driving the digitization agenda. When you start getting into technical topics related to the implementation of your vision and mission statement, bringing in tools such as **AI**, **IoT**, **cloud**, **Digital Process Automation (DPA)**, low-code platforms, engineering teams, and project managers while lacking clarity on the business and process architecture layers of the DTX, things are going to get complicated very quickly.

Avoiding common pitfalls

During my career, I've been asked a few times to drive evangelism of process-led DtC programs, and such assignments taught me the following lessons:

- DtC efforts usually span multiple business and tech areas, with numerous stakeholders owning the outcome, which may be defined differently based on the business group.

- The topic of DTX can get very big very quickly, and people will challenge your authority to discuss programs so large in scale. Leaders don't like to discuss initiatives that span the whole enterprise; such problems are simply too big to tackle.

- Many times, people involved in digitization projects have been exposed to failed implementations in the past, facing leadership skepticism about any new work or technology that reattempts to drive the same type of change. Remember the statistic cited by Boston Consulting Group of 60-70% of large transformation projects failing (*Flipping the Odds of Digital Transformation Success | BCG* (https://www.bcg.com/publications/2020/increasing-odds-of-success-in-digital-transformation)). No one likes to fail more than once, and no one wants to risk a career betting on another shiny vision of reality. The rule of thumb is that organizational memory retains information about failures for ~2 years, and if you attempt to relaunch process transformation projects that failed too early, you will struggle. Engaging in multiple root cause analyses to probe possible causes of failed digital change initiatives makes a lot of sense. Many times, prior failures are not attributed to technology and can be corrected if adequately diagnosed. The first instinct of any organization that failed DTX is to blame the software vendor providing the platform and tools; however, except for a few scenarios where DPA vendors were indeed to blame, most issues leading to failures were internal. This is not to say that software vendors don't cut corners or overpromise on tech capabilities. Some do, and cleaning up after such projects is usually not much fun. Such projects can be great lessons learned, but tend to be very stressful and technically challenging.

- In many organizations, IT units hold bigger budgets than businesses and feel that this funding provides them with a stronger voice to drive DtC. Companies yield the best results with DTX or DtC in a business-led, technology-facilitated mode of operation. Try to address this dynamic before launching any major initiatives.

- When organizations jump on the automation bandwagon, excited about the high potential, they often approach knowledge-intensive work in the same way as repeatable tasks and activities. Due to a lack of experience, it's easy to treat case-based scenarios like structured workflows. These mistakes can paralyze complex industries, such as law and healthcare. Designing end-to-end flows for work that's inherently variable leads to rigidity, workarounds, and user pushbacks. This pitfall occurs when work predictability levels are not considered, and the Fit Assessment service is skipped during the opportunity evaluation phase of the project. What's needed for the automation of knowledge work is a stateful, context-aware model that gives users control while guiding work toward the right outcome. Some leaders and execs will drink the software vendor Kool-Aid, which comes with much vendor-infused flavor, at times overpowering the true objectives of the transformation. It's only through the adoption of technology platforms and interactions with consulting teams that we learn about the authentic culture of the company brought in to help out or the true transformational power of their technology. Unfortunately, at the point of adoption, such discoveries come late.

For example, if, as an employee of a company responsible for driving the vision of the DtC for your organization, you find yourself at odds with vendors courting or competing with you for access to decision-makers, even your best strategies will fail regardless of whether your strategies are superior to visions offered by external vendors. The situation can be even more complex if your company works with multiple "strategic" advisors, vendors, or IT service companies. Some vendors will pursue their business agendas aggressively, and sifting through the track record of projects to back up claims made by these companies can be impossible and impractical.

To help you avoid all the challenges mentioned, I'd like to propose a model of a process-led DTX that, when applied correctly, guarantees success regardless of politics, technical complexities, or vendors brought in to help. Following this conceptual model to harness forces in the enterprise will ground most agendas on a shared view of DtC, ultimately leading to DTX.

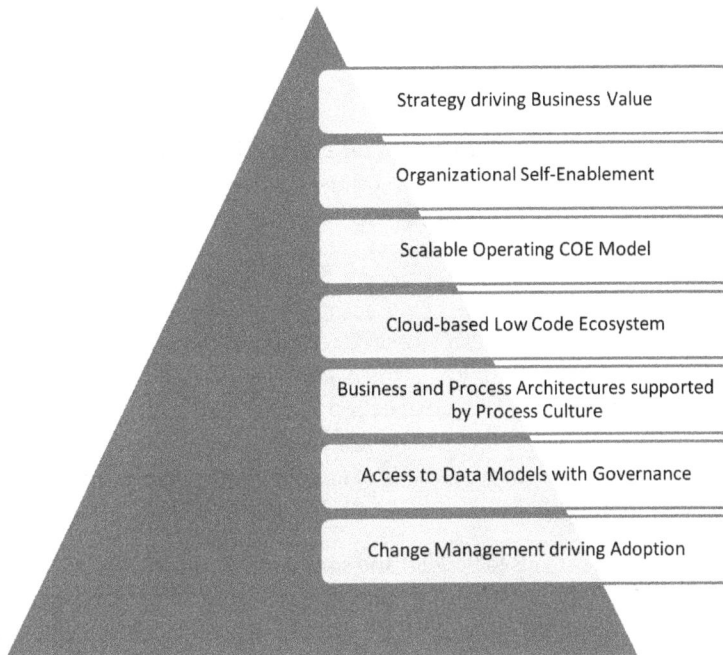

Figure 2.6 – Seven pillars of a DTX

So far, we've learned that even discussing and driving awareness of the need for DtC can be a political minefield requiring careful navigation. To ensure that our efforts will have desired and lasting effects, the seven pillars of DTX, a conceptual framework, will help establish boundaries for multiple workstreams, calming often erratic agendas and creating the right environment for our transformation.

How does DTX start?

In this section, I will focus on the five types of scenarios that can lead to the launch of a DtC program. Some efforts may ultimately lead to the DTX program involving parallel workstreams, and some never get enough support for enterprise-wide adoption. All five scenarios are based on real-life examples of large companies embarking on digitization projects.

Top-down transformation

Top-down transformations have been mastered by software vendors who usually pursue monetization of opportunities from the sale of software licenses. This style of transformation involves an executive leader stepping up to announce the massive effort to redesign business processes at a large scale in the organization. Many times, the vision and know-how behind the plans come from software vendors who aggressively pursue their own agendas by introducing digitization platforms. While, on the surface, this style seems the least risky due to the centralized level of control, this style of transformation is the least enjoyable to employees and does not get into all corners of your company's operations.

The vision, the know-how, and any specialized knowledge required to drive the adoption of the vendor's software comes directly from the vendor, putting workers at a significant disadvantage when they start realizing the need to complete work with external delivery providers or consultants who very quickly establish themselves as the go-to people for business knowledge. The organization's politics also tends to get a lot messier, with vendors starting to get a lot of face time with your executives, talking the talk but not genuinely understanding all the intricate details of your business.

The messaging from your leaders tends to be solid and consistent, yet the results promised by vendors don't always match the realities of sales PowerPoint decks you've seen at the beginning of the project. Top-level execs tend to be convinced that such challenges are only temporary while their business decision and leadership reputation is at stake. The other challenge with this transformation style is related to sponsorship from a single leader. If the top leader leaves the organization or the company is acquired, transformation efforts will stall or stop completely.

Pros	Cons
• Clear vision and messaging driven from the top of the company	• Tend to be costlier and more challenging to realize the promised ROI
• Internal program prioritization tends to be easier	• Put software-delivering tools in the driving seat
• Transformation investments have a long-term horizon	• Less collaborative
	• Higher risk of job loss for employees

Table 2.1 – Advantages and disadvantages of a top-down transformation

While top-down transformations emphasize centralized control and strategic vision, grassroots transformations rely on empowering individuals across the organization to drive change from within.

Grassroot transformation

This transformation style is most often associated with the citizen developer style of digital change programs. Companies sponsor citizen developers, bringing their ideas to DPA **Centers of Excellence (COEs)**. DPA COEs, through a portfolio of expert services, including ideation and project pipeline creation, enablement, process landscape assessment, solution consulting, risk management, ROI analysis, standards definition, and governance, support the roll out of these distributed initiatives all the way to their go-live. The role of the DPA COE or multiple COEs is to become the team that supports other groups with quick and timely services, unblocking **citizen developers (cit-devs)** on their journeys. While the COE is ultimately accountable for the overall DTC, and its funding depends on strategies and the quality of services provided year after year, the actual analysis and delivery work is performed by citizen developers and citizen architects. If your transformation initiative is led by the IT department, your company might establish a **Center for Enablement (C4E)**, which offers a limited set of services compared to a **Center of Excellence (COE)**. C4Es focus on promoting collaboration, reusability, and the sharing of reusable patterns. The main difference between COEs and C4Es lies in their functions: COEs provide expert-driven governance to ensure quality and compliance, while C4Es aim to empower teams and enable faster innovation and collaboration. In some cases, COEs may extend their mission to include functions typically associated with C4Es. However, it is rare for C4Es to expand their roles to encompass the full mission of a COE.

In the early stages of grassroots DTC, citizen developers' work may be described as shadow IT if not given enough recognition by company leaders. Don't get discouraged, as this is just a sign of the lack of maturity of the company's DTC strategy. Many companies successfully transformed their shadow IT programs into VP-accepted citizen developer adoption of digital process automation technologies, turning small improvement opportunities into large and successful projects. If your initiatives are not getting enough leadership attention, don't give up. This book provides you with several techniques intended to help you succeed. While these types of programs can be the most challenging to launch, they offer the deepest penetration of DPA technologies and address the most demanding challenges faced by your organization. Frequently, pain points uncovered by cit devs don't even get recognized by company leaders who prioritize their initiatives at the highest level, never getting into the weeds. The power of identifying and solving problems by people who live them every day can be mighty.

Pros	Cons
• Stronger and easier to prove adoption ROI • Transformation gets into all corners of the company • Bottom-up prioritization surfaces true business pain points	• Requires a significant level of investment in self-enablement and training • Requires familiarity with the COE operating model, which may be harder to operationalize without prior experience • Easier barrier to entry cost-wise, higher barrier to entry skillset-wise • Securing funding and resources to build can be a challenging and tedious process

Table 2.2 – Advantages and disadvantages of a grassroot transformation

While grassroots transformation delves deeply into organizational engagement and cultural shifts, legacy modernization efforts focus on the structural backbone of critical systems, presenting a contrasting approach to driving change.

Legacy modernization efforts

This less common but still popular trigger of DTX comes to life as the outcome of a decision to either replace or integrate with a major system of records, such as EPR, CRM, claims processing engines, or SAP. These types of systems tend to be harder to replace due to their business criticality and the complexity of the volume of business processes they support. Complete system replacement, while feasible in technical terms, assuming unlimited resources, tends to be both risky and very costly.

Pros	Cons
• More clarity about transformation objectives • Possibility to reuse already implemented business processes and established practices • High ROI	• Treated more as a project than a true business transformation program • Has a lot less impact on the transformation culture • Programs carry high business risk due to the criticality of these systems

Table 2.3 – Advantages and disadvantages of a legacy modernization transformation

While legacy modernization focuses on revitalizing existing critical systems, acquisitions or mergers introduce a dynamic interplay of integration challenges and opportunities.

Triggered by an acquisition or merger

This type of DTX usually involves two companies: one acquiring and one being the acquisition target. In this situation, there is typically a bit of time allowed to prepare the execution as the business side of planning and negotiation does take ample time, creating enough signals about what's to come a long time in advance. The business and technology teams of the acquiring company can focus on getting the complete inventory of their business processes with a thorough understanding of the technical capabilities of existing platforms.

Taking on new business models and additional volumes of work to support the populations of new customers will more than likely put significant stress on your technology, forcing leaders to reconsider or, in some cases, even accelerate any process redesign plans that have been put on the back burner for months. To be successful and land the strategic business objectives that drove the acquisition, companies need to launch several very critical projects, driving the need for the tight integration of the business processes of both companies. Most of the time, the acquiring company will have a deciding voice in how such process integrations will proceed. One of the mistakes that can be made at this stage has to do with the perception that the acquiring company's business processes should completely replace the processes of the target company. This type of thinking may prevent the acquiring company from harvesting and learning about innovative business processes that drove business in segments of the market that were not accessible to the acquiring company. In other words, it's prudent to plan for a thorough analysis of existing business processes before making decisions about what processes should stay, get extended, integrated, simplified, or discarded.

If the acquiring company can quickly get access to an understanding of business processes driving the target, integration decisions become a lot easier. It's also worth noting that many mergers or acquisitions approach such projects as system integrations of existing technologies, further complicating and delaying the business benefits of the integration.

Integrating systems versus integrating business processes can sound like the same type of activity, but it's not – the work is usually driven at a different layer of the enterprise architecture, and the types of decisions and issues that come to the forefront are different. Many people, though, still confuse these two styles of integration. I suggest taking the process-first approach, and this is an area where process mining can genuinely shine, given the scale, complexity, and pace of parallel workstreams that unfold. In some large-scale integrations, the pace of the change forces both companies to start from scratch entirely and to build new processes, but these types of primary new legislation-driven use cases are still not very common (i.e., in the healthcare industry, the occasional and frequent legislative change forces companies to reinvent themselves quickly). Most acquisitions involve integrations with large-scale legacy systems, which cannot be dropped without a significant impact on business operations (aka the loss of business).

Another variant of such a scenario involves a situation in which an acquisition or a merger stops the ongoing DTX, which can be very frustrating if you've been incubating and building internal support for your program over an extended period. These scenarios do happen, and they happen more frequently than one would hope for. In these scenarios, companies throw away hard-earned insights and reusable IP only because the acquiring company assumed their processes were better.

Pros	Cons
• Can be executed with advanced planning • Significant focus on execution eases portfolio prioritization conflicts • Opportunity to harness the intellectual property of both companies	• Usually stops ongoing transformation initiatives at the acquired company • Involves more external consultants • Exposes blind corners in the existing process architecture and compounds existing technology issues

Table 2.4 – Advantages and disadvantages of a transformation triggered by acquisition

While acquisitions often come with structured planning, transformations initiated by accident highlight the unpredictable yet impactful nature of serendipity in driving change.

By accident

As challenging as it may be to accept such a scenario as a possibility, there are situations when DTX efforts start by accident and continue moving forward in an uncontrolled fashion. How is that possible, you may ask? Well, I sometimes wonder about the impact of serendipity on DTX as well, but I can certainly attest from my professional experience, having been part of such a program myself, that such scenarios do happen and, in some situations, can lead to spectacular outcomes. There are usually a few factors that are needed to tip the scale or to tempt the proverbial fate, so to speak. Still, it all usually starts with a use case, a set of requirements addressing some very severe pain points in the organization, a working culture that favors experimentation, healthy and supportive team dynamics, and one or two change agents who are relentless about challenging the status quo. While the culture of heroes in the business usually carries some stigma attached to it, the culture of challengers, the so-called revolutionaries, can support accidental triggers of DTX.

In 2005, working as part of the e-commerce team at Prescription Solutions, the pharmacy benefits management company, I was assigned to work on a project implementing experimental technology intended to optimize the operations of a high-volume call center. This team was constituted of two vendor companies and two .NET developers, one of them being me. At that time in my career, I was keeping my eyes open to new technologies, wanting to extend my Microsoft web and development skills with an additional skillset. Working on the team with Pegasystems and Cognizant consultants opened my eyes to a brand-new world of digital process automation, which both excited me and set my career in an unexpected direction.

Fast-forward six years, our six-month project in Southern California created the small wave that created another wave that fed into another wave, ultimately leading to the enterprise-wide transformation of UnitedHealth Group with the use of the BPMS platform and related know-how. This was one of the most enormous process-led digital transformations in the world, creating multiple new job opportunities within the company, great learning projects, lots of excitement, and a few very innovative projects that gained attention from outside of the company. At the same time, the scale of this transformation created several headwinds related to the overall cost, technical and operational scalability, and challenging promotion paths for insiders involved in these efforts. You see, despite helping to release a force that digitized many parts of the organization, ultimately resulting in multi-million dollar returns on investment, many program participants did not win career-wise. As the news of the successful transformation started to do the rounds within the enterprise, pulling other business units and segments into the wave of business process management, organizational politics started to play a more prominent role, outshining true results.

"Success has many fathers and failure is an orphan" still rings true in companies with more traditional corporate cultures. Many new leaders, encouraged by the success of our very challenging transformation, quickly raised their hands, inspired by the excellent results reported by my IT director and business sponsor. Corporate leaders started to follow in the footsteps of our segments, stepping into the same set of mistakes of early adopters, self-promoting, and trying to take the credit for the transformation force that was already unleashed. Many "self-proclaimed" visionaries came out of the woodwork, connected to centers of corporate power, literally elevating their careers through PowerPoint slides built on top of the hard work of our unit. There is nothing wrong with building on the success of others; a lot of innovative companies do it. When you, however, start taking credit for the accomplishments of other people who paved the way for you, that's not leadership; that's a strategy taken directly from Machiavelli. It's a known but not very well-publicized fact that DTX programs test corporate cultures for ethics and transparency because the business value unlocked can be very high. These high ROI programs can attract all types of corporate buffoons who thrive in corporate environments by attaching themselves to successful initiatives. However, if you asked them to raise their hands to help when the going was demanding and involved risk-taking and commitment, they'd prefer to hide behind recycled PowerPoint slideware.

Our initial implementation team was small, mighty, hardworking, and committed to the bone to the success of the project. In the professional world of business and technology, such commitment should be evaluated by the number of overnights, family sacrifices, and weekends spent supporting DTX; however, these rarely see the light. Today, reflecting on the work accomplished during PAS implementation, I take my hat off to the team responsible for accidentally launching the most extensive process-led transformation in the world: Qing, Wendy, Solita, and Stacy. These ladies took this healthcare insurance giant to a place where not many companies ever went before, and I was fortunate to work alongside them.

Pros	Cons
• High levels of innovation and creativity • Can result in significant business ROI and positive results • Minimizes political turf wars in the early stages • Driven internally by FTEs increases work satisfaction	• Higher costs to launch, coupled with a number of early adopter mistakes • Insufficient preparation puts stakeholders and teams in a situation where they have to both prepare for and launch projects in parallel • Heavier dependency on software vendors drives implementation costs up and blocks specific initiatives from launching due to the lack of know-how

Table 2.5 – Advantages and disadvantages of an accidental transformation

While understanding the pros and cons of accidental transformations sheds light on their challenges, crafting a clear vision of DtC provides a strategic roadmap to navigate and mitigate these complexities effectively.

How do I craft a vision of DtC for my business group?

Now that we understand that DtC programs need a little bit of foresight to be successful, let's talk about the creative process that preempts the planning phase. Jointly crafting and socializing a vision of DtC is a step that's very often overlooked, which can have far-reaching consequences for your DtC program. Rallying people around fuzzy and ill-defined visions won't generate enough support in the organization intending to transform itself. Let's face it: changing the way companies operate can be difficult. Visions rally people around common goals while bringing perspectives that might have been overlooked. They also define future benefits and the reasons behind the work that's just about to start and continue for months, if not years. Visions should be drafted by a leader who stands behind the idea of the transformation, who understands the business and challenges faced, and who can identify metaphors that generate clarity versus muddying the waters. Let's review the following three examples:

- **Vision Example 1 – Senior Director**

  "Our goal is to provide a scalable digital solution that empowers employees to move quickly in a way that works for them, which will, in turn, improve the speed and quality of work delivered, providing the best customer experience possible while raising employee morale."

- **Vision Example 2 – SVP of Engineering**

  "We are aiming to deliver solutions that unleash and connect our people and accelerate the business."

- **Vision Example 3 – Director, Workforce Enablement**

  "Our goal is to increase employee satisfaction and productivity by enabling a fast, frictionless, and empowering digital workplace."

The process of creating and socializing the vision should take time and involve most stakeholders of the impacted organization to avoid the perception of *"this is what we are going to do to you"* versus *"this is what we are going to do with you."* If you manage to avoid the dreaded feeling that DTC is pushed on teams from the top versus being jointly defined, half of your future battles are already won.

Bringing external consultants to help craft the vision is also not the best idea, even if they have more experience and carry the weight of the top 5 consulting brands. While this may sound illogical, please remember that the process of defining, obtaining buy-in, and support goes hand in hand. Having a senior director communicate the vision of your group's digital operations will carry much more weight and set you up for long-term success. Use consultants to learn from and to expand your awareness of what is going on in the market while leaving the definition of the North Star map to your direct leadership with the right level of authority and influence.

How to plan for the future

The World War II leader and U.S. President Dwight D. Eisenhower made a paradoxical statement about preparation. Here are two versions:

- Plans are useless, but planning is indispensable.

- Plans are worthless, but planning is essential.

The advice of the leader of the free world should be considered when anticipating all potential impacts of DTX. Planning is a creative exercise that helps to prepare for the future without fully knowing what the future holds. Each business leader usually relies on their past experience and competitive research when anticipating the future; however, I'd like to call out the following common scenarios, which will require some careful consideration.

Plan for continuous adaptability

In today's economic environment, the primary value of digital change programs revolves around supporting strategic adaptability. Your company can no longer rely on the economies of scale and drastic efficiencies that drove CTO digitization agendas for process improvement just a few years ago. In today's environment, it's the companies that adapt the quickest to changing market conditions while at the same time supporting scale and efficiencies that win in the marketplace. Such strategies require a different thinking style, one aligned with experimentation and total empowerment of your workforce. Strategic adaptability also calls for a drastic rethink of the approach to the business and solution architectures in the enterprise. If you've ever tried to standardize the adoption of citizen development low-code platforms in your company, you understand how these tools call for a set of new governance paradigms that push boundaries and break the relationship between business and traditional IT.

If you extend the same paradigm to business and process analysis and empower business users to actively participate in the design of your business processes without the involvement of teams of process architects, we are talking about unleashing a mighty innovation force that not only experiences business pain points daily but one that is actively empowered to tackle their own issues. Of course, the adaptability of the employee onboarding process will mean something else in a global environment where local workforce rules and regulations change more frequently than in a process that supports the operation of a local county or province, so it's always good to keep the scale in mind.

A company's need for adaptability should be considered through the lens of enterprise-wide process architecture, and I am a massive proponent of companies investing resources into this capability. Investing but not overinvesting, as we don't want to create ivory towers of business professionals who carry with them pages of diagrams telling everyone to look at the world through the process lens. When you upskill enough people and start treating process skills in the same fashion as you would have treated presentation or negotiation skills, you will start noticing a shift in team thinking about business areas they support. It's like people start communicating about their work and business challenges using the same visual language, creating shared understanding of projects and processes they support, and helping to spot-check and diagnose issues. Speaking about, but more importantly, understanding the same process notation can be very powerful since visual notations can be easier to comprehend than pages of written work instructions. Citing the field experience of Igor Jericevich, Managing Director, ShareDo, Australia, who implements advanced case management solutions in the legal industry: *"One of the core challenges I see repeatedly is the obsession with trying to nail down every permutation of a process before implementation. Analysts would draw boxes and lines, arguing over every exception and alternate paths, until the process became more of a prison than a guide."*

Igor started to use the following analogy with his clients: *"You've laid railway tracks, and now your business is the train. But what happens when a tree falls on the tracks? Process maps appear elegant and planned until the real world intervenes. Adaptability does not mean abandoning structure; it means embedding intelligent flexibility within it."* He suggests users stay cautious and don't turn adaptability into an excuse for chaos. Guardrails are critical, and the best adaptive systems still have a strong definition of what "good" looks like. They allow multiple paths to get there.

Embrace the disruption of your workforce

DtC programs can drive very aggressive optimization of work, changing the way people perform their day-to-day activities. The fear of being displaced by AI or software is real. That fear, though, is not founded on any data, and we should be fearful of how our jobs will change rather than how we will be able to compete against machines in our day-to-day work. Thomas Davenport, in his book titled *Only Humans Need Apply: Winners and Losers in the Age of Smart Machines*, mentions a couple of strategies that professionals can apply to rediscover themselves in the workplace that's getting disrupted. Work automation implementation teams driving the adoption of DTX platforms are closely familiar with change management, which some describe as "fear management."

Emotions can inhibit the adoption of disruptive frameworks and solutions, creating the drag expressed by Forrester and Boston Consulting Group through the mind-boggling statistic of more than 60% of large-scale transformations failing. This is a very high number to ponder, especially considering the amount of hours and dollars that go into such programs.

The other type of disruption faced by your workforce has to do with skills development. As digital change programs gain acceptance, new roles emerge, requiring the reskilling of your workforce. Business process owners, business process architects, and digital change managers are examples of such roles.

In addition, your own business professionals will need to pick up or update their skills as well. While many good professional certificates specialize in DTX and DtC tracks, most graduates of business schools do not get enough exposure to these topics during their education, with vendors frantically trying to fill in the gaps by offering commercial courses packaged for college students.

Digital Change initiatives leave plenty of opportunities for HR and resource management professionals to step in and fill in the knowledge gaps created by aggressive project launches.

Plan to generate and manage lots of intellectual property

Business process discovery, definition, and redesign create lots of metadata about the work performed by your organization. The number of attributes, questions, and KPIs that can be brought to light can be mindboggling. Many times, this is the first time many professionals have started seeing all of the attributes defining their business processes; many people discover that they've been using incorrect taxonomy and terminology, or did not consider the full scope of work. Stepping outside of your core work area to look at the operations of your business process end-to-end can be a scary proposition, primarily because we've been pigeonholed into our jobs, thinking about the work in terms of **RACIs**. Well, this is a mistake that's caused by years of indoctrination by **Master of Business Administration (MBA)** and **Project Management Professional (PMP)** programs.

> **Note**
>
> **RACIs** refers to the **RACI** matrix, a project management and process tool used to clarify roles and responsibilities. **RACI** stands for: Responsible – Who does the work, Accountable – Who owns the outcome, Consulted – Who gives input, and Informed – Who needs to be kept in the loop.

RACIs were designed for different reasons, not to look at work end-to-end. If you ever step outside of your core role or team to learn about how the activities and work of others impact your daily job, I guarantee it will be an eye-opener. Smart companies recognize the fact that business processes, their attributes, and interdependencies reflecting group relationships create the imprint of your business, and this knowledge is extremely valuable. Why rely on external consultants to capture and model your organization's intellectual property, only for that knowledge to walk out the door with them at the end of the project? I've always struggled to understand the business rationale behind outsourcing process discovery and modeling to third-party firms. These consultants often leave with a deep understanding of your operations embedded in their "muscle memory"—not yours.

Instead, empowering your own employees to discover, model, and categorize business processes is a far more sustainable strategy. Yes, it may feel riskier or more resource-intensive at first, but the long-term benefits will be substantial.

What's a better approach? Bring in experienced process architects not to do the work for you, but to teach, mentor, and guide your internal teams. Their expertise will accelerate your transformation while ensuring your people build lasting skills and process awareness. It's a true win-win: your workforce grows more capable, and your organization gains a deeper understanding of how it operates.

The tricky part is that you need to be able to capture, present, and continuously enhance this great knowledge, but the spectrum of solutions ranges from SharePoint sites with highly organized folder structures reflecting layers of your company's process architecture to specialized software repositories such as the ones from ADONIS or iGrafx. When choosing the vendor of choice, think about reusability, ease of access, and the compatibility of the product with the overall DtC strategy. You'd not want to invest in a cloud-based process repository from IBM if you were thinking about driving digitization using Microsoft's Power Platform suite of tools. While all vendors offer some level of interoperability, placing the **Business Process Model and Notation** (**BPMN**) in the center, standard compatibility between tools from different camps can vary product by product. Some vendors, such as Pega or Microsoft, offer direct uplift in application design if the business process modeling starts in Visio.

Plan for the long term, but focus on the short term

DtC initiatives usually carry tons of risk, and for the right reason. Between technology, people, scope, and business constraints, the list of things that can go wrong is long. One of the primary objectives of the person creating strategic plans for such initiatives is maintaining executive support throughout the program. Anyone can create a multi-month schedule in MS Project; however, it's the track record of hitting multiple milestones that will sustain the executive support throughout the length of the program.

Project managers and engagement leaders don't own crystal balls, but they understand that the tides may change, and they may change quite frequently, impacting the work of a team. Keeping milestones manageable will ensure the risk is properly managed and deadlines are met. This approach will build momentum to help you spread your wings a little. Another factor that can hinder the progress of your project is the scrutiny caused by the financial pressures of your sponsors. When your business sponsors invest millions of dollars into licensing and consulting labor, their expectations for the ROI will be super high, and the slightest project issue will get their attention. DTX projects can get very challenging technically, despite vendor promises of technological nirvana. Transforming businesses, even with the most expensive and sophisticated technology in the world, still depends on factors that mostly exist outside the realm of technological platforms. Old-fashioned project prioritization, lack of access to APIs and interfaces, an inability to get access to SMEs, leadership turnover, burnout, and the high turnover of resources on the project can successfully halt implementations for the best teams using the most sophisticated technology.

If you don't consistently deliver on your short-term goals, even the smallest ones, your credibility to deliver the long-term view will tarnish. Success builds on top of success, even the smallest ones, and in the initial stage, it's super important to pay attention to credibility building.

Plan to regularly adjust your plans

This may sound like a cliché, but build learnings from experimentation as a phase into your projects. As you step into the operations of your company and discover details that have not been considered in the past, your plans and thinking about your project will change. It's best to make changes to your plans from a place of having data and knowledge on hand. There are a few situations that will cause shifts in strategy generated by worldwide issues, such as wars, geopolitical shifts, natural disasters, and shortages. These large grain shifts affect the DTX efforts and the ongoing work. While at Microsoft Finance, we've been faced with a situation requiring us to rapidly adjust our payment ecosystem caused by the war in Ukraine, trying to support all the great work of Microsoft partners. These unforeseen events delayed the execution of our optimization projects by weeks.

Plan to size and scope properly

Digital process transformation projects tend to grow in scope, and they can quickly multiply. Even the ones that start as tiny, itsy bitsy business process improvements can touch a nerve and expose business processes of monumental sizes. There are multiple reasons for this phenomenon, but the ones I'd like to call out are the interconnectedness of business processes, lack of experience with process-led design, lack of familiarity with the estimation of DPA projects, and a lack of understanding of the maturity of the underlying architectural landscape of the business unit targeted for transformation.

While at Nordstrom, I've seen process prototype ideas that turned into projects driving company-wide supply chain operations. I've also seen large-scale transformations that lasted for months due to the business criticality of the work they were improving. Don't get into projects assuming you already know the scope; arriving with an open mind to allow for enough experimentation should expose the true size of the program, allowing you to properly size the work.

The other critical detail of scoping has to do with the timing of when effort estimates get made. It's usually best to approach sizing in an iterative fashion, starting with T-shirt sizing, then moving to **Rough Order of Magnitude (ROM)**, and finally providing budgetary guidance as you continue to receive more information about the scope and constraints, allowing you to apply technical contingencies (50%, 15%, 5%). Depending on field-proven estimation models that consider scaling factors grounded in the realities of your organization or similar organizations from the same industry will help increase the quality of your estimates. We touch on the topic of estimation in *Part 3, Chapter 11*. Knowing when to size is as important as knowing what to size. Keep that in mind. Such an approach may be hard to explain to leaders who want quick answers, but quick answers usually damage credibility. I've seen this scenario repeat itself repeatedly; a business architect pushed for quick answers creates a shiny Excel spreadsheet with the final schedule and cost information, damaging the reputation of the transformation program by not delivering projects on time due to incorrect assumptions and wrong timing of when assumptions and estimates were made.

Plan for growth

From my experience, business process owners and sponsors who undertook digital change initiatives experienced significant business growth as process inefficiencies and kinks were worked out during the program. While it may not be easy or even possible to forecast upfront how much additional revenue will be generated in the future, we can safely anticipate business growth based on the following:

- Business optimization will make the operations of your business more efficient, initially increasing the volume of work handled by the business process.

- Elimination of waste, inefficiencies, and manual workarounds implemented as Excel spreadsheets will speed up the pace and the quality of the work flowing through business processes.

- A higher quality of work usually reflects higher customer satisfaction. Increased satisfaction leads to additional work or projects. Take advantage of the old adage that good work creates more work, and good services or products generate more business value and additional sales opportunities.

- Increased transparency offered through the digitization of business processes will create real-time metrics about ongoing operations. Such metrics can be used to analyze the process retroactively and also to support future process simulations.

Digital change initiatives, if sustained to the end, will advance the organization's operations to the fourth-fifth level of process maturity (managed/optimizing). At the optimizing stage, companies start experimenting with existing business models, introducing and piloting new ideas and models that can bring more revenue or cut costs.

- Many digital change initiatives involve the introduction of new technology platforms to streamline and optimize business processes. As technology matures, new ways to increase capacity become available to support the global scalability of your processes through services such as Azure Autoscale or Azure SQL Database Hyperscale, further driving the scalability of business processes implemented on low-code platforms. Let's not forget that cloud-based, on-demand services support growth while decreasing the need for constant IT resources consumed, helping to avoid overinvestments into infrastructure and energy and pushing the ROI of DtC initiatives to new highs.

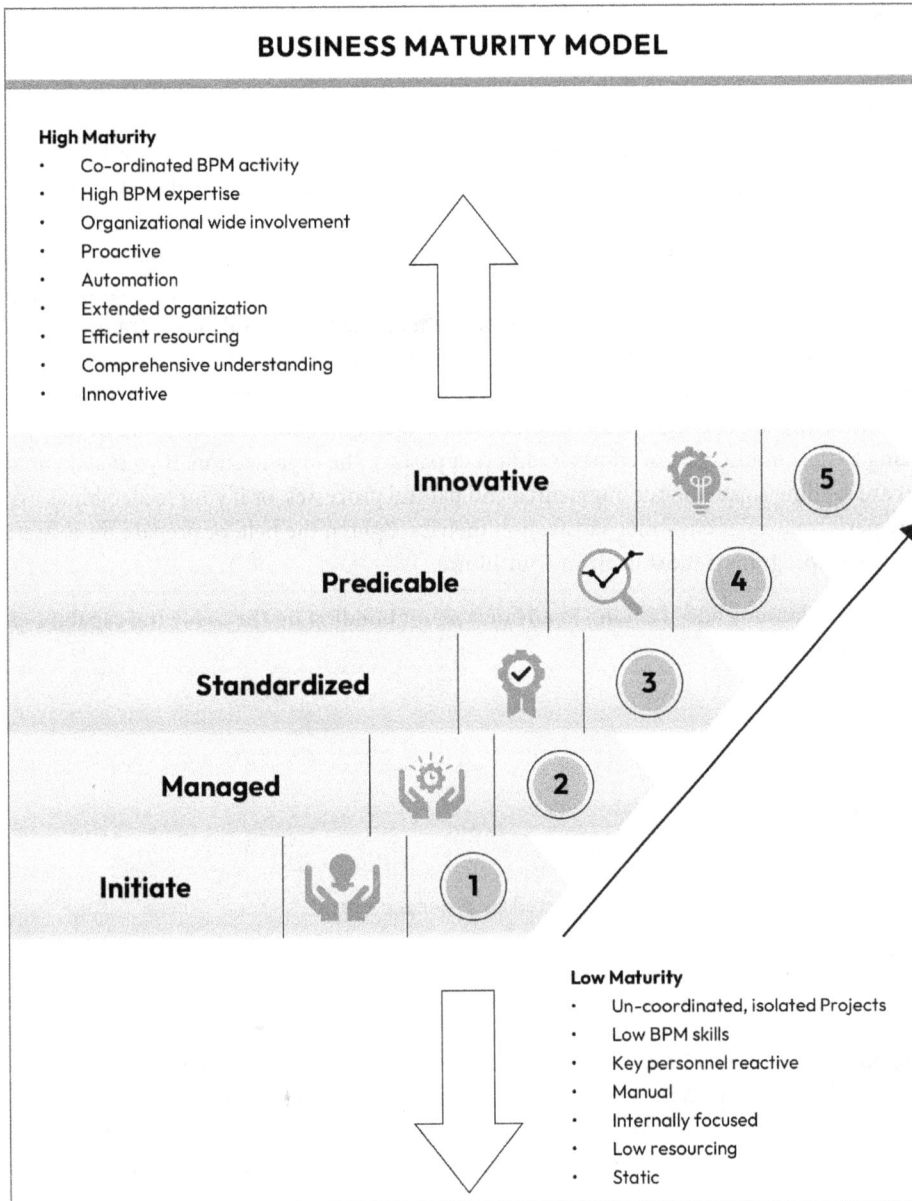

BUSINESS MATURITY MODEL

High Maturity
- Co-ordinated BPM activity
- High BPM expertise
- Organizational wide involvement
- Proactive
- Automation
- Extended organization
- Efficient resourcing
- Comprehensive understanding
- Innovative

Innovative — 5

Predicable — 4

Standardized — 3

Managed — 2

Initiate — 1

Low Maturity
- Un-coordinated, isolated Projects
- Low BPM skills
- Key personnel reactive
- Manual
- Internally focused
- Low resourcing
- Static

Figure 2.7 – Business process maturity

To fuel the expansion of process transformations, to create that self-sustaining pendulum of use cases, companies need to incubate and master the right approach to business science called business process management.

Summary

DTX within a company will mean different things to different audiences based on people's roles in the organization and the overall size of this topic. That's why it is essential to craft the vision of the transformation that's shared and to obtain buy-in from executives who are going to stand behind your execution plans. DTX initiatives don't always start in a top-down fashion, and if they do, they require a tremendous number of resources to push everyone in the same direction. Process transformations can also start in an ad hoc manner with different timing and different organizational maturity; thus, once your efforts are underway, it's important to organize work around workstreams that will support major pillars of the DTX, sustaining your efforts month after month within this stable framework. DTX requires both tons of commitment and a long span of planning. Professionals who have participated in such efforts compare them to marathons versus short sprints, following the sports metaphor. Timing the momentum of the DTX program inception can be challenging; however, there are usually many signs leading to the culmination of efforts in different parts of the organization. If your stakeholders and teams are sending signals about fragmented and painful processes, or if your leadership is asking to raise the performance or customer satisfaction metrics, tighten the belt, or prepare for a strategic initiative – a DtC program is most likely in your future.

It's smart to start planning and thinking in advance about building up the following capabilities, as they take time to mature:

- Strategy
- Organizational self-enablement
- Scalable COE operating model
- Cloud-based low-code ecosystem
- Business process architectures supported by process culture
- Access to data models
- Mature change management practices

Launching business-critical DTX initiatives while at the same time working on your transformation pillars will resemble the Tough Mudder race more than participation in the Seattle Marathon. For those of you unfamiliar with the Tough Mudder races, these extreme races include a number of signature obstacles, including electroshock therapy, plunging into a dumpster filled with ice water, climbing monkey bars slicked with butter and mud over a pit of cold water, and running up a pipe slicked with grease. Think and plan ahead to get your pillars ready in advance; no company ever succeeded in its DTX efforts without ample preparation. We are going to introduce BPM, its ramifications, and our philosophy in the next chapter.

**Unlock this book's
exclusive benefits now**

Scan this QR code or go to `packtpub.`
`com/unlock`, then search this book
by name.

Note: Keep your purchase invoice ready
before you start.

The Wheel of BPM Driving Your Competitive Advantage

Enterprise-scale **digital transformation (DTX)** requires strategic planning and **business process management (BPM)** practices, an essential component of digital change initiatives. By embracing BPM, companies can adapt to the rapidly changing landscape and drive innovation through new levels of automation-driven agility with the help of AI. As a scientific practice, BPM helps prepare and sustain wave after wave of digital change programs. It focuses on people, their expertise, and the many non-technical skills crucial in successfully implementing DTX initiatives. This contrasts with the common misconception that DTX is solely about technology. It's about people, processes, and technology working together to drive business value.

In this chapter, we will guide you through initiating and executing a BPM transformation in your organization.

You will learn how to do the following:

- Recognize the signs that indicate the need for a BPM transformation and the factors that influence its timing and scope

- Define the objectives and expected outcomes of the transformation

- Identify the current state of your processes, including the gaps and opportunities for improvement, using various techniques and tools

- Develop a compelling business case and a realistic roadmap for the transformation that outlines the benefits, costs, and risks

- Align the vision and strategy of the transformation with the key stakeholders and sponsors to gain their support and commitment

- Establish the governance and roles for the transformation and define the accountabilities of the different parties involved

- Pitch the transformation to the decision-makers and influencers, and overcome the potential objections and barriers

By the end of this chapter, you will have the skills and knowledge to plan and initiate a successful BPM transformation that will drive your competitive advantage and prepare you for the digital age. You will also learn from the best practices and most common mistakes of other organizations that have embarked on similar journeys. This chapter will help you build a solid foundation for your BPM transformation and set the stage for subsequent chapters covering the details of the BPM life cycle and methodology.

> **Note**
> This chapter is authored by BJ Biernatowski.

How do transformations start?

BPM is a discipline that aims to improve the performance, efficiency, and agility of business processes. By automating business-critical processes, BPM can help organizations achieve strategic goals, optimize resources, and deliver value to customers. However, BPM is not a one-time project or a quick fix. It is a continuous journey that requires a holistic and systematic approach to managing and improving organizational processes. This journey is a BPM transformation, ultimately leading to DTX on a grand scale.

Can you attempt to drive such programs without focusing on BPM? You can try. However, your results will remind us of an attempt to build a metro system akin to London's Subway by building lines between 3–4 stations only instead of covering all 270 of them, omitting the maintenance facilities, and not planning for enough electric lines to power your trains. To paraphrase, engaging in DTX without consideration and focus on BPM will create partial results without the ability to expand your project into the automation program, effectively transforming work performed along major process routes supporting your company's value chains. Such a lack of foresight may also inhibit your business's ability to scale your company's efforts to reach the full potential of the transformation.

It would be best to approach DTX as a change initiative involving adopting BPM principles, methods, and tools to discover, redesign, automate, monitor, educate, and improve business processes. To paraphrase, a successful BPM transformation will also serve as a precursor to DTX, executed as a wave of multiple digital change projects driven by citizen developers and project teams. The foundation laid by the BPM transformation creates a shared vision and a common language for various parts of the organization.

A BPM transformation can bring multiple benefits to your organization:

- Reduction of costs and waste by offering a continuously self-optimizing vision of your enterprise

- Increased productivity and quality by planning for growth and change, eliminating bottlenecks, and streamlining work handovers

- Enhancing customer satisfaction and loyalty by designing processes from the customer's point of view using the outside-in perspective

- Aligning processes with strategy and vision to ensure that resources deployed offer maximum return on investment

- Creating a culture of continuous improvement

- Preparing the organization for the launch of digital change programs focused on the automation of work with the assistance of digital business platforms and AI

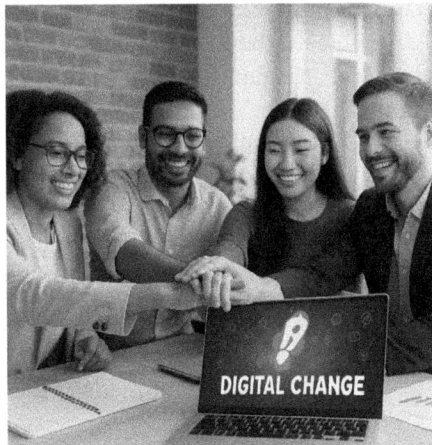

Figure 3.1 – Launching Digital Change projects is a team activity

Initiating a BPM transformation is neither straightforward nor easy. Such initiatives generally demand a clear vision, decisive leadership, a supportive culture, strong governance, and a long-term perspective. The launch process includes tackling numerous challenges, such as engaging stakeholders who might be uninterested in process methodologies, designing process architecture for significant portions of the business, standardizing and enhancing existing processes, and gaining and maintaining executive support to ensure that your efforts receive acknowledgment from company leaders.

Additional challenges may involve managing change at a scale. How you manage change will ultimately decide the fate of your transformation projects, tipping the scale of success in your favor. In addition, you will need to learn how to demonstrate business value, invest time and resources into learning and development, and carefully navigate organizational politics.

How can you initiate and plan a BPM transformation to deliver optimal outcomes for your company?

In the next sections, I will explore the key steps and best practices to start a BPM transformation, such as the following:

- Timing the inflection points for the transformation
- Defining the scope and objectives
- Developing the business case and roadmap for the transformation
- Communicating and aligning the vision and strategy
- Establishing the governance and roles for the transformation

Timing the inflection point

One of Massachusetts' most lucrative yet controversial industries was whale hunting. From the 17th to 19th centuries, thousands of sailors braved the Atlantic and Pacific in search of oil, baleen, and ambergris. It was a perilous pursuit requiring courage, endurance, and skill. Whalers faced storms, shipwrecks, disease, and the sheer power of the whales themselves. Many never returned. Those who did often carried scars, both physical and emotional, and stories of survival that few others could imagine.

Launching BPM transformations can feel daunting, complex, resource-intensive, and full of unknowns. Like the historic New England whalers, transformation leaders navigate through risk in pursuit of immense value.

Such projects can be exhilarating; they require lots of endurance and continue to tempt many by promising bounties of unlimited potential in the form of almost unlimited **return on investment (ROI)**. Who in their right mind would not be drawn to the modern hunt for the digital *whale-sized* BPM transformation?

Having experienced firsthand the tremendous appetite of companies in pursuit of process digitization strategies, I've been fascinated by the idea of the inflection point in which the company decides to launch and pursue process-driven DTX, also referred to as an automation program with an enterprise-wide scope. The strategic inflection point is a business trigger that can be described as witnessing company executives look for the bounty of never-ending efficiencies, three-digit ROIs, and new business models promised by the fifth stage of process maturity resulting from advanced digitization. External factors, such as technological innovations, regulatory shifts, competitive moves, or internal pressures, such as changes in strategy, vision, or culture, can all cause it. A strategic inflection point can be an opportunity or a threat, depending on how well a company responds to it. A company that anticipates and embraces change can gain a competitive advantage and emerge more robust. In contrast, a company that resists or ignores the change can lose market share and relevance.

Launching your enterprise program at the wrong time, without much preparation, or with the wrong digitization platform can cost you and your sponsors a promotion or even a career.

Andy Grove, the cofounder of Intel, described inflection points as events that *"change the way we think and act."*

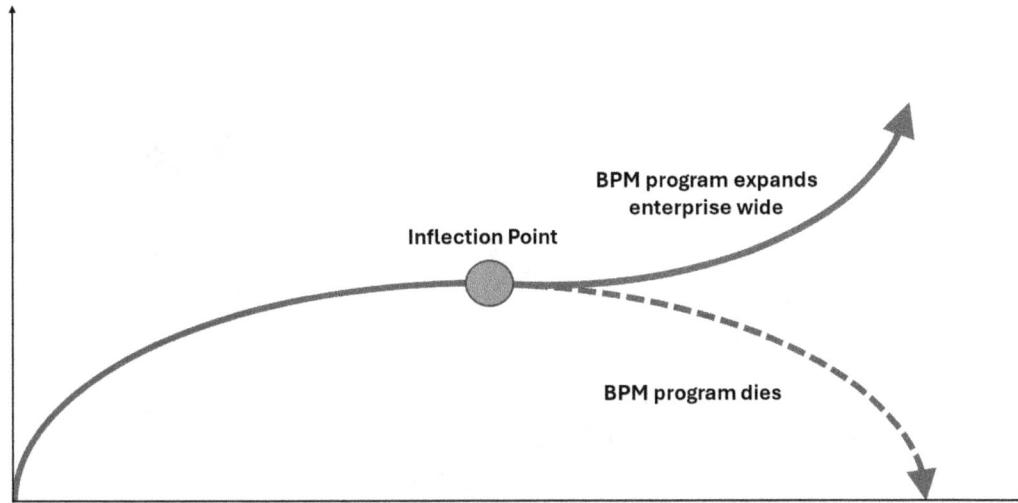

The strategic inflection point theory was introduced by Andy Grove, Intel CEO in his book 'Only the Paranoid Survive'

Figure 3.2 – The inflection point of a BPM transformation indicates the right time to expand the program

What business conditions led to this inflection point, and how can you predict the right mix of conditions to help you launch your program at the most opportunistic time?

The answer to this question is relatively simple. However, it took me a few job changes to experience the correct set of conditions that led to the proverbial *perfect storm of digitization*. Companies that get their DTX launched properly focus on preparation and equipping employees with the proper set of skills. They also have a forward-looking view of the mission backed by the support of a bold executive, who helps drive executive alignment. These companies create their favorable timing by paying attention to business conditions that impact their environment. As prominent global consulting companies would want you to believe, until you prepare for the DTX hunt, you may never know whether the creature down below is the size of Moby Dick or a school of sardines when estimating the size of the transformation scope. Thus, just like 200 years ago, large consulting firms, much like transformation whalers of old, often deploy teams in pursuit of *high-value engagements* —the modern *oil*.

However, without careful planning, such efforts can lead to inflated costs and missed opportunities, diminishing the business impact of your program. When local workforce engagement is minimal and delivery costs are high, the business case for transformation can weaken, resulting in less impact than initially projected.

Figure 3.3 – Timing the inflection point of the business transformation can be risky

Just as whale hunting once defined Massachusetts' industrial legacy, the East Coast also gave rise to early advancements in process analysis, thanks to pioneers such as Frederick Winslow Taylor, whose scientific management principles laid the foundation for modern operational thinking.

Today, there are many more ways to pursue digitization, but not all paths lead to sustainable transformation. Through this book, we encourage you to consider a different route, one that avoids the fate of the "modern whale hunter." Just as no bounty is worth risking the natural world, no DTX should jeopardize your workforce or outsource your operational knowledge in the name of efficiency.

Too often, transformation programs rely on *highly specialized, opaque skill sets* that are only accessible through formal partnerships with global consulting firms. These skills, packaged and sold as part of implementation services, may deliver results, but at what cost? When your internal teams are excluded from training, governance, or design, key knowledge may walk out the door with external partners if not intentionally transferred or retained.

This isn't to say consulting is unethical or unnecessary. Far from it—many partnerships add real value. But overreliance on proprietary expertise can unintentionally displace local teams, increase implementation costs, and reduce the long-term ROI.

The issue isn't that your people can't learn these skills. The issue is that without access to the same materials and learning pathways offered to strategic partners, your teams are left at a disadvantage. And if you're launching a DPA platform without that internal capability, how can you be sure your team's roles—and even their jobs—won't be sidelined?

It's one thing to benefit from a consultant's experience. It's another to build a program entirely around knowledge you can't access or sustain.

To counter these risks and build a lasting digital foundation, organizations must take a more deliberate approach. To lead a successful transformation, you need safeguards: open access to knowledge, hands-on learning, and a deliberate effort to keep your people at the center of the journey.

We also hope that by being aware of the forces pulling your employer into such never-ending modernization programs and applying the tips and strategies in this book, you can anticipate and perhaps even time the inflection points of your company's BPM program expansion. I also hope to convince you to prepare yourself for the scale of support needed before your program reaches the critical mass of enterprise-wide DTX by putting the BPM practice at its center. Based on experience gained from other businesses, it will be just a matter of time before your company expands its process digitization to an enterprise-wide scale. If you do it at the wrong time, with the wrong platform, or without the right level of preparation and support, the program will start declining.

The race for DTX is a matter of survival and competitive business advantage for most companies worldwide. Bear in mind that some transformations can be driven by market forces that occur quickly and without much warning, dragging companies into multi-month efforts to digitize operations rapidly. Some transformations can be planned years in advance by a visionary executive, supported by the enterprise architecture or business transformation office. Some transformations happen by accident, and many result from an effort by very astute sales teams, regularly feeding and recycling visions of business benefits between companies and customers unaware of the events they are about to trigger. The most conventional but still somewhat uncommon way of creating the momentum behind DTX is to make a strategic investment in the practice of BPM, creating the process-centric culture that permeates most areas of your company through process champions. Although a bit effort-consuming, this approach involves teaching groups of employees about the value BPM can bring to their day-to-day work while connecting the vision and the practice with the pain points of your business areas.

BPM is a vast practice, and depending on the starting point, you and your team may have quite a bit of learning to do. Your colleagues will ask many critical questions about how BPM can help them in their day-to-day jobs and what's in it for them and their careers.

In a fast-paced world that is used to instant results, the infusion of this scientific practice can sometimes be perceived as overly theoretical and disconnected from the more exciting act of building apps, executing projects, and managing software and cloud systems. It is also not as exciting as executing "automation" projects, hiring consulting companies, evaluating vendors, and investing in digital process platforms.

All the preceding activities involve *doing* rather than *learning* and making strategic plans to prepare for the long-term execution of future digital change initiatives. People usually get more satisfaction at work *doing* than *planning and strategizing*, yet it's the latter that helps accomplish strategic long-term objectives.

Some negative perceptions of BPM may last until leaders experience firsthand the benefits of this science, such as challenging projects hitting targets for the first time, unsolvable problems getting fixed, and the slowly growing hype that follows successful implementations hitting or exceeding their objectives.

To your surprise, you may also be challenged by Gen Z professionals who are known for their efficiency and preference for quick results, finding traditional, lengthy learning processes less appealing. The influence of social media has shaped a generation that values streamlined and efficient workflows. For instance, the simplicity of the online pizza ordering process (click, order, pay, and deliver) exemplifies their expectation for quick and effective solutions. Therefore, it's important to adapt training methods to be more engaging and time-efficient to meet their expectations. The generation that grew up on the internet-powered pizza ordering process does not want to learn about the internals of the "order to deliver pizza" business process if that means hours of discovery and training.

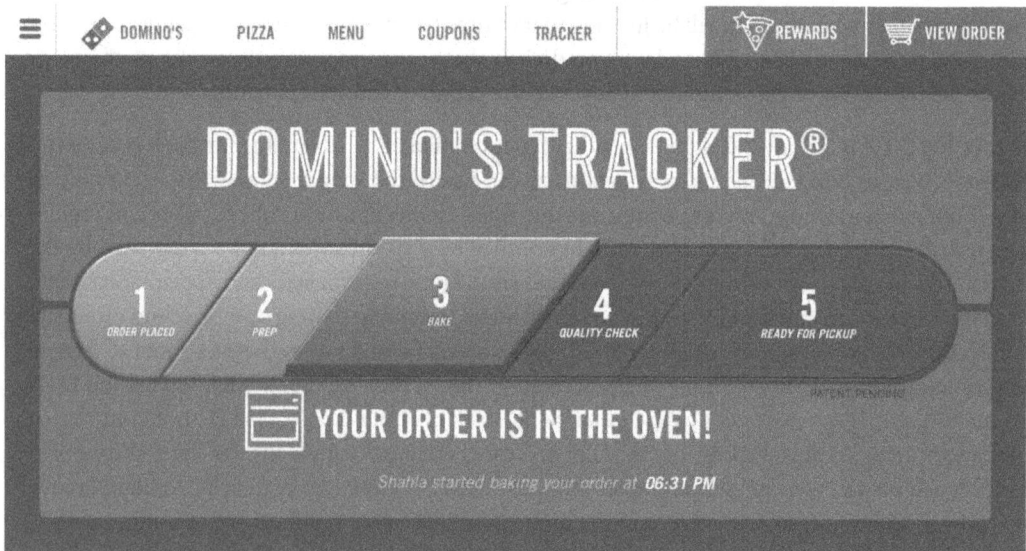

Figure 3.4 – Domino's Pizza order tracker is one of the most popular business processes

The primary challenge with BPM lies in its extensive nature, which includes numerous theoretical areas that may only become relevant as needed. Not everyone can afford the luxury of time and resources to pursue a two-year BPM master's program at institutions such as the University of Illinois, Springfield, or other schools offering BPM through professional education courses. Effectively packaging and delivering training to the appropriate audience will be crucial for the success of your DTX. Additionally, you must tailor your messaging to capture the attention of different user groups within your organization. It is well known that companies often find it hard to get enthusiastic about process improvement programs and business processes. The trend is toward building low-code apps or engaging with AI, often overlooking the essential foundational knowledge required to integrate such applications into adaptive and intelligent end-to-end process ecosystems that enable the digitization of enterprise value chains.

Indeed, you can build a low-code app or even a few without knowing anything about the theory of the business process. However, if you genuinely want to transform your company's operations and business processes, you must understand a few additional non-technical concepts. There are no shortcuts here.

In addition, like any science that can depart too far from pragmatic outcomes, measuring the ROI from the investment into the BPM transformation program alone can be challenging and non-trivial. This book devotes a whole chapter to this topic.

Great leaders know instinctively that long-term investments in BPM can yield results that other competitors can only dream of. But how do others do it? There are many published case studies of successful BPM transformations and fantastic results generated by such companies. Getting desired results—firstly, being able to define what such results should look like—can be initially easier said than done, as this task can be overwhelming.

To simplify this concept, I propose that we start thinking about BPM transformations using the wheel metaphor, which will be used throughout the remainder of the book.

Wheels are straightforward to grasp; whether in Tonka trucks, on the *Wheel of Fortune*, or referenced in religious texts, they have consistently held a crucial place throughout the history of civilization.

At most organizations, the wheel of BPM will be organized around three phases:

1. Process discovery, definition, and reuse.
2. Automation, covering a wide variety of use cases. Many companies start their transformation journeys from this point, getting themselves into trouble quickly.
3. Optimization, which is followed by phases 1 and 2, as the wheel spins continuously.

As the wheel of BPM transformation continues to spin through these three cycles in the right order, with each successful turn, your program's growth should amplify.

The growth and reach of your program will be fueled by subsequent releases of digital change projects when *launched and change managed correctly*, and with *the increasing population* of the citizen developers community, who will become your biggest ally.

While many organizations turn to external consulting firms for expertise, this approach should complement, not replace, the internal knowledge and commitment required to sustain meaningful transformation.

In other words, the successful growth of your program will be related to the level of success you get with your digital change initiatives and the level of empowerment citizen developers will have. Once you reach the critical mass of the citizen developers population and your company's unmet automation needs start to get addressed, the wheel will begin fueling continuous improvement initiatives, pushing your digitized processes to their next level of maturity.

As this momentum builds, the wheel of BPM becomes more than a metaphor—it becomes a practical framework for guiding DTX.

The wheel will keep turning for months and years until your company reaches the highest level of process maturity. Still, even at that time, a new tech or science development may push BPM to the new frontier, searching for the next best thing in process management and work automation. It is best to consider BPM as a business practice rather than a software category or a set of tools, even if both are intimately intermingled. The BPM adoption formula previously presented will drive the grassroots model of DTX in contrast to the top-down model still practiced by some consulting companies. While top-down transformation models remain common, particularly in consulting-led programs, more organizations are turning to citizen developer approaches that foster grassroots innovation, build internal ownership, and keep talent at the center of change.

The wheel of BPM supports this shift by offering a practical, repeatable framework that anchors your DTX strategy in real-world process understanding and team-driven execution.

The following illustration offers a visual representation of these phases:

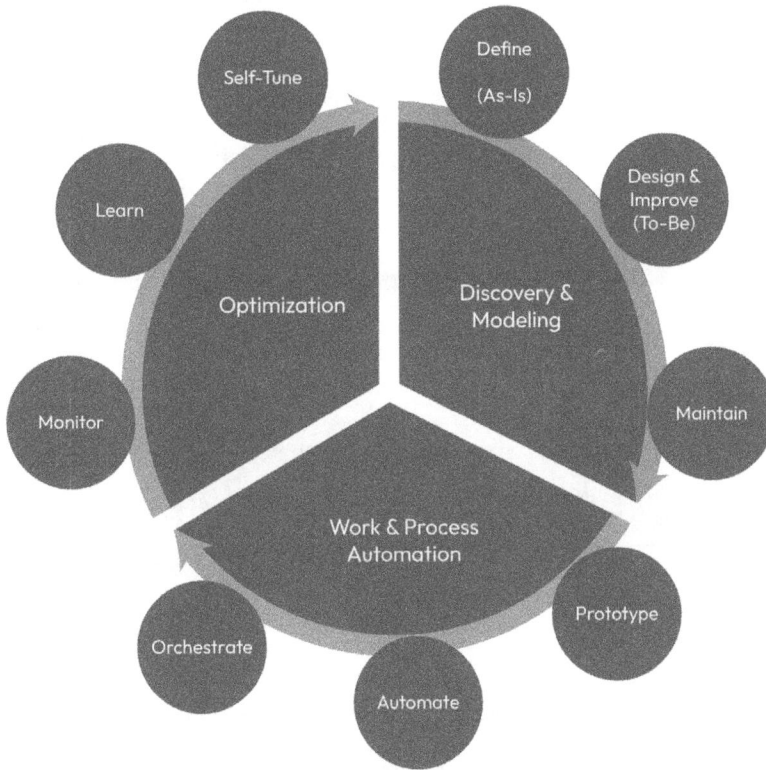

Figure 3.5 – The wheel-based view of a DTX based on an example of a US-based retailer

For the whole company to get comfortable with these concepts, the wheel must spin a couple of times, each creating the inflection point that leads to accelerated adoption of process-led solutions, a culture of continuous improvement, and genuine excitement created by successful projects. When BPM creates results, you will hear and feel the positive buzz in all parts of the company as many project teams start announcing their successes. It is a gratifying and fun part of the program as the success of others brings other use cases out of the woodwork, reenergizing everyone about the possibilities of improving operations. Success breeds more success, so you should prepare for it upfront and consider the potential scale of your program.

The wheel of BPM can be adjusted to each company's approach, as depicted by the following example:

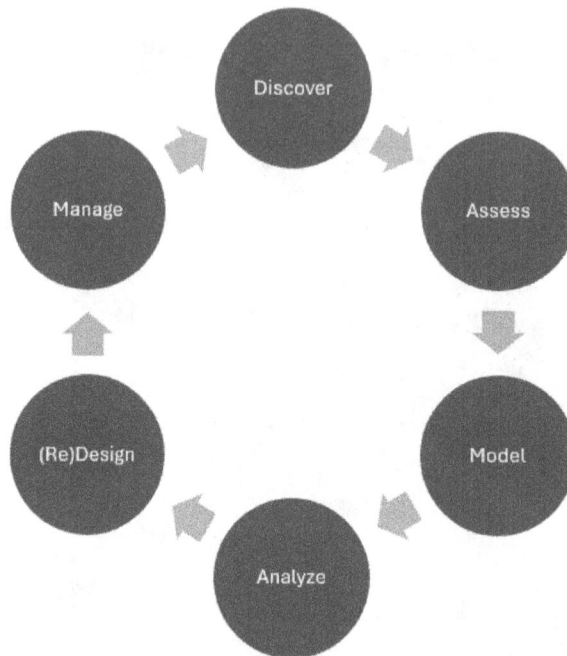

Figure 3.6 – The Process Excellence framework defined by a global software company

Jumpstarting the program can initially take some effort, so visualize the early stages of the practice adoption as a team exercise that involves pushing the boulder up a small mountain. The size of the hill (and your boulder) will vary based on where you work and how much executive support you get. Through this visualization, I am trying to help you envision the type and strength of drag your program will be exposed to, also defined as the stakeholder pushback. The first few pushes are the hardest; when you start, the boulder is still standing, with the force of gravity almost pushing back against you. Pushing the rock forward (jumpstarting the program) will require focus, grit, skills, a team, a bit of a budget, a strong sense of direction, and the unshaken sense of belief that what you are doing is going to work and create substantial results for your employer.

Figure 3.7 – Jumpstarting a BPM program is best done with a team

It is essential to have a strong belief that successful BPM programs will yield numerous unexpected and positive outcomes, acting as a beneficial force that propels the company's efficiency forward, even during difficult times. As your goals become clearer, resistance diminishes, and progress begins to build momentum on its own. Each phase that demands extra effort to tackle organizational challenges can reinforce the role of BPM programs in strengthening operational efficiency. When implemented well, these programs contribute to measurable improvements in business performance and strategic alignment—in some cases, influencing the company's stock value.

Why does this happen?

Because BPM provides a structured and repeatable approach to enhancing how work is done, it brings clarity to complex operations, supports cross-functional collaboration, and helps reduce waste. Over time, this leads to measurable gains, lower operating costs, faster decision-making, more effective use of talent, and a clearer understanding of what works and what doesn't. These are the building blocks of ROI, and in many cases, they enable companies to take on more ambitious goals, including new business models. AI will only amplify these effects by turning well-structured processes into intelligent, adaptive systems. While it's not always possible to pinpoint how much BPM alone contributes to a company's valuation, improved operational discipline consistently leads to better execution, and that shows up in bottom-line results.

We've seen companies generate meaningful business outcomes by embracing BPM practices:

- **UnitedHealth Group** (**UNH**) is a leading health care and well-being company providing health benefits, technology-driven care solutions, and pharmacy services to improve access, affordability, and outcomes. UNH launched its BPM initiatives to improve end-to-end care models, consolidate customer care, integrate clinical data and analytics, and simplify administrative processes while enhancing operational efficiency in its segments. Between 2007 and 2014, UNH's stock increased 87.1%.

- **Heineken** (**HEINY**) is a global brewing company that produces and distributes beer and other beverages across multiple markets. Heineken has utilized process digitization to drive employee innovation, improve productivity, enhance safety audits, and improve its point-of-sale systems. Between 2019 and 2025, HEINY's stock price increased by 4.65%.

- **Goldman Sachs** (**GS**) is a global investment banking, securities, and asset management firm that provides financial services to corporations, governments, and individuals. Goldman Sachs has utilized AI-driven automation for algorithmic trading, risk management, compliance monitoring, and fraud detection. GS's stock price saw an approximate 116.9% increase between 2015 and 2022.

It is important to recognize that pure financial performance, including stock prices, is also influenced by broader market trends, economic conditions, and industry-specific factors.

Other leading companies that also launched BPM programs to enhance their competitive advantage, embed operational discipline, and lay a foundation for sustainable DTX include the following, and many others:

- Google (and its parent company, Alphabet)
- Nordstrom
- Amazon
- Coca-Cola
- Microsoft
- NHS Healthcare
- Conoco-Philips
- ABN Amro
- NATO

To unleash such forces, you and your team, if you are lucky to work with one, will need to firmly believe in the transformation's vision. Without the ultimate commitment to the vision, the magic of BPM will not work. These projects usually require strong leadership skills, lots of grit, and the ability to collaborate with almost anyone, as your program, collective skill set, and its reach within the enterprise undergo multiple iterations and experience occasional roadblocks along the way.

Before you decide that pushing your boulder up the mountain is worth the effort, you must firm up the scope and objectives of the transformation for your business unit or department. I would strongly advise against starting with BPM at the enterprise-wide level unless you and your team have successfully launched similar initiatives in the past and/or your program has excellent leadership support. Even under these two conditions, starting smaller and gaining momentum with each wheel spin is strongly advisable. While there are known case studies of companies launching enterprise-wide automation programs almost overnight, such initiatives usually involve massive teams of consultants, and these scenarios are not in the scope of this book, as it's hard to estimate the realized ROI.

The approach to BPM presented in this book focuses on empowerment and democratization so that you and your company may capture the value of business transformation on your terms without the additional expense of large consulting teams.

Going big right at the start involves tackling problems on a large scale, coupled with severe corporate political winds encountered at the very top of each organization. It is always less risky (and more fun) to learn and experiment within your immediate environment, realizing that the same business practices can be applied over time to problems at the highest level of your organization. My advice to you is, don't rush it.

There are a few very large companies out there that successfully transformed themselves overnight with the help of BPM. Even the most successful ones often iterate on their models, learning through experimentation before achieving long-term BPM success.

Defining the scope and objectives

Defining the scope is a crucial step during the program launch phase. The scope and objectives should be clearly defined and aligned with the overall business strategy and vision of your organization. If the business strategy does not exist, search for it or find people accountable for defining it.

You will need to study both to help you identify critical processes and areas of the business to be impacted by the transformation. Discuss desired outcomes and benefits that BPM transformation is expected to deliver with others. This activity involves thinking big and making connections across different parts of your company. The more connections you make, the more successful your program will be over time, as you will start running into other like-minded change champions attempting to solve similar problems.

Reflect on the following objectives from a global high-tech business:

> *"The end state objective of BPM is for our company to become process-centric, with end-to-end processes defined, analyzed, and optimized continuously. Technology investments should align with business objectives as expressed by business process requirements, leading to increased predictability, agility, reduced failure rates, lower risk, and operational costs."*

Assessing the current state and maturity of business processes will involve creating an inventory with a central repository and then evaluating the existing business processes to determine the quality and accuracy of artifacts representing the coverage area. Pay attention to the names of people who created such artifacts, versions, date stamps, policy manuals, and other supporting documentation. Business process maps are like vegetables in the grocery store; most will have an expiration date as work evolves, and some artifacts may not be up to date. Working with process models over one year old most likely means you will have to validate them. Six months to one year old is a good benchmark for the need for some rework.

Your assessment can help identify gaps and opportunities for improvement, providing a baseline for measuring the transformation's progress and impact. Don't stop with business processes alone; you could expand this step into a full-blown maturity assessment to gain a better understanding of the collective process IQ and digital business platform adoption readiness across different parts of the company. Stakeholder maps, historical information about old programs, and especially intelligence about transformations that did not go as planned will equip you with invaluable information. Most process consultants know that stepping into the footsteps of a program that did not deliver on its promise will require extra time, effort, and severe recalibration with your stakeholders. Recovery projects can be challenging, as the institutional memory will keep penalizing you for the mistakes of your predecessors. Field experience suggests that you would not want to restart new programs in the ashes of the old, failed initiative if at least two years have not passed since the program folded. Sometimes, unsuccessful efforts are associated with a particular digitization software vendor or technology, especially if the company attempts to transform parts of its operations without establishing the proper theoretical foundation, or the collaboration with the vendor does not go as planned. You could be surprised to learn that your strategic software vendor is more interested in subsequent go-lives and securing the next set of license seats than in enabling you and your team.

Many companies also make a mistake by associating investment in digital process automation or low-code platforms with the actual work required to build the BPM practice. Once you make the first investment in a set of licenses, the ROI clock will start ticking, making the new shiny software toy too tempting not to be used.

Businesses would have done themselves a huge favor and saved lots of investment dollars by investing in BPM training and skills before they decided to invest in software licenses. To make a comparison, you'd want to get your driver's license, which teaches you how to get from point A to point B, before you buy a new car unless you are already an experienced driver. In this case, driving and launching BPM transformations have a lot in common. A weeklong boot camp course could get you up to speed with all necessary topics and back it up with some hands-on practice.

This preparation phase will take some time, and you should consider your relationship with BPM as a long-term journey. Future phases and likely challenges faced by your program will benefit from this preparation. While it's true that BPM shines in combination with the citizen developer style of software delivery, you may not realize that the lifespan of BPM in your organization could be many years, creating many new jobs in the future, coupling or extending the practice with other tech inventions.

As shown by multiple examples of people in the field, when applied correctly, the BPM skill set can lead to bigger and better things in one's career. In a broader sense, think about investing in BPM as taking the insurance policy to ensure that such newly created jobs will stay within your company and will not end up cannibalized by professional services companies, each wanting to take a piece of the program pie that was started and nurtured by you. Your hard work and evangelism can translate into significant profits for service vendors if your company loses its grasp on the skills required to bring everything home.

If you are in a leadership role, don't lose sight of what's at stake. You will want to invest in BPM to raise the competitiveness of your workforce and benefit local communities where you do business. There are many examples of transformations that hollowed out the internal job market, putting employees at a disadvantage after digital change programs started taking off quickly, one after another. Many such scenarios usually go hand in hand with digitization efforts performed with proprietary and hard-to-learn low-code DPA platforms.

Ask yourself the following questions:

- If BPM and digitization are so critical to my employer's strategy, why is it that third-party software vendors own and drive most projects within my company? Is any "secret sauce" knowledge required to run these programs and platforms?

- What's so special about the knowledge and technology powering our business processes that it requires a regular contingent of long-term consultants supporting these systems all the time?

- How challenging is learning and experimenting with the vendor's low-code platform?

- How aligned is the platform with the process-oriented view of the enterprise? Are we going to create technical debt quicker, or will our solutions align with the enterprise process architecture breaking the siloes and streamlining operations?

- With proper training and some support, can I successfully lead BPM transformations and subsequent digital change initiatives on my own?

- Does the platform or consulting company share the same vision of empowerment and democratization of DPA?

- Is the same training set available to users, customers, and partners?

Identifying the gaps and opportunities for improvement

This step involves assessing and analyzing the inventory of processes and creating the initial heat map of your business. Try to determine the state of the enterprise process architecture across the enterprise. Can we see one emerging?

Can we identify areas for improvement, enumerate benefits and business pain points, and define strategic goals and transformation drivers in both business and technology domains?

Which parts of the company are prepared to undertake BPM as practice, and which ones are leading as opposed to playing catch-up? Where do we see the most pushback, and why?

Which business areas are too busy to take on new challenges, even in the form of additional self-development, due to significant initiatives, staffing issues, or ongoing reorganization? You don't want to launch your initiative with the wrong group at the wrong time. *Figure 3.8* is an example of a graphical representation of business processes across an organization. This heatmap serves as a tool to identify gaps and opportunities for improvement in the organization's enterprise process architecture.

The heatmap uses color coding to highlight areas of strength and weakness across benefits, costs, and volume, allowing stakeholders to pinpoint processes that require optimization or strategic focus. You may also categorize processes based on their alignment with strategic goals, level of preparedness for BPM initiatives, or the degree of pushback from different business areas. This visualization forms a foundation for crafting actionable plans, such as creating a compelling business case and a roadmap for transformation. By doing so, it facilitates the alignment of priorities and the organization of projects around business objectives, all while rallying stakeholder support for BPM-driven transformations.

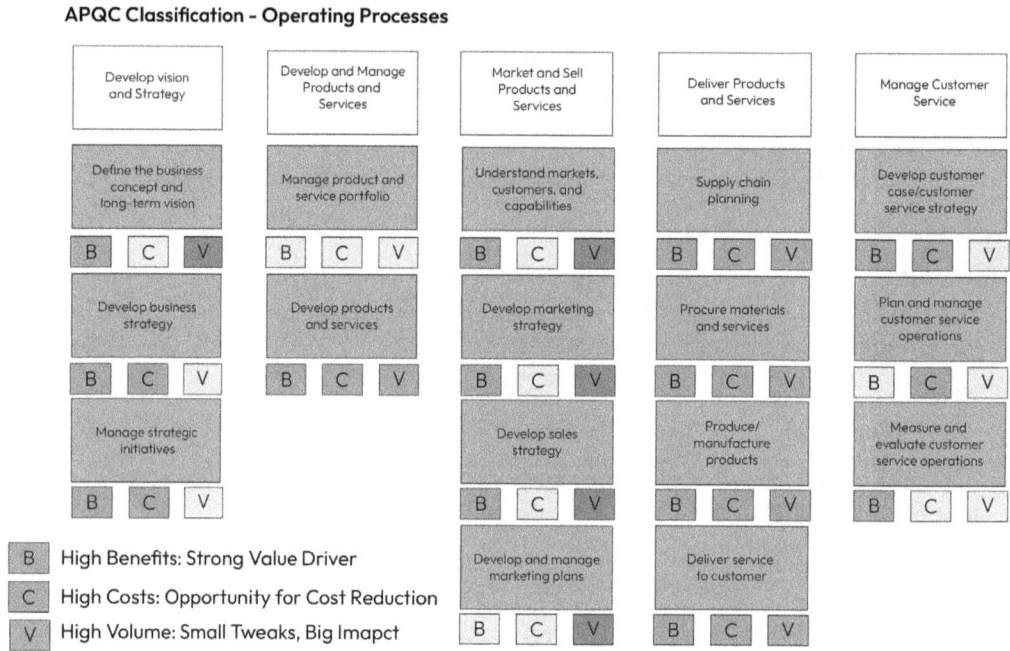

Figure 3.8 – Operating processes heatmap example based on the
American Productivity & Quality Center (APQC)

Once the gaps and opportunities have been identified and a comprehensive heatmap of operating processes is developed, the next step involves translating these insights into actionable plans by crafting a compelling business case and a clear roadmap for transformation.

Developing the business case and a roadmap

This step will involve creating a forward-looking roadmap for the transformation while keeping it regularly updated. The roadmap aims to organize individual projects around business objectives, generate clarity, and align multiple stakeholders around the same set of priorities. Transformation roadmaps should also serve as a stabilizing backbone, helping to assess progress against a set of objectives, steering efforts through the uncharted territory of organizational changes, and helping to educate stakeholders about the work being done.

Your business case should demonstrate the transformation value and benefits, as well as its urgency and identified risks. Many budgetary requests follow such business cases, so you want to make sure that you scope and plan your team size for a suitable duration and the right level of effort.

Your business case should also mention the need for a BPM strategy that will be used to accomplish your goals. This could be a *Catch-22* situation where you must have pieces of your strategy before coming to your executives for funding. That's why the launch of a BPM program can, at times, feel so challenging. Everyone will expect you to have answers to many questions, even before you start discussing transformation goals with your stakeholders. Hopefully, before the wave of questions comes your way, you will have a good grasp on your organization, its business needs, and long-term goals. Keep in mind that you are not inventing anything new; you are trying to rally support behind using the practice of BPM to transform your company over the long term with the help of low-code and other process digitization technologies.

Gaining support and motivating your communities is effective only if you persuade stakeholders that their objectives align with yours and that they have a crucial role in the democratization of technology. Your communities should not rely on enterprise ivory tower teams to address their business challenges, as these teams typically operate slowly and do not prioritize business needs according to customers' timelines.

Review the following example of a strategy to help you organize your thinking when preparing for a business case. The activity of developing the business case varies from company to company:

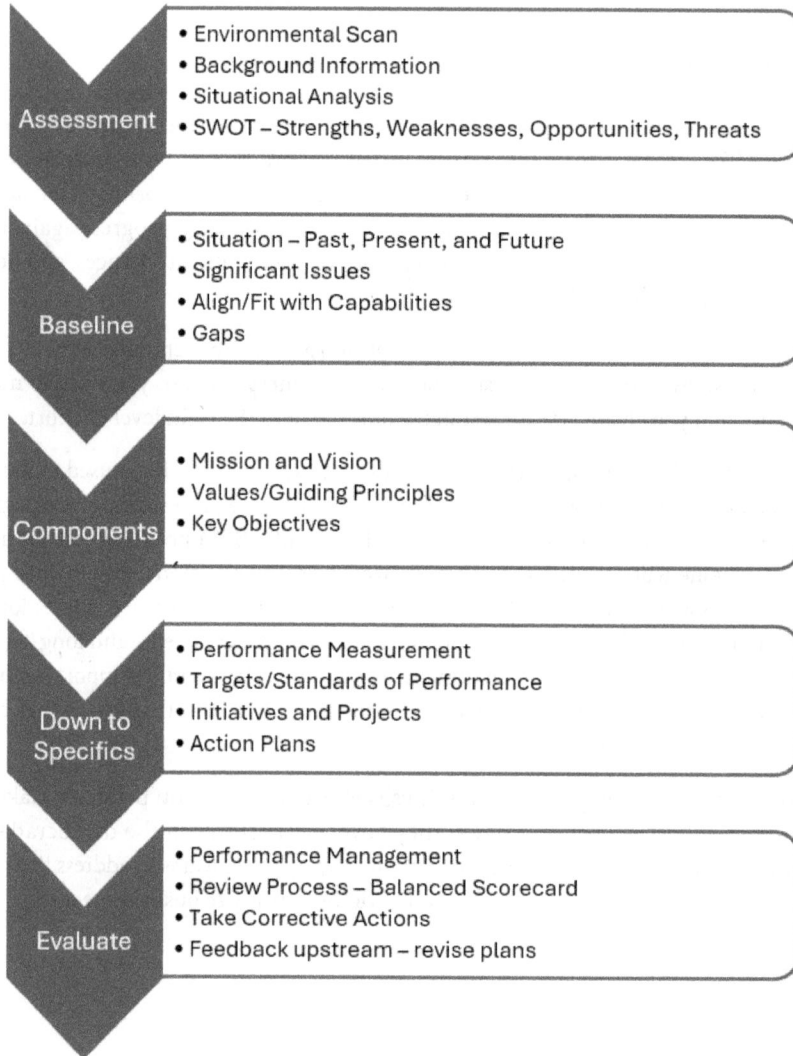

Assessment
- Environmental Scan
- Background Information
- Situational Analysis
- SWOT – Strengths, Weaknesses, Opportunities, Threats

Baseline
- Situation – Past, Present, and Future
- Significant Issues
- Align/Fit with Capabilities
- Gaps

Components
- Mission and Vision
- Values/Guiding Principles
- Key Objectives

Down to Specifics
- Performance Measurement
- Targets/Standards of Performance
- Initiatives and Projects
- Action Plans

Evaluate
- Performance Management
- Review Process – Balanced Scorecard
- Take Corrective Actions
- Feedback upstream – revise plans

Figure 3.9 – Example 1: Strategy development process

Communicating and aligning the vision and strategy

As with most projects in the business world, communication plays a key role. What remains unseen does not exist, and what's communicated poorly usually does not get support.

Launching a successful transformation takes quite a few activities, and if you are scrambling for resources, the timing of everything can make execution even more challenging. To help you succeed, start small, then expand to road shows, office hours, newsletters, workshops, project go-live celebrations, and perhaps even DTX days to create multiple opportunities to communicate your team's mission and the opportunity for your company.

If you start by prioritizing the right level of executive sponsorship and building the foundation of your citizen developer community, you will find yourself involved in discussions about potential project opportunities. These conversations will offer further validation that your pursuits are pertinent, necessary for the company, and appealing to the correct audience. By concentrating on recognizing genuine business challenges and addressing them with your skills and enthusiasm, individuals will respond positively to your message and embrace BPM as a practice that tackles real business issues.

While working for one of my previous organizations, I was able to launch and grow a digital process automation practice to complement our process **center of competency (CoC)** under challenging business conditions in an environment that was IT-centric and did not support citizen developer initiatives. I accomplished my objectives on a shoestring budget with the support of my CoC director, who understood the power of process-led transformations and suggested taking a very entrepreneurial approach. My boss built a robust process culture, and he was trying to spin the wheel of BPM into its next cycle, expanding on the vision of the process-oriented enterprise into automated and optimizing stages. I helped the team carry the wheel momentum to the next program cycle, building the adoption wave from 0 to 60 citizen developers, navigating through meanders of corporate politics and not always opportunistic timing. Growing grassroots programs is not easy; it can take a bit of time and requires a long-term view of the place of the business process in the company strategy.

Experienced leaders, enterprise and business architects, and management consultants typically recognize that BPM and business processes lay the groundwork for successful DTXs. It's not merely about AI, low-code platforms, or the cloud; all technology aims to aid companies in executing their business processes more efficiently, quicker, at a lower cost, and with greater adaptability. Numerous technologists will attest that when business processes evolve, they often do so rapidly, causing the tech sector to race to support these changes.

Process models and process architecture provide clarity to various stakeholders about current and potential workflows, identifying any bottlenecks.

Digital Process Automation 101

Take your process automation skills to the next level

Course content

- Intro to Business Process Automation
- Terminology
- K2 Five Platform:
  - ✓ Concepts
  - ✓ Hands-on exercises
  - ✓ How to get support
  - ✓ Design clinic with K2 Architects

Preregister your interest via SharePoint:

https://nordstrom.sharepoint.com/sites/BPA/Lists/Digital%20Process%20Automation%20101%20Class/AllItems.aspx

10/31/2018   9:00 AM – 12:30 PM

Ala Moana Training Room, Store 807

1617 6th Avenue, Seattle, 98101

Each class participant will receive a free digital copy of "Digital Transformation with BPM" and "Data-Driven Process Excellence: Special Edition" courtesy of Future Strategies, Inc (https://bpm-books.com).

Figure 3.10 – Example of evangelism and training activities

The visual representation of a workflow, where tasks are mapped across various IT systems, helps create a unified vision or "North Star" that connects individuals from different parts of the organization within the same business process paradigm, breaking down artificial barriers and silos. When people start communicating in the same language and appreciate the efficacy of well-formed BPMN visual metaphors, it ignites optimization, standardization, and automation initiatives aimed at enhancing efficiencies.

However, it's important to acknowledge the effort and preparation needed for this phase—you will have significant work ahead. Unless your organization has already reached a mature stage in BPM, support for the practice needs to come from the highest levels of leadership, with its value clearly recognized among the C-suite. Although discussions about process optimization, automation, and transformation are common among leaders, practical skills in BPM are less so, as they were historically not included in MBA programs. While some progress has been made globally, only a select few business schools prioritize the BPM curriculum.

Your executive team may lack direct experience with BPM's theoretical and transformative potential. Executives with consulting backgrounds and firsthand knowledge of BPM's benefits will be your greatest allies. It's also important to recognize that while BPM is exciting, it struggles to sustain itself long-term without integration into the business architecture and process automation domains. These programs might be merged during cost-cutting periods. Your strategy should involve embedding the BPM practice within the organization, developing it into a robust process culture, and then leveraging it as citizen developer programs gain traction. In corporate settings, sustaining funding for specialist teams is challenging unless these teams directly contribute to the bottom line. Seek individuals who are not only passionate about processes but also excel in relationship-building, sales, and technology, as these attributes will enhance the likelihood of success. Despite its evolving scientific nature, the pragmatic goal of BPM is to support DTX programs, unless operating within an academic setting focused on the theory of work and process.

Establishing the governance and roles for the transformation

The roles and governance models can vary from company to company; however, the following lineup will be required regardless of the size of your organization. Some roles can be played unofficially, some can be shared, and some can take time to evolve, all based on your company's level of maturity. With so many processes driving your company, it's common to find processes without owners, even at vast and mature companies:

- **The BPM sponsor**: This senior executive plays a crucial role in supporting and advocating for the BPM vision and strategy. They provide direction and guidance, while also securing the necessary funding and resources. Your executive sponsor is the most important advocate for your program; it's not just about obtaining financial support. Sponsors help raise visibility and protect your initiatives from outside influences that could undermine your work. Finding the right executive sponsor may take some time, so don't be too concerned if you don't have one immediately. It's more beneficial to find a leader who aligns with your vision rather than to be continually sidelined by someone whose priorities differ from yours. You might also discover some initial funding in the budgets at the director level. However, it's the support from a VP that will truly help you access the right opportunities.

- **The BPM leader**: This is the person who leads the BPM transformation program, coordinates the activities and projects, and reports on the progress and outcomes. They are the coach, the salesperson, the one who knows it all, and the face of the program.

- **The BPM team**: This is a group of specialists aiding the BPM leader in implementing the transformation plan by providing expertise in process analysis, design, improvement, automation, monitoring, and governance. Given the complexity of the field, individuals often specialize in different areas, making it uncommon for one person to possess comprehensive experience across all BPM facets. If you have a team of two members, consider yourself fortunate; if your team is larger, count yourself very lucky and make the most of this opportunity. When building your team, avoid the pitfall of isolating them in an "ivory tower" or adopting a consulting approach within your organization too soon. You are not acting as a consultant unless you have earned the trust to be seen as an advisor by your internal stakeholders, a feat that takes time within a company. External consultants can quickly establish credibility but may also lose their positions once the project concludes. While developing your reputation internally takes longer, it better equips you to navigate internal politics and align with the core operations of your company as an insider.

- **The BPM community**: Community-building activities will help you gain visibility, look for supporters, and identify new projects. If you organize your team correctly, you can solicit innovative ideas and tap into specialized knowledge. Come up with ideas to evangelize your mission and make it resonate with the needs of your community. Think about your community as the extension of your **center of excellence (CoE)** team, and don't call your team a CoE from the start. A CoE needs secure executive support, a suitable service-oriented model (a team that supports other teams), and credibility from different company areas. Calling your team a CoE too early can attract the wrong type of attention from other parts of the company trying to accomplish the same. Trust me when I say it: in an average-sized company, there are many change champions, all full of innovative ideas, knowledge, and experience, who are getting ready to take on the challenge of digital change. You need to find these folks, establish relationships, offer them help, and expand your view of a team. These folks are the reason your practice exists. Don't put yourself on the pedestal of the CoE; the right way to get there is to get elevated by your community to this role. You will know you are the one person destined to spearhead and introduce BPM to your business unit when your community says so. That usually takes many conversations, projects, help offered, evenings spent troubleshooting processes and apps, and building credibility. In this profession, like in any other, credibility is essential.

- **The process owners**: These are the business managers who own and are responsible for the performance and results of the processes within their domain and work with the BPM team to identify and implement improvement opportunities or launch new transformation projects. This role may not be clearly defined in companies that are still new to process thinking. Search for business owners of critical applications and systems; these folks will step into such roles as your transformation accelerates.

For example, the director of a call center at a national healthcare insurance company can be accountable for new member onboarding, benefits and claims processing, and prior authorization processes.

- **Process participants**: These are the employees who execute tasks and activities within processes while providing feedback and suggestions for enhancements. If your participants have the interest and technical ability, you might consider expanding your program with the citizen developer pillar. Your participants are at the core of the action; by staying connected with them, you can gain valuable insights into your processes, discover improvement opportunities, and receive appreciation for your work. There's great satisfaction in being acknowledged for proficiently managing processes involving multiple people, machines, and occasionally external companies.

- **Citizen developers**: BPM programs should support citizen developer initiatives, eventually merging into a unified digital process CoE. The method you choose, the duration required, and the funding source will vary based on your company's strategy. Often, the business endorses BPM initiatives while citizen developer platforms receive funding from IT budgets. It is essential not to let this create discord between your teams; within the broader practice, citizen developers belong in the *work and process automation* segment of your transformation framework. A critical issue to avoid is competition between the business and IT sectors of the CoE, as it can hinder the progress of transformation. The CoE's operations should be directed by a strong and competent leader capable of managing any political influences at this level. Failure to do so may lead to a ripple effect that destabilizes your promising practice. At this organizational level, you will encounter individuals with significant egos seeking recognition and fame. Managing such personalities requires considerable skill and, at times, might be impossible. While searching for highly recognized and experienced experts to collaborate with and support your company, prioritize those who are modest and can manage their egos. When some individuals are promoted to work on the CoE team, they transform into Lord Farquaad from the movie Shrek. You should identify digital change champions—individuals with a healthy ego grounded in their successful career trajectory. The distinction between a champion and a BPM Lord Farquaad lies in their ability to both articulate their vision and deliver consistent results.

Farquaads typically advance their CoE careers through numerous PowerPoint presentations, attracted to the high-visibility role while reluctant to acknowledge their lack of experience, which poses risks for a high-stakes team.

Figure 3.11 – BPM CoEs can attract high-ego personalities

Creating a clearly defined and compelling governance structure and role definition for the BPM transformation is vital to ensure alignment, collaboration, responsibility, and transparency among various stakeholders. It is fundamental for achieving the sought-after outcomes and benefits. Don't worry if formalizing all roles takes some time. The main point is that your program requires individuals to fulfill these roles, and eventually, they will fit in. For larger organizations, this model can extend into a hub, evolving the BPM community into multiple communities of practice. In such cases, maintain clear communication channels and ensure standards and best practices are shared freely among all communities. Your communities might operate more democratically; however, the most experienced and capable leader with aspirations should take on leadership roles. If things aren't working or your program needs changes, you can find new leadership for different phases of your transformation. Nonetheless, it's crucial to maintain continuity of knowledge and build upon past work.

How do you pitch a transformation?

A BPM transformation as a strategic initiative requires the support and buy-in of the senior management and the critical stakeholders of the organization. Without their endorsement and sponsorship, a BPM transformation can face many obstacles and risks, such as the following:

- Lack of funding and resources
- Lack of alignment and coordination
- Lack of accountability and ownership
- Lack of trust and credibility
- Lack of motivation and engagement
- Waning executive support
- Competing strategic priorities taking over the long-term focus

Thus, it is crucial to present a BPM transformation in an engaging and persuasive manner that clearly illustrates its value and advantages to your organization. How can you successfully pitch a BPM transformation? In this section, we will cover the main components and strategies for effectively pitching a BPM transformation, including the following:

- Identifying the audience's needs and expectations
- Emphasizing the current challenges and pain points
- Depicting the vision and advantages of the future state
- Utilizing stories and examples to demonstrate the impact and success of the transformation
- Implementing "quick win" projects to achieve initial successes

- Presenting the business case and roadmap for the transformation

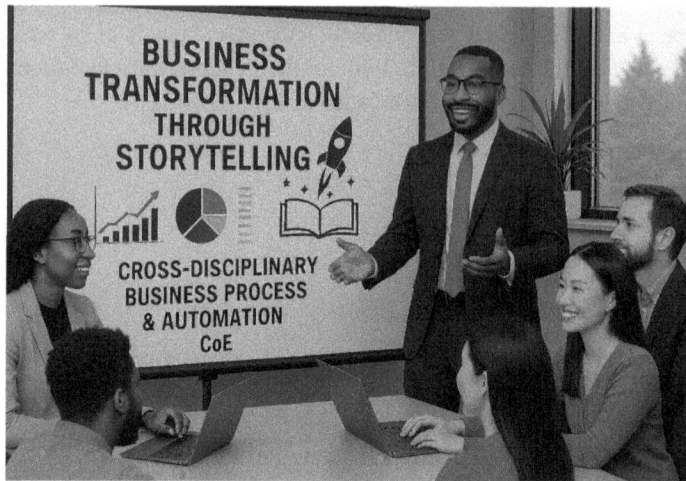

Figure 3.12 – Pitching business transformation is best done through storytelling

Prior to embarking on any new project, evaluate your current business landscape and contemplate whether the timing is right. Here are a few real-world examples that led to the establishment of a robust BPM practice, except for the last one:

- A company that invested in the process automation platform from the vendor Zeta discovered within 2–3 years that the product was difficult to use. The anticipated ROI remained out of reach, and the consulting teams responsible for driving transformation left behind a series of failed projects. These setbacks created a negative perception of BPM and automation.

- A company faces intense market pressure resulting from new regulations, shifting business environments, or key strategic initiatives that necessitate a comprehensive revamp of its core operating processes to maintain economic sustainability. This situation is referred to as the *automate or die* scenario.

- Your new VP previously had successful experience with BPM at their former company and is eager to replicate that success at your organization.

- Faced with highly demanding business objectives, you recognize that achieving these targets will be impossible without implementing work and process automation. Consequently, your leadership encourages you to initiate the automation program.

- A successful business process automation project with the consulting firm Beta brought process-oriented thinking to your organization, leading to high satisfaction levels because of the positive ROI achieved. Other leaders within your company have heard about these successes and are interested in replicating them in various areas of the business.

- An adept process practitioner is promoted to a leadership position and chooses to apply greater rigor and discipline to business operations, drawing from their experience.

- Lacking hobbies outside of work, you decide to use insights from recent sales and marketing webinars to influence your colleagues' thinking. So, you propose the launch of the BPM CoE to your boss for recognition and advancement.

All but the last one of these scenarios are correct, and you would tailor your pitch differently for each one. While your starting position doesn't dictate your objectives and endpoint, it's beneficial to be aware of it. The following tips can help you devise your action plan:

- Define BPM using terms and language compatible with your company culture. Avoid corporate jargon that does not explain concepts.

- Align your BPM terminology with the language of business architecture and the business itself. Avoid acronyms.

- Don't use scientific papers or presentations; your initial messaging needs to be crisp and businesslike.

- Connect the vision and value of BPM with your company's strategic DTX goals.

- Address the "What's in it for me?" for the following:

    - The sponsor

    - Business leaders

    - Process owners

    - Citizen process architects

    - Citizen developers

- Develop a collection of reusable slides and maintain control over them. Avoid cluttering your presentation with content taken from vendors' decks unless you are intentionally managing your partnership with the company.

- Ensure that your training materials are vendor-neutral; avoid using resources from specific software vendors to teach BPM. You might be astonished at the number of vendors necessary for a successful BPM implementation in your company. It's common to begin with one vendor, say Zeta, only to later find that another vendor, Alpha, provides the tools and capabilities better suited to your company's needs.

- Start by presenting your proposal to the business team; the most effective BPM programs are usually led by the business side, even when they involve a high degree of technical detail.

- Pay attention to the underdog. Occasionally, areas of business that have traditionally lacked funding can provide significant visibility by presenting solutions to problems that other regions have been grappling with.

- Refrain from making bold pitches and avoid mentioning enterprise transformations unless you have the backing of executives. Such discussions and plans are generally meant for executive audiences.

- Avoid exaggerating BPM's capabilities. BPM is a disciplined approach that can lay strong groundwork for your digital change initiatives, ultimately driving your company's DTX. Like any science, it is applied practically to solve real-world issues.

- Avoid becoming too comfortable with any one vendor; some companies base their sales strategies on engaging the most promising BPM advocates to adjust their strategy later. Build solid relationships with multiple vendors, but refrain from acting as their informant. There's a delicate balance between being an advocate and turning into part of the software vendor's sales force trying to penetrate your account. Teams that use these tactics lack true loyalty.

- Understand that the pitch that was successful with your previous employer or client might not be effective with your current one. Businesses, similar to individuals, react differently to various messages.

- Integrate the story of BPM with the specific requirements of your business and avoid overwhelming your audience by pitching too much initially. Keep in mind that BPM can become quite complex for those unfamiliar with it.

- Maintain your high standards; you're aware that BPM is effective, so don't consent to any shortcuts in process modeling, process architecture, or the quality of your presentation materials. Recognize your value, even if those around you haven't yet seen the full extent of what you bring to the table. In time, your worth will become evident, even if you're unable to demonstrate it immediately. As a practitioner, be rigorous in your standards but adaptable in other aspects.

- It's great to have the advantage of a well-prepared pitch, but sometimes this can lead to complacency, emphasizing perfection over actual needs. I strongly advocate for pitching BPM within teams or programs during challenging times. Although focusing on intellectual work is more difficult under these conditions, the necessity and potential of BPM are easier to communicate when a business is in a phase of transformation. These programs will engage you with their narrative and create opportunities for rapid results. Conversely, presenting BPM to a stable business that isn't expecting significant changes might require prolonged periods of advocacy, possibly spanning months or even years. Prosperous times often marginalize BPM, whereas challenging periods draw in practitioners along with their expertise.

- When pitching BPM, invest some time to create a library of pertinent case studies from companies and sectors similar to your business. These resources may develop fresh ideas, motivate your decision stakeholders, and inform you about potential benefits and pitfalls. Quality case studies from the local market can demonstrate how your peers are addressing business process management issues.

- Exploring LinkedIn for BPM roles will reveal companies that are looking for your expertise and identify the programs that are becoming popular.

- Attending vendor conferences online and in person will reenergize and educate you about market trends. Some worthy events to track include *PEX Process Excellence*, *Gartner and Forrester* webinars, and conferences hosted by specific software vendors.

- Keep in mind that tangible results are more impactful than any PowerPoint presentation. Utilize the "quick win" project method to generate an initial wave of success, which you can then expand upon with additional projects. The purpose of your "quick win" is to demonstrate the effectiveness of BPM in a low-risk environment, leveraging your initial success. This quick win might be exemplified by a prototype process implementation, identifying a new process from hidden data logs, or carrying out a feasibility study that recommends a technical approach based on business unit performance analysis. The critical aspect of a "quick win" is achieving swift success. Ensure you clearly understand what constitutes success for your stakeholders.

After achieving a few successful projects and finalizing your business case, you should present it to senior management to secure their support for the BPM transformation. Carefully plan your presentation and customize it according to the audience, taking into account their objectives, challenges, and expectations. Here are some guidelines to help you prepare and deliver an effective presentation:

- **Timing**: Choose when your audience is most receptive and attentive. Avoid scheduling your presentation right before or after a significant event, such as a board meeting, a product launch, or a holiday. Also, avoid cramming too much information into a short time slot. Ideally, you should allocate at least 30 minutes for your presentation plus 15 minutes for the Q&A.

- **Approach**: Use storytelling to engage your audience and make your case compelling. Start with a clear problem statement highlighting current challenges and gaps in your business processes. Then, show how BPM can help solve those problems and deliver value to your company. Use concrete examples and data to illustrate your points and showcase the benefits of BPM. Finally, present your roadmap for the BPM transformation, outlining your project's scope, timeline, resources, and expected outcomes.

- **Audience**: Know your audience and anticipate their queries and concerns. Understand their motivations and provide information that builds support. Address objections and risks early, using evidence and testimonials. Highlight the benefits, such as increased efficiency, quality, customer satisfaction, and innovation. Communicate in a way that resonates with them, using familiar terms and concepts.

How do you grow your BPM expertise?

A BPM transformation is an educational journey that involves cultivating and refining the process skills and competencies of those involved. These BPM skills and competencies encompass the knowledge, abilities, and behaviors necessary for the effective identification, execution, and management of business processes, including workflow automation. They can be categorized into four distinct groups aligned with the BPM life cycle:

- **Process design**: The skills and competencies to analyze, model, and redesign business processes

- **Process implementation**: The skills and competencies to automate, integrate, and deploy business processes as workflows

- **Process monitoring**: The skills and competencies to measure, evaluate, and control business processes

- **Process improvement**: The skills and competencies to identify, prioritize, and implement process improvement

In addition to these categories, there is a subset of equally important skills, such as presentation and public speaking, strategy development, critical thinking, and evangelism.

How can you grow your BPM expertise and become a BPM professional? How can you acquire and improve the BPM skills and competencies that are relevant and valuable for your role and organization?

In *Chapter 4, Long-Term Trends and the Impact on Your Job*, we will explore the various sources and methods to increase your expertise, such as the following:

- Learning from BPM literature and research

- Participating in the BPM training and certification programs

- Joining the BPM communities and networks

- Applying the BPM tools and techniques

- Practicing the BPM principles and methods

- Receiving feedback and coaching

How do we drive measurable results?

A BPM transformation is a performance-focused effort designed to achieve quantifiable results that validate the investment and labor involved. These measurable outcomes are concrete, quantifiable indicators reflecting the success and influence of the BPM transformation. According to the balanced scorecard framework, measurable results and outcomes are categorized into four types:

- **Financial**: The results and outcomes that affect the financial performance and profitability of the organization

- **Customer**: The results and outcomes that affect customer satisfaction and loyalty to the organization

- **Internal**: The results and outcomes that affect the operational efficiency and quality of the organization

- **Learning**: The results and outcomes that affect the innovation and growth of the organization

How can you drive measurable results and outcomes from a BPM transformation? How can you define and track the **key performance indicators (KPIs)** that can measure the value and benefits of the BPM transformation?

In the following section, I will emphasize the most effective practices and strategies to achieve tangible results and outcomes from a BPM transformation, such as the following:

- Aligning the BPM transformation goals and KPIs with the organizational strategy and vision

- Setting the **specific, measurable, achievable, relevant, and time-bound (SMART)** objectives and targets

- Collecting and analyzing the data and evidence to monitor and evaluate the BPM transformation performance

- Reporting and communicating the BPM transformation results and outcomes to stakeholders and users

- Recognizing and rewarding the transformation's achievements and successes

- Learning and improving from the transformation's feedback and lessons

Establishing CoEs

A BPM transformation is a collaborative initiative that requires coordinating and integrating the BPM activities and resources across the organization. A CoE is a centralized and dedicated unit that provides the organization with BPM leadership, guidance, and support.

A CoE can help to facilitate and accelerate the BPM transformation as follows:

- Evangelizing the need for business process transformation and ongoing support
- Defining and enforcing standards and policies
- Providing and managing tools and platforms
- Developing and sharing knowledge and best practices
- Building and nurturing a process culture and community
- Leading and sponsoring projects and initiatives
- Coordinating and aligning BPM stakeholders and partners

How can you establish and run a CoE for your BPM transformation?

When is the right time to start one? What are the key elements and factors to consider when designing and operating a CoE? What is the difference between a BPM CoE and a citizen developer CoE?

In this section, we will explore the steps and challenges related to establishing the CoE for your BPM transformation, such as the following:

- Determining the scope and functions of the CoE
- Securing the funding and resources
- Selecting and organizing the team and roles
- Developing and executing the strategy and plan
- Measuring and improving the CoE performance and value
- Adapting and evolving the CoE to the changing needs and expectations

CoE timing dilemma

One of the most pressing questions I've heard asked when companies are either amid a transformation or considering starting one is when a good time is to establish the BPM CoE.

Why would we want to invest in one if we only have a single project in motion?

For many professionals and leaders, creating a CoE when they are either just starting to adopt low-code DPA tools or are simply discussing the need and potential benefits is a bit of a chicken-and-egg discussion. Which one should come first?

Figure 3.13 – Do I need a CoE to be successful with my BPM initiative?

When you are just beginning your journey, you have not yet established yourself as a business process champion, let alone have a team to support the mission. At this part of your journey, you are most likely looking for any free support you can get.

You'd like to start small and gain experience with new concepts and technologies without attracting attention to your mistakes. It seems like a bad idea to throw the CoE discussions into the mix unless you are in a group of companies that already have their CoEs firmly established.

While requesting CoE funding might seem ambitious, I want to share some insights from other companies' experiences to shift your perspective.

Planning and strategizing for the CoE should be a thoughtful exercise that incorporates strategy, meticulous planning, and several targeted assessments. This comprehensive preparation will position you well to request funding. However, planning for the CoE does not imply that you'll immediately create job postings for it.

The long-term value of strategic planning aids in adapting your transformation approach, even amid changing plans (which are inevitable). Planning is essential; without it, we set ourselves up for failure.

Initiating small does not mean brief efforts. Many companies demonstrate that BPM transformations are extensive, spanning several months to years.

When I started my first BPM project in 2005, I never imagined managing BPM at an enterprise level years later. With nearly two decades of experience across four employers, I see BPM as a practice that has grown significantly. My initial BPM transformation expanded from a single implementation to over 35 programs across various business domains over 6 years. Initially, my employer was unprepared for the need for a CoE as those BPM projects began. Recognizing this requirement earlier could have saved substantial person-hours, though it doesn't mean forming teams for yet-to-exist initiatives. Many projects weren't conceived at the beginning.

Over the years, there has been persistent confusion between BPM transformations and technology-driven transformations due to rapid developments in DPA software platforms, low-code tools, AI, and marketing campaigns. Technology transformations tend to attract more attention due to their innovative and appealing software elements.

Concentrating on CoE planning activities enables you to foresee the changes that will unavoidably impact you and your initiatives. In my experience as a BPM professional, I have witnessed significant enhancements in various areas, such as the following:

- Intelligent automation

- Cloud-based processes

- Robotic process automation

- Low-code platforms

- Process mining

- AI-driven adaptive processes

- The sprawl of social channels and chatbots used to interact with our businesses

- CoE-in-a-box accelerators

- The advent of process frameworks

- Standardization of DMN and CMMN

- Universities starting to offer advanced BPM degrees, such as Stevens Institute of Technology, **Queensland University of Technology** (**QUT**), University of Liechtenstein, and the University of San Francisco

When I embarked on my BPM journey in 2005 at a pharmacy benefits management company in Southern California, I couldn't have anticipated the developments that would follow. In 2025, BPM practitioners and citizen developers entering this field can expect significant technical innovations over the next two decades, closer integration of practice areas, and increased automation capabilities at progressively lower costs. However, these advancements will not necessarily make it easier or less effortful for practitioners to grasp the fundamental principles involved.

Viewing BPM as an evolving science is essential for sustaining your team, advancing your career, and supporting your employer's transformation initiatives. Shift your perspective from short-term goals and deliverables over the next 1–3 months to a long-term vision because you, like me, might find yourself dedicated to this field for many years.

Initiating CoEs can often be politically sensitive. Without firm executive support, it might be wise to initially refrain from labeling your efforts as a CoE. Proclaiming excellence too early can draw scrutiny and questions for which you may not yet have prepared answers. Instead, refer to your work as a *community of practice* while you concentrate on establishing the CoE operating model. When the time is right and your executive sponsor recognizes your efforts, you can seamlessly transition into a fully-fledged CoE.

For the CoE to become formally recognized by your organization, you will need the following:

* Official support and backing from your leadership
* Broad peer recognition
* A couple of successes behind your belt, demonstrating your expertise and your level of influence
* Clearly defined service offering that's relevant and mature enough to be offered to other parts of your business
* Several tools and best practices that will keep the wheel of BPM in motion

Direct engagements with the CoE champion or team should clearly showcase the benefits, the value proposition, and the high standards of services provided by the team. Effective selling should primarily be through actions rather than slide presentations, with the latter serving as supporting materials. Prematurely claiming the status of CoE can have negative repercussions, as corporate dynamics generally do not favor self-proclaimed centers of influence.

In any organization, several teams might aspire to establish themselves as the CoE. This is because many individuals face similar challenges, and comprehensive information on addressing these issues using low-code technologies is widely accessible. Additionally, your company is likely targeted by software vendors promoting their tools and the concept of CoEs. Many perceive working on the CoE as more appealing than their routine responsibilities. After all, who wouldn't want to be part of a team that garners attention from across the entire organization?

That's why securing executive buy-in is so essential. Don't let multiple CoEs emerge, as this will lead to chaos and indicate misaligned leadership. I have worked at a large company where an IT-sponsored BPM CoE and a business BPM CoE were competing for resources, projects, and recognition, due to leaders being unable to collaborate toward a common objective. This approach undermines the principles of BPM, which aim for unified operations between business and technology practices. It also highlighted the inexperience of key executives who couldn't unite for a greater purpose. Ideally, you want a single BPM CoE, even with multiple satellite teams executing parallel functions within a *tribe of tribes* model.

These tribes should optimize company resources by consolidating and sharing IT assets such as competitive intelligence reports, cloud services, and teams conducting shared tasks such as testing. Each BPM CoE should offer a mix of business-oriented and technical services. If you allow BPM to break into separate teams, your projects will become fragmented as well.

It's best to think of the CoE as a cross-disciplinary team dedicated to establishing a long-term plan of execution in support of the executive vision. It systematically handles BPM and automation projects that align with your company's culture and limitations. Additionally, it is responsible for defining and assessing the ROI of the transformation, providing a comprehensive perspective of your units' initiatives.

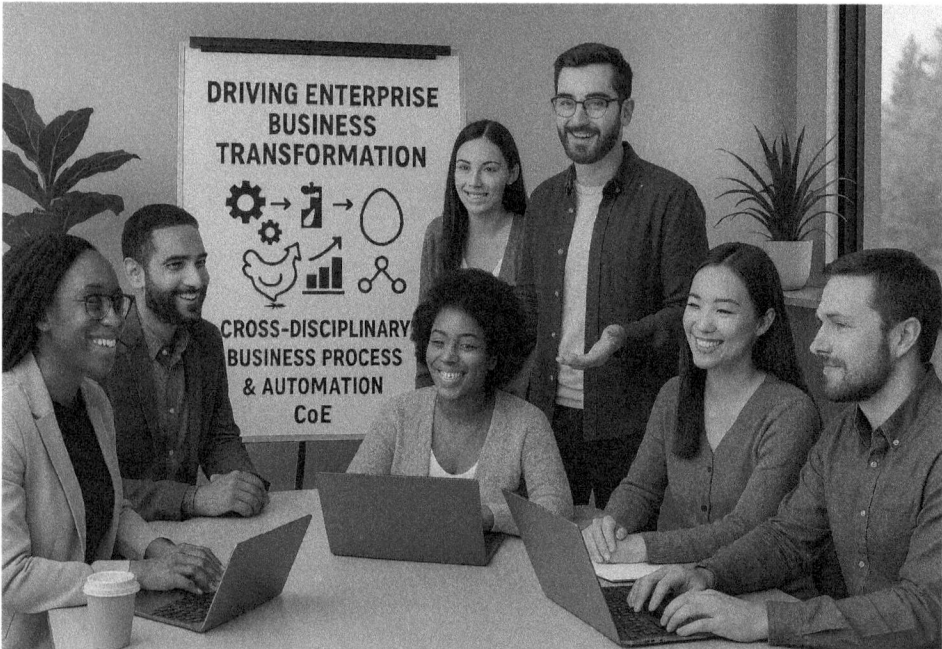

Figure 3.14 – Driving enterprise business transformations requires a cross-disciplinary CoE

The CoE must demonstrate to its sponsors that the allocation of company resources has effectively achieved strategic objectives while delivering the desired ROI. Typically led by a senior manager or director, a well-established CoE has a mission that aims to capture and disseminate knowledge and best practices, ensure consistent standards, support various projects, and manage the shared services utilized by the program. The CoE evolves into a team dedicated to aiding other teams with advocacy, enablement, and technical assessments. It also acts as an informational hub for leaders seeking to align their initiatives with different segments of the company.

CoEs may oversee relationships with software vendors, delivery services, and consulting firms; however, they must remain vigilant in preserving the objectivity and independence of their vision and the company's interests.

How to select a digital business platform

Markets and business requirements change over time, and the technology revolution consistently uncovers new capabilities that eventually enhance process digitization. Such progress frequently occurs through rapid, significant advancements rather than gradual evolution. Few software vendors are capable of supporting both the current technological landscapes and quickly emerging areas of innovation.

Choosing the wrong digitization platform could reveal that your vendor's vision does not align with yours; they may struggle to keep up with new market trends or fail to scale their resources to meet your business needs. You might also discover that your organization is at odds with the culture of the software vendor providing their expertise and tools. This could be due to differences in company culture, the relationship between your sponsor and the vendor's account executive, or biases within leadership teams.

It's also easy to fall into the trap of making the BPM CoE a launch pad for software sales teams promoting process and workflow automation tools. In such cases, recall that even highly reputable vendors will push their agendas to boost platform adoption success. If a vendor's transformation vision and track record don't deliver results for your organization, you may ultimately need to seek alternative solutions with similar capabilities.

The following visual illustrates the approach to selecting the best software platform for your company to support your long-term DTX strategy:

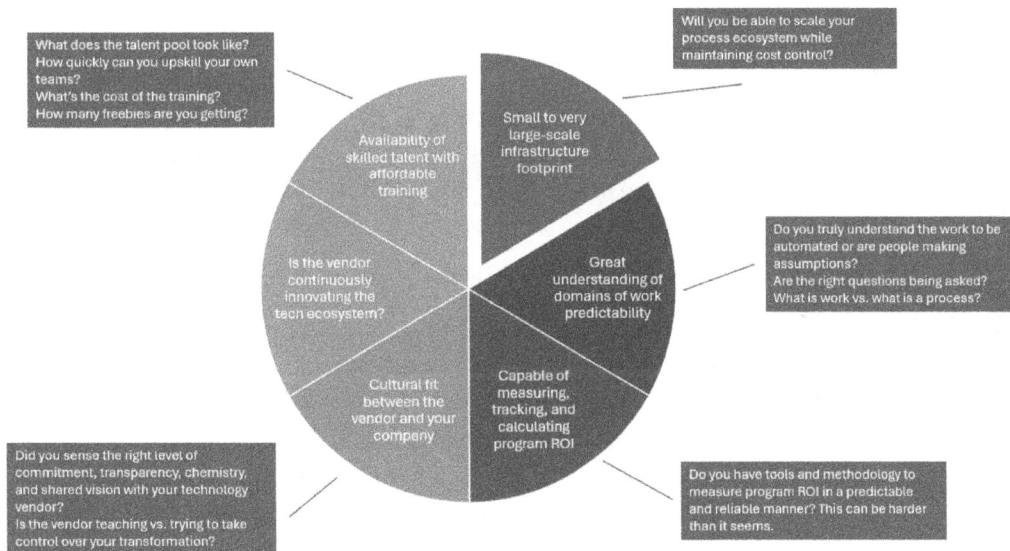

Figure 3.15 – How to pick your DTX ecosystem

While I'm not suggesting that vendors are working against you—most have the best interests of their customers at heart—the reality is that many still exaggerate their capabilities by claiming they can fully automate a wide range of business processes to enhance their appeal. Typically, customers engage with two to three digital business software vendors to mitigate such risks, each provider focusing on specific areas of automation or addressing particular needs within the BPM framework. Analyst firms such as Forrester, Gartner, and IDC offer specialized tool rankings and commercial reports that shed light on the capabilities of various platform vendors, helping to manage these risks. However, it's important to note that these assessments do not always consider project execution factors. Drawing from experience in implementing BPM across multiple companies, using a portfolio of tools deemed best-in-class by analysts does not invariably result in superior DTX outcomes. Practitioners often have divergent views on what constitutes value and excellence compared to those of analysts. Nonetheless, resources from Gartner and Forrester should not be disregarded; they provide valuable insights into market trends and the broader scope of process digitization.

BPM CoE mission statement examples

Let's review a few examples of CoE mission statements highlighting roles and responsibilities.

Here is example 1:

"We exist to drive VALUE to our customers and shareholders.

We exist to remove friction and gain stakeholder alignment in our core and strategic processes."

Here is example 2:

"We believe that a mature BPM program unlocks our ability to deliver customer wins and improve the efficiency and effectiveness of business activity. We accomplish these things by partnering with our stakeholders to embed BPM best practices that include: process discovery & architecture, analysis & improvement, work automation, process performance management, and optimization."

For example 3, let's review a mission statement from a hypothetical company headquartered in the Pacific Northwest of the United States:

"The business process center of excellence team provides expertise in BPM practices and related automation technologies to drive efficiencies across our company. We drive best practices, process culture, and risk management services to help you drive successful digital change programs at optimal cost."

As demonstrated by the preceding examples, mission statements usually remain broad and avoid mentioning specific tools or vendors, instead concentrating on the capabilities offered by the team in line with the wheel of BPM. After creating your mission statement and solidifying a transformation strategy that links the CoE's mission to your organizational transformation goals, it's time to identify the expert services you and your team can provide from the service catalog. These expert services will encompass business, process, and technology, delivered through the BPM playbook.

The BPM playbook serves as a reference guide for BPM implementation programs, covering all aspects of the BPM implementation life cycle with a focus on business-driven activities and responsibilities. It is designed to instruct business teams on the *when*, *what*, *who*, and *why* for each phase of a BPM program, providing best practices and recommended checklists. When utilized properly, such a playbook addresses many of the fundamental issues behind BPM program failures.

A comprehensive BPM playbook would provide advice in the following areas:

- Program fundamentals
- Strategy and vision alignment
- BPM program success factors
- Process readiness assessment
- Business readiness assessment
- Solution fit assessment
- Design review criteria
- Effort estimation models
- Training plans
- Project support templates, including RACI
- Business value analysis methodology
- Methodology guidance
- Digitization platform onboarding guide
- Implementation guidelines
- Governance models for citizen developer-led delivery
- Role-based training paths

BPM playbooks can take the form of websites, PowerPoint slides, Excel sheets, accelerator services provided by consulting teams, applications, or any combination of these. They serve as guides for citizen process architects and developers through the transformation framework, ensuring repeatable results and converting the experience gained from internal projects into future best practices.

Consider the following statistics:

- A survey indicates that 60 to 80% of process transformation projects fail. Another source mentions that 50% of BPM projects fail due to a lack of collaboration between business and IT.

- 96% of executives who fail at BPM attribute this to a deficiency in employee buy-in (*What Business Process Management Statistics Experts Want You to Know*. Cflow. March 6, 2023. `www.cflowapps.com/business-process-management-statistics/`).

- Over 50% of companies not using BPM software consider it too costly.

- Only 26% of organizations employ process mining to evaluate their process performance.

Companies investing in thorough employee training for BPM programs are 2.1 times more likely to see an increase in their ROI compared to those that do not adequately train their employees.

When you initiate transformation programs, it's crucial to specify a few specialized services you plan to provide across the organization. These expert services deliver targeted transformation objectives for your program participants. They can be grouped into service plays, assisting clients in achieving precise transformation goals based on their maturity, current needs, and overall business readiness for transformation. Some vendors incorporate expert services into their CoE consulting packages, aiding customers in transforming their operations. Microsoft provides its CoE Toolkit as a software package available to Power Platform customers. The extent and nature of each CoE offering will differ depending on the vendor's digitization strategy and their target audience. Many companies prefer to develop their service offerings internally to retain their intellectual property. However, this can resemble reinventing the wheel. From my experience with various transformations and CoE teams, organizations generally follow similar practices, with technology-specific variations.

The following figure provides both a template and an example of a BVA service provided by the CoE team I was involved with. This template helped define over 30 services included in our BPM CoE portfolio.

EXPERT SERVICE: BUSINESS VALUE ANALYSIS
Version 1.0   Maturity:2 of 5

Service description

Effort estimation can be performed at multiple stages of your project, each time providing critical information to your business sponsors and program leadership. Our team can provide you with 2 types of estimates: order of magnitude (aka T-Shirt sizing) and budgetary guidance. Each type of the estimate will require a different level of effort from the project team. It is not uncommon to spend between 1-4 weeks of time collaborating on the budgetary guidance estimates as they will require thorough understanding of your vision and requirements. T-Shirt sizing estimates can be performed in a matter of 3-5 days. Keep in mind that CoC estimates are not replacing delivery team estimates and should be treated as a baseline. Through close relationships with BPMS and workflow technology providers, we are in possession of proprietary models and best practices, which can be used to provide you with high quality estimates. Through internally developed scaling factors, we tailor external estimation models to Nordstrom realities.

Business value

Many times, new business ideas cannot advance and flourish without the knowledge of how to approach their implementation. T-Shirt sizing will help you asses initial work complexity, helping to quickly navigate and reconfirm any assumptions being made at this critical time. Proper estimation techniques increase predictability of success by employing common criteria and methods. Hiring external consultants with the expertise for sometimes iterative, ad hoc work is not always feasible and will be costlier. Our service reduces risks of misestimating effort of business critical initiatives. We will also tell you like it is, and you will not have to worry about the conflict of interests like in the case of estimates produced by consultants.

Inputs, requirements and assumptions

Vary based on the type of the estimate.
Requirements Evaluation and Fit Assessment Expert Services are required for the budgetary guidance.
Business use cases, iGrafx process models with their complexity, technical requirements describing SLAs, notifications, org design, reporting requirements, number and complexity of interfaces, UI requirements required to branding and type of the UI (speed of use vs. high aesthetics).

NORDSTROM

Figure 3.16 – Example of a business value analysis expert service

A comprehensive BPM program encompasses end-to-end support provided by an array of on-demand services, such as the following:

- Requirements evaluation
- Process landscape assessment
- Process discovery and analysis
- Fit assessment
- Environment onboarding
- Prototyping
- Design review
- Automation governance
- Licensing consultations
- Effort estimation

- Training plan

- Project and process RACI

- Methodology review

- Business value analysis

The statement-of-work approach and its benefits

For large organizations, I recommend using statements of work to organize the service plays for your customers. These internal documents help clarify expectations, timelines, assumptions, and success criteria. When the service play meets its goal, it's easier to evaluate satisfaction and share lessons learned. Avoid a self-service approach without guidance, as it's crucial to integrate insights into your BPM playbook. In addition to custom playbooks, BPM CoE-in-a-box accelerators are available, offering best practices to quickly establish BPM CoEs. These toolkits can save time and effort with a proven framework, providing guidance on the following:

- Business process governance

- Project status reporting

- Tracking delivered business value

- Design and estimation standards

- Access to reusable components and utilization

- Simplifying automation platform onboarding

- Learning paths for key CoE roles

- Training for citizen developers

What is the difference between a BPM CoE and a citizen developer CoE?

Depending on your exposure to BPM, you might find it challenging to differentiate between a BPM and a citizen developer CoE. A BPM CoE is a centralized business unit that offers leadership, direction, and support for process transformation within your company. It streamlines and quickens BPM transformation by coordinating activities, services, and resources. BPM CoEs are more closely linked to the business side. Conversely, a citizen developer CoE is an extension of the BPM program designed to enable employees to create their solutions using low-code and no-code platforms, such as Power Platform. Supported by a community nourished by the BPM program, the citizen developer CoE evolves alongside the BPM transformation. While BPM CoEs emphasize broad transformation, citizen developer CoEs empower staff to develop solutions and focus on technology, bridging ties to IT. In some instances, a citizen developer CoE can exist independently of a BPM CoE, which may suggest a gap in strategy or a still-developing program.

Without proper management, low-code solutions can lead to unconnected technical debt and a lack of alignment with business strategy or process architecture. Ideally, both BPM and citizen developer CoEs should operate under the same leadership and approach. Given that budgets often influence decisions, it's typical for IT to manage the budget for the citizen developer platform and Azure resources, while a different part oversees funding for the BPM CoE. Both teams should work together harmoniously, sharing the same vision and transformation goals.

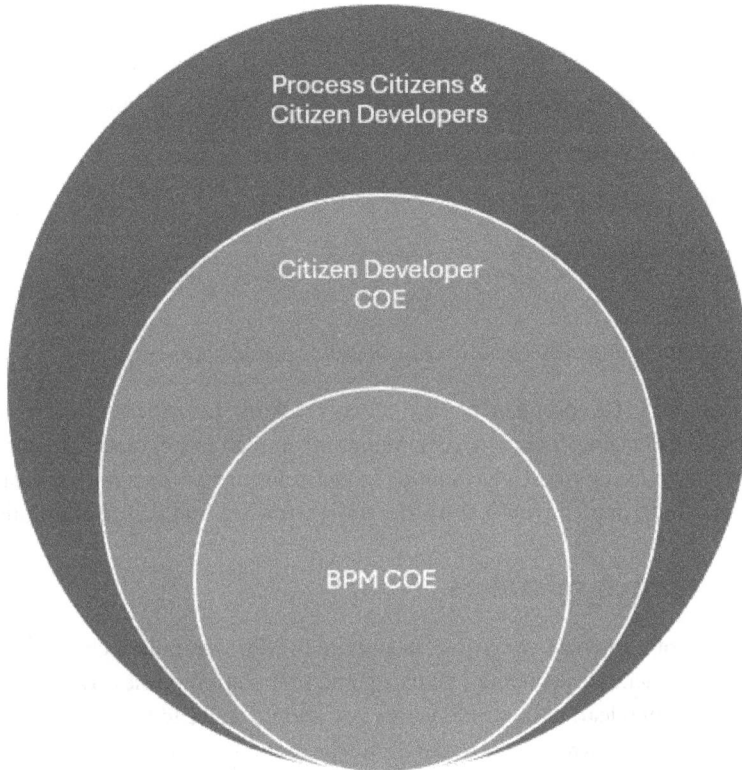

Figure 3.17 – Overlapping relationships between groups of BPM practitioners

CoE KPIs

To evaluate the effectiveness of the CoE and ensure ongoing funding, BPM CoEs can monitor several key metrics, such as the following:

- Number of processes discovered
- Percentage of process discovery coverage
- Number of projects completed
- Number of workshops conducted

- Number of business areas engaged in BPM
- Number of process practitioners
- Rate of process reuse

Conversely, citizen developer CoE KPIs can be assessed through the following:

- Number of projects completed
- Number of groomed ideas in the pipeline
- The ROI of implemented processes
- Number of engineering hours saved
- Number of citizen developers
- On-time and on-budget delivery
- Reuse rate of process and application artifacts
- Percentage of digitized processes indicating overall transformation progress

It is evident that these KPI sets complement each other. Tracking these measures across a growing portfolio of projects is challenging; thus, when beginning with a small scope, you might not gather data for all metrics. When introducing your CoE operating model, prioritize two or three key measures based on sponsor guidance and expand as you mature, develop your team, and secure additional funding.

BPM program launch mistakes

As detailed earlier, various business scenarios can initiate BPM program launches. However, these scenarios do not always facilitate sequential planning and preparation phases, as one might ideally prefer. These instances often lead to common errors you should strive to avoid. The most effective strategy is to pause, assess the current stage of the BPM wheel, and step back if necessary to ensure no essential activity is overlooked. Here are some frequent mistakes made by those new to BPM practice:

- Advancing from the *competency* phase to *excellence* too quickly or too slowly.
- Failing to align your CoE strategy with the company's maturity level.
- Approaching transformation solely through a technological perspective (i.e., focusing on automation for technology adoption rather than business transformation driven by strategy, process, and technology).
- Failing to secure two to three "quick win" projects and then successfully converting them into tangible outcomes.
- Not adjusting external process and methodology standards to fit your company culture and existing practices.

- Equating BPM with BPMS:

  - BPM is the discipline focused on driving efficiency, optimization, and process improvement

  - BPMS is the technology aimed at enhancing collaboration, real-time insight, intelligent decisions, and process agility

- Treating the CoE as a shared tech resource management organization without emphasizing business analysis, BPM consulting, project, and change management.

- Allowing management consultants to dominate your program. While they can offer valuable ideas and perspectives, they often lack the technical connection between problem solving, process improvement, change management, and solution architecture.

Summary

In this chapter, you explored BPM as a discipline aimed at enhancing the performance, efficiency, and agility of business processes. A BPM transformation encompasses adopting principles, methods, and tools to discover, redesign, automate, monitor, and refine these processes. Each iteration of the BPM wheel contributes to the quality and scope of the business transformation. Such a program necessitates a clear vision, robust leadership, an effective operating model, a dedicated team, and a supportive culture. Establishing a CoE can offer BPM leadership, direction, and support across the organization. Over time, the citizen developer CoE can complement the BPM CoE by promoting the DTX of business processes in an inclusive manner.

The next chapter will delve into various sources and methodologies to advance your BPM skills and become a BPM professional, making you an essential component of your company's DTX strategy.

Further reading

- *Business process management* – Wikipedia: `http://www.wikipedia.org/wiki/Business_process_management`

- *The Modern Definition of BPM* – Poster by Fujitsu: `http://social-biz.org/2014/09/30/bpm-poster/`

- *UnitedHealth Group (UNH)* – Yahoo Finance historical stock data: `http://finance.yahoo.com/quote/UNH/`

- *Heineken Brews Digital Future at Lightning Speed with the Power Platform* – Macaw case study: `http://www.macaw.net/eng/cases/heineken-brews-digital-future-at-lightning-speed-with-the-power-platform`

- *Heineken (HEINY)* – Yahoo Finance historical stock data: `http://finance.yahoo.com/quote/HEIA.AS/`

- *Goldman Sachs Delivers Automation at Scale* – Camunda case study: `https://camunda.com/about/customers/goldman-sachs/`

- *Goldman Sachs (GS)* – Yahoo Finance historical stock data: `http://finance.yahoo.com/quote/GS/history/`

- *JALLC staff improves Business Process Management skills*: `https://www.jallc.nato.int/articles/jallc-staff-improves-business-process-management-skills`

- *Conoco Phillips Using BPM to Focus on Core Business - ProcessForum Nordic* presentation: `https://www.slideshare.net/slideshow/conoco-phillips-using-bpm-to-focus-on-core-businesstrack2processforumnordicnov142013/29106972`

- *NHS England enhances BPM with data analytics* – Process Excellence Network: `https://www.processexcellencenetwork.com/business-process-management-bpm/interviews/nhs-england-enhances-bpm-with-data-analytics`

Unlock this book's exclusive benefits now

Scan this QR code or go to `packtpub.com/unlock`, then search this book by name.

Note: Keep your purchase invoice ready before you start.

4

Long-Term Trends and the Impact on Your Job

In the previous chapter, we examined how the **Business Process Management** (**BPM**) discipline enhances companies' profitability and innovation while also highlighting the necessity to constantly keep pace with the evolving science of business process management and the array of technologies propelling it. As an employee, partner, or business owner, it is impossible to overlook the impact of **Digital Transformation** (**DTX**) on your profession. This reality impacts all industries and job types, demanding continuous adaptation and evolution of skills. Being aware of the long-term trends will help you stay relevant in the marketplace.

When companies aggressively embrace new DTX platforms as part of their digitization efforts, many employees encounter competition in the internal job market for which they are unprepared. A CTO's decision to rely on a strategic partnership with a software provider can significantly impact one's career trajectory with that employer. Although some companies foster cultures that support employee upskilling, digital change initiatives may progress so rapidly that employees lack sufficient time and resources to meet evolving job demands. Training is not always a budget priority, so if you find an employer who values employee self-development, you have found a company that has improved your chances of thriving amid DTX.

These are turbulent times, and hard and fast business decisions don't always align with employees' career needs. This chapter highlights strategies and skills you should pick up to help ensure your career will align with your company's long-term DTX goals based on the author's experience in the field. We will also discuss how you can leverage your existing knowledge and expertise in BPM to learn new competencies that will help you stay relevant and valuable in the constantly evolving job market.

In this chapter, you will learn about the following:

- Surprising truths no one tells you about
- Why is the understanding of digital change topics so critical?
- Definition of business process

- How major trends shape skill requirements

- The art of knowing how to learn

- How to navigate through a rapidly changing job market

- Discovering new trends

> **Note**
>
> This chapter is authored by BJ Biernatowski.

Unveiling the hidden truths: surprises you never knew existed

When participating in a digital change program, you are likely part of a major DTX initiative aimed at transforming a business unit, process, or team operations. The maturity and experience level of your team will significantly influence both the approach and outcomes of this transformation.

The way you frame the business problem and your project will ultimately determine the results you achieve. Unfortunately, many leaders driving transformation initiatives lack the core technical skills needed to effectively lead these efforts, yet they are still expected to guide the process based on their authority. While it is not necessary for directors, managers, or program managers involved in DTX initiatives to be experts in every area from BPM to DTX, these leaders and *Change Champions* should be equipped with essential skills to enhance their team's DTX IQ.

You may have heard someone say, "*I don't know what I don't know.*" The breadth and depth of a leader's experience often establish the baseline level of DTX IQ for their team. It is surprising that leaders or managers who drive major initiatives are not assessed for their understanding of DTX.

Why do students in schools undergo regular testing while those in the workforce are assumed to no longer need continued self-development? Individuals leading technology-driven initiatives should be well versed in the details of the platforms, methodologies, and frameworks relevant to their business challenges.

The greatest risk to any organization is having a leader who fails to recognize their weaknesses and attempts to bridge their knowledge gaps from a limited perspective, unaware of the areas where they lack understanding. Leaders often hesitate to openly acknowledge their shortcomings, which can become evident within a year or two of taking on new responsibilities.

Effective leadership requires a foundation of knowledge, experience, or a combination of both. The challenge with understanding DTX and BPM is that these subjects are extensive, and most existing courses are geared toward business analysts, enterprise architects, or executive leaders. As a result, they either provide excessive details or are prohibitively expensive. The industry needs a standardized curriculum that offers a sufficient level of depth without demanding significant financial investment. This approach would ensure that Change Champions have access to the necessary knowledge and training.

For $5,900, Stanford Online offers an excellent course designed for senior-level leaders. However, even in this case, Stanford has opted to divide the training into two separate tracks: managerial and technical.

The course focuses on key topics such as the following:

- Foundations of DTX
- Adapting to a changing landscape
- Managing uncertainty
- Human-centered design
- Building an AI-enabled organization
- Developing a product platform strategy

You can find the course description with enrollment criteria and the recent cost information at https://online.stanford.edu/programs/digital-transformation-program.

For *Change Agents* and BPM practitioners, courses from the BPM Institute cater to various needs, with prices for professional-level certificates ranging from $3,400 to $5,950, depending on the delivery format (on-demand, e-learning, private learning, or face-to-face sessions). The BPM Institute provides multiple self-assessment questionnaires, enabling you to evaluate your skills conveniently from your home office (https://www.bpminstitute.org/assessments/). However, the abundance of learning paths—totaling 14 certificates—can be overwhelming as you try to determine the right one for you. These learning paths focus on areas such as Agile BPM, business process analysis, business process management, operational excellence, business architecture, Agile business analysis, decision automation, process mining, and low-code/no-code or intelligent automation.

Having participated in one of the BPM Institute's training courses, I can confirm the high quality of the training materials and the thoroughness of the certification process. Gregg Rock embodies the notion that if you seek to learn about BPM and DTX, Boston is a great place to do it—even if only remotely.

If you are searching for a cost-effective learning option, a LinkedIn Learning subscription provides access to various BPM courses for just $240 per year with a Premium Career subscription. LinkedIn Learning offers just-in-time training, allowing practitioners to select the right learning paths and schedule their training according to their daily work demands. Most courses focus on Six Sigma, robotic process automation, business analysis, project management, process analysis, and Microsoft products, such as Power Platform and Power Automate. Courses such as *Business Process Improvement* by Eddie Davila, the ASU supply chain management program chair, offer a solid introduction to BPM topics at an unbeatable price.

As of 2025, there is a significant number of bite-sized training courses that offer completion certificates. However, be cautious when investing your time in classes led by individuals attempting to ride the wave of hyperautomation buzz. Occasionally, you may encounter classes that are either very generic or taught by venture capitalists seeking attention in this booming market. Many trainers who teach DTX and BPM often lack practical experience. An effective coach or trainer should have participated in 30 to 50 programs or projects before instructing others. Given the considerable hype around hyperautomation, it is crucial to verify the credibility of the information before accepting it.

Zbigniew Misiak at `http://bpmtips.com` frequently updates a list of high-quality free online resources for those seeking cost-effective BPM training. He dedicates substantial time each year to researching available BPM classes, and the insights shared on his blog can be invaluable for practitioners and organizations. *BPM Tips* has emerged as a global, vendor-independent source of information, raising awareness of BPM's value proposition as a practice. If free training is available on any BPM subject, you will likely find it on `bpmtips.com`.

In addition to the various free resources, many software providers now offer complimentary online DTX training. Nevertheless, despite their positive intentions, these courses often dive into technical and implementation aspects without providing adequate foundational knowledge. Typically, vendor-specific training tends to focus on promoting their all-in-one platform solutions while overlooking the underlying reasons for DTX. Most software vendors I have encountered have rushed through their technical curricula, understandably motivated by the desire to drive the adoption of their platforms.

It's important to understand that adopting a platform does not guarantee success in digital change or DTX. If you choose to begin your learning journey with these resources, be aware that there may be hidden costs down the line. Ultimately, you may end up focusing more on learning about the tools rather than addressing the practical business challenges that necessitate the use of these platforms.

I greatly enjoy the buffet-style and modular training courses offered by Microsoft Learn: `https://learn.microsoft.com/en-us/training/browse/`. Microsoft provides flexible training career paths that can be tailored to your professional experience, interests, products, or desired career directions. This approach enables you to create a custom curriculum without being limited to a specific job description, which may not align with your future roles. However, it's worth noting that Microsoft Learn does not cover DTX topics in detail and you will need to complement your studies by reading blogs by a wide ecosystem of Microsoft's **Most Valuable Professionals** (**MVPs**). There are plenty of interesting blogs and podcasts to choose from. I highly recommend Mark Smith's (nz365guy) *Microsoft Innovation* podcast running for over 8 years. Mark features expert guests, including thought leaders, industry innovators, and community specialists, who are redefining the world with advancements in AI and cloud technologies. His website can be found at `http://www.nz365guy.com`.

After spending considerable time reviewing and comparing various training programs, I observed that many vendors design their courses to prepare students for specific roles. In my experience, this approach can sometimes limit job seekers' opportunities in the market. Throughout my career, I have preferred a skills-based approach over a role-based one, ensuring that my focus on digital technologies did not confine me to a particular niche within vendors' sales strategy.

At a certain point in my career, I concluded that I did not want to become an architect specializing in a single vendor's platform, despite the compelling training materials suggesting otherwise. Having worked with platforms from various companies, I respect the credibility of innovations endorsed by Forrester and Gartner rankings. As I moved away from vendor-specific allegiance to adopt a more generalist approach, I realized that the scope of DTX and digital change was too vast for any single software vendor to dominate. Therefore, I chose to specialize in digital change, leveraging both business and technology expertise to drive DTX initiatives. This allowed me to navigate different toolsets and platforms more effectively.

If you possess the fundamental skills outlined later in this chapter, you'll be able to implement workflow automation solutions across a variety of platforms, such as **ServiceNow**, **Microsoft Power Platform**, or **Bizagi**. In contrast, specializing in tools such as **Pega** or **Appian** typically involves a longer-term commitment. These platforms are more complex and proprietary in nature, often requiring a steeper learning curve and deeper technical immersion. In a rapidly changing job market or because of technological advancements, having a versatile core skill set can make it easier to adapt and enhance your skills.

Developing a core DTX skill set will also help you adapt to various automation platform vendors, as companies frequently invest in multiple platforms to mitigate the risks of vendor lock-in. Being an expert in one DTX platform today enhances your chances of working with others. Despite differences among vendors, the majority of platforms are centered around business processes that can be mapped using **Business Process Model and Notation (BPMN)**. While switching platforms requires flexibility and a willingness to relearn, it's entirely achievable and provides valuable insights into BPM and business process automation from diverse perspectives.

Another advantage of this strategy is that working with BPM exposes you to various topics, including cloud technology, AI, data science, change and program management, team leadership, information security, strategy building, evangelism, and other aspects of DTX. As your employer's needs evolve, this exposure can significantly advance your career.

Today, work and process automation are once again in the spotlight due to advances in AI. AI is poised to transform work, automation, and enterprise architecture profoundly. The key question on everyone's mind is how extensively will AI transform work, automation, and enterprise architecture?

With appropriate career planning and the right learning model, you may be able to pivot yourself into another career as your aspirations or the job market's needs change. Committing to one vendor's path is a risky proposition; if you choose to do so, invest time in researching the market size, future job opportunities, and your earning potential. Spending a decade within one vendor's ecosystem could lead you to miss advancements and opportunities arising in other market segments. Choose your work automation ecosystem wisely, as there are significantly more options available today compared to a decade (or even half a decade) ago, considering that digital processes now dominate most business operations.

Understanding the importance of digital change topics

Why am I emphasizing the importance of familiarity with BPM science for people who drive digital change programs?

Throughout my career, I have collaborated with numerous seasoned leaders, architects, and program managers who, thanks to their extensive experience, could easily helm a large-scale project in a different industry, such as building construction, purely through their leadership abilities. These leaders have exceptional organizational and leadership skills, and irrespective of the industry, a project remains a project; scope, risks, and issues hold the same significance.

Transforming physical objects is different from changing business models or operations because the outcomes in the digital world are less tangible. Digital business can be abstract, especially with software, and involves navigating complex, multi-dimensional concepts. Unlike a physical object such as a brick, the unit of work in digital business can vary widely in meaning among different groups. This field requires metaphors, effective metamodels, and various diagrams to illustrate workflows, systems, and outcomes.

When you present a brick to the construction crew, an inspector, or the homeowner, they all perceive the same object. However, if you show a business process or requirement to a business analyst, process architect, engineer, or citizen developer, their interpretations often differ. This variance is influenced by their individual experiences, cognitive abilities, the tools they use to document requirements, and their capacity to connect relevant information. When emotional and human factors are considered, it becomes clear why over 60% of digital transformation initiatives fail. Frequently, our stakeholders do not share the same vision.

For the sake of an example, if you are building a fence, you will most likely use bricks or wooden planks to illustrate the design of your construction.

Figure 4.1 – Farm fence in Watlington, Norfolk ("Farm fence in Watlington" by Lewis Collard, licensed under CC BY-SA 3.0)

Bricks or planks have multiple properties; it is possible to join them into walls or larger structures surrounding land or houses. In the world, there are many substitutes for clay bricks; for example, in Ireland, many walls are built with natural stone, resulting in beautiful landscapes in addition to their functional purpose.

A small brick can be the foundation for an enormous structure. For instance, the Malbork Castle in Poland, the world's largest brick castle, was constructed from clay bricks by the Teutonic Order in the 1400s

Figure 4.2 – Malbork Castle, Poland is the largest brick castle in the world

> **Note**
>
> Here is the copyright information for the preceding figure—*Panorama of Malbork Castle, part 4.jpg*, Wikimedia Commons, GNU free documentation license, version 1.2: `https://commons.wikimedia.org/wiki/File:Panorama_of_Malbork_Castle,_part_4.jpg`.

The brick has been tested as a very flexible and sturdy building block over the last few centuries.

In the process of designing and planning your business, you must establish a foundational building block. This element will also aid in expanding the reach of your company.

We suggest that you regard the metamodel of a *business process* as this fundamental building block. However, there are several caveats to consider:

- Enterprise business processes, unlike fences or castles, are constantly changing and require flexibility. Some are still hiding in data logs, work instructions, or as tribal knowledge exercised daily.

- A business process applies to a transformation of the unit of work, so you need to be able to describe both the work and the business processes that can be used to transform your work. I worked with many architects from different companies during my career, and only a handful could explain what work was using plain language. The number of architects who knew how to connect the unit of work to a process-driven business transformation and then launch one into motion is even smaller. This is caused by too many software applications designed in an ad hoc fashion, the lack of a uniform approach to the practice of enterprise **Business Architecture (BA)**, and not pushing enough information about BA concepts from the Ivory Towers of EA into the trenches of the enterprise. In that part of the company where pain points are lived daily, projects are executed without delivering their full value and people spend time continuously fixing and improving—the part of the company where we operate daily.

- Let's consider that the term *business process* can be defined differently by the marketing department, engineering team, process architecture, and program manager. It is the same business process, each time defined using different visuals, words, and meta models. All these folks may not see the BPMN diagram underneath, which gets into the nitty gritty of work. There is a BPMN, **Case Management Model and Notation (CMMN)**, or **Decision Model and Notation (DMN)** diagram (or a few of them) for each business process discussed in the universe. Sometimes, it just takes a bit of effort to discover it.

Let's switch gears for a second now to the task of envisioning the blueprint of our company. What is the equivalent of the *brick, stone, or wood plank* that can be used to represent our business?

Is it a business process? No, because if you know something about business process naming, those are represented by a verb (a thing that's being *done*). What we are looking for is the item on which the business process applies its transformation magic, converting inputs into business outputs.

To quote the wisdom of Copilot, *the business process emerges as a foundational thread in the intricate tapestry of organizational dynamics.*

Defining business process

A **business process** represents a sequence of interrelated activities or tasks that collectively achieve a specific organizational goal. These processes span various functions, departments, and roles within the organization.

Examples of business processes include **order fulfillment, inventory management, customer onboarding**, and **financial reporting**. It's important to consider the role of verbs in naming conventions for these processes. Let's take some time to discuss the characteristics of business processes to clarify the definition further:

- **Fundamental role of business processes**:

  - **Operational efficiency**: Business processes streamline operations, ensuring that work is executed consistently and efficiently. They minimize redundancy, reduce errors, and enhance productivity.

  - **Value creation**: Processes directly contribute to value creation for customers, stakeholders, and shareholders. Whether it's delivering a product, providing a service, or managing resources, processes drive outcomes.

  - **Alignment with strategy**: Effective processes align with the organization's strategic objectives. They translate high-level goals into actionable steps, ensuring that everyone moves in the same direction.

  - **Adaptability and agility**: Well-designed processes are adaptable. They can evolve to accommodate changes in technology, market conditions, and customer preferences.

  - **Continuous improvement**: Organizations thrive when they embrace a culture of continuous improvement. Business processes provide a canvas for optimization, innovation, and refinement.

- **Process-centric view**:

  - Some schools of thought emphasize a **process-centric view** of organizations. Here, processes take center stage, and organizational structures adapt to support these processes.

  - In this paradigm, roles, hierarchies, and functions exist to serve the efficient execution of processes. The focus shifts from silos to seamless flow.

- **Holistic perspective**:

  - While business processes are fundamental, they don't stand alone. They interact with other organizational elements, such as **people**, **technology**, **data**, **culture**, and **strategy**.

  - The synergy among these components creates a resilient and thriving organization.

In essence, business processes form the backbone of an organization, weaving together its fabric of functionality and purpose. It is also relatively easy for a person in the business to go from a definition of the business process (a thing that transforms inputs into the business value) into a process map, then into a larger collection of business processes (architectures) representing capabilities of the whole business unit, into actual projects that drive implementations resulting in workflow ecosystems. I'd like to also propose that we look at a business process as a string of activities and tasks that can do the following:

- Learn

- Be adaptive

- Change colors and distribute coffee and candy (not really, but wouldn't that be nice?)

Imagine now that the Order of Teutonic Knights attempts to design their next headquarters in Europe in 2025. If they took the business process-led design approach, the following could apply to their next castle:

- It could have a few shape-shifting towers and moats, and be able to adjust to changing weather conditions, inside temperature, and the number of visiting guests. The Order of Teutons enjoyed entertaining their guests so the ability to flex the quarters by a few additional rooms would be worth a premium.

- The design would also learn from Navajo, Spanish, Irish, British, French, Portuguese, South Indian, and Aztec castle designers about different architectural styles and layouts, selecting the most optimal building style for their needs depending on the occasion, situation, or the level of threat. The Teutonic Order had many enemies due to its aggressive stance toward non-Christians, and its location in Central Europe emphasized protection over openness.

- The bricks would be made from LED-like material, charging from the sun. They could also change colors and translucency (adaptive and self-sustaining properties).

- The castle could be built by peasants who were not part of the Teutonic Order and contributed a few hours per week to help create this fortress in their spare time.

- The new castle could be built in 6 months on a parcel in the neighboring city, then overnight, the old structure would be destroyed and replaced by a new design.

The preceding mental exercise is intended to overlay the qualities of a business process into the physical structure deployed at a large scale as in the enterprise-wide process transformation.

Now, consider that there are some leaders who attempt to design and digitize core business processes without the right level of appreciation of process architecture, modeling, and execution. What they build is individual moats and bridges (they'd call such projects *automation*), hoping that, over time, these bridges will somehow connect and create the whole *castle* of their enterprise or a business unit.

In other words, if you are invested in your career and would like to play an active role in digital change programs, you need to understand quite a bit about the foundational *brick* of the transformation and the theory of the business process itself. Look at the business process and learn it from every possible angle to later apply this knowledge to your company's transformations.

Carry the understanding that your core foundational skillset will need to be extended with technical skills based on your role, which may be closer to the implementation work (castle construction vs. castle design). The tech capabilities of digitization platforms change every few months, and you will need to stay on top of these features and refresh yourself with new certifications occasionally. One thing that will keep you grounded and allow you to navigate through new tools, new jargon, and, often, confusion is your understanding of the business process and BPM fundamentals. Such knowledge will put you ahead of 70% of your colleagues who claim that they are *transforming and automating* business processes without understanding what such business processes are, why they exist, and being aware of their life cycle. Such colleagues can be recognized by flowchart artworks full of logical errors that waste time and spread confusion. Many business professionals still do not understand and value basic process mapping notation and its purpose; they look at swim lanes as a necessary evil, getting satisfaction and a sense of empowerment when producing slideware. Democratization of domains creates the need to start treating areas of process design, mapping, and architecture as common skills that supplement MBA programs.

Navigating major trends and their impact on skill requirements

There are many trends affecting BPM and DTX, such as the following:

- AI
- Cloud computing
- Big data
- Blockchain
- Internet of things (IoT)
- Robotics, 3D printing
- Decision management
- Customer journey mapping
- Robotic process automation
- Process mining
- AI chatbots

These trends are not isolated phenomena, but rather interconnected and interdependent forces that create synergies and feedback loops. They also have different impacts and implications depending on the industry and application.

However, there are some common characteristics and consequences of these technological trends that are often overlooked or underestimated by most people. Here are some of them:

- The technological trends are exponential, not linear. This means they are growing at an accelerating rate, doubling their performance and impact every few years. For example, Moore's law states that the number of transistors on a microchip doubles every two years while the cost halves. This leads to an exponential increase in computing power and a decrease in cost. Similarly, other trends such as AI, big data, and IoT follow exponential curves of improvement and adoption. This implies that the future will be radically different from the present and that the changes will happen faster than we expect.

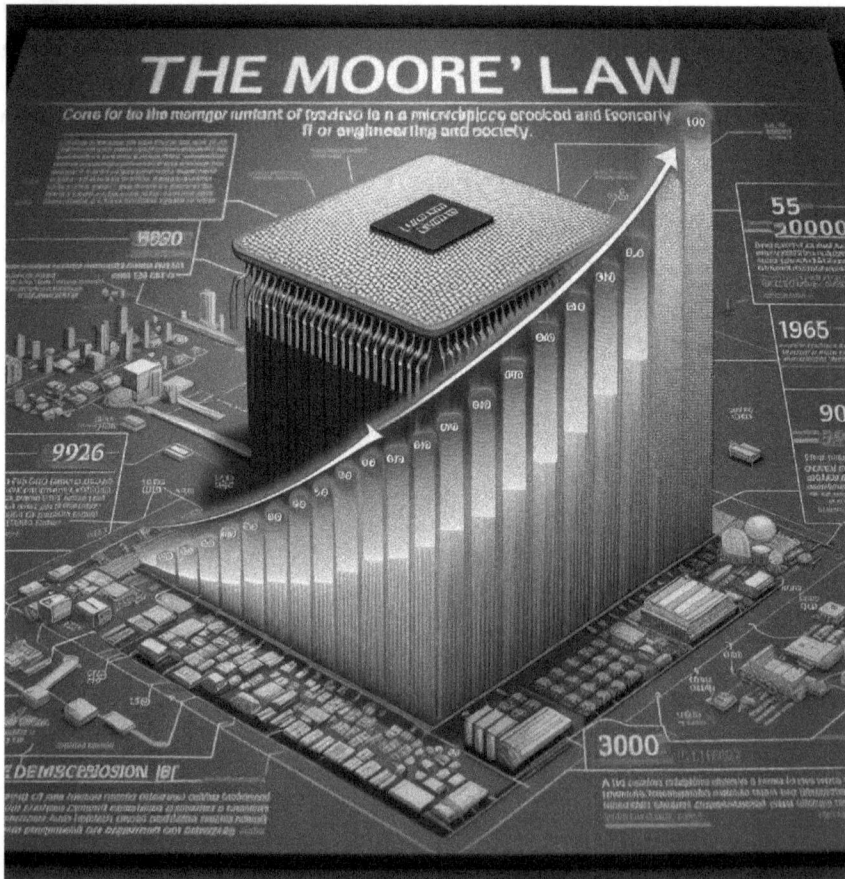

Figure 4.3 – The influence of Moore's law on DTX

- Technological trends are convergent, not divergent. This means that they are merging and integrating with each other, creating new combinations and possibilities. For example, AI and cloud computing enable the analysis and processing of massive amounts of data, which can be used to optimize and automate business processes. Blockchain and IoT enable the creation of decentralized and distributed networks of smart devices, enabling new forms of collaboration and coordination. AR and VR enable the creation of immersive and interactive digital environments, which can enhance customer and employee experiences. These convergence scenarios create new value propositions and business models that transcend the boundaries of traditional industries and sectors.

- The technological trends are also disruptive, not incremental. This means they are creating fundamental shifts and transformations in how things are done rather than minor improvements or modifications. For example, AI and robotics enhance human capabilities and augment human tasks and roles, creating new challenges and opportunities for workers and organizations. Cloud computing and blockchain provide more efficient and secure ways of storing and transferring information and enable new forms of governance and trust, challenging existing institutions and regulations.

Many vendors aiming to lead in DTX often rapidly add new capabilities to digital business platforms. This results in high-density features that are difficult to master and sometimes even hard to discover, let alone comprehend. Such technologies challenge users, making staying on top of new and emerging features difficult. From the market perspective, vendors continuously innovate, playing catch up with others' feature sets. This never-ending race of technological progress takes massive engineering resources, market maturity, innovativeness, and execution strength, all needed to provide DTX support to other companies.

It is also very common to see new trends completely cannibalizing older approaches to digitization, putting a large customer base at a disadvantage, and making both customers and platform vendors rethink their digitization strategies. BPMS cannibalized workflow orchestration engines, iBPMS swallowed BPMS, low code gobbled up iBPMS, and now AI is transforming low coding and professional coding forever.

Being aware of such dynamics prompts us to ask a few questions:

- When and how will this never-ending continuum of progress end?

- Who is to decide which approach or technology is no longer applicable or better at solving a business problem?

- How do you position yourself and your future career amid constantly changing trends?

As a participant in DTX, you may find that you have limited influence over the selection of the platform or technology used to drive digital change programs. However, when considering your career, there are decisions you can make regarding where to invest your time in upskilling. This will help you remain relevant in the job market and valuable to your employer. We would like to propose a set of foundational skills that are essential for a digital change practitioner:

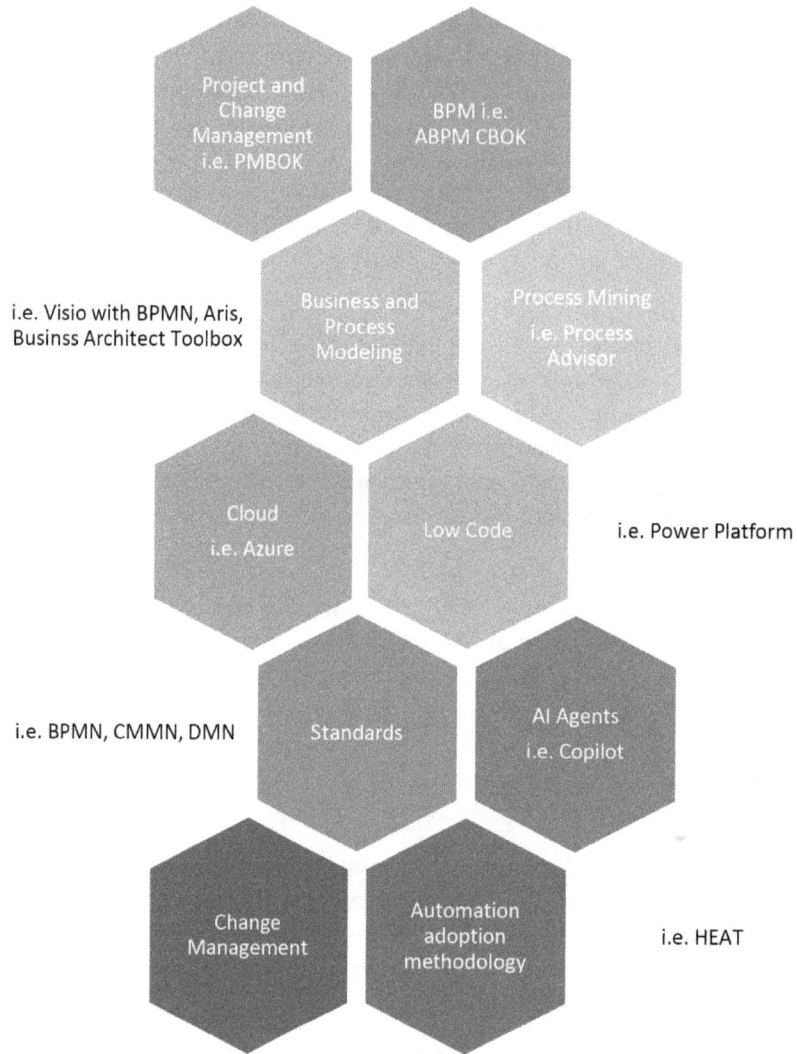

Figure 4.4 – A variety of skills and expertise is essential for successful digital change projects

Until a few years ago, the primary strategy for digitization involved collaborating with consulting firms experienced in DTX across various platform vendors. While this method proved successful for some, it also led to delays in initiatives that couldn't launch due to insufficient internal expertise or inadequate return on investment. Additionally, large workflow automation platforms often present broad solutions across many industries but frequently fail to meet expectations, attempting to impose a one-size-fits-all approach to transformation.

Project after project has proven that the **return on investment** (**ROI**) equation will take a hit if you hire process transformation and automation experts from large, global consulting companies versus reskilling your workforce that can be tapped within your organization with some consulting assistance. The hybrid approach, which initially hires consultants to jumpstart the project while simultaneously training internal staff, offered the best of both worlds.

The **citizen developer** movement, which exploded not so long ago, benefits from a new generation of tooling that is simpler to use, quicker to deliver results, and taps into underutilized software delivery resources that, until recently, were not even considered. Citizen developer programs can provide massive results; however, they are not easy to launch as they require an unconventional delivery approach and changes to compliance models governed by IT. The big elephant in the room is that IT organizations are unwilling to give up their power to masses of DTX change champions delivering digitized processes without IT's involvement. Creating cohesive business process ecosystems in this model also requires a specialized and innovative design, project, and change management approach.

The citizen developer movement is also much more empowering to the existing workforce, increasing work satisfaction and fixing pain points that have finally been properly diagnosed. No more lost in translation requirements caused by issues explaining and describing business issues to multiple teams of business architects.

Democratization of digitization technologies directly connects the issue with the solution, shortening the time to solve and the time to realize business benefits. This approach requires an entirely new work method as many companies are still used to source requirements through multiple teams, tools, methodologies, and software factories.

The citizen developer movement also unleashed a wave of direct innovation, offering more gender equality on teams historically dominated by men. When I led the citizen developer program at Nordstrom in Seattle, over the 2+ years period, 95% of citizen developers who worked with our team were females attempting to solve business pain points with the help of low code, nicely counterbalancing male-dominated engineering teams. Many of our citizen developers used the experience gained on the program to springboard into other parts of technology, such as data science. When asked about their motivation, they cited positive experiences with low code as a motivating force pushing them toward bigger and bolder aspirations in the world of technology historically dominated by men. While I would not consider my two years of casual observations as a scientific study, the number of women citizen developers designing and launching low-code solutions made me think about the positive impact of such technologies on diversity in the tech field. There are no public studies I know of on the effects of low code on workplace diversity.

The experience on a program involving 60+ citizen developers at Nordstrom in Seattle, WA, between 2016 and 2020 confirmed that by reducing the reliance on traditional engineering teams, the low-code platform allowed a broader range of perspectives and voices and improved the ROI of our work automation program, delivering quicker results and improving workforce diversity.

Embracing the strategy of continuous learning

As with any skill set, specific skills will offer higher premium value while changing more frequently, and other skills will not require frequent updates. Fundamental business analysis and process architecture, **project management body of knowledge (PMBOK)**, or **change management body of knowledge (CMBOK)** curriculum does not advance as drastically as advances and revisions in AI, low code, and the cloud curriculum.

With that information on hand, you can plan on how to build your core skills, then supplement them with technical courses, starting with generic and then diving into specialized as your career and interests develop. Building out your core skills will serve as your defense against major technological breakthroughs, which will always demand a bit of learning. One constant thing in the world of technology is the pace of change, which requires regular upskilling to stay on top of current and relevant trends.

Given the exponential, convergent, and disruptive nature of technological trends, staying relevant and competitive in the world of BPM and DTX requires a constant and proactive effort of learning and adaptation. However, learning is not a one-time event or a static state but rather a dynamic and ongoing process that involves acquiring, applying, and updating knowledge and skills. Moreover, learning is not only an individual endeavor but also a collective and collaborative activity that involves interacting with other people and sources of information.

Therefore, we propose a continuous learning strategy consisting of four main elements—curiosity, exploration, feedback, and reflection—as shown in the following figure and described in the list that follows:

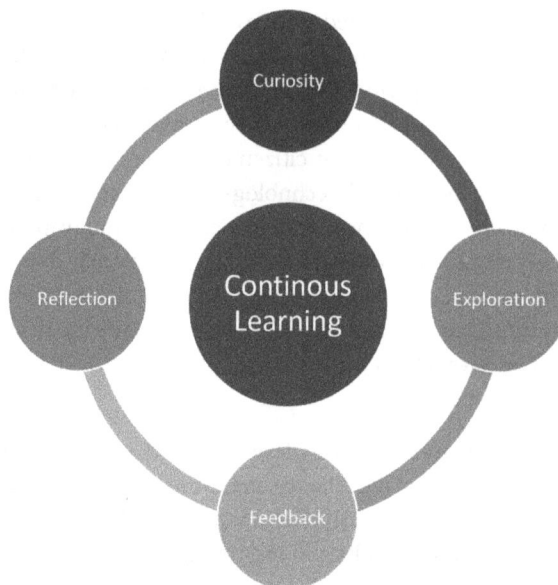

Figure 4.5 – The continuous learning framework

- **Curiosity** drives the desire to seek new information and experiences that can broaden one's perspective and challenge existing assumptions

- **Exploration** involves actively pursuing various avenues for learning, such as reading, watching, listening, experimenting, or engaging with others

- **Feedback** encompasses both receiving and providing constructive criticism and guidance to enhance performance and understanding

- **Reflection** entails thinking critically and creatively about learning outcomes, processes, and goals, as well as identifying areas for improvement and further learning

By adopting this approach, you can cultivate a growth mindset and a lifelong learning attitude, which are essential for navigating rapid and complex changes in the fields of BPM and DTX.

Throughout our parents' careers, technological change occurred at a much slower pace, which did not prepare us for the faster-changing world we face today. The technologies of their time were central to their lives and remained relevant throughout their existence. In contrast, we live in an era characterized by a remarkable acceleration in technological advancements that displace inventions more quickly than ever before in human history. This trend necessitates the development of new adaptive learning strategies.

Reflecting on the evolution of BPM over the past two decades, it has matured into a credible foundation for DTX initiatives. However, BPM has also faced criticism for being perceived as overly broad, impractical, and disjointed, often due to the methods used in teaching or implementing it within organizations. **Digital Process Automation (DPA)** platforms have emerged as key drivers of digitization, while BPM methodologies have evolved to incorporate intelligence, enabling companies to design, refine, and automate critical business processes. The market has witnessed a surge of software vendors and consulting firms entering this space, each striving to innovate and reshape the marketplace. While evolution tends to be incremental, many technological trends that shape the tech landscape progress exponentially, leading to significant market shifts that transform practices and contribute to confusion. Process transformation and associated tools do not exist in isolation, even during substantial technological advancements; they are usually influenced by and interconnected with other technological trends. As we reflect on the last two decades of BPM evolution, it is essential to examine these developments with a forward-looking perspective.

Past: transformations from paper to digital processes

Digitization has transformed organizations from relying on paper-based processes to embracing digital workflows. This shift is now accessible to a large portion of the corporate workforce, thanks to the availability of user-friendly, low-code, and cost-effective platforms for citizen developers and citizen process architects. Automation has liberated resources, reduced costs, and eliminated bottlenecks, enabling companies to explore new business models. The integration of business processes with legacy systems ensures a smooth data flow and eliminates process silos. Analytics provides insights into real-time process performance. Agility and related methodologies have influenced BPM by emphasizing adaptability and continuous improvement. The future-forward outlook on the advancements of the process sciences warrants consideration of these new developments.

Future: evolving from digital to adaptive, autonomous, and emergent processes

AI and machine learning are set to lead the way in outcome-based process automation and predictive analytics, which are essential for automating various tasks. Low-code and no-code platforms will further facilitate the digitization of business processes, allowing individuals without extensive coding knowledge to become citizen developers. This shift will encourage companies to adopt model-based enterprises. While strong enterprise processes and business architecture practices remain crucial, they will also become more accessible, putting pressure on traditional centralized architecture teams. Additionally, robotic process automation will consistently handle repetitive tasks, enabling humans to concentrate on more complex work.

The aforementioned capabilities promise a positive ROI that organizations can achieve on their own terms—something that would have been impossible just a few years ago. Long-term economic trends and the need for adaptation will continue to drive companies toward real-time process digitization. This transition creates an ongoing demand for skilled practitioners and innovative approaches that allow for quicker and more effective solutions aligned with each company's strategic objectives. However, speed does not always equate to quality. Alignment with the company's strategic goals, adherence to enterprise process architecture, and adaptability are essential for long-term success. A frequently overlooked issue is the necessity of skills and experience to manage key transformation initiatives. Affordable low-code technology, cloud services, and AI models are now readily available, offering a promising yet challenging future for those willing to learn. Given the wide range of technologies accessible to the average worker, it's important to reflect on the following questions:

- How do we integrate all of these components while keeping pace with advancements?

- How do we leverage the abundance of technologies at our disposal?

- How can we improve our chances of success in a landscape that requires constant learning and relearning, both now and in the future?

Let's take some time to discuss the acquisition of information and learning.

Mastering the art of learning

Learning involves acquiring information, applying it in different contexts, and integrating it with existing knowledge and experience. To facilitate this process, one must develop skills such as critical thinking, problem-solving, creativity, and innovation. These skills enable the transfer and adaptation of knowledge across various domains and tasks.

Learning is not a passive or isolated activity; it is an active and social endeavor. Engaging with diverse and credible sources of information, such as books, articles, podcasts, videos, blogs, online courses, webinars, workshops, mentors, peers, experts, and communities of practice, is essential for active learning.

To learn effectively, you should cultivate habits of curiosity, exploration, feedback, and reflection. These habits will help you seek out and utilize different learning sources effectively.

Furthermore, learning is not a fixed or linear process; it is dynamic and iterative. This means constant monitoring and adjustment of your learning goals, strategies, and outcomes are necessary.

Have you ever wondered why we are not taught how to learn in schools, instead of being placed in an educational system that assumes we already know how to learn?

In this context, I would like to highlight a few relevant training courses that can broaden your understanding of the learning process and enhance your cognitive abilities:

- *Learning How to Learn* by Dr. Terrence Sejnowski and Barbara Oakley: This course provides an overview of the science and practice of learning, covering topics such as memory, attention, metacognition, motivation, and emotion. It also offers practical tips and strategies for improving learning efficiency and effectiveness, including spaced repetition, interleaving, retrieval practice, elaboration, and mnemonics. Available on Coursera.

- *Learning with Your Mobile Device* by Kevin Kelly: This course demonstrates how to leverage the power and convenience of mobile devices for learning anytime and anywhere. It covers how to locate and evaluate mobile learning resources, create and consume mobile learning content, and manage mobile learning activities and goals. Available on LinkedIn.

- *Developing a Learning Mindset* by Gary Bolles: This course explores the concept and advantages of a learning mindset—the belief that one can always learn new skills and grow personally and professionally. It provides guidance on cultivating a learning mindset, including embracing challenges, seeking feedback, reflecting on failures, and celebrating successes. Available on LinkedIn.

After exploring the courses just mentioned, I recommend creating a learning map—an active document you can refer to every few quarters to track your progress. A learning map will help you organize and chunk the knowledge you need to acquire, providing clarity and guidance as you see the bigger picture of what you will learn while showcasing the connections between different pieces of information. *Figure 4.6* shows an example learning map:

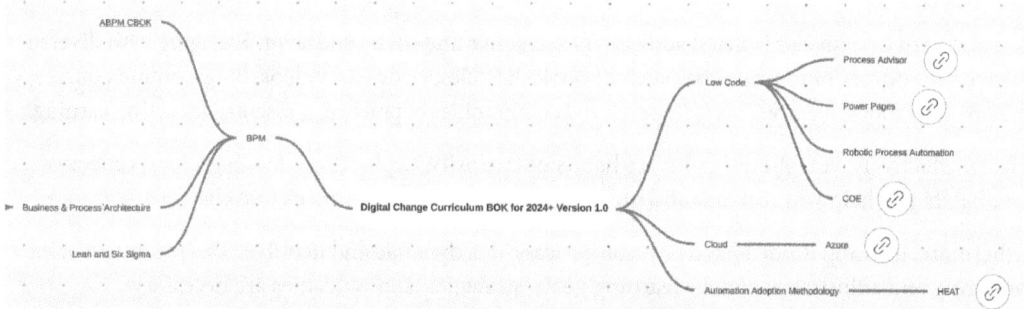

Figure 4.6 – A sample learning map for the DTX curriculum

To view the full version of this learning map, please go to this link and sign in using your email ID: `https://packt.link/8M1It`.

Navigating through a rapidly changing job market

Market forces, along with technological advancements, have led to some skills becoming more relevant while others become obsolete. In response, companies are creating new job roles and eliminating those that are no longer needed.

During major transformation initiatives, HR professionals play a crucial role in helping employees transition into new positions. Mary Claude Milot, a former chief transformation officer at Dairygold in Seattle, mentioned that HR teams aim to assist valuable employees in reskilling during times of business transformation. This strategy benefits the organization, as it is more advantageous to invest in existing employees and leverage learning and development teams rather than seeking new hires with the required skill sets.

When Dairygold implemented its Oracle-based process modernization, this 1,300-person company in the Pacific Northwest adopted a learning-oriented approach. They integrated training into new business processes, which had the added benefit of mitigating turnover during the Great Resignation. The company experienced significant staff losses during this period, and its learning management system and standard operating procedures were not updated in time to retain critical knowledge from departing employees.

Consider Dairygold's example in the context of your own workplace. Reflect on the turnover rates you observe and the expertise leaving your team each month due to reorganization, attrition, promotions, or other factors causing employees to change roles.

While this example highlights the employer's perspective, it is also important to consider how you, as a professional seeking to add value to your organization and enhance your employability, can stay relevant to current and future employers.

To stay relevant in a rapidly changing market, consider the following strategies:

- **Assess your skills**: Evaluate your current skills and competencies. Identify gaps and areas for improvement.

- **Research current trends**: Stay informed about emerging trends and demands in the BPM and DTX fields. Align your career goals with these insights.

- **Seek learning opportunities**: Look for ways to acquire new knowledge and skills or update existing ones. Consider online courses, certifications, workshops, webinars, mentorships, or hands-on projects. Learning through practice can be particularly beneficial.

- **Update your portfolio**: Revise your professional portfolio and resume to showcase your achievements, skills, projects, and interests. The portfolio can be in the form of a website, a blog, or showcased on social media sites.

- **Build your network**: Establish and maintain a network of professional contacts. This can provide support, advice, feedback, and referrals.

- **Create and promote a personal brand**: In a crowded digital landscape, staying visible to your network and recruiters isn't optional. It's how opportunities find you. A consistent presence that reflects who you are and what you stand for will increase your chances of being discovered.

- **Explore job opportunities**: Actively seek job openings that align with your interests and qualifications. Be prepared to adapt to various situations and expectations.

- **Publish your ideas**: Share your insights by writing articles on LinkedIn and Substack. Your articles could include examples of work and case studies to show your interest and proficiency in topics while boosting your relevancy to search algorithms.

- **Broaden your BPM perspective**: Treat BPM as a vendor-independent practice. Explore tools and platforms from various vendors. Remember, BPM is not owned by a single company—it's defined by standards set by committees or professional bodies. Specializing in a specific vendor's BPM solution can limit your perspective.

- **Stay updated**: Read industry reports, blogs, newsletters, and magazines that highlight the latest developments in BPM. Resources such as the *Business Process Management Journal* and *MIT Sloan on Digital Transformation* provide valuable insights.

- **Follow industry leaders**: Connect with thought leaders and experts on social platforms such as LinkedIn, X/Twitter, and YouTube for the latest insights and opinions.

- **Attend events**: Participate in webinars, workshops, and conferences focused on BPM and DTX, such as bpmNEXT, Gartner Business Process Management Summit, PEX events, or Digital Transformation World Series.

- **Learn from best practices**: Study case studies and research findings from industry leaders and other practitioners to adopt proven best practices.

- **Join professional communities**: Engage with online communities, forums, and networks relevant to BPM and DTX, such as BPM.com and the Digital Transformation Network, to exchange ideas, ask questions, and receive feedback from peers and mentors.

- **Explore job trends**: To discover new BPM and DTX roles, use online platforms that aggregate and analyze job postings, such as LinkedIn, Indeed, Glassdoor, and Dice. These platforms allow you to search with relevant keywords, filter by location, industry, and function, and compare the skills and qualifications required for different positions.

Monitoring market trends can help you identify gaps in your skill set and uncover new opportunities. By staying informed about industry trends and enhancing your skills, you can position yourself for new employment opportunities and prepare for the next wave of roles in BPM and DTX.

Discovering new trends

As a BPM and process practitioner, it is essential to keep up with the latest trends and innovations that shape the field and affect business outcomes in the workplace. By staying informed and adaptable, you can leverage the opportunities that arise from the changing market demands, customer expectations, and technological advancements. This section will discuss some methods and sources that can help you discover and track new trends impacting your career.

Online platforms

One way to track the types of DTX jobs in the marketplace is to use online platforms that aggregate and analyze job postings from various sources, such as Indeed, Glassdoor, or LinkedIn. These platforms can help you search for relevant keywords, filter by location, industry, function, level, or salary, and compare the skills, qualifications, and responsibilities required for different roles. By monitoring the job market trends, you can also identify the gaps and opportunities in your profile and tailor your resume and portfolio accordingly. Additionally, you can follow the news and updates of the leading organizations and consultancies that offer BPM and DTX solutions, such as Accenture, McKinsey, and EY, and through regular publisher reports and whitepapers, learn about their current projects and achievements.

Social media

User communities tend to group themselves around products and companies as they develop a strong affinity toward solutions from a particular vendor. Most process and DPA vendors tend to market very similar sets of product capabilities; what makes each different is the approach to the training, the ROI equation, and the size and strength of their user communities.

One of the key qualifiers I use to assess vendor strength is the community engagement level on social media.

Professional networks

Another effective way to discover and track new trends is by building and maintaining a strong professional network with other process professionals, experts, and peers. You can join online communities, forums, groups, or social media platforms that focus on BPM and DTX topics, such as BPM.com, BPM Forum, and Process Excellence Network.

Additionally, you can participate in webinars, podcasts, blogs, and newsletters that showcase insights, best practices, case studies, and interviews with industry leaders and practitioners. Some notable sources include *BPM Leader*, *BPM Institute*, and *Process Street*.

Furthermore, attending offline events such as conferences, workshops, seminars, and meetups offers great opportunities to network, learn, and exchange ideas with like-minded professionals. Popular events include BPM Conference, BPM Next, and OPEX Summit.

My preferred method of connecting with fellow professionals is through LinkedIn groups. However, it's important to recognize that many people may not openly discuss their work and projects due to confidentiality clauses and **non-disclosure agreements** (**NDAs**). By following groups and companies that engage actively in BPM, rather than merely mentioning it in passing, you'll discover organizations where genuine business transformation takes place.

Here are some examples of groups to follow:

- Business Process Management Professionals Group
- Workflow/Business Process Management
- Business Process Improvement
- Workflow Management Coalition
- World BPM Magazine
- LinkedBPM

Academic and research sources

One effective way to discover and track new trends in BPM and DTX is by following academic and research publications. These sources advance knowledge and innovation in the field. You can access journals, books, articles, reports, and white papers that present the latest findings and theories related to BPM and DTX. Notable examples include the *Business Process Management Journal*, the *International Journal of BPM*, and *IEEE Transactions on Services Computing*. Additionally, you can explore databases, repositories, or directories that collect and organize various resources related to BPM and DTX, such as the *BPM Academic Initiative*, *BPM Center*, and *BPM-Online*. Furthermore, consider engaging in courses, programs, certifications, or degrees that provide structured and comprehensive learning experiences in BPM and DTX. Options include BPM certification, DTX certification, or a master's degree in BPM.

Summary

In conclusion, discovering and tracking new trends is essential for any BPM and process professional who wants to remain relevant and competitive in the dynamic and complex business environment shaped by digital change. Technological advances in AI and work automation will continue to evolve, leading to shifts and confusion about what remains relevant and what will change. It's important to actively assess which new skills will be beneficial to maintain your value to your employer. Good business will support your efforts to reskill if you express your interest.

The rapid pace of technological advancements necessitates a new approach to on-the-job learning, allowing professionals to master many emerging and complementary areas of DTX. The democratization of access to powerful technologies, which were historically available only to a limited group of users, raises the stakes for adaptive learning. If you are tasked with leading digital change programs, your DTX IQ will set the standard for the entire team. However, keep in mind that having leadership skills alone is not sufficient. Creating learning plans and reviewing them regularly will help you stay on track and open new avenues in DTX.

BPM continues to serve as the foundation for digital change and DTX programs, enabling professionals to leverage new tools and technologies while maintaining a focus on the science of BPM. No single vendor dominates BPM, and this discipline continues to evolve. By communicating using shared standards such as BPMN, CMMN, and DMN, we can create blueprints for digital enterprises.

These blueprints can be implemented with the help of digital business platforms from various vendors, blending different solution delivery styles and developing resilient and adaptable digital business processes in a democratized and ROI-positive manner. The upcoming chapters of this book will delve into the details of business process modeling, process architecture, and modeling notation, focusing on practical how-to guides.

Unlock this book's exclusive benefits now

Scan this QR code or go to `packtpub.com/unlock`, then search this book by name.
Note: Keep your purchase invoice ready before you start.

5

Business Process 101

Business processes are key to value creation within any kind of organization. People often think about these processes only in terms of the series of steps that need to be taken. However, to reap the benefits of process thinking, you need to have a broader view of your processes. You need to understand the whole ecosystem of a process – other processes influencing your process and the ones influenced by it, but also supporting and governance processes, providing resources and guidance for your process. Without this broader view, it is very difficult to really understand a process and nearly impossible to implement meaningful improvement with long-term benefit.

In order to manage a process, we need to document it somehow. Using textual descriptions of a process is not sufficient, so usually, graphical models are used as the main way of modeling a process. Modeling can be useful for various purposes. All those purposes (known as **modeling scenarios**) have some specific requirements that influence what we will document about a process and how much detail we will need. Process models can be created in various tools and in different ways – this chapter will show the most important ones. We will also briefly mention how process models can be used.

In this chapter, we're going to cover the following main topics:

- Processes as a driver of value creation

- Leveraging a broader process perspective for improvement and digital transformation

- What is your scenario and why does it matter?

- What do you need to know about your process?

- Tools, people, and methods to create a process model and ways to use it

---

Note

This chapter is authored by Zbigniew Misiak.

Key concepts in process thinking

In *Chapter 3, The Wheel of BPM Driving Your Competitive Advantage*, and *Chapter 4, Long-Term Trends and the Impact on Your Job*, you already had a chance to learn a little bit about the history of **business process management** (**BPM**), see some key definitions (such as what BPM and a business process are), and understand a few important concepts of process management, such as the role of business processes and the importance of thinking about BPM activities as a cycle and not as a one-time activity.

In this chapter, we will revisit some basics of process thinking to give you a chance to deepen your understanding, as well as suggesting additional readings and resources. Since many of my students often ask me for recommended books and additional materials, these will be provided in *Chapters 5 to 9*.

BPM is a discipline with a long history. Not surprisingly, there are also many competing definitions of the key concepts (as was mentioned by BJ in previous chapters). Since there is no single body governing all things related to BPM worldwide, you can search for inspiration from many sources and pick the definition that works best for you and your organization.

Here is a quote from the **Association of Business Process Management Professionals International** (**ABPMP®**), which is one of the most authoritative organizations when it comes to BPM. ABPMP (`https://www.abpmp.org`) is a global, non-profit professional association dedicated to BPM. It maintains a global standard for BPM practices and offers widely recognized certification. As of 2025, ABPMP has over 17,000 members representing over 750 corporations and has 56 chapters worldwide.

In its guide to the **Business Process Management Common Body Of Knowledge** (**BPM CBOK®**), ABPMP uses the following definition:

> *"Business Process Management (BPM) is a disciplined approach to identify, design, execute, document, measure, monitor, and control both automated and non-automated business processes to achieve consistent, targeted results aligned with an organization's strategic goals.*
>
> *BPM involves the deliberate, collaborative and increasingly technology-aided definition, improvement, innovation, and management of end-to-end business processes that drive business results, create value, and enable an organization to meet its business objectives with more agility.*
>
> *BPM enables an enterprise to align its business processes to its business strategy, leading to effective overall company performance through improvements of specific work activities either within a specific department, across the enterprise, or between organizations."*

You can learn more about the guide to BPM CMOK here: `https://www.abpmp.org/page/guide_BPM_CBOK`.

> **Note**
>
> The body of knowledge needed for effective process management (especially for high-impact processes) is comprehensive and covers many aspects apart from process modeling and the usage of the models (which are the focus of this book). If you would like to learn more about aspects such as process governance, monitoring, and change management, as well as see other definitions of BPM from reputable sources, see the resources for this chapter at `https://github.com/PacktPublishing/Practical-Business-Process-Modeling-and-Analysis/tree/main/Chapter05`.

As you can see, the definition from ABPMP shares a lot of similar ideas with the definition used in *Chapter 3*. In the following section, we will cover those important ideas one by one to give you a better understanding of the key concepts in process thinking. We will start with the concept of **value creation**, since it helps with understanding many other things in process management.

Processes as a driver of value creation

The definitions of BPM and business processes that we have covered so far mention the extremely important concept of value creation. Business processes represent some work that needs to be done. However, we are not expecting simply for work to be done and then **output** to be ready. Our ambition is to generate **outcomes** that help the organization achieve its goals.

This shows a clear relationship between strategy and processes. Processes should make the strategic vision become a reality in the everyday work of an organization. The business processes should be designed and executed in a way that is consistent with the organization's **value proposition**.

The results of the process should be valuable for the customers (either external or internal). If it is a customer-facing end-to-end process, by starting with a need of a customer and finishing with a result that satisfies this need, it is easier to see what the value creation looks like.

Of course, a good process allows us to offer a product or service that a customer is willing to pay for, so the value flows both ways. There are also many important processes that are not visible to a customer. They support the value creation less directly, for example, by providing necessary resources and guidelines for the customer-facing processes and the whole organization.

The situation is a bit more complex, for example, in the public sector (or for non-profits), where people who benefit from the services may not be the ones who pay for them directly, but the idea is the same: the organization needs to create value for someone to endure and prosper. The same type of thinking can also be applied to processes that are serving internal customers: only if we create value for the customer and the organization does the process make sense.

As you can see, processes are very important for organizations that want to create value. Viewing an organization through the lens of processes helps to understand how work is done much better than using simply the perspective of organizational structure. However, there are even more aspects that we need to be aware of when it comes to processes. We will discuss this broader ecosystem of processes in the next section.

Leveraging a broader process perspective for improvement and digital transformation

In the previous section, we covered the concept of value in process management. Now, let's see how to make sure that the value is created. To create products and/or services of value, work needs to be performed by people with the necessary knowledge and skills. Those people need to use various resources, such as IT systems or equipment, and the necessary information to get the work done.

Since processes are often complex, it is not sufficient to have people from one organizational unit. We need various skills and competencies, so people from many teams, departments, or even organizations may be needed. You may also want to have a **hybrid workforce**, with people and AI agents collaborating to produce the desired outcomes (pretty soon, we may want to add robots to this as well).

To make sure all those people do their job properly, they need some guidance. Needless to say, AI agents need some guidelines as well, so that they can work effectively and in a way that is consistent with the values of the organization.

This guidance needs to cover the whole process and cannot be limited to a separate organizational unit (to avoid **silo thinking**). That's why BPM underlines the importance of **cross-functional processes** and having a big-picture view of the whole process with all the dependencies.

Cross-functional value creation is a very important concept in process management. A process does not operate in a vacuum; it is not a lonely island. There are many other processes that impact how it works. That's why, in many cases, an improvement initiative that only has a single process in scope will at best bring limited success and at worst simply move problems to some other process. We need to have a broader view of the process that will consider the process as a part of a broader ecosystem with all its dependencies.

Taking this broader view and analyzing processes together helps with identifying real causes of problems and coming up with much better ideas for process improvement/automation initiatives. We will learn more about the practical aspects of creating this broader view of processes in *Chapter 6*, which covers the concept of process architecture.

Now, let's briefly discuss how to create a useful overview (or a so-called **helicopter view**) showing the context of our process so that we can understand it better without the need to create a detailed process diagram. Out of several possible approaches, I will mention here two very popular techniques that will help you get a much better understanding of a process than focusing only on the work that we plan to do in a single process.

The first approach is **SIPOC**, which is very popular in **Lean management**. SIPOC diagrams describe the following aspects:

- **Suppliers**: Organizations or people that provide inputs for the process
- **Inputs**: Things needed by the process to run properly – information, documents, materials, know-how, and so on
- **Process**: (Key) things that need to happen in a process to generate the desired results
- **Outputs**: Results of the process (products or services)
- **Customers**: (Internal or external) organizations or people who receive the outputs

The second approach worth mentioning is the **IGOE** method, developed by Roger Burlton. IGOE considers the following aspects important for the proper understanding of a process:

- **Inputs**: Elements, such as information and materials, needed to perform the process, which are transformed or consumed by the process
- **Guides**: All elements, such as standards, regulations, and knowledge, that show us why, when (by showing which events define the scope of the process), and how our process should be performed
- **Outputs**: All the results of the process (products, deliverables, and information)
- **Enablers**: All the resources or assets (e.g., people, systems, facilities, or equipment) that we need for our process to run and that are not consumed by it

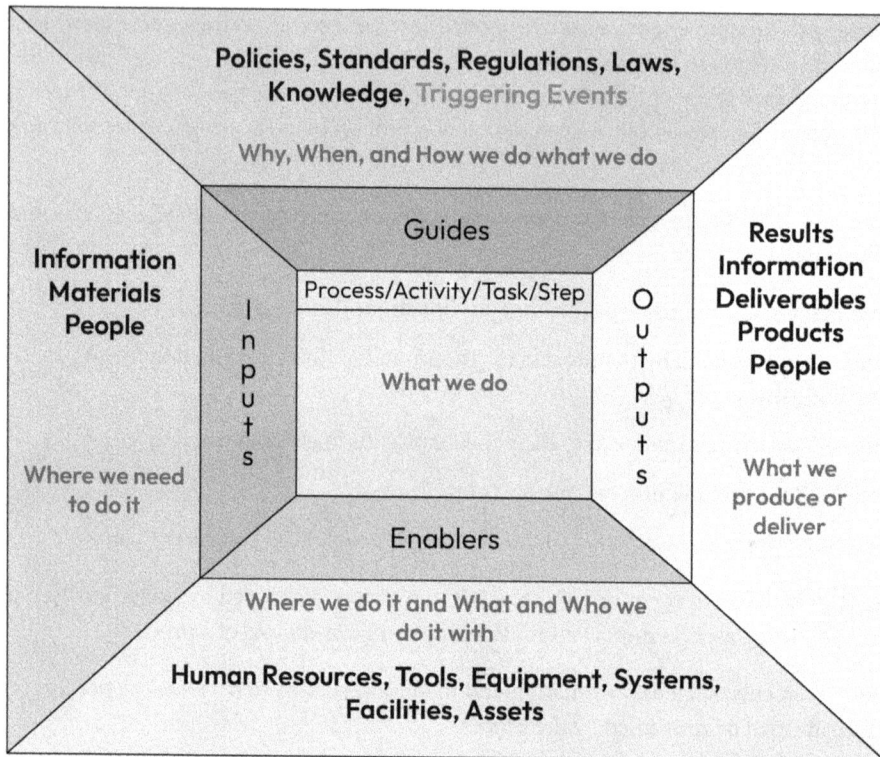

Figure 5.1 – Example IGOE diagram (by Roger Burlton)

What is important here is that IGOE doesn't just provide a list of elements for each of the areas. It also shows you the connections, that is, with other processes. That's why it is also called a **context diagram** or a **scope diagram**. In the GitHub repository, you will also find links to two helpful videos about IGOE: one from Roger Burlton and Sasha Aganova explaining the concept of IGOE and a second from Roger Tregear with an example of IGOE for a "make coffee" process. Both are well worth your time!

If you are wondering why those methods of providing a quick overview of a process (and a deeper understanding of it) are important, let's imagine that we are interested in improving the process of handling complaints in a company manufacturing customer products (this example will be used from this chapter to *Chapter 9*).

If there are problems with the complaint-handling process, perhaps the first idea would be to make it faster. While this improvement could make a lot of sense since customers will certainly appreciate faster resolution, perhaps it would be worthwhile to find the root cause of why the process underperforms and not stop with some generic solution.

Maybe employees are overloaded with customer complaints due to problems with a new delivery company that was chosen due to lower prices, but that sadly does not have a good quality of service. Or maybe the problem is with packaging because people from the logistics team work in a hurry. Or even worse, maybe the product is simply too fragile because of errors in design.

As you can see, to be able to understand the process and improve it, we very often need a lot more information than it might seem at first glance. To cope with this amount of knowledge about the process, we need a good description mechanism to ensure that we don't miss anything important. We will cover this in more depth in *Chapter 6, Establishing Process Architecture*. We also need to decide what kind of information we need to gather for our purposes. This will be covered in the following section.

What is your scenario, and why does it matter?

We already know that processes are an extremely important aspect of any organization's operations and that they are difficult to manage when we are not aware of what processes we have at all and how they are interrelated.

For this, we need **business process models**. Models provide a simplified representation of some aspects of reality (in our case, processes of the organization) in a form that helps us understand it more easily. Think of Google Maps, which shows us a digital representation of the city that helps us figure out where a location we are looking for is.

However, as the famous saying goes, *"The map is not the territory."* Our models provide valuable information, but they are not the same as the real objects that they represent. Models can also serve different purposes for different people. I will be referring to them as process modeling scenarios.

Some users are interested in basic information, while others need to consider many aspects that would be very hard to understand without models. A tourist searching for attractions in an unknown city, an architect planning a new skyscraper, a utility company worker searching for information about the detailed location of a leaky sewage pipe – they all would search for different information with different levels of detail that would suit their purpose. It works the same for business process models, *so there will be different levels of modeling and different levels of detail in those models*.

As an example, an overview of all top-level processes (process landscape) would be like the map of a whole city, while a detailed diagram of a process would be similar to the plan of a specific land lot with information about the pipes, fiber-optic cables, and other elements of infrastructure.

Each organization that decides to model its business processes makes an investment of some kind. It requires people, time, and money to create process documentation, to use it, and to keep this documentation up to date. Process models as such do not create value – they need to support some goals of the organization. The better this support is, the more valuable process modeling can be for the organization.

Therefore, it is generally a good idea to decide what needs to be done – particularly, what kind of process-related work needs to be done – before we start the actual work. Otherwise, we may do things that will not be beneficial for the organization, and our work could be perceived as a wasted effort, or we may omit some key information.

Think of providing a super detailed map of a sewage system to a tourist searching for the best place to take photos, or forgetting to add information about fiber-optic cables and other important infrastructure to a map provided to a utility worker who needs to make an excavation to replace a pipe.

Process models can document the current state of an organization (so-called as-is models) or be blueprints of the future state that we are designing (those are known as to-be models).

As-is and to-be models

As-is models document the current state of the organization. They show the baseline and allow not only training new employees, facilitating communication, and so on but also gathering requirements and ideas for improvement.

To-be models show the possible future state of the organization. They allow designing new ways of working, identifying dependencies and the impact of changes, comparing different variants, and picking for implementation the one that is the best for the organization.

Models also help with planning the transformation within an organization, especially if there are several stages to reach the desired state. Apart from being used for documentation, analysis, knowledge, and change management, process models can also be used, for example, for process automation. Models are great for improving communication and building a shared understanding of complex situations with many interdependencies and several teams involved. This can help you a lot in automation cases, such as implementing a new IT system that will support a process, preparing **robotic process automation (RPA)** bots that will take over some repetitive tasks from your employees, or maybe designing a new version of a process using AI tools and agents.

However, not all models are equally useful. We need to find the sweet spot between too little and too much information, so that they present useful content in a proper form to the intended audience. Our models must correctly describe reality (using some commonly agreed method), even though they are a simplification of it. This means, for example, that a good model should not miss key process steps. Finally, competent recipients should be able to read the model correctly without explanation from the model's author. For this, it helps a lot to establish some common language within the organization and use modeling standards.

Since many processes are getting more and more complex (e.g., due to regulatory requirements), the need for process models increases, especially when we are preparing some change in the organization and want to avoid errors caused by overlooking some important aspect, for example, focusing only on the costs of process steps and ignoring customer experience and compliance aspects.

With such a piecemeal view, there is a risk that a modification that seems to make a lot of sense from one team's point of view will result in a lot more work for other teams and worse results for the process. It may also happen that the new process will be effective and efficient from the organization's point of view but will not meet the needs of customers or not comply with laws or regulations.

Of course, models as communication tools can have different target audiences. Models documenting the processes can be aimed at new employees to help them settle into the organization, so that they can acquire the knowledge needed faster and avoid rookie mistakes. They can also be helpful for current employees and serve as procedures to remind them of the best way to work, or as a tool for planning changes in the organization. Models can help us improve processes or automate them. They can also be created for the organization's partners, to whom we need to explain our way of doing things, or for regulators, for whom the documentation will be proof of our compliance with regulations.

Each of those process modeling scenarios has requirements regarding the level of detail and attributes (documenting information about various aspects) of a process that are needed. In the next section, we will see a few examples of what it could look like in practice and how to create a method that will help create models according to a common standard used in an organization.

Understanding the process – modeling method and level of detail

If the model is to serve as a tool for communicating with others, it should contain information that is relevant to the recipient in a form that will allow the recipient to use it. But what kind of information should we cover? Isn't it enough to describe the steps of the process?

Just as in good journalism, in process modeling, we can say that the model should present information according to the **5W1H model**, also known as the **Kipling method** (**5W1H** stands for **who, what, when, where, why, and how**).

Based on many discussions with customers and training participants regarding the information they want to have in their models, I have compiled the following list (based on 5W1H) to serve as an inspiration for you:

- *Who* is responsible for performing the process steps? Who is the process owner?
- *What* is processed in the process (products, documents, or data)?
- *When* do things happen in a process? What has to happen for the process to start? Is something supposed to happen in the process at certain times or circumstances? When does the process end?
- *Where* in physical locations or information systems does the process take place (e.g., in a CRM system)?
- *Why* do we perform this process at all? What value does it create?

- *How* does the work inside the process look? What needs to be done? Are there more complex elements? How many steps does the process have? What are the dependencies between the elements of the model? For example, what are the possible paths of execution of the process? What exactly is to happen within the individual steps of the process? How is the work performed? What guidelines should be followed?

Of course, this list is just an inspiration. For some modeling scenarios, you may need less information, and for others, much more. This depends heavily on the people who will be using your process models.

Typical target audiences for your models, or stakeholders for your process-related initiative, could be directors of a process and project management departments, project managers of an ERP implementation project, business analysts involved in an RPA initiative, software engineers, programmers, quality management specialists, process improvement experts, or risk management specialists. Of course, employees who may need information on how to perform the processes should hopefully be interested in the process documentation! Each of these people may have their own expectations, based on how they want to use the process models.

To prevent everyone from creating process models that meet only their needs and the needs of their coworkers, it is helpful to create common guidelines, serving as a style guide, including, among other things, a list of topics that should be included in the models.

Such a standard set of topics will help the team create consistent process models (even if there are many process analysts/modelers), compare them with each other, and analyze the models with ease. The models, in this way, can serve as a common language across the organization, making it easier to communicate, avoid doing the same work over and over again, and achieve the desired results faster.

The following is an overview of common process modeling scenarios with information on what each scenario looks like in practice:

- **Documenting processes and creating procedures**: For such a scenario, models are usually created using a reduced number of notation elements to make them easy to read by non-experts, but with extensive descriptions of individual steps. Those models often contain information such as ownership of the process, history of changes and approvals, information about the responsibility for the steps of the process, and applications and documents used in the process.

- **Process improvement**: For this scenario, the models also tend to use a simplified notation. What distinguishes models created with **process simulation** in mind is data about times and costs, allowing us to simulate processes and compare variants to determine a method of process execution that is faster and cheaper than the one used today. Depending on the requirements of an organization, we may also want to include information about risks and controls used to mitigate those risks.

To make process improvement work, we usually need to gather some information about problems and errors in the process, as well as ideas for improvement. Frequently, process improvement and **waste elimination** techniques from Lean management are used. As an example, value analysis of the process steps can be documented in process models to show which steps are **value adding (VA)**, **value enabling (VE)**, or **non-value adding (NVA)**.

- **Process automation**: For this scenario, models are often more complex in terms of both the number of objects and the sophistication of the notation. The first step in process automation is very often an analysis of variants as part of process improvement, but models to automate processes are usually much more complex than models for business analysis. Apart from the attributes of a process model that we have covered so far, models used for automation will include technical attributes required by the specific tool used to automate the process, such as information about the forms that should be presented to people performing the process. If the automation tool also has process orchestration capabilities, you can expect additional information about RPA bots, AI agents, and many other methods that allow you to automate your process.

As you can see, process models can contain lots of valuable information. However, we need to learn how to create these process models.

Tools, people, and methods to create a process model and ways to use it

In the previous sections, we learned that process models can be very helpful for managing processes. We also know that these models can contain various kinds of information. In this section, we will discuss how process models can be created and used in an organization.

Before we dive into the details, it is worth mentioning again that process modeling should always serve some purpose. We model processes to bring some value to the organization. So, please remember that this section covers only a small part of all process management activities happening in organizations and that process modeling is usually not seen as a separate stage of the **process management life cycle (PMLC)** since it is a technique used in many such stages.

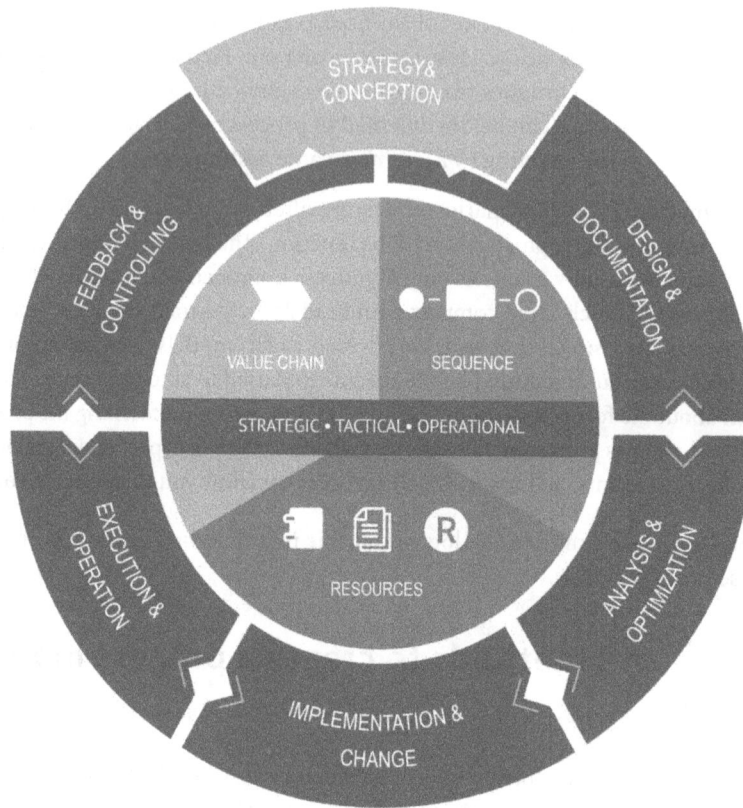

Figure 5.2 – Process management life cycle by BOC Group

For example, in BOC Group's PMLC, most of the process modeling would take place in the design and documentation phase, but the first high-level models would already have been created in the strategy and conception phase. In the analysis and optimization phase, models would be used to come up with an improved version of a process. In the implementation and change phase, models would be used for change management and process automation, and so on.

In other popular frameworks, such as **PDCA/PDSA** (which stands for **plan-do-check-act** or **plan-do-study-act**), popularized by W. Edwards Deming, and the **BPM life cycle** (described in the book *Fundamentals of Business Process Management, 2018*), it would work in a similar way. The interesting thing to note is that those frameworks suggest an iterative and incremental approach to process management and improvement.

Now, let's see how models can be created. In the following sections, you will find an overview of a few common approaches. However, this information is not exhaustive as new options, such as modeling processes with GenAI tools, are emerging.

A general overview of different roles involved in BPM was already covered in *Chapter 3*, so here I will focus only on roles involved in process modeling, especially creating detailed process diagrams (as opposed to high-level process landscapes), since this usually takes more time in an organization.

> **Note**
> One thing I would like to note is that my experience of working with people from BPM centers of excellence has been very positive, and luckily, I have not experienced any of the problems mentioned by BJ.

Modeling by employees of an organization versus modeling by outside experts

The first aspect of modeling worth mentioning is who should do the modeling, that is, who will act as the **process analyst/process modeler**. Many organizations prefer to create process models on their own. This can be done either by specialized process analysts from the process management team (the BPM CoE), by local process modeling experts in departments/teams supported by the process management team, or in a grassroots approach where people from departments/teams learn modeling on their own without support from some center of excellence.

The second approach is to involve people from outside the organization. This can be, for example, external consultants who specialize in process management or analysts working for contractors responsible for the introduction of some IT system, such as an ERP suite.

As a consultant, I often help organizations model their processes, define modeling guidelines and best practices, and train their employees to do the modeling on their own. If you need to have lots of high-quality models fast, involving external experts can be helpful. But if you want to have process documentation that is always up to date and (more importantly) involve your employees in process management and improvement, it helps a lot to have internal experts who know how to model the processes. In the following sections, I will share with you my experience with different approaches to process modeling.

Modeling based on various sources of knowledge about a process

The next aspect that we will be covering is how we come up with a process model. There are several different approaches that are possible, such as the following:

- Modeling based on your own knowledge
- Modeling based on the knowledge of interviewed **subject matter experts** (SMEs)
- Modeling based on observations of a process
- Modeling based on pre-existing documentation

- Automated process discovery

- Modeling based on workshops

- Modeling based on best practices/reference models

The first option is when a person creates a model of a process that they know well. Since SMEs usually do not know how to model processes, it is important to pick the correct people to do the process analysis and modeling as not everyone wants to learn how to model processes. Those people should also get some support from more experienced colleagues. Ideally, this would be training in modeling notation and the modeling tool, plus guidelines for creating models provided by the team of process experts. This will speed everything up and should help avoid situations where every expert creates a process model in a different tool, using different notations and different approaches.

Since training many people to do the modeling takes time, and they will not be as skilled in process modeling as experts, very commonly, organizations decide to start with a smaller team of process analysts, who will create models based on interviews with process experts. A person with more modeling experience does the modeling and asks the questions, and a person familiar with the process tells them how the process looks in practice. With this approach, the models are created faster because the person with more experience does the modeling, and the person who knows the process doesn't have to spend a lot of time learning how to model processes.

For both options, it is very important to make sure to involve the correct people in modeling, that is, make sure that all teams involved in the process include SMEs. Otherwise, you may end up with incomplete process models because your experts did not know the whole process or failed to mention some steps for various reasons.

It is also helpful to share widely the process documentation that was created and give your employees and collaborators a chance to not only view it but also provide their feedback in a convenient way. Those comments are very valuable because they allow you to see whether your process documentation is complete and accurate. As an added benefit, this approach promotes process thinking and getting people more involved (especially if they see that their feedback was heard and implemented).

One of the ways to overcome this problem of incomplete description of the process is to model based on not only what people think or say but also reliable data. Historically, this usually meant that the person creating the model would observe people performing the process and would document all the steps happening in it.

Documenting a process is not always easy, however. For example, the process analyst should not disrupt the work (too much) with questions. But without asking questions about the process, it may not always be obvious to the analyst what is happening, especially if some steps are automated.

To make things more difficult, people tend to behave in a different way when they know that someone is watching them (this is called the **Hawthorne effect**). Taking all these elements into consideration, it is often a good idea to cross-check what the analyst can see with other sources, such as process documentation.

Existing process documentation can also be helpful as a source of knowledge for process analysts. However, sometimes it is not up to date, so it needs some additional work to make sure that it is known what is really happening. It is a good starting point, but sometimes it needs to be validated and should not be used as the single source of knowledge about the process.

In the past few years, a new approach to gathering information about as-is processes has gained popularity: **automated process discovery**. By using **process mining** and **task mining** techniques, it is possible to analyze the logs from the IT systems automating the process or analyze the screens of employees performing the process to come up with a data-backed version of what the process really looks like.

Of course, you should be aware that while process mining offers you many exciting possibilities for advancing your process management to the next level, it is not a panacea for process discovery. That's because for a significant percentage of organizations, there are still many processes with parts that cannot be analyzed in an automated way.

The next approach is to create a process model by involving teams performing the process as well as the **process owner** in a workshop. This requires careful coordination because it is not easy to have several busy people attend the workshop at the same time. However, by involving all interested teams in the modeling, we create a model that considers everyone's voice. Such a model is a kind of contract between all the teams working together to document their shared understanding of a process. The participation of many people provides the opportunity to clarify any ambiguities and misconceptions. In addition, working together on the model helps build commitment among the participants.

Interestingly, some organizations also hold workshops online with copilots providing input for creating process documentation based on transcripts.

It is also worth mentioning that sometimes it makes sense to speed up the modeling by using existing reference models or best practices. This is especially helpful when we are not trying to document the existing process but want to design a new one and don't want to do it from scratch.

Processes of process modeling

Since we now know how a process model can be created, it would also make sense to briefly discuss what will happen when we already have the model. An organization that wants to manage its processes can benefit from defining some processes it will use in process management. While there are many such processes, I will mention the most common ones.

First, we need a process that will help us identify what processes we have in the organization. Once we have done this, we should plan which processes require the detailed modeling that was described previously. This may be needed because we do not have a model at all or because the process model needs to be changed, for example, due to a process improvement initiative.

When the process model is ready, usually there will be some formal steps needed for approving it by the process owner, but possibly, other roles can be involved too. The approved model should be easily available to **process performers**, so that they can use it in their daily work, but also so that they can send feedback and improvement ideas for the process.

More advanced organizations often have processes for monitoring the **key performance indicators** and/or periodic reviews of the process as well. This can trigger a need to improve a process, which will also require an update or a complete redesign of the process model.

As you can see, there are many things needed to make sure that process models are up to date and useful for the organization. To make sure that all this work is not a burden for the organization, proper tools should be used that will support working with the process documentation.

Tools for process modeling

Since we now know who can do the process modeling and how this knowledge about processes will be gathered, it's time to discuss how the process models can be created and what kinds of applications can be used.

First of all, it is worth noting that it is not obligatory to use IT tools for process modeling. There are some organizations (especially those with a strong Lean or Agile culture) that prefer to use tools such as flipcharts, whiteboards, and sticky notes.

However, in my experience, while those tools are great for workshops and making people engaged in process improvement initiatives and visual management, it is rather difficult to avoid using software if process management initiatives are broader and involve more people from different locations. That's why we will focus on software supporting process modeling.

There are many IT tools that can be used to create process models. Currently, more and more tools are available on the cloud via a browser, but there are still many standalone applications that you can download on your computer.

Organizations will have different modeling scenarios and different visions of how processes should be documented, how this documentation should be published, and how to make sure that it will be a living system capable of gathering feedback and ideas, as well as supporting changes. That's why there's no one tool that would work best in every case and help get the whole organization involved in BPM. So, instead of giving you a recommendation for one single BPM tool to rule them all, I will provide an overview of various tool categories with information about their advantages, so that you can decide what would be best for you.

Some organizations start their adventure in process management by creating process documentation with general-purpose office suites. This mix of text documents, shapes representing processes, and so on is very easy to create, but keeping it up to date is very cumbersome and time-consuming. Also, it is very difficult to keep people engaged if the process documentation is available as slides, text documents, and spreadsheets.

That's why usually, more specialized tools are used. In my experience, there are four broad categories of applications that can be used by organizations that want to document their processes:

- Diagramming tools
- **Enterprise business process analysis (EBPA)** tools
- **Model-based software engineering (MBSE)** tools
- Modeling tools linked with process automation suites

Let's look at each of these in greater detail.

Diagramming tools

As you could expect, **diagramming tools** allow for much easier creation of diagrams than office suites. Usually, they are very user-friendly tool suites with dozens of diagram types and hundreds of different templates that allow you to create a diagram for nearly any purpose you can dream of, from strategy planning to planning the layout of the office.

Of course, they also allow you to create many kinds of diagrams that can be useful for process management: high-level process landscapes, detailed process maps (using various notations), organizational structure diagrams, and so on.

Basic tools of this kind focus on creating nice-looking pictures with smooth collaboration, but they usually offer very limited features in terms of process analysis and governance (e.g., approvals).

More advanced diagramming tools can also be integrated with external systems, for example, to reach a broader audience with process documentation or to import live data and visualize it in the diagrams. This makes them closer to the next category of tools: EBPA.

Example tools of this kind that I frequently encounter are the following:

- **Draw.io/Diagrams.net** (JGraph Ltd and draw.io AG)
- **Lucidchart** (Lucid Software)
- **Visio** (Microsoft)

With Visio, it is worth noting that it has some features that exceed the standard capabilities of drawing tools. For example, Visio BPMN diagrams can be exported to Power Automate.

It is also worth mentioning that simple process documentation could also be created with **collaboration boards** such as Miro, Mural, or Klaxoon. Both diagramming tools and collaboration boards excel at visual collaboration over diagrams.

EBPA tools

EBPA tools are much more specialized than diagramming tools. They allow you to create various types of process models very easily, but they are much more focused, so you can expect many types of models that you may need to create a comprehensive process documentation, but not as much in diagramming tools.

Those models are usually much richer in attributes in comparison with diagramming tools. While a simple diagramming tool creates a diagram or a process map that is a nice-looking picture, a process model usually has strictly defined rules of what is allowed and what is not. Also, model types available in EBPA tools are much more advanced and contain special attributes, and features aimed at different roles involved in process management, and so on.

Examples of EBPA tools are the following:

- **ADONIS** (BOC Group)
- **ARIS** (Software AG)
- **iGrafx** (iGrafx)

ADONIS is the tool I used to create most of the examples in this part of the book. This is the tool I know the best, since I work at BOC Group. If you wish, you can use the free version of the tool, called ADONIS Community Edition. The registration page can be found at `https://www.adonis-community.com`.

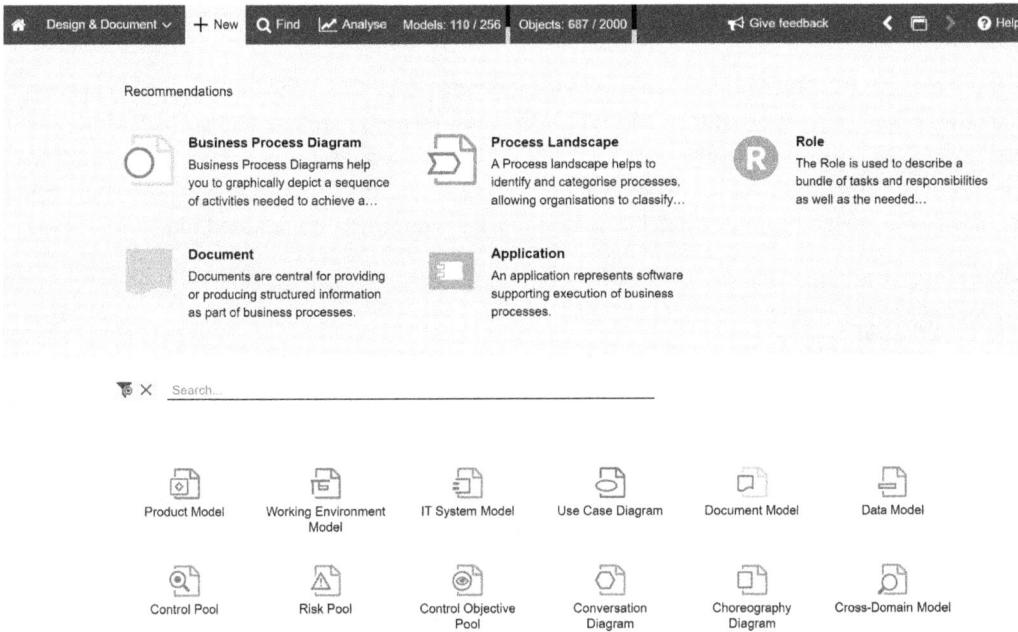

Figure 5.3 – Overview of available diagram types in ADONIS as a representative EBPA tool

MBSE tools

MBSE tools are also commonly referred to as **computer-aided software engineering** (**CASE**). As the name suggests, those tools are aimed at more technical users involved in software engineering. There are many types of CASE tools, so we will focus on those that allow modeling systems with their business context.

Those tools usually support many notations that are relevant to business analysts and IT specialists, such as **Unified Modeling Language** (**UML**) and **Systems Modeling Language** (**SysML**), but also standards more relevant to business process modeling, such as ArchiMate and BPMN. Apart from creating precise models that can be analyzed and easily updated and preparing documentation (e.g., as requirements for the IT system), they often also allow you to generate code from the models and models from code.

Examples of MBSE tools are the following:

- **Enterprise Architect** (Sparx Systems)
- **Visual Paradigm** (Visual Paradigm)

Modeling tools linked to process automation suites

The last category of tools that are often used for modeling processes is the tools linked to process automation suites (often referred to as **BPMSs**, or **business process management suites**). **Modeling tools** allow you to create process diagrams (often in BPMN notation) and enrich them with additional attributes needed for automation (e.g., information about forms, roles in a process, or integrations), often along with DMN diagrams for defining business rules important for automation.

Example tools from this category are the following:

- **Bizagi Modeler** (Bizagi)
- **Camunda Modeler** (Camunda)
- **IBM Blueworks Live** (IBM)

It is worth noting that Camunda Modeler uses the `BPMN.io` library, developed by Camunda, which is used by dozens of other tools from many companies.

Of course, apart from the tools that we have covered, there are many more tool categories that are important to companies interested in BPM. Companies managing their processes and using the **hyperautomation** approach will often use not only BPMSs and some tools for modeling their processes but also RPA tools, process/task mining tools, and so on.

Ideally, they will also have a platform facilitating process orchestration, which allows running end-to-end processes that include people, RPA bots, AI agents, and interfaces (APIs). This type of technology platform is termed by Gartner **business orchestration and automation technology (BOAT)**.

Summary

In this chapter, we learned about the basics of process thinking. We learned how processes help create value and why it is important to have a broader understanding of the processes before doing any analysis and improvement. We discussed various purposes of modeling processes and how they impact the content of the process models. Finally, we learned about the tools used to model processes and approaches to create process models and work with them. If you have a feeling that an organization may end up with many process models and that it would be helpful to arrange them somehow, you are right! This is what will be covered in the next chapter.

Further reading

If you want to deepen your knowledge of BPM, the following are suggestions of books and additional resources:

- If you would like to learn more about the history of BPM, as well as the most important concepts in this field, I would recommend *Business Process Change: A Business Process Management Guide for Managers and Process Professionals* by Paul Harmon.

- If you want to dig even deeper, have more time, and want to experience probably the widest coverage of leading BPM experts, take a look at the two-volume series from Jan vom Brocke and Michael Rosemann: *Handbook on Business Process Management 1. Introduction, Methods, and Information Systems* and *Handbook on Business Process Management 2. Strategic Alignment, Governance, People and Culture*. You can find almost everything you would want to know about BPM there.

- If you would like to learn more about the concept of creating value through processes, I suggest two books written by authors whose ideas strongly influenced BPM as a discipline: *White Space Revisited: Creating Value through Process* by Geary Rummler, Alan Ramias, and Richard Rummler, and *Faster Cheaper Better: The 9 Levers for Transforming How Work Gets Done* by Michael Hammer and Lisa Hershman.

- If you would like to learn more about the concept of cross-functional business processes, I would recommend the timeless classic *Business Process Management: Profiting From Process* by Roger Burlton, and the both insightful and fun-to-read *Elements* by Roger Tregear.

- As another recommendation for a great book about BPM, I would like to suggest *Fundamentals of Business Process Management* by Marlon Dumas, Marcello La Rosa, Jan Mendling, and Hajo A. Reijers. This book covers not just the fundamentals of BPM but nearly every topic important for process management professionals. It also offers lots of examples and case studies, plus it has a fabulous list of other BPM books if you would like to deepen your knowledge even more.

You can find more information and resources in this book's GitHub repository: `https://github.com/PacktPublishing/Practical-Business-Process-Modeling-and-Analysis/tree/main/Chapter05`.

Unlock this book's exclusive benefits now

Scan this QR code or go to `packtpub.com/unlock`, then search this book by name.

Note: Keep your purchase invoice ready before you start.

6

Establishing Process Architecture

Every organization needs to run processes to create value. To get an overview of those processes, we need to have some kind of *table of contents*. However, since processes are interconnected, it is not sufficient to have one flat list containing hundreds of processes. We need something more sophisticated—something that will show what kind of processes we have, how they are connected, and what their details are, to mention just a few important aspects. The solution is **process architecture**.

In this chapter, we're going to cover the following main topics:

- What is process architecture, and why is it useful?
- How can **American Productivity & Quality Center's (APQC's) Process Classification Framework (PCF)** and other process libraries be used?
- How can we build our own process architecture?
- How can we use process architecture to select processes for improvement and automation?

Note
This chapter is authored by Zbigniew Misiak.

What is process architecture?

In this section, we will learn what process architecture is and why it is useful for organizations to create one. Since many organizations are not sure why they should invest time and resources into building a process architecture, let's start by discussing why it is needed.

Why do we need process architecture?

In *Chapter 5, Business Process 101*, we learned the basic concepts of business process management. We learned that processes can be seen as a way to create value for an organization. However, this requires many cross-functional processes to work together smoothly.

Many organizations can identify hundreds of processes. Of course, not all of them are equally important, and often, one top-level process can be decomposed into many lower-level processes.

To make things even more complex, organizations frequently model not only the current processes (**as-is processes**) but also design various possible future process variants (**to-be processes**) to compare them and pick the right one to implement. Not to mention, they also have an archive that contains models showing how the organization worked previously (e.g., for auditing purposes).

To get a good understanding of what the entire ecosystem of processes looks like, which are interconnected in different ways, it is not enough to create hundreds of detailed process diagrams and try to organize them in a folder structure. Building a huge spreadsheet (or a wiki page) that contains a list of all the identified processes is not the answer either.

This is because processes do not exist in a vacuum; instead, they influence each other. Processes are interrelated in many ways: very often, processes form a sequence or are part of a common **value chain**.

This term can be defined in many ways; I will quote Roger Burlton, who says it is "*a set of processes that need to be performed together to make the line of business succeed.*" He also stresses that "*companies may have multiple value chains for different types of customers, such as retail and business, and wealth for banking.*"

One process provides a product that is needed for the following process (and so on) before the result can be provided to the customer. In addition, to work properly, processes need certain resources, such as trained employees, well-functioning IT systems, and more, as well as guidance that is provided by other processes. An interesting point here is that even the best technology does not create value if the process and the strategic guidance are poor.

Therefore, if we do not have the big picture of how our organization works through its processes, **silo thinking** is also a challenge, causing people to plan and act only from the perspective of their organizational unit, not the whole organization. This is extremely risky for the whole organization, because processes need the involvement of many people from different parts of the organization to create value. So, if they don't have a common, agreed-upon view of how the organization works, they may make wrong decisions.

If people simply think only about their own organizational silo, it is quite possible that a change in a process that seems to be beneficial, at least for the organizational unit responsible for a part of a whole process, will be harmful to the entire organization. This situation is called **sub-optimization**.

If people try to have a broader view, but either have some misconceptions about the work of others or simply do not know about others who are working in the same process, this can also lead to various kinds of problems, such as a solution being designed that does not provide proper support for all the interested parties or a process being prepared based on requirements that are not based on real needs.

Since processes operate within a complex ecosystem, does it make sense to model and optimize or automate a single process in isolation from others? Or, looking at the situation from another side, if we want to improve the performance of an organization within a certain process area, how do we know what processes exist there, and how do we choose which ones to analyze?

The solution is **process architecture**. It is a comprehensive way of identifying and presenting processes that provides a common and agreed-upon definition of the organization's processes.

Process architecture has many levels and allows us to easily navigate from the general overview to more specific models that provide more details. It is also multi-dimensional since it shows different categories of processes and their interdependencies, but also takes other dimensions into account—aspects such as connections between processes and IT architecture, the impact of strategies and goals on processes, relationships with risks and **environmental, social, and governance** (ESG) requirements, and many other issues.

In the following section, we will look at an example of a top-level process architecture model. We will expand it throughout this chapter so that you can see important concepts in practice.

Process categories

Organizations that create a process architecture usually divide their processes into different categories. Typically, three categories are used:

- **Management processes** (sometimes also called **guiding processes**): Management processes guide the other processes by giving them direction, constraints, and rules.

- **Core processes**: Core processes implement the organization's strategy and create value. For commercial organizations, these are the processes that provide products and services that customers are willing to pay for.

- **Support processes** (also known as **supporting** or **enabling processes**): Support processes provide reusable resources that are needed by other processes, allowing them to work as expected.

Figure 6.1 shows an example of the top-level overview model (sometimes called **Level 0**) within the process architecture. Here, generic processes are arranged graphically to show which category they belong to. In addition, shapes (chevrons or arrows pointing upward or downward) and colors are used to make the distinction clearer. However, this is not always the case; for some organizations, consistency is more important, and they use the same shape throughout (it's usually blue, right-facing, and wide chevron-like).

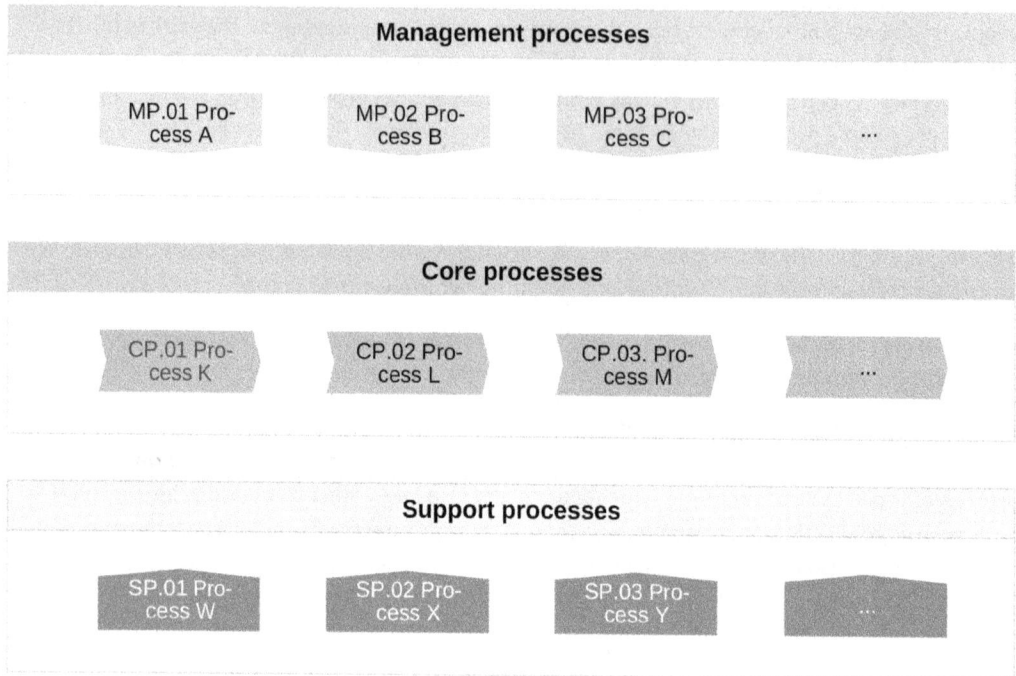

Figure 6.1 – Example of a top-level model for process architecture

Sometimes, the process category may also be indicated by an alphanumerical prefix—for example, the different process categories may begin with **MP**, **CP**, and **SP**. As we will see later, in the *Building custom process architecture in practice* section, it is not obligatory to use prefixes in process names. For some organizations, it may even cause some misunderstandings if the process types are shown in names. Prefixes can also include numerical identifiers, something we will cover in more detail in a moment.

Process hierarchy

The next important element of process architecture is **hierarchy**. Just as for construction planning, we can look at maps and plans that provide different levels of detail, such as a city plan, a plan of the plot of land on which we are building something, a plan of individual apartments within a building that contain information about the layout of electrical, plumbing, and air-conditioning systems, and more, and move between those levels as needed (zoom in and zoom out). Process architecture also implies multiple levels of documentation in the form of connected models.

This is useful because, to support process thinking in an organization, we need to involve many different stakeholders with different information needs. For some people, it is important to have a quick overview and a general idea of the process and how it relates to other processes. Others need much more precise information about a process to do their work or to improve and automate this process.

There is no one-size-fits-all approach to several levels in a process architecture. Some experts suggest that there should be a fixed number of levels. This may be the case when an organization uses a certain standard and wants to compare its processes to other organizations using this standard.

Others suggest that the number of levels may differ even within a single organization. This allows some flexibility to go deeper where needed. Also, there is no common agreement regarding how many levels of processes can be shown within one model. Therefore, what I will be presenting here is a best practice based on my experience.

How could this process hierarchy work? When we have a top-level model showing an overview of our process architecture (e.g., similar to *Figure 6.1*), it usually shows 10-20 groups of processes, which could also be called **process areas** or **mega-processes**. Each of those could be decomposed into more detailed models showing several levels of *children* processes.

Finally—at least for some of the processes—we may want to document them by providing detailed process diagrams, often described using BPMN notation—perfect for documenting how we perform the process, but not suitable for showing high-level process architecture. This is something we will cover in *Chapter 8, BPMN—What You Need to Know*, and *Chapter 9, Advanced BPMN*. These detailed diagrams can also be decomposed into even more detailed sub-processes and can be enriched with instructions for individual process steps. Such instructions can include **Standard Operating Procedure (SOP)** documents, which are frequently used even in organizations that do not use process thinking but just want to help their employees by providing precise information and ensuring quality of work.

Each of the processes can also contain more information apart from the connections with other processes. We will cover those process attributes in the next section. This way, we can provide necessary information about the processes to interested people without having to create detailed diagrams for every process. This is crucial because creating and updating detailed diagrams can be very time-consuming.

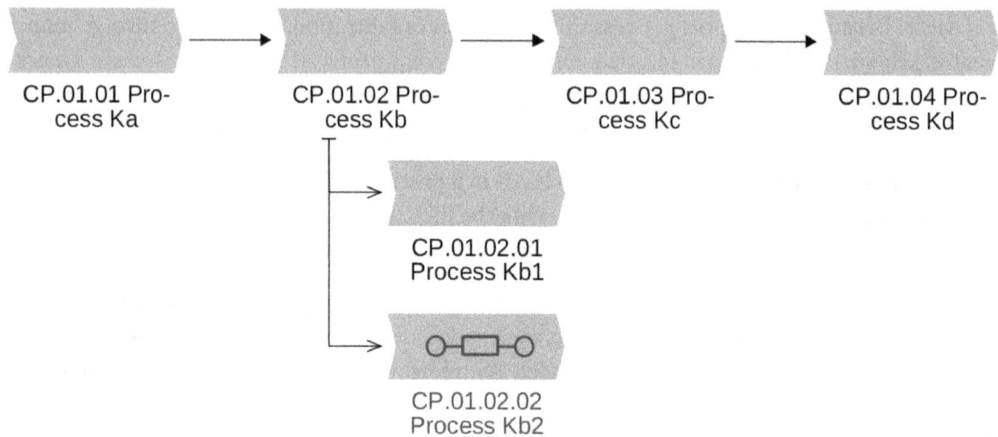

Figure 6.2 – A more detailed model showing the decomposition of a top-level process

Figure 6.2 shows an example of a lower-level model describing the contents of the **CP.01 Process K** process, which we saw in *Figure 6.1*, in more detail. In this case, we can see that this process has four processes as its children (**Ka**, **Kb**, **Kc**, and **Kd**) that form a single value chain (they follow each other sequentially). Apart from the visual aspect, you can also see that these processes are on the same level by looking at their prefixes (**CP.01.01**, **CP.01.02**, **CP.01.03**, and **CP.01.04**), which show that their parent process is a (core) process with **CP.01** as its prefix. In addition, one of the processes (**Kb**) has children (**Kb1** and **Kb2**). Those processes can also be described in the form of a more detailed BPMN diagram so that you can drill down for more information.

Please bear in mind that you can create a process architecture without using prefixes. Prefixes can be helpful since they immediately show where our process belongs and make parent-child relationships clearer, which is often very convenient. That's why I am using them in this section; they make explanations much easier for a multi-level process architecture.

On the other hand, without some kind of IT tool support, it can be a daunting task to make sure all the prefixes for process models are up to date when, for example, new processes are created or existing processes are split, merged, or deleted, which causes changes in IDs that people become accustomed to.

Generally speaking, it may be better if people treat prefixes as support and not a part of a real process name, especially if they do not focus on the prefixes, thereby forgetting the true meaning of the processes at hand. If people can recall the number of a process but do not remember its name and what exactly the process does, this is often a bad sign.

Several levels of process architecture...

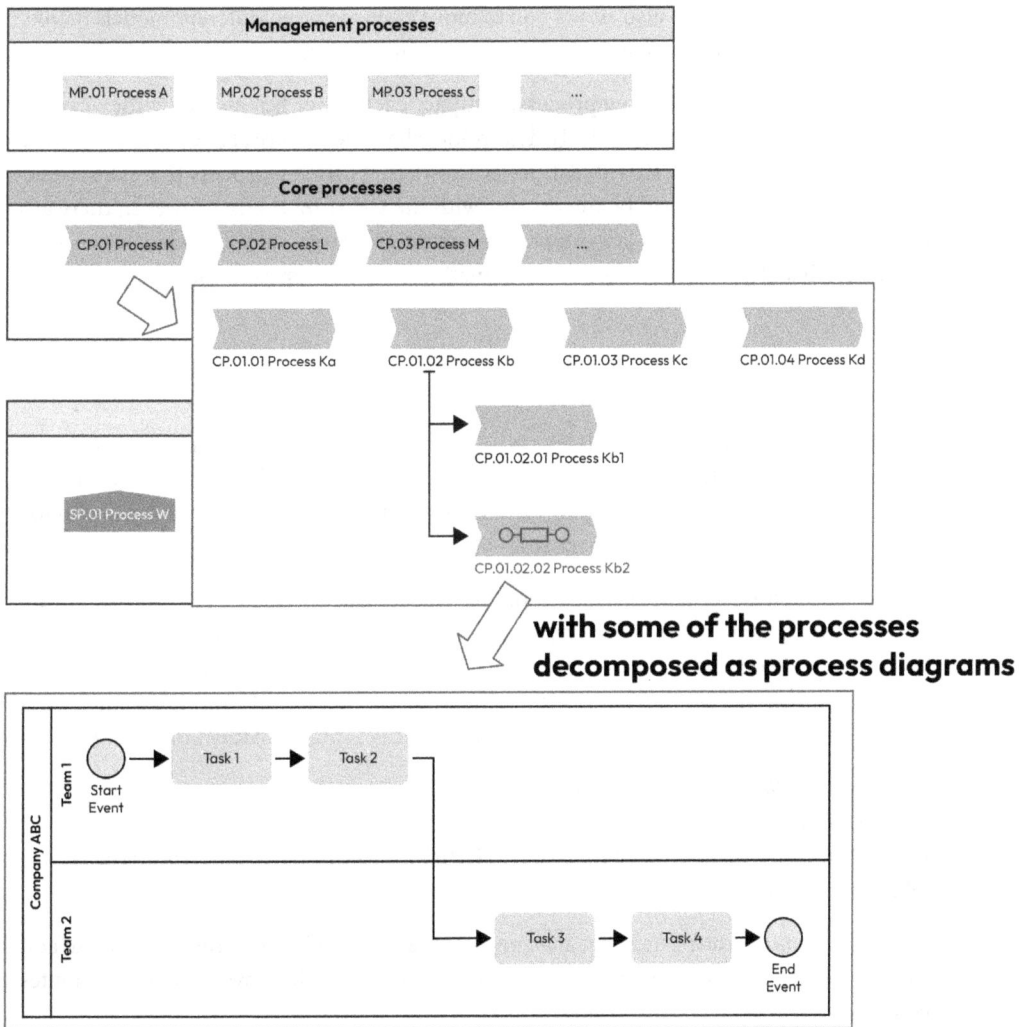

Management processes

MP.01 Process A   MP.02 Process B   MP.03 Process C   ...

Core processes

CP.01 Process K   CP.02 Process L   CP.03 Process M   ...

CP.01.01 Process Ka   CP.01.02 Process Kb   CP.01.03 Process Kc   CP.01.04 Process Kd

CP.01.02.01 Process Kb1

CP.01.02.02 Process Kb2

SP.01 Process W

with some of the processes decomposed as process diagrams

Company ABC

Team 1

Start Event

Task 1 → Task 2

Team 2

Task 3 → Task 4

End Event

Figure 6.3 – The multi-level structure of a process architecture and its navigation

Figure 6.3 shows an example of the multi-level process architecture. It gives an easy overview of the dependencies between processes, but also allows you to move easily between different models thanks to hyperlinks, which make it easy to navigate in depth with a single click.

In our example, we showed not only how processes impact each other but also how they can be decomposed further. Prefixes allow us to quickly determine what level we are at and what the *parent* of our process is. For example, the **CP.01.02.01** prefix shows that this is a process that's described at the third level and that its parent will be the process with the **CP.01.02** prefix. However, there are also more sophisticated ways to capture key information about processes, such as their relationships with other processes, that allow us to change the information about the process without the need to change its name.

Process attributes

At first glance, models such as those shown in *Figure 6.1* and *Figure 6.2* may appear to be just pretty pictures, but a process architecture is much more than nice-looking graphics that allow for easy navigation. Usually, each object representing a process has many more attributes that are useful for information, management, and analytical purposes.

Figure 6.4 shows an example of additional information that a process architecture could contain (using the ADONIS BPM tool). Apart from the process name (**CP.01.02.02 Process Kb2**), we could also have a link to a more detailed process landscape or a BPMN business process diagram and description that provides more information about what is happening in this process and how is it executed (this is especially important for processes that do not have linked models that provide more details).

However, this is not all. We could also state what the goal (or aim) of the process is, what triggers the process, and what the results of the process are. If we state a process goal, it will also make a lot of sense to consider the **key performance indicators** (**KPIs**) for this process. For some processes, a **Service Level Agreement** (**SLA**) can also be added.

Apart from the aforementioned attributes that are shown in the **General information** tab, we can add much more information. Names of other visible tabs can give you hints about what kind of attributes can be placed there.

A very important aspect of process management is the connection between processes and organizational structure. Ideally, for each process, we should define ownership and responsibilities—who the **process owner** is, who supports the owner, what units are involved in performing the process (often called actors or **participants**), and more.

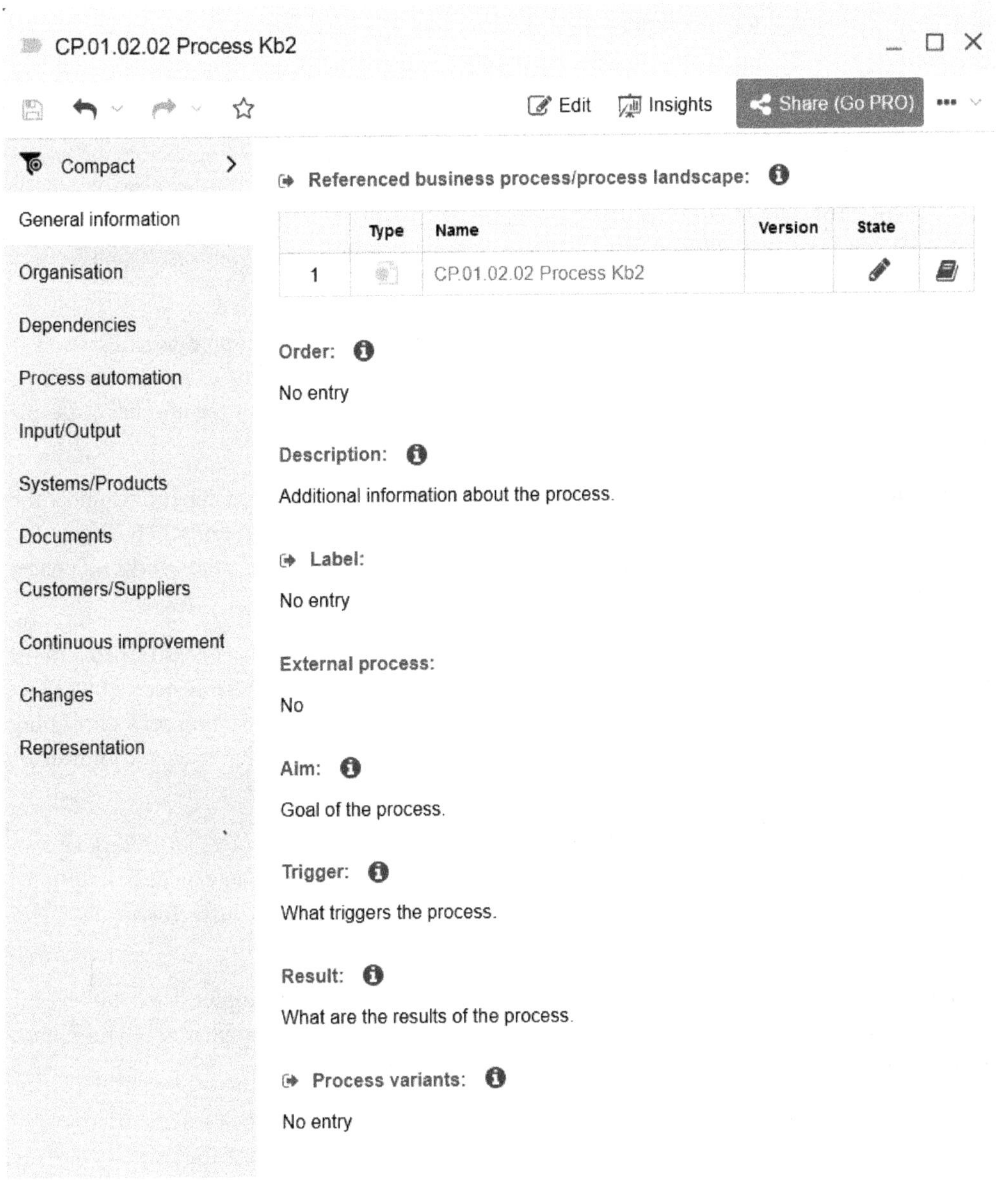

CP.01.02.02 Process Kb2   _ □ ✕

   📷   ↩ ⌄   ↪ ⌄   ☆   📝 Edit   📊 Insights   **◄ Share (Go PRO)**   ••• ⌄

🔦 Compact	❯

General information

Organisation

Dependencies

Process automation

Input/Output

Systems/Products

Documents

Customers/Suppliers

Continuous improvement

Changes

Representation

↪ **Referenced business process/process landscape:** ❶

	Type	Name	Version	State	
1	📷	CP.01.02.02 Process Kb2		✏️	📘

Order: ❶

No entry

Description: ❶

Additional information about the process.

↪ **Label:**

No entry

External process:

No

Aim: ❶

Goal of the process.

Trigger: ❶

What triggers the process.

Result: ❶

What are the results of the process.

↪ **Process variants:** ❶

No entry

Figure 6.4 – Example of process attributes (screenshot from ADONIS)

We may also like to have documented dependencies of our process (which processes precede and succeed our process in a value chain, what the parent of our process is and whether it has any children (or sub-processes), and perhaps which processes it influences or is influenced by).

If we want to use process architecture for decision-making, such as prioritizing change initiatives related to customer-centricity or digital transformation, we could also use additional classifications and assessments. This would allow us to, for example, distinguish critical processes for which any improvement and automation is a priority, or to rank processes in terms of customer satisfaction, cost, quality, regulatory compliance, and more.

When it comes to automation, we could rank the costs and potential benefits of process automation or calculate the automation potential of a process based on its predictability, complexity, and frequency, to name just a few potential options. Some organizations also like to document the number of people involved in the process by using **full-time equivalents** (FTEs).

Of course, each organization is different, so selecting the attributes to be used depends on how the organization wants to use the process architecture and what management systems will be integrated with process management within the organization. Note that the way the organization works influences this significantly.

For example, an organization that takes a more centralized approach to process improvement initiatives, seeking synergy and using a broad organization-wide view, will probably need a bigger set of attributes that are obligatory for many areas. On the contrary, if the organization prefers running individual projects initiated by leaders of organizational units that seek quick results, a common set of attributes may be much smaller.

Note that topics relevant to the organization will impact what will be documented. So, if the goal is to provide employees with basic information and convenient navigation, you can expect descriptions, links to related processes, ownership information, links to documents (procedures, forms, etc.), and a handful of additional attributes.

For organizations where risk management and compliance are important topics, we could expect information about risks and controls, links between processes, and various compliance requirements, as well as information needed for **business continuity management** (BCM).

On the other hand, for an organization that uses process architecture to select processes for improvement and automation as part of digital transformation initiatives, apart from the attributes we've already mentioned, links to the applications used by the process would also be needed, as well as information about the projects. In the *How to use process architecture* section, we will learn how various attributes can be used to classify processes.

To summarize, process architecture is very useful if we want to ensure that we are providing a common reference point for an organization's many different management systems. While modeling individual processes allows for their standardization and improvement, creating a process architecture, maintaining it, and using it to manage an organization is necessary to achieve a higher level of business process management maturity.

Standards for process architecture

As we learned in the previous section, process architecture is an important aspect for successful process management. It is also linked to many other management systems in organizations. Of course, this may make you wonder whether there is a universally recognized list of topics that process architecture should address and ways to show them graphically, and whether there is a standard way to create a process architecture.

Interestingly, there is no single universally accepted approach to its construction. Some organizations find it sufficient to only focus on the processes, along with all their attributes and links to organizational units. Others use more topics, such as applications, risks, KPIs, and others.

However, other organizations use the **ArchiMate** standard for enterprise architecture management, in which *process* (more precisely, **Business Process**) is just one of dozens of available object types used to describe the organization and the interrelationships between its elements. Those elements can be grouped with different layers that represent categories, such as business or technology, as well as aspects such as passive structure or active structure, all of which help categorize the elements of a diagram.

In ArchiMate, as shown in *Figure 6.5*, business processes are part of the business layer and contain elements such as **Business Actor, Business Role, Business Function, Business Event, Business Service, Business Object**, and **Product**. Note that here, **Value Stream** is in the **Strategy** layer.

Figure 6.5 also shows just a few of the ArchiMate objects that are available, such as the **Strategy, Business,** and **Application** layers. For a complete overview of ArchiMate's notation, which contains over 60 object types and 11 relationships, check out the image provided in this book's repository: https://github.com/PacktPublishing/Practical-Business-Process-Modeling-and-Analysis/tree/main/Chapter06.

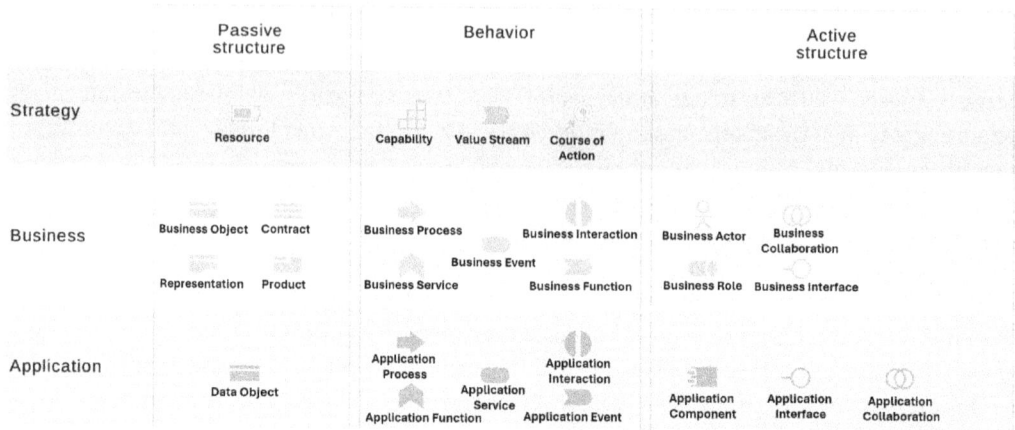

Figure 6.5 – Elements of the ArchiMate notation (image from the free Enterprise Architecture Management tool ADOIT: Community Edition)

🔍 **Quick tip**: Need to see a high-resolution version of this image? Open this book in the next-gen Packt Reader or view it in the PDF/ePub copy.

📖 **The next-gen Packt Reader** and a **free PDF/ePub copy** of this book are included with your purchase. Scan the QR code OR go to `packtpub.com/unlock`, then use the search bar to find this book by name. Double-check the edition shown to make sure you get the right one.

Apart from ArchiMate, several other approaches aimed at business architects, such as **Business Architecture Body of Knowledge (BIZBOK®)** and Object Management Group standards such as **Value Delivery Modeling Language** and **Business Architecture Core Metamodel**, can be valuable sources of inspiration, but so far, none of them can be seen as the de facto standard as they do not provide comprehensive guidance on how to create a process architecture.

For many organizations that I have had a chance to work with, those standards may be a bit too much to implement immediately since they need a certain level of organizational maturity and a group of people who know how to use them. In this situation, my suggestion would be to cross-check the BPM method that the organization creates against such standards to make sure nothing important is missing at this stage.

Now, let's cover the topic of how to document the process architecture. Apart from the cases where organizations avoid graphical modeling and maintain textual lists of processes, typically, processes are indicated by arrows or chevrons. However, this is not standardized in any way (unless you use ArchiMate), so it is only a common practice and something that's inspired by Michael Porter's work.

The last question that remains is, how do you create a process architecture? In practice, I see two main approaches. The first is to take advantage of best practices and use available process libraries. The second is to prepare a process architecture tailored to a specific organization.

In the following sections of this chapter, we will cover both options. We will use both approaches to build a process architecture for a fictional company, *BPMT Dishes*, that manufactures and sells bowls, plates, and other dishes. This example will also be used in *Chapters 7* to *9*, where we will be using the complaint-handling process of this company. Of course, this example will be simplified since it's for illustrative purposes.

APQC's PCF® and other process libraries

Let's begin by discussing what the process libraries are and how they work. We will cover the most popular one, APQC's PCF, in more depth, but several others will be mentioned as well.

Introducing the process libraries

The most commonly used set of reference processes is a library offered by APQC called the PCF. Documentation in the form of Excel and PDF files for the PCF is available for free after registering at www.apqc.org/pcf.

APQC describes the PCF as a taxonomy of processes. It can be used for many purposes—often, organizations start by describing processes or, as we will see later, they may want to verify the completeness of process descriptions. However, often, process improvement and standardization become important use cases. But that's not all: the PCF can be used to categorize content that has been created within an organization and for process **benchmarking** purposes, such as comparing the organization's results with the peer group.

APQC offers more than a dozen types of PCFs. The most basic is the generic **Cross-Industry** type. However, there are also versions tailored to specific industries, such as **Airline**, **Automotive**, **Banking**, **City Government**, **Consumer Products**, **Education**, **Healthcare Provider**, **Life Sciences**, **Retail**, **Telecommunications**, and **Utilities**.

Content within the PCF is divided into five levels:

1. **Category**.
2. **Process Group**.
3. **Process**.

4.   **Activity**.

5.   **Task**.

Let's use the Cross-Industry version to see those levels in practice. To make things more fun, we will use the **13.0 Develop and Manage Business Capabilities** category since it contains elements related to process management.

Categories are the broadest groupings of the processes in the PCF and represent the first level. Each of them contains process groups, which represent level two.

In our example, there are nine process groups, and the first one is **13.1 Manage business processes**. Other process groups include **Manage portfolio, program, and project (13.2)**, **Manage enterprise quality (13.3)**, **Manage change (13.4)**, **Develop and manage enterprise-wide knowledge management (KM) capability (13.5)**, **Measure and benchmark (13.6)**, **Manage environmental health and safety (EHS) (13.7)**, **Develop, manage, and deliver analytics (13.8)**, and **Manage sustainability (13.9)**.

As you may expect, process groups contain processes. Our 13.1 process group contains five of them: **13.1.1 Establish and maintain process management governance**, **13.1.2 Define and manage process frameworks**, **13.1.3 Define processes**, **13.1.4 Manage process performance**, and **13.1.5 Improve processes**. We will focus on 13.1.3 in our example. Processes represent level three, as indicated by their prefixes.

Processes can be further decomposed into activities (level four). Our activities would include **13.1.3.1 Scope processes**, **13.1.3.2 Analyze processes**, **13.1.3.3 Identify and denote process control points**, **13.1.3.4 Model and document processes**, and **13.1.3.5 Publish processes**.

Sometimes, activities need to be decomposed even further. For this purpose, tasks, representing level five, are used. Please note that not every activity has tasks. In our example, *13.1.3.1 Scope processes* is not decomposed any further, while *13.1.3.2 Analyze processes* has one task: **13.1.3.2.1 Identify published best practices**.

If you would like to see additional examples of how those levels work, check out the *PCF levels explained* section of the PCF files.

In the current version of the PCF (7.4), there are 13 categories of processes, as shown in *Figure 6.6*. Instead of the classic division into management, main, and support processes, the PCF divides operational processes presented in the form of a value chain, where management and support processes are grouped.

Each element, in addition to its name, has a unique identifier, as well as a hierarchical identifier, which makes it very easy to find out on which level of the architecture it occurs and what its parent is.

Selected processes also have descriptions available. What's very useful for organizations interested in process measurement is that, for selected APQC process areas, the PCF also includes proposed metrics along with ways to calculate them.

In this way, the PCF provides a common language for process practitioners. It can be used to process comparisons between different companies and benchmark process metrics (KPIs).

When you consider how much valuable information the PCF contains, and the fact that many sector variants have about 1,000 process elements described, it's no wonder it's a common choice for many organizations preparing process architectures. Importantly, the PCF can be used not only as a template for the process architecture structure but also to categorize an organization's various types of information resources. For this last aspect, you can think of the analogy of a library catalog, where each book is assigned to a specific category.

It is worth remembering, however, that the lower levels of the PCF should be viewed as a list of elements that can occur in a given process, rather than a detailed description of processes that can be used one to one. Nor does the order of occurrence of elements within a list necessarily translate into a sequence.

APQC's PCF is an extremely valuable resource for process management teams in organizations since it helps them avoid many mistakes and allows more value to be delivered quickly in process initiatives.

However, you should not expect to simply apply the content contained in the PCF one-to-one in every case. Rather, it may be necessary to make some modifications and tailor the content to the specific industry, organization, or legal environment in which the entity operates.

Here, I will quote Roger Tregear, who says that "*Even if management and support processes may be similar or even identical in different organizations, core processes may be different or perhaps even unique, and it helps a lot if they are named using the terminology of the organization.*" This increases resonance and buy-in.

> **Note**
>
> More information about the PCF, along with a wealth of resources about its usage, can be found on the APQC website (`https://www.apqc.org/process-frameworks`).

APQC's PCF in practice

In this section, we will see how our fictional company, *BPMT Dishes*, could use the APQC's PCF to build a process architecture. The first issue would be the decision of which version of the PCF to use: the Cross-Industry one, or any of the industry-specific variants.

As mentioned earlier, while the highest level, with its 13 process categories, is quite similar, but not identical, the lower we go down, the more differences there are between the different versions of the PCF.

Since our example company, *BPMT Dishes*, produces and sells dishes, we can easily identify two industry-specific variants that could be relevant for us. Comparing the Cross-Industry variant with the Customer Products and Retail versions, we can see that while we have 13 categories in each of these variants, the names of these process categories are tailored to the specific operations of the organization. These differences are shown in the following table:

Process Category (Hierarchy ID)	Cross-Industry (PCF 7.4)	Customer Products (PCF 7.2.2)	Retail (PCF 7.2.1)
1.0	Develop Vision and Strategy	Develop Vision and Strategy	Develop Vision and Strategy
2.0	Develop and Manage Products and Services	Design and Develop Products and Services	Develop and Manage Customer Experience
3.0	Market and Sell Products and Services	Market and Sell Products and Services	Market Products and Services
4.0	Manage Supply Chain for Physical Products	Deliver Products	Merchandise Products and Services
5.0	Deliver Services	Deliver Services	Deliver Products
6.0	Manage Customer Service	Manage Customer Service	Deliver Services
7.0	Develop and Manage Human Capital	Develop and Manage Human Capital	Develop and Manage Human Capital
8.0	Manage Information Technology (IT)	Manage Information Technology (IT)	Manage Information Technology (IT)
9.0	Manage Financial Resources	Manage Financial Resources	Manage Financial Resources
10.0	Acquire, Construct, and Manage Assets	Acquire, Construct, and Manage Assets	Acquire, Construct, and Manage Assets
11.0	Manage Enterprise Risk, Compliance, Remediation, and Resiliency	Manage Enterprise Risk, Compliance, Remediation, and Resiliency	Manage Enterprise Risk, Compliance, Remediation, and Resiliency
12.0	Manage External Relationships	Manage External Relationships	Manage External Relationships
13.0	Develop and Manage Business Capabilities	Develop and Manage Business Capabilities	Develop and Manage Business Capabilities

Table 6.1 – A comparison of the process categories in the PCF for three selected variants

Based on this comparison, *BPMT Dishes*, which manufactures and sells its products to customers, could select the Customer Products version. The company could then create its process architecture based on the process categories taken from the PCF. An example of this is shown in *Figure 6.6*.

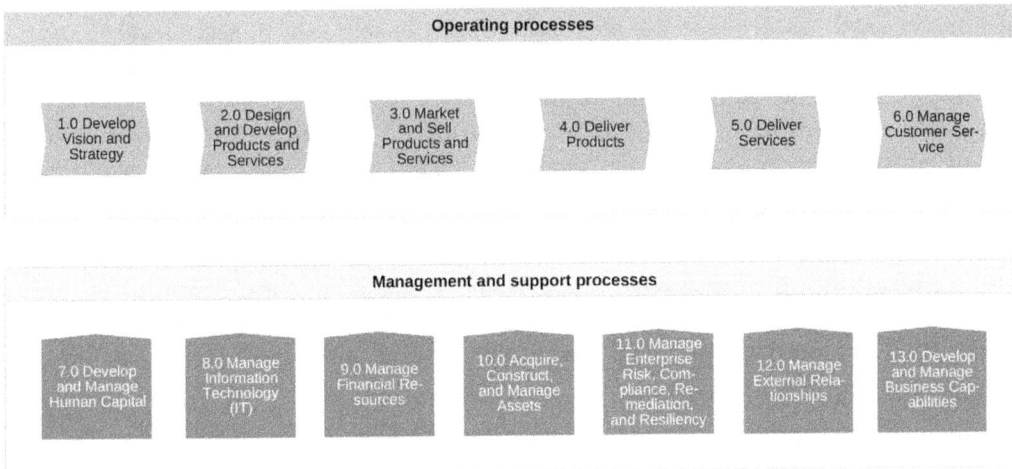

Figure 6.6 – A top-level model for process architecture based on APQC's PCF

The next step would be to describe what happens in each process category. In our example, we'll focus on the area related to customer service, because that's where the area related to handling complaints is. It would be a process group named **Service products after sales**, with hierarchy ID 6.3:

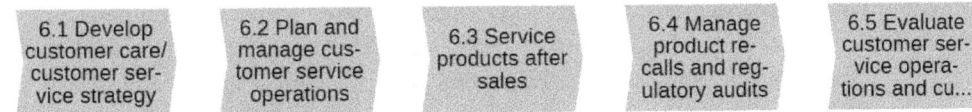

Figure 6.7 – Example decomposition of the process category

As shown in *Figure 6.7*, our process group not only has a name and hierarchy ID, but also a description that helps us better understand its scope. In addition, for our 6.3 process group, there are also lower-level elements that provide additional information: five processes (**6.3.1 Register products**, **6.3.2 Process warranty claims**, **6.3.3 Manage supplier recovery**, **6.3.4 Manage customer self-service materials**, and **6.3.5 Service products**) and more than 30 low-level elements (activities and tasks), such as **6.3.2.3 Investigate warranty issues** and **6.3.2.3.1 Define issue**.

As you can see, APQC's PCF contains a real wealth of elements describing processes. For example, the taxonomy for the Customer Products version contains almost 2,000 elements at the five levels, of which more than 1,800 contain descriptions. The PCF is an invaluable aid for identification, documentation, standardization, and process improvement purposes, as well as for many other applications, such as benchmarking and organizing content.

Given all this, it should come as no surprise that the PCF is the most popular process library in the world. However, it is not the only option available. Telecommunications companies frequently use **Enhanced Telecommunications Operations Map (eTOM)**, companies for which logistics is an important aspect of operations use **Supply Chain Operations Reference (SCOR)**, and IT departments use **Information Technology Infrastructure Library (ITIL)**. In addition, reference process libraries can be provided alongside IT systems (e.g., ERP from SAP) or by consulting companies.

Many of those sources of process knowledge can also be used by AI, so it is technically possible to use GenAI solutions to prepare first drafts of the process architecture based on those process libraries. Or, perhaps even better, AI-enabled tools can be used to make sure that no important group of stakeholders or other business concept that should be covered in a process architecture is forgotten.

However, so far, there is no way to *automagically* create a good process architecture that people will be using without involving employees. Therefore, if you are interested in automating your processes and want to make sure you do not miss something important, it makes sense to create some kind of process architecture before you start the technical part of automation.

For many organizations, a process library such as the PCF is also very useful for making sure that the company will not spend months trying to reinvent the wheel and making common mistakes. Sometimes, it is also easier to make everyone agree on one global standard approach to processes than to reach a consensus internally, especially if the organization has a strong silo culture.

For some organizations, adapting the process library to their needs is not sufficient for ensuring that employees feel that the process architecture is tailored to their needs. The next section will show how to handle such situations so that we can have better employee acceptance and keep the benefits of using global standards.

How to build your own process architecture

In this section, we will learn how to build a custom process architecture. We will begin by discussing when it makes sense to do so, and then we will see what building a process architecture could look like for our fictional company.

Why does it make sense to create a custom process architecture?

As mentioned previously, for some organizations, a process architecture tailored to their needs is a very compelling option. As in the previous cases, this also involves a multi-level structure of connected models. Typically, they are created during workshops with organization employees. As you may expect, it takes more time than adopting the PCF, but if done correctly, it can help build a stronger process culture in the organization.

For those who want to benefit from the best practices available and have the custom look and feel of the process architecture, a hybrid approach is also possible. A process architecture can be created based on input from workshops, but with additional verification of completeness based on reference processes such as APQC's PCF. This helps to speed up the whole process and improve its quality.

The construction of the process architecture often benefits from an analysis of the organization's strategy. This is because processes should ensure the operationalization of this strategy, as well as consider the stakeholders and the products and services through which the organization creates value for them.

Interestingly, often, it turns out that, within an organization, there are frequently many conflicting ideas about through which processes value is created and for whom, who the organization's stakeholders are, and how the organization intends to meet those expectations.

A common vocabulary is also a very frequent problem for many organizations. This can lead to situations where different units do not have a common definition of who the customer is! You can easily imagine how harmful this can be for important initiatives.

Discussions about different aspects of building the process architecture help develop a common understanding of how the organization works and how its processes fit into the overall value creation ecosystem. This is simply invaluable. The outcome of the architecture work itself—for example, a set of dozens or hundreds of identified and described processes documented in the form of interconnected models—is very useful, but the most important thing is to ensure that these models are the result of agreements between all stakeholders.

It is possible to prepare a process architecture very quickly via a small group of specialists from the BPM CoE, but the real value is an architecture that results from a common understanding and agreement between people involved in process management in the organization. This acts as a contract that summarizes the way of working and provides a common view of the organization that has been agreed upon.

It is also worth cautioning against the frequent temptation to speed up the work that's done on the process architecture by using the organizational structure to identify top-level processes. Value-creating processes run through the organization and require cross-functional cooperation, so building a process architecture based on the organizational structure would be fruitless.

Building a process architecture is an extremely interesting area of process knowledge that has many approaches and possible solutions. To see what various process architectures might look like in practice, I invite you to visit `https://bpmtips.com/process-architecture-real-life-examples`.

In addition to some additional examples from process architecture experts such as Roger Burlton and Roger Tregear, on this page, you will also find links to other useful resources, such as interviews on process architecture with Roger Burlton and Professor Marcello La Rosa. These provide lots of valuable insights.

Building a custom process architecture in practice

At this point, we know how to create a process architecture with APQC's PCF. Now, let's discuss how our fictional company, *BPMT Dishes*, could approach building a custom process architecture.

Of course, it is worth stating again that building a custom process architecture doesn't mean we have to start from scratch and invent everything ourselves. Libraries such as APQC's PCF can and should also be used to check whether we are overlooking any important process areas.

A valuable input for building the first level of a process architecture could be information about the strategy and operations of our company. For our fictional company, we could say that it is a family business with a strong customer focus that produces dishes (such as plates and bowls) and sells them to customers directly or via partners.

To make things easier, we will only focus on producing dishes and selling them to customers directly. In real life, our company would probably also offer some other products from partner companies, such as cutlery, table linen, and so on, but we will not cover that in this book.

As you can probably already see, there are two main areas where we produce value for our customers. The first **end-to-end process** would cover the full life cycle of product development from idea, through production, to managing the product, with decisions being made about changes or possibly retiring the product. This would guarantee that the company has great dishes that can be sold to customers.

The second end-to-end process would focus on serving customers while also covering the full life cycle from making the customer aware of our products, selling and delivering them, to handling complaints if something goes wrong. This process should guarantee that the dishes produced in the first process reach the customers.

Both processes would be an important way of making the company's mission come true. This mission could be *creating delightful products that help customers have unforgettable moments around the table*

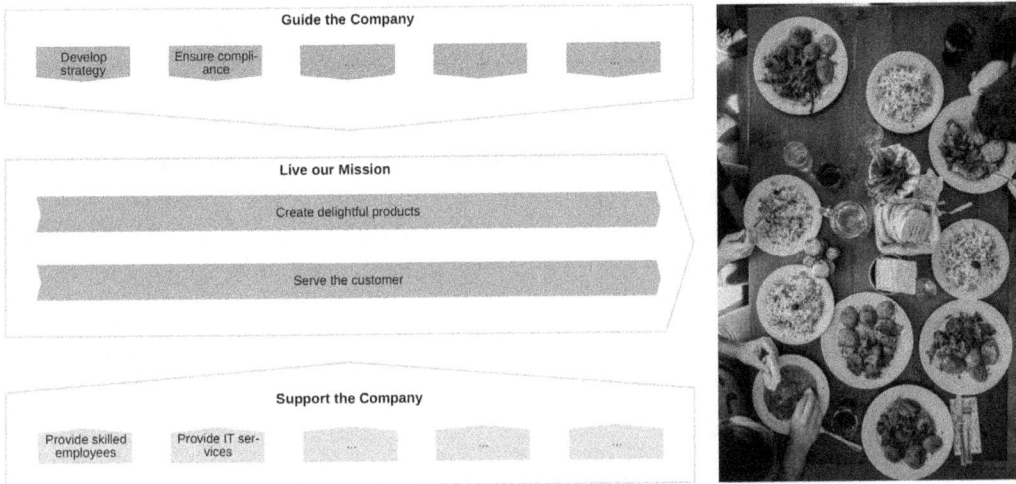

Figure 6.8 – Example of a custom top-level model for process architecture

Quick tip: Need to see a high-resolution version of this image? Open this book in the next-gen Packt Reader or view it in the PDF/ePub copy.

The next-gen Packt Reader and a free PDF/ePub copy of this book are included with your purchase. Scan the QR code OR go to packtpub.com/unlock, then use the search bar to find this book by name. Double-check the edition shown to make sure you get the right one.

Figure 6.8 shows what a top-level model for a process architecture could look like. As you may have guessed, such models differ a lot from company to company. The names of process categories, the number of process levels within one model, visual aspects such as graphics and logotypes, deciding which attributes should be shown (e.g., process owners), and providing additional navigational support to other related models describing the organization—these are only some of the aspects that impact what the top-level model of the process architecture looks like.

Discussions regarding the placement of a given process in the management or support category are also common. For some people, even the positions of the processes they see as their own can be important. Usually, the top-left element will have something to do with defining the strategy and vision, and making sure it guides the whole organization. In many organizations, this process would be called **strategy management**, even though this name is not very specific. This process could be followed by some other processes that guide the organization. For the support processes, this isn't as obvious. Do we start with people (our employees), IT, or something else? It is often a matter of perceived importance.

Luckily, as the people in an organization get used to process thinking, things such as more or less prominent positions of certain processes no longer matter. This is a good indicator that people grasp the concept of process management as a team sport, where the focus is on managing cross-functional processes to create value.

Naming conventions are also tricky. A frequently used approach is the **verb + noun** naming convention (e.g., **Develop Strategy**). However, you will also notice other approaches (e.g., **Strategy Management**) or nouns that are not very precise (e.g., **Manage Strategy**). Well-known BPM expert Alec Sharp warns against using names that do not clearly state what the purpose of the process is because they do not help create a common understanding. A catchy name for this problem that was used by Alec in his acclaimed book, *Workflow Modeling: Tools for Process Improvement and Applications Development*, is **mushy verb fuzziness**.

While the aforementioned options are not as clear and elegant as the first example provided, where we used an active verb, and they do not show precisely what the result of the process is, sometimes, it is hard to avoid them for several reasons. Sometimes, they are simply taken from a process library. Other times, the people responsible for some areas are used to such names (e.g., **Risk Management**). Usually, the result is a compromise of some kind, but this is typically widely discussed and a result of a common agreement.

Of course, what we *see* in a graphical model is just the tip of the iceberg; it is simply not practical to make all the information that was gathered about processes visible. Based on discussions, each process would be enriched with the necessary attributes. When the overview model is ready, usually what follows is a decision that specifies in which order processes will be decomposed further.

In a perfect world, every process from the top level of the process architecture would have a model showing lower-level processes. However, often, organizations start by picking only the most important ones and documenting them in more depth. Only after this approach shows visible results and the organization learns how to approach the creation of process architecture can the remaining process areas be tackled.

How to use process architecture

Earlier in this chapter, we discussed some of the benefits of having a process architecture. We already know that process architecture provides an overview of how an organization creates value and how processes are related to each other and other organizational resources. This is the **informational function** of the architecture. This is very helpful for training new employees and making sure that everyone is on the same page.

Process architecture also allows you to easily drill down from overview models to models that show what is happening in a selected process area. This is the **navigational aspect**.

If we add the issue of the huge opportunities that arise from standardization and the use of common procedures (reusability) and synergies in many places, we can see that we have a situation where several other business areas can serve as sources of good practices.

For example, practitioners of **business process management** could find inspiration in domains such as **enterprise architecture management** (in particular, application portfolio management), **product portfolio management**, or **project management**, which at higher levels turns into **program management**, so that individual projects work well together, and **portfolio management**, so that practitioners can select the right projects for their implementation.

In each domain, reusability and seeking synergy are important topics, so the methods that work there could also be useful in process management.

This is especially important for organizations that plan to launch new products and enter new markets because they do not need to prepare everything from scratch; instead, they can reuse some of the existing processes. This helps reduce costs, speed everything up, reduce risks, and increase the overall agility of the organization.

Also, companies planning mergers and acquisitions can greatly benefit from process architecture as it allows them to figure out which elements are redundant, where standardization can be used, and where separate processes are still needed.

In the *Process attributes* section, we learned that, within a process architecture, each process is often described by a set of different attributes that are usually not visible in a graphical model at first glance, although they can be used for process analysis.

In this section, we'll look at what other practical applications of process architecture might look like and how process architecture can be useful in an organization's digital transformation initiatives.

Let's start with a topic that is often central to selecting processes that should be included in further architectural work: evaluating processes in terms of their importance. Depending on the specifics of the organization and the goals guiding the initiative within which the process architecture is being built, it can be helpful, for example, to classify processes in terms of their business value, level of customer satisfaction, IT support, compliance with regulatory requirements, and more. Such information can, for example, be visualized as a heat map using colors, which helps in the discussion of priorities for further work. An example of such an approach is shown in *Figure 6.9*.

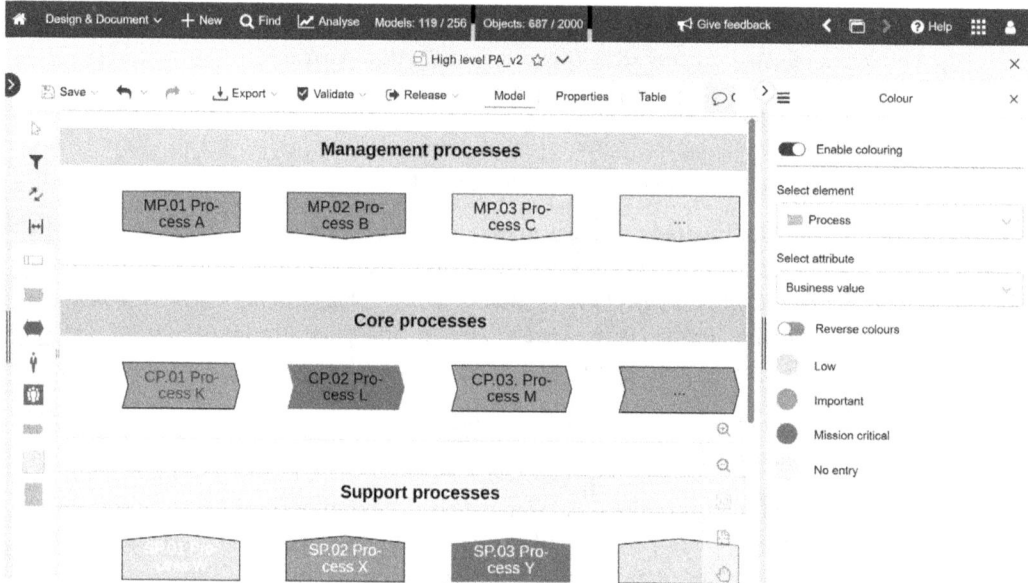

Figure 6.9 – A heatmap analysis of a process architecture based on business value

More sophisticated analyses using multiple data dimensions are also possible. For example, a common way to select processes for improvement might be to evaluate them based on two criteria: importance and urgency (i.e., the **Eisenhower Matrix**) or pain and gain. When selecting processes for **Robotic Process Automation** (RPA), on the other hand, attention is often paid to the frequency of process execution and the degree of standardization (or business relevance).

Another example set of attributes would involve assessing the benefits of automating a given process and the costs of that automation. For this type of analysis, the results are often presented in the form of a graphical analysis showing process evaluations as bubbles in each element of the graph. *Figure 6.10* shows what this approach to process selection could look like.

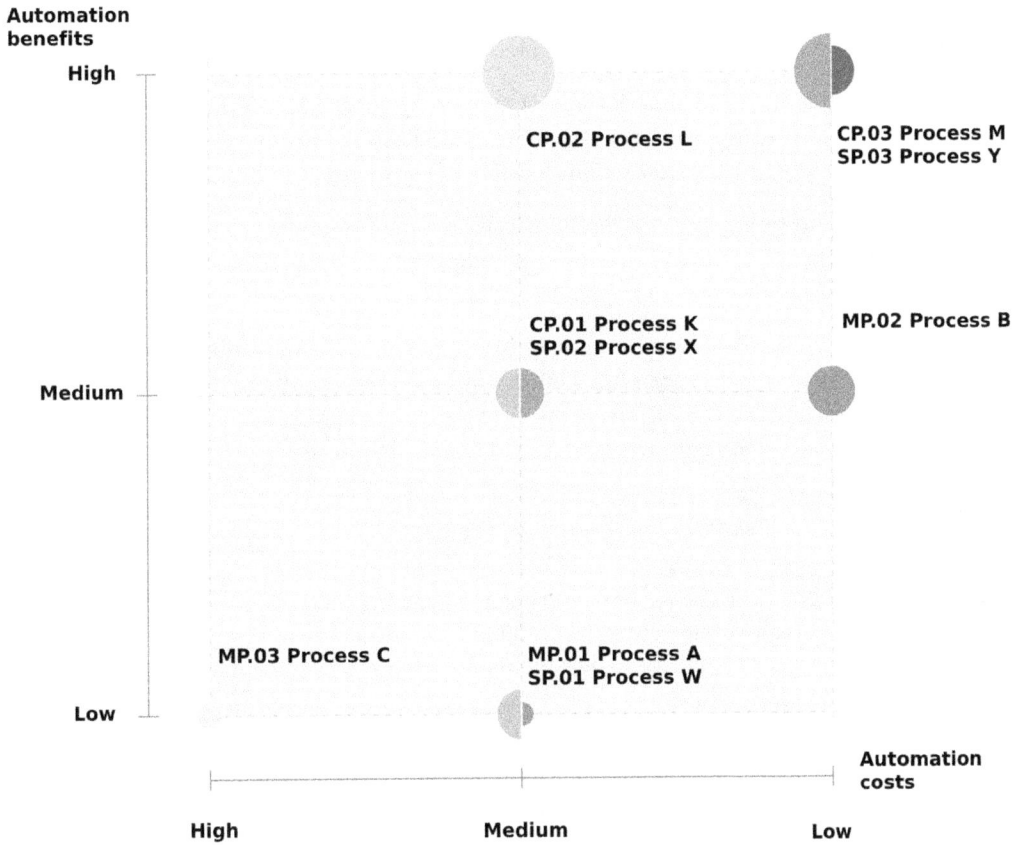

Automation costs vs Automation benefits vs Business value

Figure 6.10 – Selecting processes for automation based on multi-level analysis
(automation costs versus automation benefits versus business value)

By taking this approach to process selection as part of a digital transformation initiative, the chances that the right processes will be included increase, rather than processes being loudly advocated by a high-profile person in the organization. As an additional benefit during further analytical work, those involved in designing new solutions will know more about the process.

Knowing who the process owner is and what other processes our process is linked to makes it possible to determine who to involve in planning. Being aware of what applications and data the process uses can also help with avoiding costly mistakes due to a lack of knowledge.

Because process architecture provides a comprehensive description of the process, along with key attributes and relationships, the risk of designing piecemeal solutions that do not provide the entire organization with optimal results significantly decreases.

Another benefit of having a process architecture is that the aforementioned attributes describing the process, such as the process goal, process description, process owner, and others, can be used not only as part of design work but also daily. By using the right approach to process documentation, we can ensure that all interested parties have access to the knowledge they need.

> ### How to show the benefits of the process architecture
>
> As discussed previously in this section, process architecture can be very helpful not only for documenting processes but also for improving and automating them. Once we've picked the right processes (e.g, high-volume processes with big improvement potential that are possible to automate), the next step would be to pick the right approach to automation.
>
> For some processes that are high-volume, standardized, and do not require unstructured data to be handled, more traditional automation approaches such as ERP and CRM could be sufficient. For others, where volume is not as high, but processes are relatively standardized, you may want to use the BPMS tools/workflow automation. Of course, it is also possible that you will need to orchestrate many technologies, such as RPA bots and AI agents, while ensuring your employees are working together on your process.
>
> Having a good understanding of your process will help you decide how to automate your process properly. This way, you will avoid creating a fancy and expensive solution with AI agents for a process where a CRM system would be perfectly fine.
>
> Information about the process will also help you design and implement the solution. Here, apart from the high-level process architecture, a detailed diagram showing the workflows will be of use. We will cover this topic in more depth later in this book.
>
> An additional exciting opportunity that can shorten the time needed to deliver the value of the process architecture (e.g., running successful automation projects) is **process mining**. This concept, mentioned in *Chapter 5*, allows you to discover your processes based on process logs and improve them. For mid-sized and large organizations, such projects can bring significant benefits, and having a process architecture may help with deciding which areas should be tackled first.

Depending on the specifics of the organization, this can be organized through a process tool, most likely using one of the repository-based **enterprise business process analysis** tools mentioned in *Chapter 5*, publishing to a solution such as SharePoint or Confluence, or creating printable documents that contain key information about the process.

With this type of approach, it is possible to gather the necessary process information without creating a detailed diagram for each process, which saves a lot of time both in terms of creating and updating.

Summary

In this chapter, we learned what process architecture is and its role in process management. We learned how an organization's process architecture can be built: either by using popular process libraries such as APQC's PCF or by building a process architecture tailored to the specifics of the organization. We also had the opportunity to see how process architecture can be used in practice and learned about the benefits of having one.

In many places, we also had the opportunity to see that process architecture allows us to choose which processes we should describe in detail, or that process architecture allows us to choose processes to optimize or automate, which often requires that we describe them more elaborately. But how can we describe processes at a greater level of detail? This is what we will address in the next chapter.

Further reading

- If you would like to learn more about the naming of processes and the topic of building a business architecture that encompasses process architecture and how it's related to business capabilities, I strongly recommend the great book *Business Architecture: Collecting, Connecting, and Correcting the Dots*, by Roger Burlton. An additional awesome book is *Reimagining Management: Putting process at the center of business management*, by Roger Tregear. Both books are pure gold!

- If you are interested in building an organizational architecture that merges business process management and enterprise architecture management, check out the book *Successful Architecture Implementation: A practical guide on how to implement your EA/BPM program*, by Roland Woldt.

- If you are interested in real-life cases showing how organizations implement BPM, I do not know a better book than *Business Process Management Cases Vol. 3: Implementation in Practice*, whose editors are Jan vom Brocke, Jan Mendling, and Michael Rosemann. In particular, I recommend that you read the interesting case about building the process architecture at Poland's Ministry of Finance to see different approaches to a process architecture.

- You can find additional examples and best practices for creating a process architecture in *Holistic Business Process Management: Successful with BPMN 2.0 and OCEB 2 Fundamental*, by Serge Schiltz. This book is also a great choice if you are interested in gaining a BPM certification. More on this topic will be covered in *Chapter 11*.

- Finally, if you would like to learn more about ArchiMate, I would like to recommend *Mastering ArchiMate Edition 3.2: A serious introduction to the ArchiMate® enterprise architecture modeling language*, by Gerben Wierda.

Unlock this book's exclusive benefits now

Scan this QR code or go to `packtpub.com/unlock`, then search this book by name.

Note: Keep your purchase invoice ready before you start.

7

Process Modeling Notations

Chapter 1 provided a great overview of the main reasons for graphical modeling. Process management has a long history, so it should be no surprise that during this time, many ways of modeling processes – so-called modeling notations – emerged. As we discovered in *Chapter 6*, process modeling can be used on various levels. Models can also be aimed at different audiences.

Because there is no single notation that is sufficient for all users and all purposes, in this chapter, we will learn how to model processes and discuss the differences between those notations.

Since there are dozens of process modeling notations, we will not be able to cover all of them in depth. We will instead go through the history of process modeling, discussing the important notations that are still relevant today, and briefly mention those that are not very popular currently but had an impact on the most popular process modeling notation today – BPMN.

In this chapter, we're going to cover the following main topics:

- The basics of process modeling
- Going beyond flowcharts – an overview of other notations
- BPMN – how we got there and why it is relevant to us

> **Note**
> This chapter is authored by Zbigniew Misiak.

The basics of process modeling

It's hard to imagine, but the modeling of business processes can be traced back over 100 years. In 1921, Frank and Lillian Gilbreth (brilliant industrial engineers and efficiency experts) proposed a new way of presenting processes in a presentation for the **American Society of Mechanical Engineers** (**ASME**) titled *Process Charts: First Steps in Finding the One Best Way to do Work*.

What is fascinating to me is that the article starts with a point that is still valid today:

> *"The process chart is a device for visualizing a process as a means of improving it.*
> *Every detail of a process is more or less affected by every other detail; therefore, the*
> *entire process must be presented in such form that it can be visualized all at once*
> *before any changes are made in any of its subdivisions".*

Apart from suggesting an approach for process modeling, they also proposed several dozen standard symbols (shapes) for the process charts. Their ideas gained traction, and in 1947, process charts became an ASME standard (in a simplified form with fewer shapes, which was supposed to be less prone to errors).

ASME process charts used shapes such as circles, arrows, squares, and triangles. This way of modeling processes was very simple, and this was done on purpose. Those diagrams were meant to be used not only by managers but also by the people performing the process so that they could understand the process better, find errors, and propose a more streamlined version of the process.

A great quote (which I found in the article named *People Come First* on: http://www.worksimp.com/articles/keynoteworkflowcanada.htm) from Alan Mogensen, who used this way of modeling in consulting projects, shows clearly how process improvement was considered a democratic activity, not restricted to managers or experts:

> *"The person doing the job knows more about it than anyone else in the world and is*
> *therefore the one person best fitted to improve it."*

Most likely, you have seen some flowcharts already. However, if you decide to check the image showing the original flowchart shapes, which is available on the GitHub page with resources for this chapter, (https://github.com/PacktPublishing/Practical-Business-Process-Modeling-and-Analysis/tree/main/Chapter07) you may not be familiar with all the shapes. That's because flowcharts kept evolving, especially after it was discovered that they are very useful for creating diagrams representing computer code.

There are several standards specifying shapes used in flowcharts, for example, ANSI's *Flowchart Symbols and their usage in information processing* from 1970 and ISO 5807 from 1985: *Information processing – Documentation symbols and conventions for data, program and system flowcharts, program network charts and system resources charts.*

However, still, in various programs, you may encounter some differences. Since we will be comparing different notations, we will use a common style of table that will allow you to see similarities and differences more easily. In this table, you will see an overview of objects (shapes) frequently used in diagrams, but please note that they also need some connectors (arrows). Each notation uses its own style of connectors, but as you will see, connectors showing how the process flows are usually drawn with solid lines.

Modeling concepts	Shape and name	Description
Start of the process diagram	Start	First element of a process diagram. Start and end shapes look the same.
Process step (simple)	Process	A simple process step representing some work to be done in a process.
Process step (complex)	Subprocess	A more complex step of a process, which can have several sub-steps – often shown in a separate diagram.
Process split	Decision	The place where a process splits into two or more paths on the basis of some decision.
End of a process diagram	End	The last element of a process diagram. Start and end shapes look the same.

Table 7.1 – Flowchart shapes (basic)

As you may imagine, the shapes shown in the preceding table are very useful and allow you to document many interesting aspects of processes, but they are not everything that flowcharts have to offer. The following table shows some less frequently used modeling concepts:

Modeling concepts	Shape and name	Description
Document creation	Document	Step for creating a document

Modeling concepts	Shape and name	Description
Handling inputs or outputs	Data or input/output	Data or materials entering the process from the outside, or the output of the process
Navigation – the same page	On-page reference	Jump to another part of the flowchart
Navigation – another page	Off-page reference	Hyperlink to another page of the flowchart

Table 7.2 – Flowchart shapes (more advanced)

Now, let's see in practice how a business process could be documented as a flowchart. We will continue using the process of complaint handling of a B2C company that you saw in the previous two chapters.

The process is initiated by a communication from a customer who reports a complaint (via email, phone, or chat on the website). The complaint is checked by a complaint specialist for validity (within a system that automates this entire process). If the complaint is invalid, the customer receives a message about its rejection, with a justification (the justification should have been prepared by the specialist in the previous step). If the complaint is valid, the customer receives information about approval of the complaint, and then the specialist determines which solution will be satisfactory to the customer: refund (part of) the payment or replace the product with a new one. If the customer opts for a refund, the corresponding order goes to the financial team to make the refund. If the customer prefers a replacement, the order goes to the logistics team to ship the appropriate product. The process can thus end in three ways:

1. The customer may receive a message about the rejection of the complaint (along with a justification).
2. The customer may receive a monetary refund.
3. The customer may receive a replacement product.

As you can see, it is pretty difficult to get a good overview of what is happening in this process simply by reading the text. *Table 7.3* allows you to see how the tabular form of a process description may increase the readability a bit. While this is a step in the right direction, it does not make a huge difference either (e.g., the reader needs to guess that after step 5, we finish the process and do not continue with step 6, as they represent two mutually exclusive process flows).

#	Name of the step	Responsibility
1	Complaint valid? Yes – go to step 2 No – go to step 8	Complaint specialist
2	Inform the customer about the complaint's validity	Complaint specialist
3	How to handle a complaint? Replacement – go to step 4 Refund – go to step 6	Complaint specialist
4	Order shipping of the replacement product	Complaint specialist
5	Ship product	Logistics specialist
6	Order refund	Complaint specialist
7	Process a refund	Finance specialist
8	Inform the customer about the rejection	Complaint specialist

Table 7.3 – Tabular description of a process

Now, let's take a look at the same process shown as a flowchart.

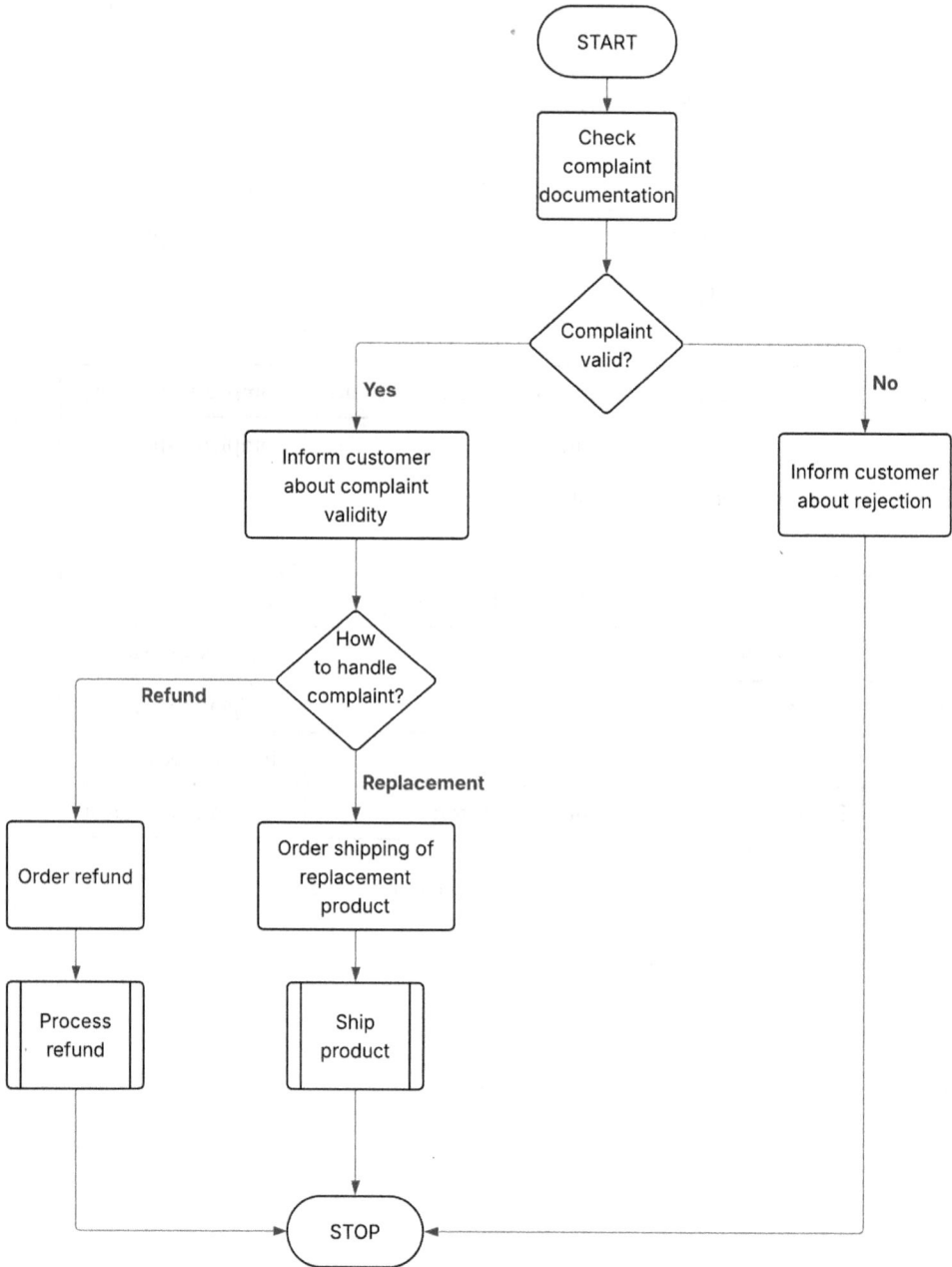

Figure 7.1 – Example process as a flowchart (created in Lucidchart)

As you will immediately see, it is clear what the steps of the process are and what the logic of the process is, including where the process splits into exclusive paths (i.e., only one path can be taken: the complaint is either valid or invalid).

This simple flowchart shows in practice several things important for reading process diagrams:

- The process needs to have a specific place showing its start and end
- You read the process diagram by following the arrows connecting the objects
- Process steps, that is, work that needs to be done, are usually shown as rectangles
- Places where the process splits into several paths are usually shown as diamonds
- If a certain part of the process is complex, it may be helpful to simply mark it in what is called a subprocess, that is, a process of a lower level, instead of trying to show everything in one big diagram

Simple flowcharts do not show responsibilities for process steps, but this was added to more advanced versions of flowcharts (cross-functional flowcharts) later on.

Going beyond flowcharts – overview of other notations

While flowcharts provided a nice way to show what is happening inside a process, it quickly became apparent that there are additional ideas regarding how processes can be modeled.

Notations that I think are worth mentioning in this section are the following:

- IDEF
- LOVEM
- UML
- EPC

IDEF

The **Integrated DEFinition (IDEF)** method is a family of modeling notations developed for the US Air Force and the Department of Defense in the 1970s. It contains several model types serving various purposes – among them, IDEF3 is meant for modeling processes. It is not very popular nowadays outside the US but it shares some of the characteristics that we have already covered, such as representing activities as boxes and connecting them with arrows. You can learn more about IDEF3 and see examples at `https://www.idef.com/idef3-process-description-capture-method`.

LOVEM

Line of Visibility Engineering Methodology (LOVEM) was introduced by IBM in the mid-1990s to model processes for the purpose of reengineering initiatives. As process reengineering lost its appeal, LOVEM also stopped being used frequently. Just like IDEF, LOVEM also had several types of charts (so-called **Line of Visibility Charts (LOVCs)**). You can see examples of various LOVCs and learn more about LOVEM from the (archived) publication by IBM available thanks to the Internet Archive: `https://web.archive.org/web/20140309022748/http://www.redbooks.ibm.com/redbooks/pdfs/sg242590.pdf`.

Just like in IDEF, LOVEM also used boxes representing activities and arrows, but also **swimlanes** showing who does what. The innovation in LOVEM is the **line of visibility** – a special line in a diagram showing the border between the company and the customer. Apart from this, LOVEM also helped show additional information such as data flows inside a process.

UML

While IDEF and LOVEM are not used often, our next notation is still popular. **Unified Modeling Language (UML)** is a modeling standard still popular among IT specialists for documenting various aspects of software development. Just like the previous examples, UML also has many diagram types (14 in version 2.5) serving various purposes. Unlike other notations, UML is a standard supported by an independent body – the **Object Management Group (OMG)** – which oversees the standard and maintains it.

UML also boasts a long history – version 1.0 was proposed in 1997, and the latest update (version 2.5.1) was published in December 2017. You can learn more about UML on the standard's website: `https://www.uml.org/`.

Out of the many diagram types, **activity diagrams** could be used for modeling processes. In the following figure, you can see an example of a UML activity diagram.

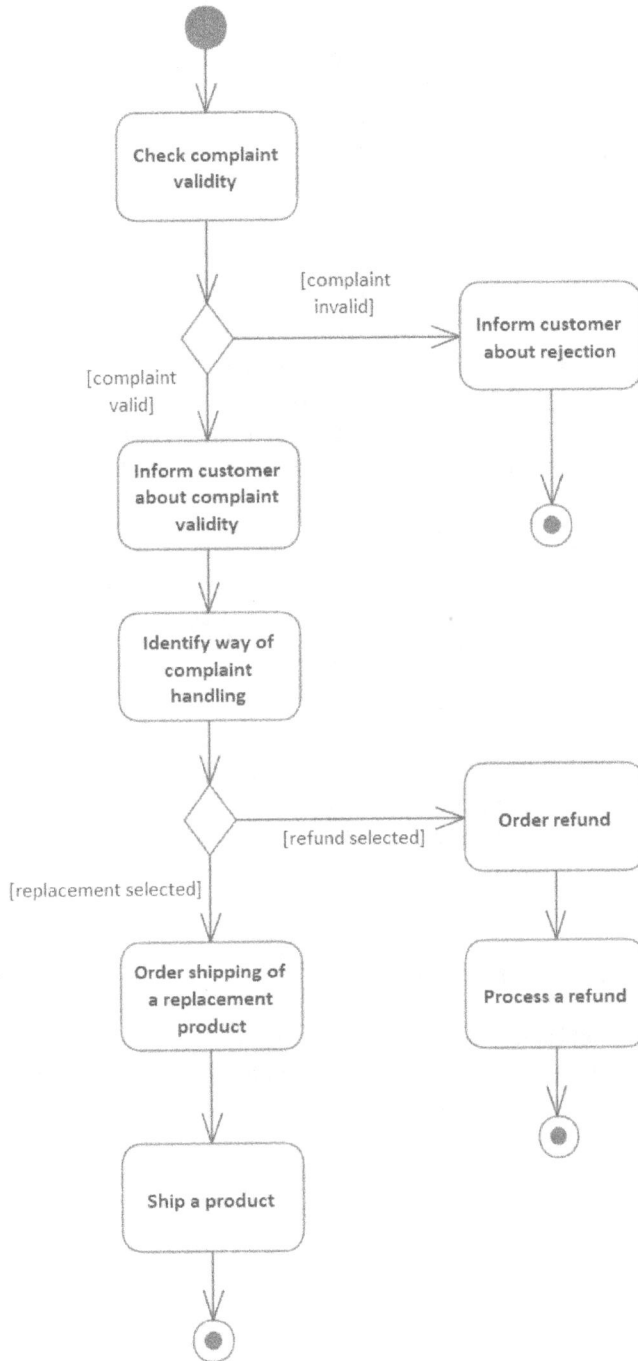

Figure 7.2 – Example process as a UML activity diagram (created in Enterprise Architect)

As you can see, activity diagrams preserve the rules we have mentioned so far. In addition, they introduce different visualizations for start and end nodes (circles) and use rounded rectangles for the process steps instead of normal rectangles. However, much more importantly, UML provides a metamodel and an XML-based interchange mechanism so that diagrams are not only pretty pictures but can also be shared among other tools.

EPC

Finally, I want to mention a notation for modeling processes that for a long time was one of the most popular among business professionals: **Event-Driven Process Chain** (**EPC**). EPCs are part of the **Architecture of Integrated Information Systems** (**ARIS**) method, developed by Professor Scheer in the 1990s for the purpose of documenting organizations and their processes. Of course, it was not the only notation serving this purpose (e.g., the **BPMS** method was proposed by Professor Karagiannis around this time), but EPCs were popularized by their usage in SAP **Enterprise Resource Planning** (**ERP**) software.

As the name suggests, EPCs put a strong emphasis on events in a process; however, they also introduce several other elements that allow you to show who performs certain process steps (in case you are wondering: EPCs can also use swimlanes to show responsibility, which documents and IT systems are used, and so on). This allows conveying much more information in comparison to plain flowcharts.

> **Note**
>
> To learn more about EPC and see an example diagram prepared by Roland Woldt, visit the GitHub page with resources for this chapter: `https://github.com/PacktPublishing/Practical-Business-Process-Modeling-and-Analysis/tree/main/Chapter07`.

BPMN – how we got there and why it is relevant to us

In a previous section of this chapter (*Going beyond flowcharts – overview of other notations*), you had a chance to see how complex it was to communicate with others using process models even 20 years ago. Numerous ways of describing processes made communication within and between organizations difficult because everyone used their own way of modeling. This resulted in the classic Tower of Babel syndrome. Local efforts to solve this problem (e.g., the creation of a standard process modeling notation for the German public administration) did not lead to a universally recognized modeling method. The BPMN notation was conceived as a solution to this very problem.

The first version of the standard was published by the **Business Process Management Initiative** (**BPMI**) in 2004 as Business Process Modeling Notation. Since 2005, when BPMI merged with OMG, an organization known for developing and maintaining many technology standards, BPMN has been developed by OMG. As part of this work, version 1.1 of the standard was published in 2008, followed by version 1.2 in 2009.

However, the most important moment in the development of BPMN was in 2011, when version 2.0 of the specification was published, which, with minor modifications (the latest version of the standard is 2.0.2, published in 2014 as the ISO/IEC 19510 standard), is still in force today.

Version 2.0 of the BPMN standard brought a lot of significant changes; many new object types and icons were added and some of the elements introduced in the earlier version of the specification were changed. So, in this book, we will be dealing with the current version.

The first important thing to know about version 2.0 is that the BPMN acronym now stands for **Business Process Model and Notation**. This name change naturally has a deeper rationale, which we'll address in a moment, but for those uninterested in the technical details, it has brought one very important benefit: if, in the course of searching for answers to questions related to BPMN, you find an article in which the author uses a different acronym expansion than Business Process Model and Notation, it's quite likely outdated content that doesn't take into account the latest version of the specification.

Another extremely important change introduced by version 2.0 of the standard was the definition of how data is exchanged between different tools supporting BPMN. This is very important as well. While earlier versions of the standard allowed generating – for some types of process diagrams – code to automate processes in **Business Process Execution Language** (**BPEL**), there was no reliable way to go from BPEL code to a BPMN diagram that would work for every process diagram. For a while, another technology standard served as a workaround for this problem: **XML Process Definition Language** (**XPDL**), developed by the – unfortunately no longer functional – **Workflow Management Coalition** (**WfMC**). However, this was not an optimal situation, because not all elements possible to describe in BPMN could be exchanged between different tools using XPDL.

Version 2.0 of the standard introduced a special data exchange format, using the XML file format and described in the Diagram Interchange section (*chapter 12.1*) of the standard, which is often referred to as BPMN DI or BPMN XML. This ensures that any business process diagram can be saved as an XML file for data exchange with other modeling or process automation tools.

In addition, to take care of efficient data exchange, a special **BPMN Model Interchange Working Group** (**BPMN MIWG**) was established – for more than 10 years, it has provided a forum for tool developers to collaborate, conducted annual diagram exchange demonstrations, and maintained and developed a library of test models through which it is possible to verify the level of support of BPMN notation by a given tool. Test results are presented in the form of a table, the current state of which, at the time of writing this book, is shown in the following screenshot.

BPMN Tools tested for Model Interchange

Search:

Vendor	Tool	BPMN 2.0	Import	Export	Roundtrip	Demo Participation	Last Test Submission	A Results Submitted	B Results Submitted	C Results Submitted	Schema-valid
Camunda	bpmn.io (Camunda Modeler) 18.6.1	O	Diff	Diff	Details	2024, 2022, 2020, 2019, 2018, 2017, 2016, 2015, 2014, 2013	2025	24/24	3/8	24/24	14/14
BOC Group	ADONIS 17.0	O	Diff	Diff	Details	2024, 2022, 2020, 2019, 2018, 2017, 2016, 2015, 2014, 2013	2025	24/24	8/8	24/24	14/14
Trisotech	Trisotech Workflow Modeler 12.6.3	O	Diff	Diff	Details	2024, 2022, 2020, 2019, 2018, 2017, 2016, 2015, 2014, 2013	2025	24/24	3/8	24/24	14/14
OMNINET	OMNITRACKER BPMN 12.3	O	Diff	Diff	Details	2024, 2022, 2020	2025	24/24	8/5	24/24	12/14
vladee Unternehmensberatung AG	BPMN-Modeler for Confluence Enterprise 3.38.0	O	Diff	Diff	Details	2024, 2022, 2020	2024	24/24	8/8	24/24	14/14
Software AG	ARIS 10.0.22	O	Diff	Diff	Details	2024, 2022, 2020, 2019, 2018	2023	24/24	8/8	24/24	14/14
SAP Signavio	SAP Signavio Process Manager 17.5.1	O	Diff	Diff	Details	2024, 2022, 2020, 2018, 2017, 2016, 2015, 2014, 2013	2023	24/24	8/8	24/24	9/12
Esteco S.p.A.	Cardanit (prev. BeePMN) 4.9.1	O	Diff	Diff	Details	2024, 2022, 2020, 2019, 2018, 2017, 2016	2023	16/24	0/8	24/24	10/10

Figure 7.3 – An excerpt from a table summarizing the results of tool tests performed by the BPMN MIWG

The purpose of the BPMN is to provide a common language for stakeholders interested in the process. In the specification document, the authors state that their goal was to create a notation that would be a *common language* for various groups of users: business analysts, developers, and business users, both in terms of designing a process and automating it. They wanted to simplify communication between various process stakeholders: people running the process, implementers, customers and suppliers. To do so, they aimed to create a standard notation based on other already-existing notations and using their tried and tested elements.

This is a rather bold assumption, because on the one hand, it should support business users who are interested in creating easy-to-read diagrams, and on the other, it should enable one of the notation's goals, which is to allow any diagram to potentially serve as a basis for preparing process automation.

The solution proposed by the specification is the concept of compliance levels (inspired by Bruce Silver's method of teaching BPMN), which divides the elements of the notation into three groups. The first group consists of the most basic elements for documenting processes at the **descriptive level**. Diagrams using these elements are not much more complicated than flowcharts, but they ensure the transmission of information in a clear and standardized way.

The second group includes elements that go beyond what users of flowcharts may be used to – they allow the creation of more sophisticated models, aimed more often at an audience interested in analyzing processes for automation. These elements belong to the **analytical level** of BPMN.

The last group is generally made up of the most advanced elements, which are intended to automate processes, although nothing prevents you from using them for documentation and analytical purposes.

We will learn much more about elements of the BPMN notation in the following chapters (there, you will see more object types described, as well as information about the categories used in BPMN), but for the purpose of comparing it with other notations, we will start by reviewing the basic elements, which will be used in our example diagram. Please note that BPMN diagrams are usually drawn horizontally, but I am using a vertical representation to make it consistent with previous examples.

Modeling concepts	Shape and name	Description
Start of the process diagram	Start event	The first element of a process diagram representing an event that starts a process. Please note that all events are circles, but each type has a distinct look.
End of a process diagram	End event	The last element of a process diagram representing that an event is the result of a process. Please note that all events are circles, but each type has a distinct look.
Process split	Gateway	Split of a process into multiple outcomes. Please note that in BPMN, several types of gateways are possible with different icons inside. A diamond without an icon inside represents the most common type: exclusive gateway.
Process step (simple)	Task	A simple process step representing some work to be done in a process. Please note that both tasks and subprocesses are shown as rectangles, but each type has a distinct look.
Process step (complex)	Subprocess	A more complex step of a process, which can have several sub-steps – often shown in a separate diagram. Please note that both tasks and subprocess are shown as rectangles, but each type has a distinct look.

Table 7.4 – Basic shapes of BPMN

Apart from the basic shapes of BPMN, which represent the most important modeling concepts, there are, of course, more, which will be covered in depth in *Chapters 8* and *9*. In the following table, you can see two more shapes, which you will see in the following figure.

Non-standard modeling concepts	Shape and name	Description
Data	Data object 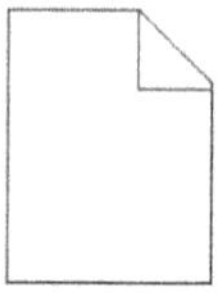	Data used in a process (also serving as an input or an output for the process)
Storage/IT system	Data store 	Permanent storage of data in a form such as a cabinet or IT system

Table 7.5 – More advanced shapes of BPMN (selected)

As you can see, there are many similarities between BPMN and previous notations. Now, let's take a look at the complaint process modeled in BPMN.

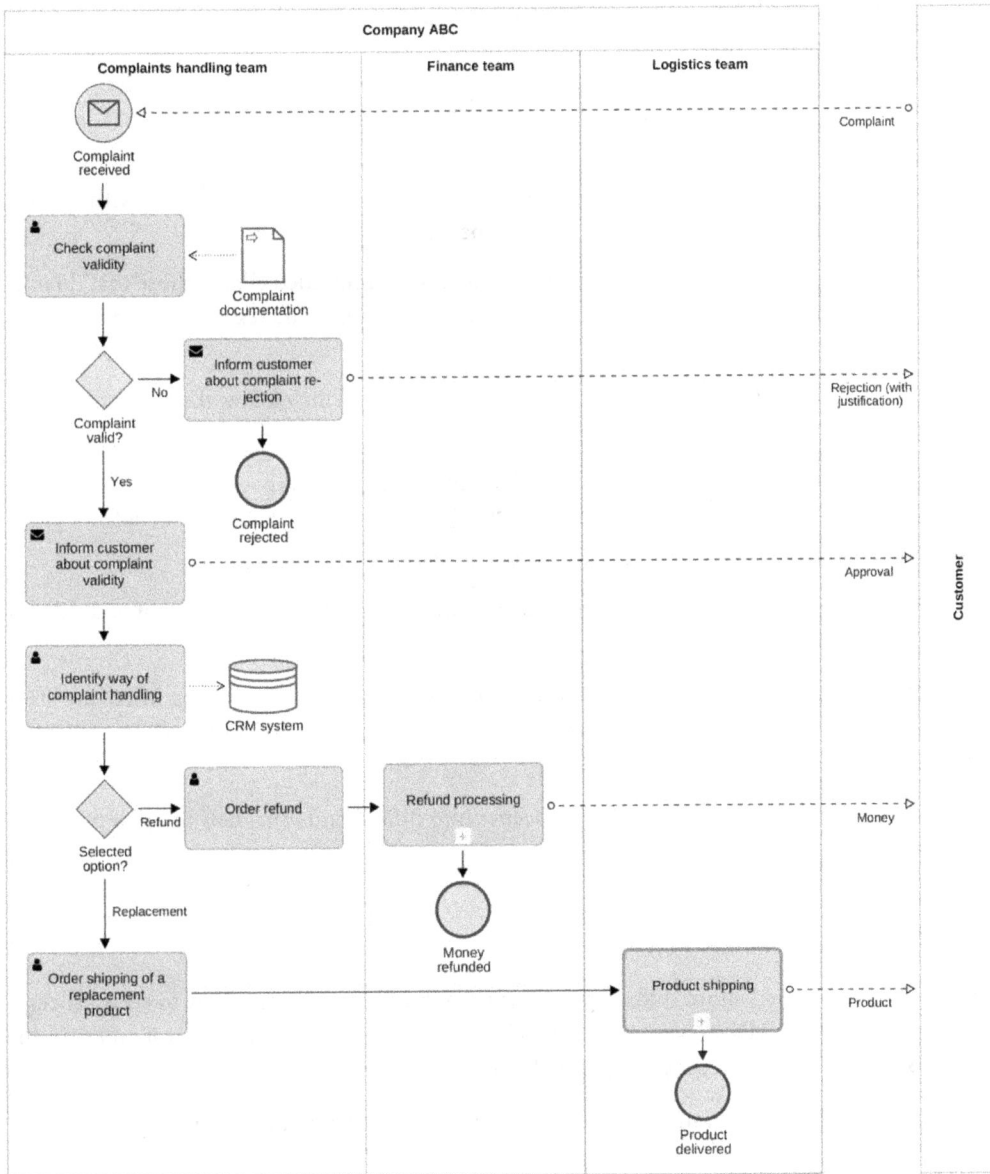

Figure 7.4 – Example process as a BPMN business process diagram (created in ADONIS)

As you can see, BPMN took many of the proven methods introduced by other notations and extended them, so that the following apply:

- Start and end events are both represented as circles but can easily be distinguished from one another based on the border thickness.

- You read a process diagram by following an arrow called a sequence flow drawn with a solid line (we will cover additional types of flows in the following chapters).

- Process steps (also known as activities) are rectangles with rounded edges. Those that do not need to be decomposed are called tasks, and those that are more complex (usually marked with a "+" icon) are called sub-processes.

- Places where a process diagram splits are called gateways, and they follow the common shape of a diamond.

- You can easily see who does what because elements of the BPMN diagram are placed inside pools and lanes representing process participants (e.g., companies) and more detailed logical divisions of those participants (e.g., departments or teams).

Therefore, if you have already modeled a process using other notations, chances are that you will be able to read BPMN diagrams pretty easily.

However, BPMN offers you many more options in comparison with other notations. There are also pitfalls – places where shapes and parts of models may look familiar, but in BPMN, they have a slightly different meaning.

That's why in the following chapter, we will dive deeper into BPMN and learn how to use it properly – beginning from the basics.

Summary

In this chapter, you learned about different ways of modeling processes and how to read process diagrams. You saw how BPMN uses proven approaches from other notations and how it differs from those notations so that you can easily grasp visual differences in diagrams.

In the next chapter, we will learn more about the things that you need to know about BPMN to use it in practice.

Further reading

If you want to learn more about the modeling notations covered in this chapter (and more), I suggest you check out the following books and resources:

- If you would like to learn more about the history of BPMN and its relationship with other standards, such as XPDL, I would recommend a very interesting free paper, *Business Process Model and Notation—BPMN*, by Mark von Rosing, Stephen White, Fred Cummins, and Henk de Man, available at `https://www.omg.org/news/whitepapers/Business_Process_Model_and_Notation.pdf`. You can also read the full book, *The Complete Business Process Handbook: Body of Knowledge from Process Modeling to BPM, Volume 1*, by Mark von Rosing, Henrik von Scheel, and August-Wilhelm Scheer.

- If UML is something you would like to explore further, I would suggest checking out this resource from my go-to expert in UML Filip Stachecki. Visit `https://www.uml-diagrams.org/` for a great overview of what UML has to offer.

- If you prefer learning from books, on `https://modeling-languages.com/list-uml-books/`, you will find a list of many great titles. This website offers many useful resources about UML modeling (and more) as well.

- Finally, I would recommend `https://agilemodeling.com/` by Scott Ambler.

- For more resources, visit the GitHub repository for this book: `https://github.com/PacktPublishing/Practical-Business-Process-Modeling-and-Analysis/tree/main/Chapter07`. You will also find information about notations such as VSM or UPN that we did not cover in this chapter.

BPMN – What You Need to Know

In *Chapter 7*, we briefly covered the history of process modeling notations and learned about the most important shapes of BPMN. BPMN is a very logical and easy-to-learn process modeling notation if you know how to approach it. In this chapter, we'll cover its basics, including both its most crucial elements – that is, objects that can be used in a model (events, activities, gateways, swimlanes, artifacts, and data objects) and fundamental concepts that are important for having a proper understanding of BPMN diagrams.

In this chapter, we're going to cover the following main topics:

- How to read a BPMN diagram

- When and how to use gateways in BPMN

- How start and end events can be used

- How to show work in a process diagram with tasks and sub-processes

- How to add more meaning to your BPMN diagram with additional elements, such as swimlanes, artifacts, and data objects

> **Note**
> This chapter is authored by Zbigniew Misiak.

How to read a BPMN diagram

Let's go back to the complaint handling process you know well from *Chapter 7*. This time, we'll spend some more time discussing the basics of BPMN and explaining the usage of the key elements of the notation based on this example.

The following is a horizontal version of the BPMN diagram. While BPMN allows both horizontal and vertical orientation of diagrams, the horizontal orientation is much more common:

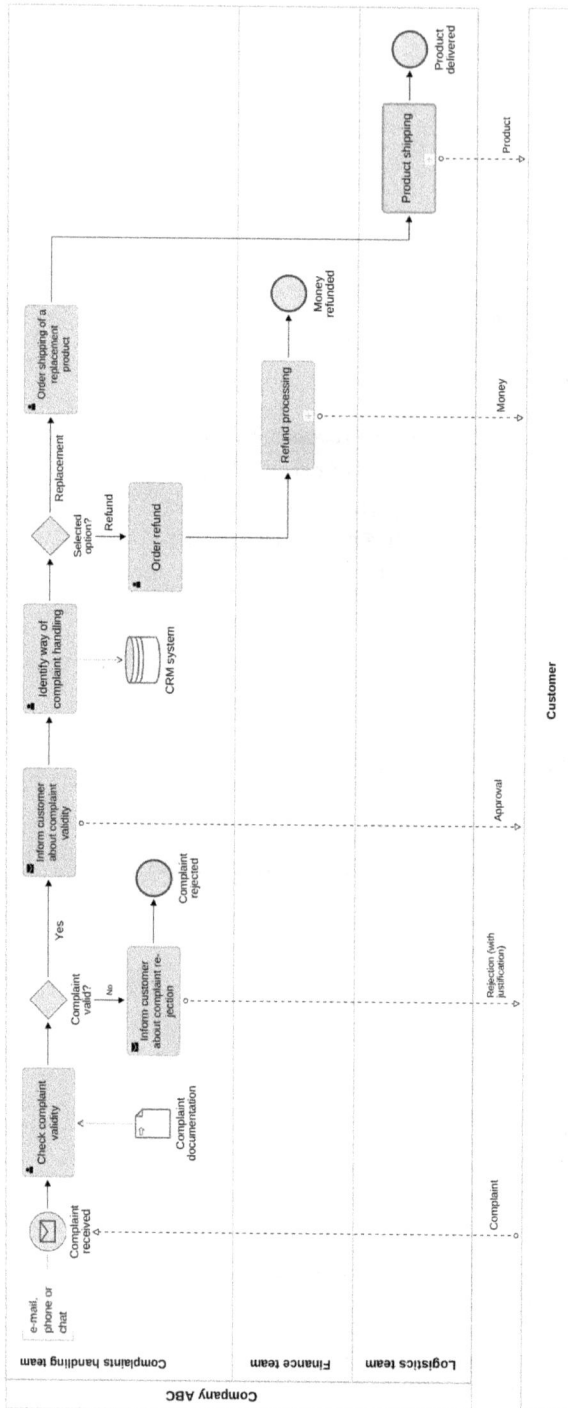

Figure 8.1 – Complaint handling process in BPMN

The following two figures (*Figure 8.2* and *Figure 8.3*) will help you learn more about the most important shapes you can see in *Figure 8.1*:

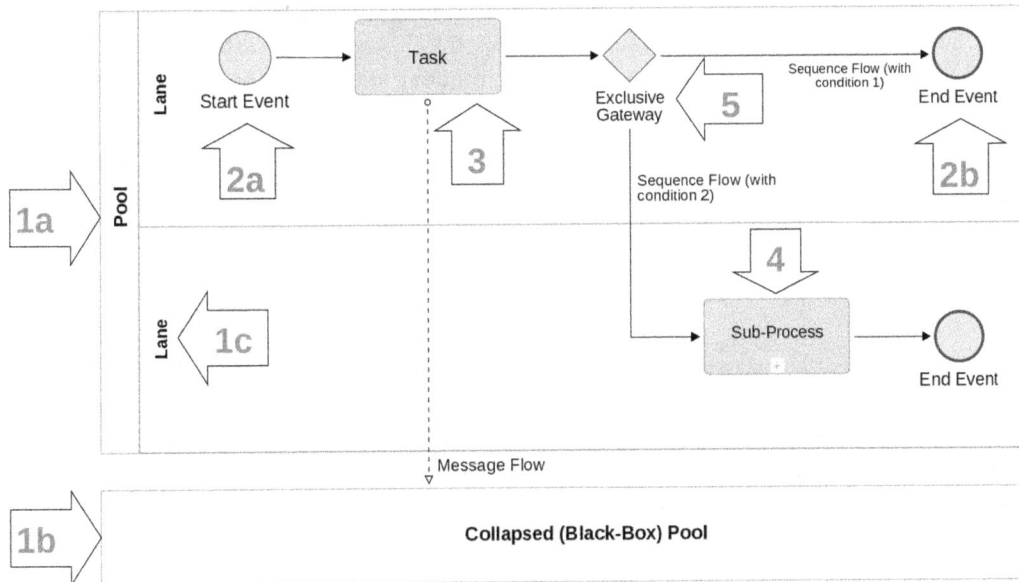

Figure 8.2 – Basic elements of BPMN (part 1)

Pools and lanes

Let's begin by looking at the two large rectangles that are visible in *Figure 8.1*: **Company ABC** and **Customer**. In BPMN, we call them **pools**. This name is meant to suggest that the process flows inside the pool (just like people swim inside a swimming pool). This is a very important concept that we'll develop further in a moment.

As you can see, the diagram can contain several pools if you want to show the different participants involved in the collaboration, each with its own process. The pool can contain lots of elements inside, describing the process in more detail (this is visible for element **1a** in *Figure 8.2*), or just representing that there's such a participant, without specifying how it performs its process (this, in turn, is option **1b**).

For **Company ABC**, we can see not only elements representing what happens in the process but also some kind of structure showing us who performs what steps. Modeling **lanes** (see element **1c**) are used for this purpose.

It's worth noting that the name **lane** is another reference to a swimming pool; it can be divided into lanes to organize the way people swim. In our case, we have a lane representing the **complaints handling team**, an additional one for the **finance team**, and finally one for the **logistics team**.

The second pool, representing the customer, doesn't contain any visible content. Such a pool is often called a **collapsed pool** or **black-box pool**. This suggests that from the point of view of the diagram, we either don't know what the performer does or we don't need to describe it in this diagram. Just in case you're concerned about missing some important insights regarding customer activities, for example, the idea is to make a diagram more readable by hiding unnecessary details. However, they can be captured in another connected diagram.

As you'll see later in this chapter, pools (and lanes) are great not only for showing the responsibilities in a process but also for showing what the cooperation between different entities involved in a process looks like. Pools and lanes are part of the BPMN category called **swimlanes**.

Events

While pools and lanes allow us to understand who does what in a process, we still need to understand the scope of the process, especially what makes the process start and how it ends. For this purpose, BPMN offers us events – elements that are always shown as circles. In our example diagram (*Figure 8.1*), we have two types of events: a **start event** (**2a**) and an **end event** (**2b**), which have a thin single border and a thick single border, respectively.

BPMN also allows you to create slightly more complex intermediate events, something that will be covered in the following chapter (*Chapter 9, Advanced BPMN*). However, all the events represent some state of reality that's important for the process. Unsurprisingly, start events represent situations that cause our process to start. End events, in turn, show the results of the process, its products, or final states (positive or negative). In our example, we have one start event, **complaint received**, and three end events: **complaint rejected**, **money refunded**, and **product delivered**. This allows us to see the scope of the process right away, even without knowing the individual steps of the process.

It's worth noting that if a process flows through several organizational units represented by modeling lanes, we model it to show continuity within the process – subsequent lanes don't begin with start events and don't have end events at the stage of transferring work to a further lane.

Activities

Now that we know how to represent the scope of the process, it's time to cover an equally important aspect: how to represent work that needs to be carried out in a process. Those steps representing work (called **activities** in BPMN) can be described as **tasks** and **sub-processes** and are shown as elements **3** and **4**, respectively. Without them, modeling a process diagram would be nearly pointless.

Tasks and sub-processes are always shown as rectangles with rounded corners. Tasks represent simple, indivisible process steps that we don't need to decompose further for a more detailed description. Sub-processes, on the other hand, represent more complex process steps. These steps could be described in a more detailed model (this approach allows us to navigate from the main model to the lower-level diagrams) or simply serve as placeholders showing places where such decomposition could potentially take place.

Often, sub-processes are useful when we have many diverse things (tasks) to do, and they're carried out by different roles in the organization. Sub-processes are usually marked at the bottom with a + symbol, indicating that they may hide **something more** than ordinary tasks.

We can see the division between simple and more complex elements in our example, where steps such as **Check complaint validity** and **Order refund** are tasks. On the other hand, more complex steps such as **Refund processing** and **Product shipping** are sub-processes because we could probably define at least several tasks for each of them, most likely being something more than a sequence of activities (for example, in the case of a payment refund, we perform it differently when the customer makes the payment by bank transfer and differently when the payment is made by credit card).

Gateways

As we just mentioned, processes are rarely simple sequences of consecutive activities. Therefore, to be able to separate a process into different paths (splitting) and to connect these paths (merging), we must use another type of object in the BPMN: **gateways**. Gateways (see element **5**) are always represented as diamonds (rhombuses) with incoming and outgoing arrows representing process sequence flows.

In our example, the simplest type of gateway is used – that is, an **exclusive gateway**. Exclusive gateways represent places in the process where we have two or more paths available, of which only one can be selected. In the case of the **Complaint valid?** gateway, we have **Yes** and **No** as options, while for the **Selected option?** gateway, there are two mutually exclusive options for handling complaints: **Refund** and **Replacement** (of course, in practice, we would have more paths presenting other possible ways to handle a complaint, but this would make our diagram a bit harder to read).

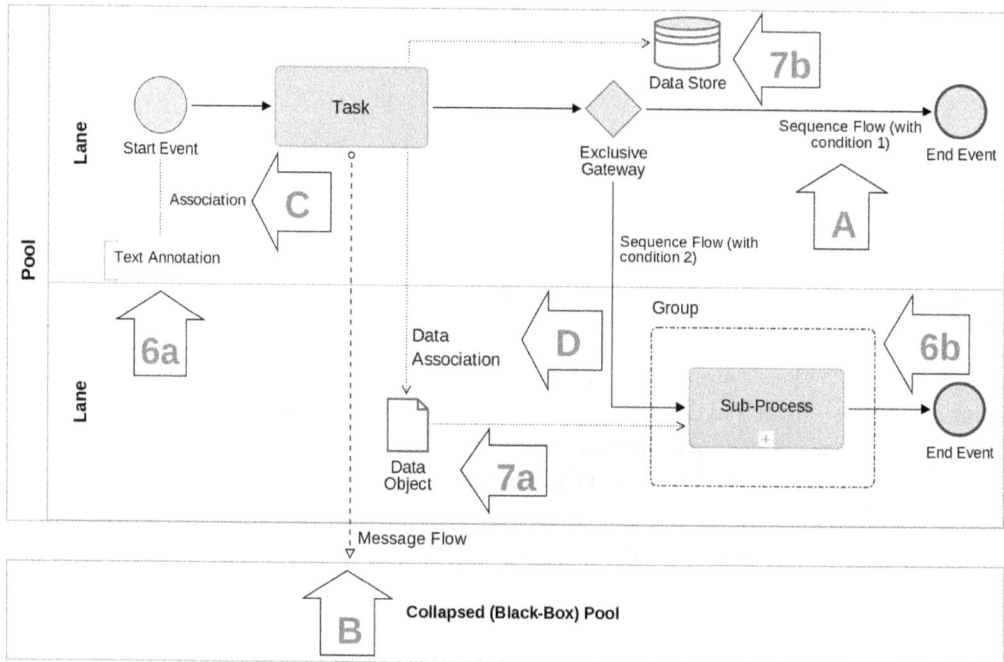

Figure 8.3 – Basic elements of BPMN (part 2)

Activities, events, and gateways are called **flow elements** in BPMN and they allow us to document what happens during the process flow. However, simply placing those elements one after another wouldn't allow us to figure out what the logic of the process is.

Connecting objects

For this purpose, we would need an additional category of BPMN: so-called **connecting objects**, or colloquially speaking, arrows. The most important type of arrow in BPMN is the **sequence flow**, which is always marked by a black solid line with a full triangular arrowhead at the end (shown as element **A** in *Figure 8.3*).

As the name implies, this kind of arrow shows us in which sequence elements are activated as it connects events, gateways, and activities within a pool so that it's always clear what comes before and what comes after the given element in the process. The sequence flow shows us the control we have over the elements of the process – either implemented by the process automation tool or by the process owner, who controls what happens in the process.

Usually, the sequence flow is just a line without additional markers or texts but if it's used where the process paths split (most commonly after the gateway), you'll often see textual labels on the arrows that help you figure out which path represents which flow (in our example, it will help you figure out what will happen if our process needs to support the **Refund** option, and what will need to be done for the **Replacement** option).

To summarize our principle regarding the process flow, we can say that a process always flows within a specific pool and can move between different lanes: from the start event through various activities and gateways to the end event, always following the sequence flow arrow (no **gaps** or **jumps**).

Since a sequence flow can only occur within a single pool, how do we show that different entities work together? This is where an additional arrow type – **message flow**, labeled as element **B** – comes in handy.

Unlike the sequence flow, we can only use it between pools. The message flow is always marked with a dashed line. At its beginning is a circle filled with white, and at the end is a triangular empty arrowhead.

A different type of line might suggest that this type of flow behaves differently from a sequence flow, and indeed this is the case. While a sequence flow tells us about control and suggests that a process has a defined course that can be enforced one way or another, a message flow shows that different entities exchange messages, or information, with each other. However, those exchanges are more like requests, proposals, or suggestions to another entity. A customer has the right to make a complaint but can't force an organization to acknowledge it if it's unfounded.

The elements that we've discussed so far allow us to describe the logic of the process and show how it interacts with other participants. With this knowledge, you can now read the vast majority of BPMN diagrams. However, apart from those key building blocks of the notation, there are also other categories of objects that give us more options in two additional areas – conveying additional information about the process and describing how to use data in the process.

Artifacts

To provide additional information about the diagram for the people reading it, so-called **artifacts** are used in BPMN. There are two types of artifacts: **text annotation** and **group**. These are visible as elements **6a** and **6b** in *Figure 8.3*, respectively.

These objects allow process modelers creating AS-IS or TO-BE diagrams to capture useful comments relating to how the process currently works or what we want to change about it. However, note that artifacts don't change the meaning of the diagram, which is based on the elements that we discussed previously. So, for diagrams serving as documentation and for those used for automation, artifacts only provide more information without influencing the core message that's captured in a process diagram.

A text annotation is an element that allows you to place some text in the diagram. It has a very characteristic shape of a left square bracket with text inside. Text annotations can be placed anywhere inside a process diagram or connected with a particular diagram element. The former option makes sense if your comment is relevant to the whole process. The latter option is useful if we want to show that the comment applies to some specific diagram part. In this case, an additional type of arrow – an **association** drawn with a dotted line (element **C**) – is used. In our example, text annotation is visible next to the start event and shows the following text: **Email, phone, or chat**.

A group, in turn, allows us to visually distinguish certain elements of the diagram to emphasize that they have something in common and belong to some specific category. A group is shown as a rectangle with rounded corners, drawn with a line composed of dots and dashes (which reminds me of Morse code). The group isn't connected to other elements of the diagram by arrows, so it's easy to distinguish it from (nearly) all other elements of the notation. Groups can have labels that show what the contained elements have in common.

The last category of BPMN objects is **data objects**, which (not surprisingly) allow us to show how data flows in the process. There are several types of data objects with different visualizations, but usually, they look like a sheet of paper with the top-right corner folded (in our example diagram shown in *Figure 8.1* it's **complaint documentation** – that is, element **7a** from *Figure 8.3*).

In our example (*Figure 8.1*), we can also see a specific type of data object (**CRM system**) that looks like a cylinder with three stripes at the top (element **7b**). To show how data flows from or to an activity in a BPMN diagram, we can use the **data association** arrow. This looks very similar to a plain association, but it has an arrowhead drawn with a black line (element **D**).

As shown in *Figure 8.1*, objects in BPMN can differ within each type. For example, tasks may have icons in the top-left corner indicating what type they represent; inside the events, there may be special icons indicating how the process starts (for example, our start event has an envelope icon inside, which means that the process was triggered by a message from the customer); and sub-processes may differ, for example, in the style of the border. This way, BPMN allows us to convey additional information about the process. We'll cover those shape differences in this and the following chapter.

Overall, if we tried to count all the possible combinations of allowed shapes, icons, and line styles, there would be over a hundred shapes that have a specific meaning. Luckily for us, not all these elements are equally popular. Therefore, in this book, we'll start with the most useful and popular elements and devote the most attention to them. For those that are less frequently used, we'll allocate less space, but we'll point out when and for whom they could be useful.

How does the process flow?

As we know from the previous section, one of the more important issues is to understand what work needs to be done in a process and what the relationships are between the various elements, or, more simply, what needs to be done and when.

It seems trivial, but for someone who doesn't know the whole process well, the mere information about what is to be done won't be enough. It's like giving a person learning how to cook a recipe for a dish but without information on when to add which ingredients. The mere fact that we'll perform all the necessary steps isn't enough – we can't perform them in the wrong order or do something that wasn't needed in that situation.

Process models can be small or large, simple or very complex, but regardless of their size and complexity, when we analyze them, we can distinguish certain recurring patterns. The concept of workflow/process **patterns**, which were created for analyzing process automation (workflow) solutions, proves to be very useful in analyzing processes and learning modeling notations too. That's why we'll be using them in this book.

While discussing various process patterns, we'll be using an additional concept since it's part of BPMN specification – the **token**. This isn't one of the notation elements that can be used when drawing a BPMN diagram since it's only a theoretical concept. However, it's very useful for understanding how a process is executed, especially when there are several paths within a process. In case you're curious, there are BPM tools that allow you to use tokens in practice – either for simulating business processes or for visualizing the progress of work in a process. However, BPMN specification doesn't require tokens to be implemented in modeling or automation tools.

A token is born when a start event is triggered and then flows through the process along the sequence flow arrow until it reaches the end event, where it's consumed.

Sequence

The simplest possible pattern is a **sequence** – a series of actions that are performed in succession. This sequence shows what should happen first so that it's possible to move to the next stage of the process. To discuss this sequence, we'll once again refer to the concept of a token.

Imagine that we're building a house. First, we must prepare the foundation. Only then can the walls be put up. Once the walls are standing, we can think about the roof. Common sense tells us that the idea of speeding up construction by putting up walls on an unfinished foundation and covering this with a roof is risky.

Let's look at an example of such a simple sequence:

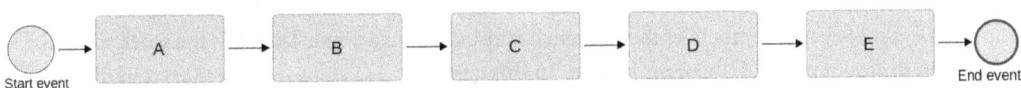

Figure 8.4 – Sequence

When the process is started, the token goes to task A and makes it activated. This is a formal name from specification In practice, this doesn't necessarily mean that someone has already started working on task A (for that, you still need a resource, such as an employee assigned to that task), but that if all the circumstances are favorable, you can start working on task A (as opposed to task B, which isn't feasible yet).

Then, at some point, the work on task A begins and, after some time, when it is still in execution, it is completed. When modeling, it's important to be clear where the scope of one process step ends and the next begins. When task A ends, the token flows along the sequence flow arrow to task B, and so on until the last task. When the last activity in the process is executed, the token reaches the end event and is consumed by it. Within a process instance for a sequence, we have only one token, so the moment this only token is "consumed," the life of the instance ends, and we can consider that we have nothing more to do.

If our process wrote a log or a diary (or if we had a system that documented what tasks were performed), we would always have the following entries in such a **process log**: ABCDE. There could be differences in who performed the tasks, when they were performed, and how long they lasted, but for such a process, it isn't possible for steps to be skipped (ACDE), duplicated (ABBCDE), or to occur in a different order (AEDCB).

Now, let's turn to complaint handling and look at a slightly different example of a sequence – a simplified version of the diagram we've been working with so far, in which only one of the paths is included (we assume that the complaint is always valid and that we always make a refund):

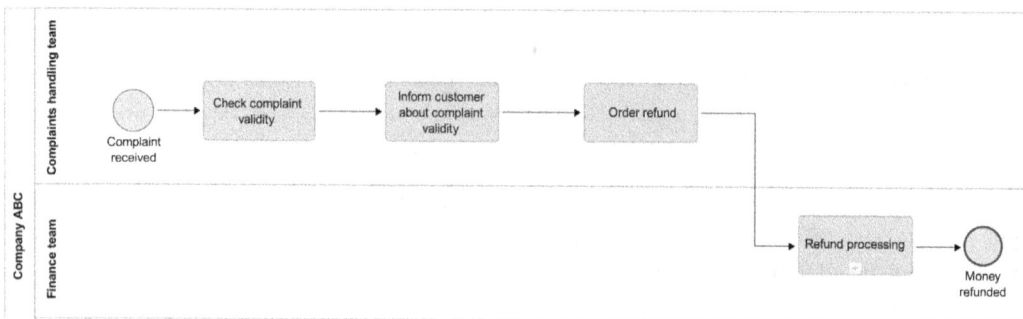

Figure 8.5 – Example of a sequential process with process steps in different lanes

As shown in *Figure 8.5*, the elements of the sequence may be within a single lane, but the work may also flow between different units of the organization. In this case, process steps may be placed in different lanes. From the point of view of the sequence, this placement isn't important – what's important is that the moment one element of the process ends, we move on to the next – that is, only after analyzing the validity of the complaint can we inform the customer that their complaint has been accepted as valid, and only after that can we set up a refund order, without which payments can't be processed.

Exclusive gateway (XOR)

In the previous section, we dealt with processes that were a simple sequence of steps. However, usually, our processes are more complex and some fragments are only performed if some condition has been met. The most common way to model such a situation is to use the exclusive gateway. This is often called the **XOR gateway (exclusive OR)**:

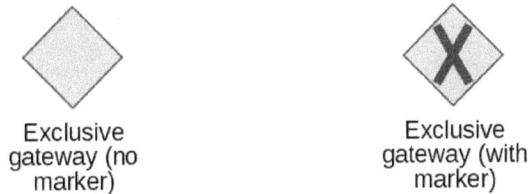

Exclusive
gateway (no
marker)

Exclusive
gateway (with
marker)

Figure 8.6 – Two possible visualizations of the XOR gateway

The XOR gateway can be a simple diamond, or it can have an X marker in the center. Interestingly, while these two visualizations are allowed, they shouldn't be mixed within a single model. Within the organization, it's good practice to determine how XOR gateways should be drawn to avoid confusion. I'm in favor of using XOR gateways without the X marker in the middle, but I know that for many people, the X is a great mnemonic to help them remember that it's an XOR gateway.

Naming

The BPMN specification doesn't impose a specific way of naming exclusive gateways. So, in practice, you can encounter different approaches, as shown in *Figure 9.7*. In one approach, you don't name XOR gateways, instead only making sure that the conditions/labels of the arrows coming from the gateway are sufficiently clear (for example, **Complaint valid** and **Complaint invalid**).

I prefer the second approach, in which the XOR gateway is named with a question (for example, **Complaint valid?**), and the answers to this question are placed on the sequence flows coming out of this gateway (for example, **Yes** and **No**).

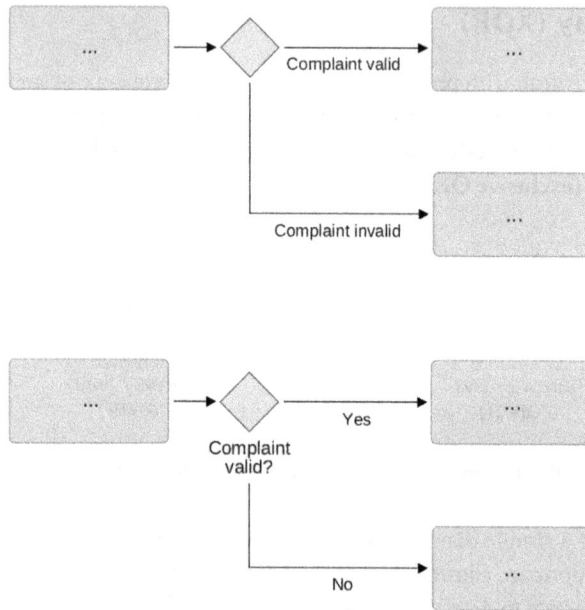

Figure 8.7 – Possible naming conventions for paths outgoing from the XOR gateway

It's worth remembering that while we have some freedom regarding the way we name the conditions for sequence flows that come out of the exclusive gateway, we aren't allowed to use tasks to represent which paths need to be taken and avoid using conditions on arrows. Such an anti-pattern is shown in *Figure 8.8*:

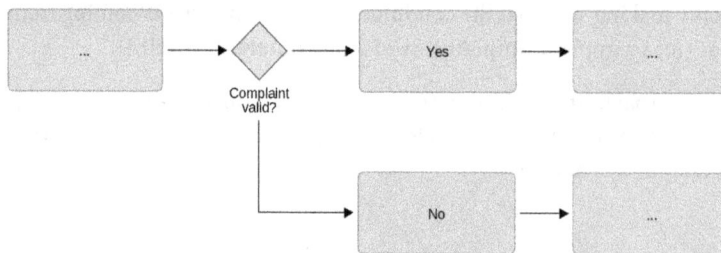

Figure 8.8 – Anti-pattern – describing paths by tasks

Alternative process paths

We already know that the exclusive gateway is used to split the process into several mutually exclusive paths. But what can happen further down the process? From a notational point of view, each of these paths may lead to its end event. We had such a situation in our example process – the first gateway led to the **Complaint rejected** end event, or further, to the section where we dealt with an acknowledged complaint, where the process split into two paths, ending with the **Money refunded** and **Product delivered** end events:

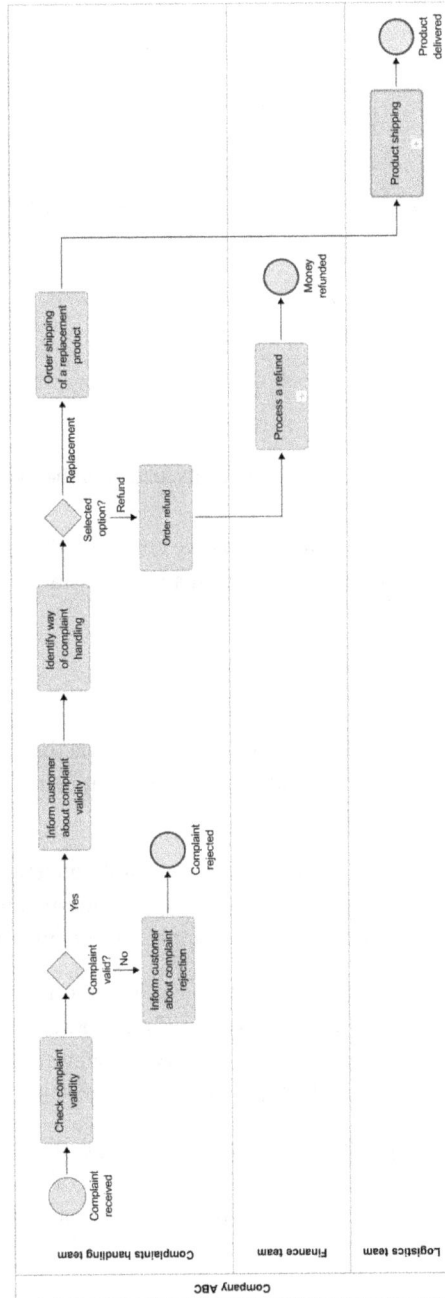

Figure 8.9 – Example process with exclusive gateways and multiple end events

Using a simplified process with tasks named using letters, we could present the situation of multiple paths that don't meet again and lead to different end events, as shown in *Figure 8.10*:

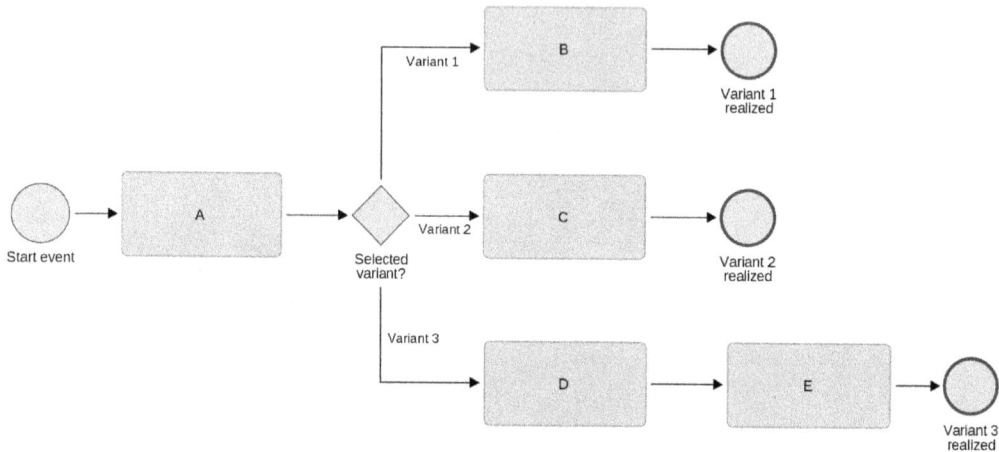

Figure 8.10 – A process with multiple end events following the exclusive gateway

Depending on the selected process execution variant, we could get the following process logs: AB, AC, and ADE. Two/three paths can't be executed within a single instance, so we would never get an ABC, ABDE, or ABCDE entry.

Merging

In addition to the situation where our paths split and don't come together again, it's also possible that only a certain part of the process differs, depending on the variant being executed; the rest remains identical because the process paths merge.

As we'll learn in a moment, merging is an extremely important concept in processes where more tokens are created. However, the exclusive gateway, as we know, doesn't multiply the token – it only redirects the token to the correct path. So, how can we approach merging in this case?

The specification gives us two possibilities. On the one hand, we can skip the XOR merging gateway and attach sequence flows directly to the next process step. On the other hand, we can insert a second exclusive gateway that will merge the process paths. This merging gateway doesn't need to have a name. It's also worth knowing that it passes through all the tokens that enter it.

As you may imagine, the fact that the specification has given us such possibilities has led to the emergence of two schools of modeling with very strong views. Representatives of the first one opt for modeling without a merging XOR because it makes the diagrams simple and easy to read, plus it saves space.

Representatives of the second school, on the other hand, claim that XOR gateways should always be inserted in pairs – opening and closing – because only this makes diagrams readable.

In my experience, the first approach is closer to those with **business** roots. The second, on the other hand, is more common among people with either IT or academic backgrounds. I hypothesize that those users associate closing gateways with closing parentheses in code, which becomes a habit.

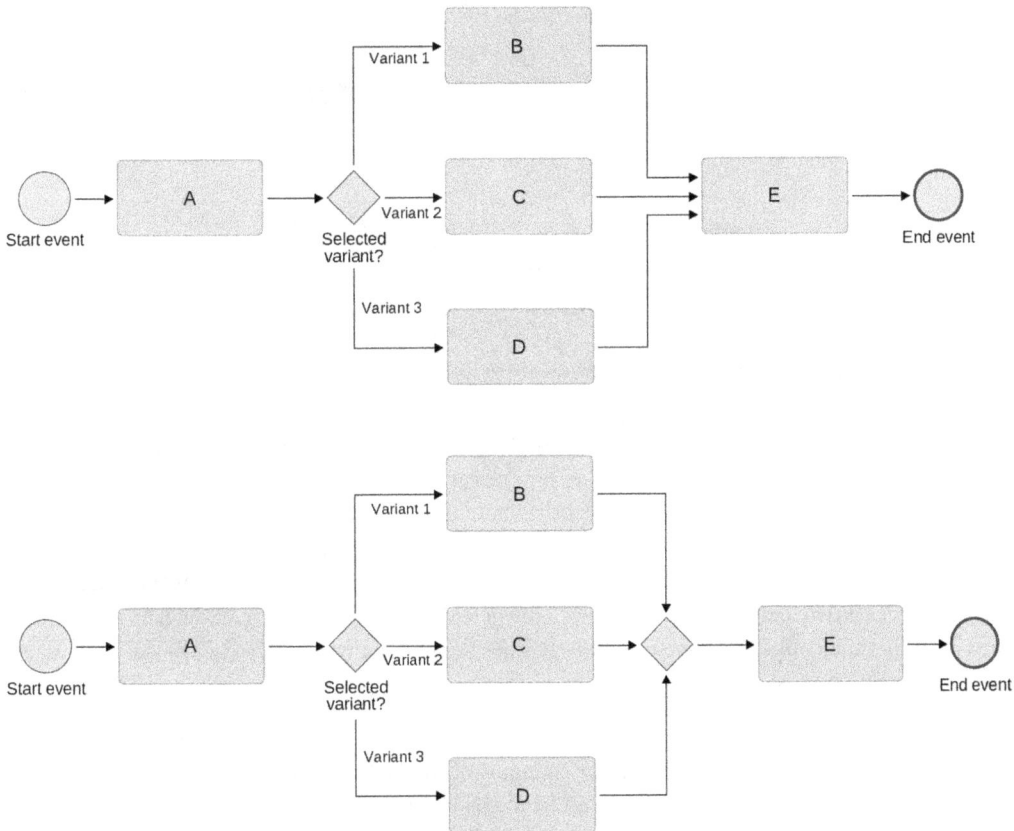

Figure 8.11 – Two possible approaches to modeling a process with mutually exclusive paths

Regardless of which way we choose to model, the preceding two diagrams have identical meanings and could generate the same process logs: ABE, ACE, and ADE.

XOR gateways in practice

Let's return to our business scenario and see how the exclusive gateway works in practice (using the simplified example shown in *Figure 8.12*). As you can see, if the complaint is considered valid, then we proceed to the **Inform customer about complaint validity** task. Alternatively, it can be considered invalid, at which point we perform the **Inform customer about complaint rejection** task. It isn't possible to perform both tasks within a single process instance.

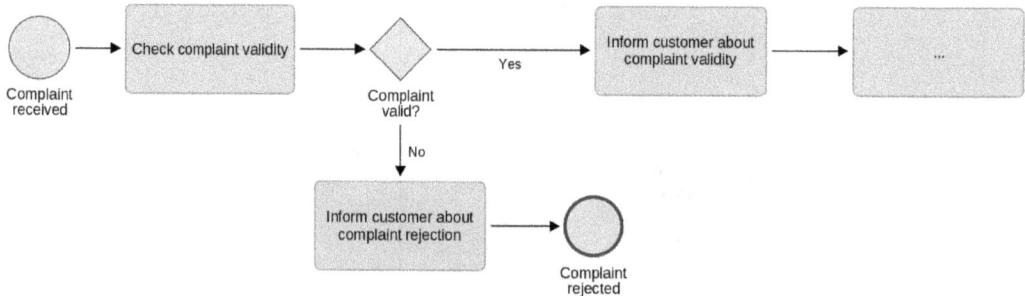

Figure 8.12 – Part of the example process – exclusive gateway in practice

One interesting feature of BPMN is worth highlighting here. While in many modeling approaches, such as flowcharts, there are diamonds representing places where decisions are made, information is verified, and so on, BPMN gateways have a slightly different meaning. Although gateways are referred to as decisions according to the BPMN specification, it's worth noting that the types of gateways that are often used in practice fall into a category called **data-based gateways**. This means that a gateway – especially an exclusive gateway – is something like a streetcar track gearbox. It determines which process paths get their token. By itself, a gateway doesn't generate work, increase the duration of a process, or increase its cost.

But how does the gateway *know* which flow should receive the token? This is influenced by comparing the data coming into the gateway from earlier elements of the process with the conditions found on the sequence flows. This data is often obtained from tasks or sub-processes before the gateway, but it doesn't have to be this way – it could have been obtained much earlier before the occurrence of the gateway that will handle it. Again, let's refer to our example – it could be that the **Identify way of complaint handling** task will provide us with the data based on which we'll proceed further along the path of **Replacement** or **Refund**.

From a technical point of view, the user in charge of the **Identify way of complaint handling** task, who's working in the IT system, would have a radio button on the case handling form where they would select the correct option – **Replacement** or **Refund**. This selection would affect which task would be received upon completion of the current task. It could also work like this in the earlier part of the process, where the user would have to mark whether the complaint is legitimate or not.

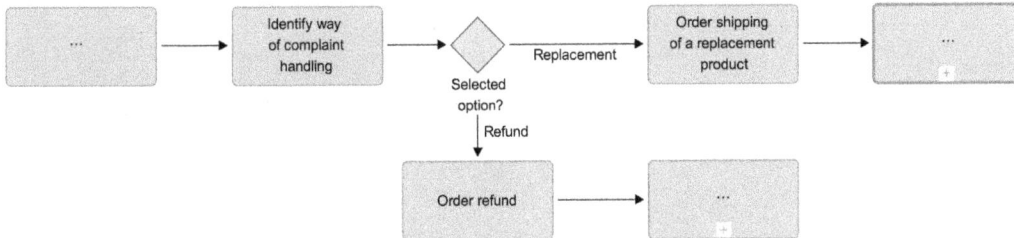

Figure 8.13 – Part of the example process – gathering data in a task that's been placed before a gateway

However, it's also possible to have a situation where the customer is asked to specify the preferred way to resolve the complaint earlier in the process. If we assume that the customer always completes the relevant fields in the form (and doesn't change their mind afterward), our process will look like this: the data as to the preferred way of resolving the complaint is obtained in the **Receive the form** task and only affects the process in the **Selected option?** gateway. At this point, our employee would have to choose whether they recognize the complaint as valid or not. Whether they'd get the **Order refund** or **Order shipping of a replacement product** task wouldn't depend on what they *click* in the system because the data would already be available.

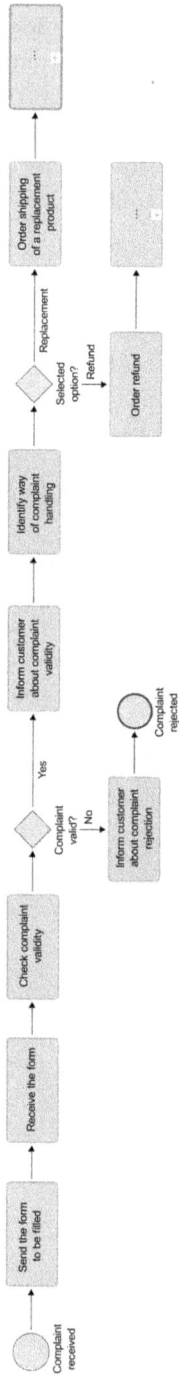

Figure 8.14 – Part of the example process – a gateway using data
that was gathered in the earlier part of the process

Once we have the data, and the token has reached the gateway, the conditions that were defined for each path of the process are analyzed. In the case of an exclusive gateway, the first path whose condition is met will receive the token and the process will proceed. Naturally, such exclusive gateway behavior makes it very important to define the conditions on the paths properly. Therefore, a very popular approach is to try to document processes in such a way that exclusive gateways have only two outgoing paths, representing **Yes** and **No** options for the question asked in the gateway. We saw an example of this approach in *Figure 8.14* for the **Complaint valid?** gateway.

However, BPMN allows us to separate process paths in other ways so that process flows coming out of a gateway have conditions that are more complex than **Yes** and **No**. This gives us more options (especially if we have three or more possible flows in our process) and makes the diagrams more readable (otherwise, we might have to insert gateways one after the other), but it also forces us to take more care with well-thought-out conditions.

Watch out for errors with conditions

Let's use a slightly more elaborate version of our process to analyze an anti-pattern of how to handle this situation. Let's assume that our organization has decided to simplify the claims handling process so that claims for low-value goods are automatically accepted so that no employees are involved. *Figure 8.15* shows us that complaints with a value of less than 100 USD will be automatically accepted, and a refund will be issued (we assume that this is the condition of our **fast track**), while complaints of more than 100 USD will be analyzed by an employee.

However, what about complaints worth exactly 100 USD? Unfortunately, our process would encounter an error in such a situation and won't be able to continue because none of the provided paths supports such an amount. For the reader of the process, this is confusing, but for the automation of the process, it's an even bigger problem.

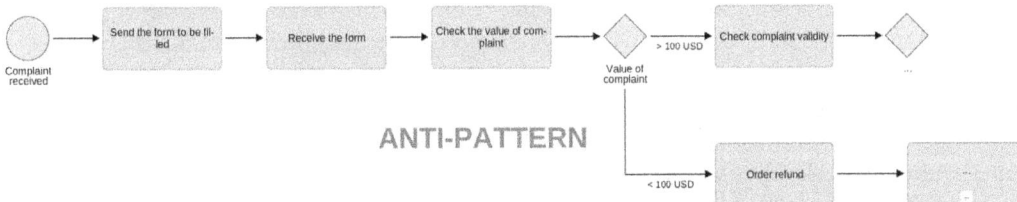

Figure 8.15 – Anti-pattern – unclear conditions regarding the amount of the claim

It would also be problematic if our conditions overlapped. Such a case, however, would be less troublesome than the previous one, because then you can take the first path for which the condition was met.

Default sequence flow

But what if we can't anticipate all the options that might exist? Here, BPMN offers us a solution that's ingenious in its simplicity – the default sequence flow. We often use it to refer to process flows that are coming out of an exclusive gateway. The default flow has an additional designation that's visible as a diagonal crossed line near the beginning of the arrow.

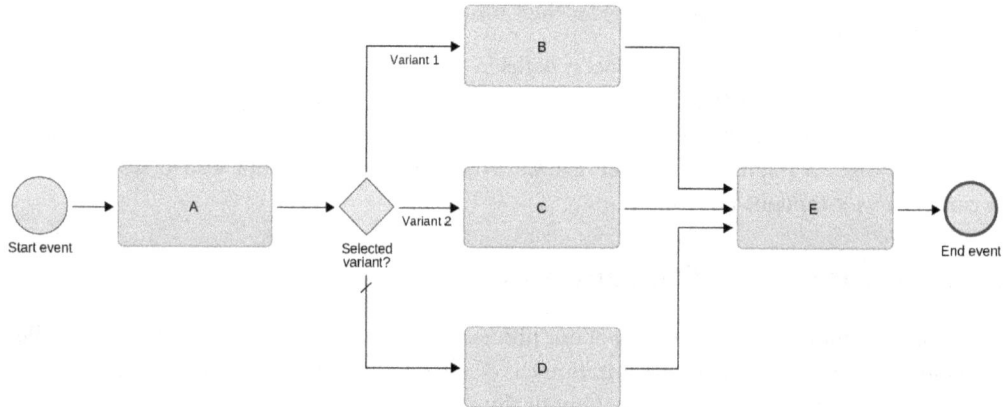

Figure 8.16 – Default sequence flow

The default sequence flow allows us to indicate which path the process should take if none of the conditions that have been defined on the other arrows are met. This guarantees that our process will never get stuck due to receiving data we didn't expect.

It's worth remembering that the default flow doesn't necessarily mean the most common way to execute the process or the option that's most expected from the point of view of the organization (the so-called happy path). It's simply a designation – if none of the defined conditions are met, take that path. IT professionals may associate it with the ELSE command present in many programming languages.

Parallel gateway (AND)

Another type of data-based gateway is the **parallel gateway**, also referred to as an **AND gateway**. This gateway is denoted by a + symbol in the middle. However, unlike the XOR gateway, this symbol isn't optional, so in the case of this gateway, the + symbol must always be present.

A parallel gateway is used to mark process paths that must be executed before the process can move on. Interestingly, this doesn't mean that the activities along these paths must run at the same time (as its name might suggest), but simply that they must all be completed, before we can continue. The key point is that the order isn't important to us (if it was, we could use a simple sequence), but that all the elements must be executed.

The AND gateway has a simple interpretation and behavior, so often, there's no need to show its name on the diagram (although this is allowed). The principle is simple: when a token enters the parallel gateway, it's multiplied so that each of the sequence flows coming out of the gateway gets its token (without checking the conditions). Since the token is generated independently of the conditions, it makes no sense to add conditions on the paths coming out of this gateway.

However, what happens next with the tokens that are created in this way? Each of them flows further through the process and activates further tasks. This sounds harmless, but one of the biggest pitfalls lurks here for people new to BPMN. Let's look at *Figure 8.17* and consider what would happen in such a process.

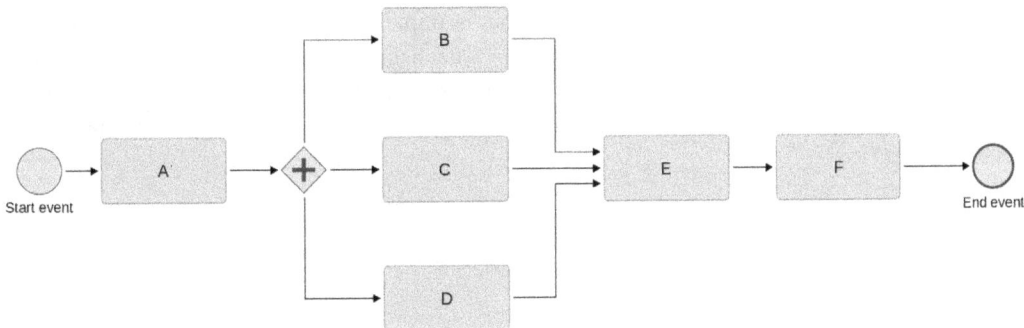

Figure 8.17 – A risky way of modeling – using only the opening (diverging) AND gateway

To make it easier to describe this situation, let's assume that task B takes 5 minutes, task C takes 10 minutes, task D takes 15 minutes, and tasks E and F take 1 minute each. There's no problem with the availability of the resources responsible for these tasks.

The beginning of the process is as we expected: after task A was performed, our token reached the parallel gateway and split into three tokens – one for each path – and thus activated tasks B, C, and D. After 5 minutes, task B was completed (our log is AB for now). Next, the token reaches task E and activates it. After another minute, task E is completed (our log is ABE) and the token reaches task F, which is activated. Another minute passes and the token reaches the end event, where it's consumed. At this point, our process log is ABEF. Another 3 minutes pass and task C is executed (so we have ABEFC). Its token also goes to task E and activates it, after which it continues until the end event (when the second token disappears; we already have a log of ABEFCEF). Something similar will happen with the third token that goes out of task D. When the last token reaches the end event and thus the process instance (that is, its specific execution) ends, our process log will look as follows: ABEFCEFDEF. As you can see, we have executed tasks E and F three times!

Paradoxically, this situation isn't a mistake from the point of view of BPMN but the way of modeling, in which we have a splitting AND gateway without a closing (merging) gateway will likely be highly confusing for most people because they won't expect multiple executions.

Of course there may be processes where we aim for such behavior, but usually, when people think about parallel process paths, they tend to expect a situation where we must wait until all the parallel parts are done before we move on. This behavior is extremely useful from a business point of view because it shows us that we can assemble a device only when we have all the parts ready, or that we can only prepare an offer to a customer when we have both the business part and the financial part ready. So, how can we get this behavior?

The solution to our problem is the concept of synchronization. Unlike exclusive gateways, where the use of a merging gateway was optional, for parallel gateways, we'll often want to insert a parallel merging gateway as well.

Let's see what inserting such a gateway will change in our example. For simplicity's sake, I'm no longer inserting task F, which was previously intended to show what happens when tokens flow through the process uncontrolled. This time, we're no longer assuming how long tasks take or what the availability of resources is because we want to focus on how synchronization using a merging parallel gateway looks like in practice.

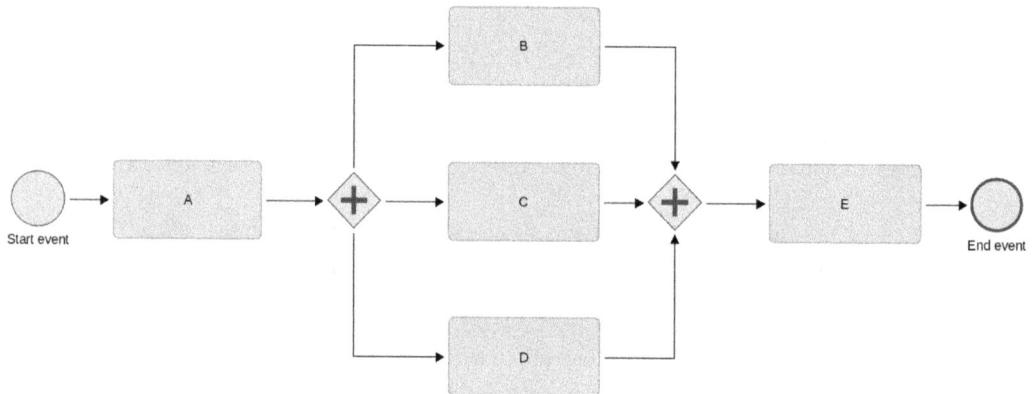

Figure 8.18 – Synchronization with a merging AND gateway

The beginning is familiar: after task A is completed, the token arrives at the AND gateway. At this gateway, it's multiplied (we can jokingly say that the token is photocopied) so that each of the sequence flows leaving the gateway gets its token. Then, each token flows independently and activates tasks on the paths. The availability of resources determines the order in which they're performed. Thus, the ABCDE, ABDCE, and ACBDE orders are possible.

But how do we know that we can already perform task E? And why do we perform it once? It's all due to the merging parallel gateway, which provides synchronization. The moment the first token reaches the synchronizing gateway, it's stopped because the gateway waits for tokens from all sequence flows that enter it. In our case, only when the third token arrives at the gateway will the gateway merge all of them into one and allow it to pass.

To make it work like this, we need to use a merging parallel gateway. That's because using the exclusive gateway for merging would miss the mark as it would let every token through.

A common question related to modeling parallel gateways is that by changing the position of tasks in the diagram, can we suggest what should happen earlier and what should happen later?

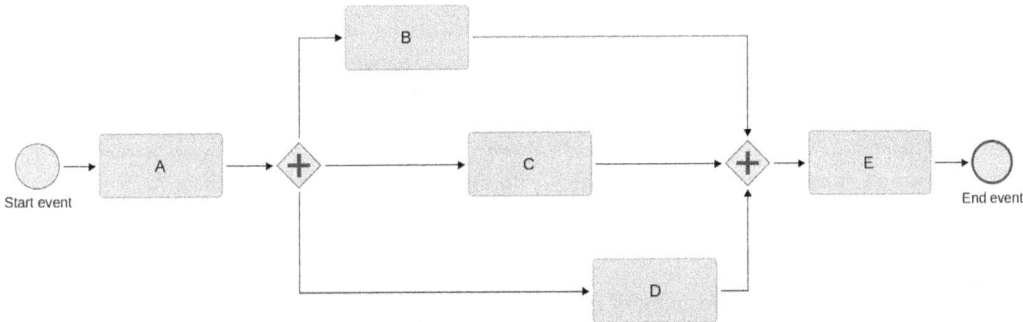

Figure 8.19 – The placement of tasks within parallel paths doesn't determine the timing of their execution

BPMN suggests timing of the process steps by showing the logic of the flow. So, by following the sequence flow arrow, we can see that task B must happen after task A and before task E. However, whether we arrange tasks B, C, and D in a single line vertically, or they're placed in some other way (like what's shown in *Figure 8.19*), it won't affect how the diagram is interpreted.

The order of execution depends solely on the resources performing the tasks and how the tokens arrive at the process steps to activate them. So, it's worth remembering that if we want to guarantee a specific order of execution of process steps, the sequence is a good choice. On the other hand, a parallel gateway should be used when we want to guarantee some flexibility in the order of execution of certain process steps while ensuring that the process can only continue after selected elements are executed.

Inclusive gateway (OR)

So far, we've discussed the two most common types of gateways: the exclusive gateway, which allows us to describe the situation where only one of many options can be selected, and the parallel gateway, in which all paths leaving the gateway must be executed for the process to continue. In practice, however, we also encounter processes in which certain paths are always executed and some only under certain circumstances.

Naturally, we may be tempted to describe them as a combination of XOR and AND gateways, but we can also use another type of gateway – an inclusive gateway. An inclusive gateway behaves like a combination of XOR and AND gateways, thus allowing more complex process flows to be described more compactly.

An inclusive gateway is often referred to as an OR gateway. Like all gateways, it's shown as a diamond, and the icon in the center indicating its type is a circle (which can be associated with the O in OR).

How do you read the processes with an OR gate? Simply put, if a condition isn't defined on the path coming out of the gateway, then this path will always get a token (that is, it will behave like an AND gate).

If, on the other hand, a condition has been defined on the sequence flow coming out of the gateway, it will only get a token if the condition is true. Importantly, an OR gateway can have multiple outgoing paths with conditions that can be mutually exclusive but can also overlap.

In practice, this means that when you see an OR gateway, you should take a closer look. In a situation where we have an OR gateway with sequence flows without conditions, it behaves like an AND gateway. If, on the other hand, we see an inclusive gateway whose paths all have mutually exclusive conditions, its behavior will be identical to that of an XOR gateway.

Most often, however, the inclusive gateway is used in situations where multiple paths may be active. Since we'll be reading the conditions found on the paths, it's usually useful to give the gateway a name – just like exclusive gateways, and unlike parallel gateways.

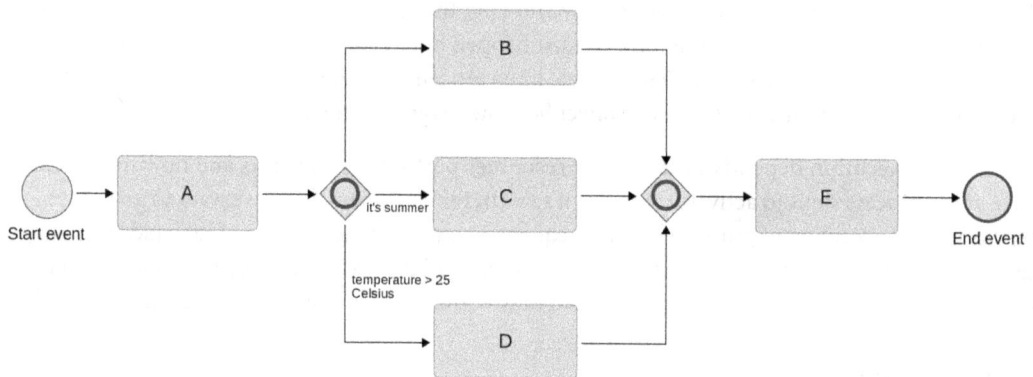

Figure 8.20 – Example of an OR gateway

How will this work for our example? Since the sequence flow leading to task B has no condition, this path will always get a token. On the other hand, as we can see, the conditions for sequence flows leading tasks C and D are constructed in such a way that all, only one or neither of them can be satisfied at the same time.

So, our process log could look like this: ABE (for cold spring), ABCE (for cold summer), ABDE (for warm spring), and ABCDE (for warm summer). However, there could be no ACE (because B must be executed since there's no condition for this path) or AE (because the synchronizing gateway won't let us through).

However, if a diagram doesn't contain a path without a condition following an OR gateway (that is, the path that would always get a token), it might be a good idea to add a default sequence flow to prevent a situation where none of the conditions are met and there's an error in a process causing the deadlock.

It's worth noting that our process could be modeled in a slightly different way: since task B is always performed, we could try to move it in front of the OR opening gateway. Of course, the requirement for this would be that tasks C and D can't be performed before B.

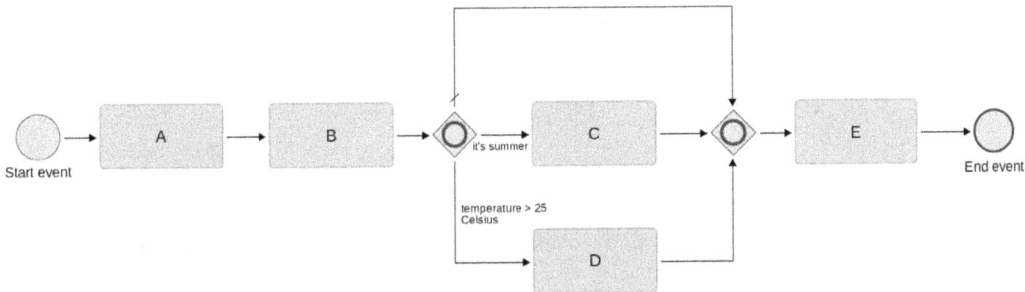

Figure 8.21 – Default sequence flow for an OR gateway

While modeling in BPMN, it's generally a good practice to make sure that the closing gateway is of the same type as the opening gateway. This is because if we were to insert a closing AND gateway, then in a situation where the opening OR gateway doesn't generate a token for each path, our process will get stuck.

Modeling without gateways

One of the interesting aspects of BPMN is how much freedom the specification authors left to users by giving them many ways to model. However, as we've already mentioned, such freedom and having many options to choose from aren't always helpful to us when we're wondering how to model a particular process.

In this section, we'll address the issue of modeling without using gateways. The idea behind this is laudable – if we don't use gateways, our models will be smaller and thus more user-friendly. However, as we'll see in a moment, a smaller model isn't always easier on the eyes. Therefore, the ways of modeling that are presented in this section shouldn't be taken as recommended. I only want to show what's allowed according to the rules of notation so that if you encounter such a model in practice or on an exam, will know how to interpret it.

Let's start with the parallel gateway. As we know, a token entering the AND gateway *multiplies* in such a way that each process path leaving the gateway gets its token. A similar effect can also be achieved in another way – we just need to add several outgoing sequence flows (without conditions) to a task or sub-process. Then, each of the paths will get its token!

In practice, both diagrams in *Figure 8.22* have the same meaning. The diagram on the left – with an AND gateway – takes up a bit more space, but you can immediately see how to interpret the model. In the case of the diagram on the right, you need to take a closer look at the process flows to make sure they don't have conditions and that each path gets its token:

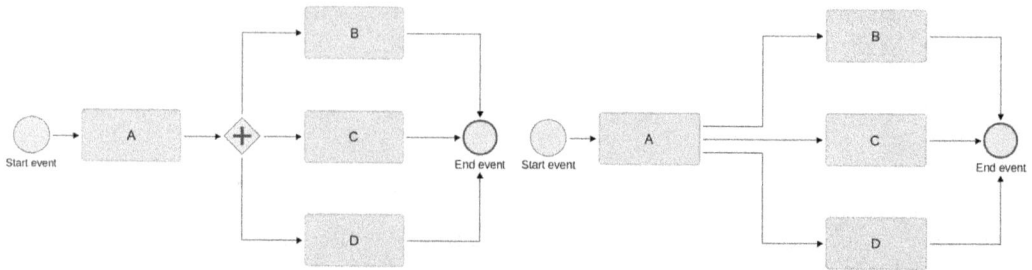

Figure 8.22 – Comparison – splitting process paths with and without an AND gateway

As we mentioned earlier, while it's possible to split paths without gateways, in most cases, skipping the synchronization gateway isn't a good idea. For example, *Figure 8.23* shows a situation in which nothing synchronizes the three tokens that were created in task A, which of course results in task E being executed three times.

As we mentioned for *Figure 8.17*, such a way of modeling is formally allowed, but you must be aware that many people will consider it a mistake and even more people will misread our intention, so this isn't recommended.

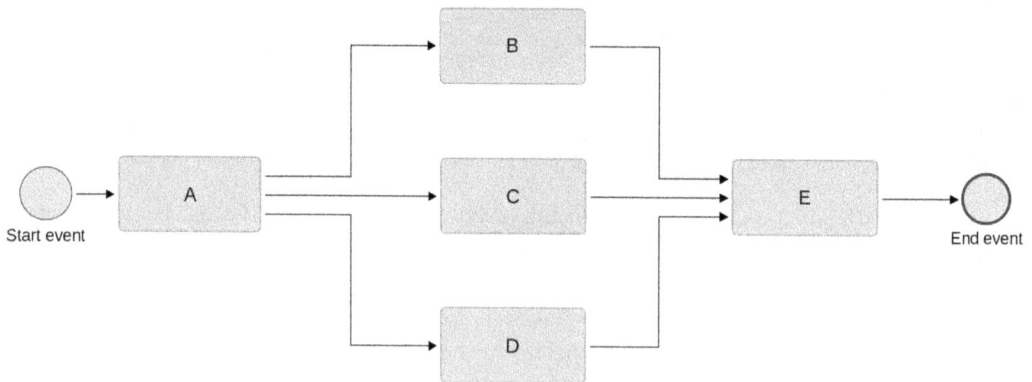

Figure 8.23 – A risky way of modeling – lack of synchronization

It's also possible to avoid using gateways when there are multiple flows with conditions (that is, the situations we discussed with XOR and OR gateways). In this case, a new type of sequence flow is needed – a conditional sequence flow. A conditional flow can come out of a task or sub-process, but it can't be used after gateways (for obvious reasons). Its appearance suggests that it's used to replace gateways since it has a special symbol of a small diamond at the beginning.

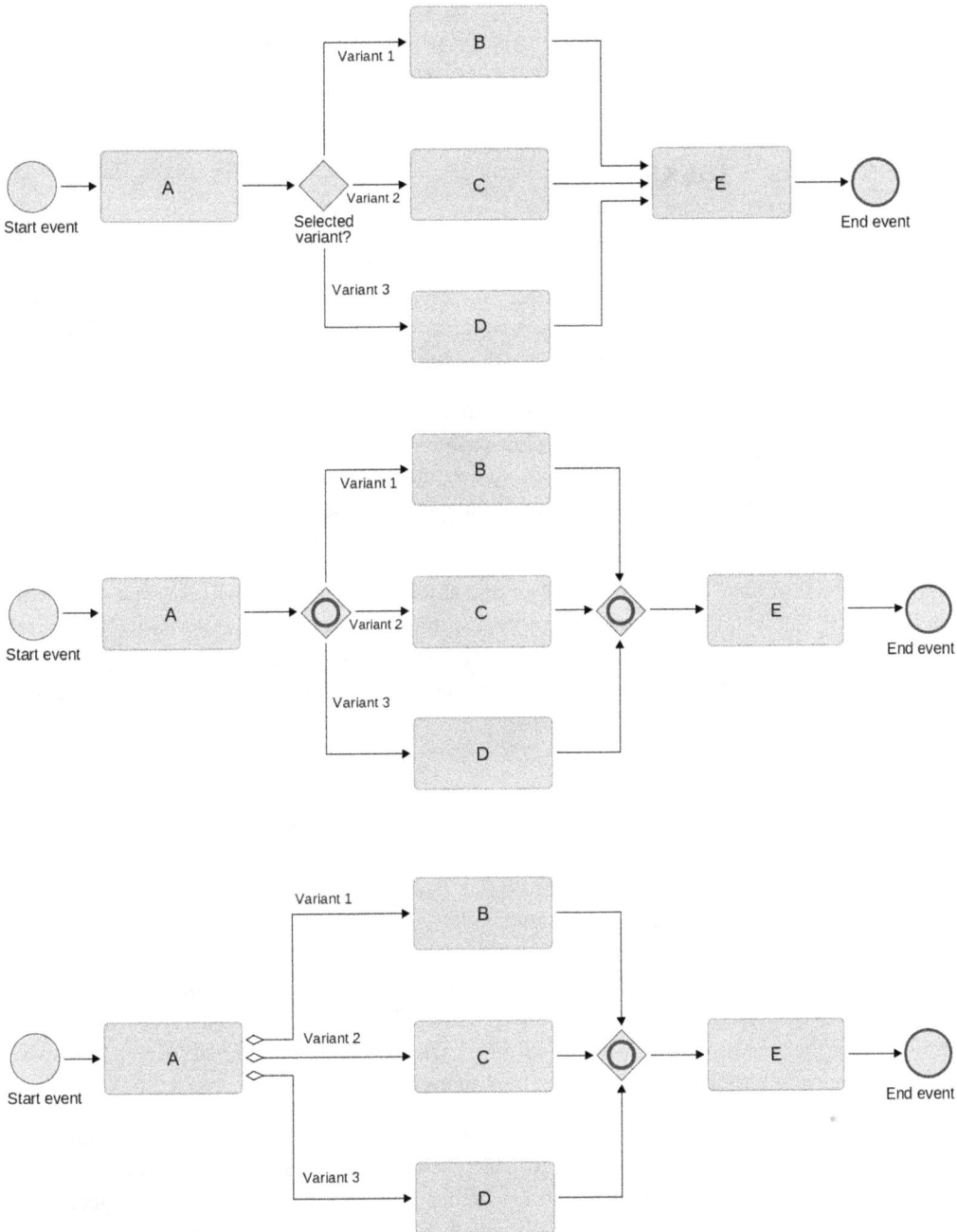

Figure 8.24 – Comparison of modeling with gateways (XOR and OR) and conditional flows

Figure 8.24 shows a comparison between a diagram in which we used an exclusive gateway, a diagram in which we used an OR gateway, and a diagram in which we used only conditional flows to split the paths. Naturally, these aren't fully equivalent diagrams because, for the exclusive gateway, we take the first path whose condition is true, while for the OR gateway and conditional flows, we check all conditions to determine which one is valid. In the first diagram, we can immediately see that only one of the conditions can be true. In the second and third, it isn't obvious unless we examine the conditions.

Process steps – tasks

We already know how to read the various types of process flows in the diagrams, but that's not all we might be interested in. One of the basic things we need to know about any process model is what work needs to be done in it. For this, we use tasks. A task represents an indivisible piece of work to be done in a process. Why indivisible? As we mentioned at the beginning of this chapter, BPMN offers two types of objects (activities) to describe the work to be done – tasks and sub-processes.

When our work is complex, can be broken down into multiple steps, and potentially performed by different actors, we should use a sub-process whose content can be described in a separate diagram. When there's no need to add more details in such a way, the task will suffice, especially since we can add a description documenting what's supposed to happen in a process step.

Tasks are represented as rectangles with rounded corners, most often with a name in the center. As with most elements of the BPMN, we can either stop at using a simple task with no type specified, which is perfectly sufficient for models that serve documentation purposes. Alternatively, if we're thinking of automating a process or need it for analytical purposes, we can set a specific type, which is symbolized by an icon in the top-left corner of the task. Those types tell us more about how the work of the task is done.

Figure 8.25 – The most common types of tasks – none, manual, user, and service

There are many different types of tasks, but it's useful to start learning about them with three basic ones: a manual task, a user task, and a service task. While an ordinary task, without a type, tells us that a specific step of the process must be performed, any of the three types mentioned previously allows a simple analysis to be performed of the degree of automation of our process.

At this point, it's worth mentioning one of the quiet assumptions of the BPMN specification authors. Their idea was that any diagram described in BPMN could potentially be the basis for process automation (there's even a special attribute stating whether a diagram is executable or not). Hence the name **task** – after automation, each task could potentially be routed to an employee to be performed.

User task

Let's start describing the three basic types of tasks by looking at the user task. A user task is marked by the user avatar icon in the top-left corner. This icon is commonly used in applications, where it represents the user of the application. It also commonly allows the user to access personal settings in their account.

The user's task is performed by a person in the information system through which the process is coordinated. Such a system can be, for example, a workflow/BPMS tool, but also a CRM, ERP, or "helpdesk" system such as Jira.

The important thing is that such a system controls the entire process. So, when a user performs the first task, the system, knowing what comes next based on the logic of the process, will assign the next task to the same or another user.

Service task

An even more advanced automation option is described by a service task. It's marked with an icon of two cogwheels in the top-left corner of the task.

A service task is a process step that's performed fully automatically, without any user involvement. These tasks can include automatic calculations, document generation, data exchange between systems as part of integration, and more.

Formally speaking, however, from the point of view of the specification, not every automatic activity is a service. By definition, a service is an element in which an engine that automates a process calls out other software that provides some service. We can refer to the concept of **service-oriented architecture** (**SOA**) or the more contemporary concept of microservices.

Manual task

As we well know, not all process steps and processes are automated. In this situation, a third type of task – a manual task – comes in handy. A manual task is indicated by a hand icon in the top-left corner.

But what exactly should we consider manual tasks? The specification doesn't give us much help here as it gives an obvious example of a technician installing a phone. What's more, in addition to the obvious statement that a manual task is performed without support from a process automation engine (which is clear – otherwise, it would be a user task), the specification includes the note *nor any application*, while elsewhere it only states that a manual task isn't performed or managed by a process automation tool. In an additional document accompanying the specification (*BPMN by example*), we can see examples of manual tasks that, while not coordinated by a process automation tool, require IT support (for example, by sending an email).

Unsurprisingly, I'm often confronted with the question of whether manual tasks are those in which we don't use a computer at all. In my opinion, this isn't necessarily the case. Since the key issue is whether the task is coordinated by some kind of process engine, I use manual tasks where there's no coordination from the IT tool.

For me, an example of a manual task could be preparing an offer for a customer – that is, unless it's done in a CRM system, where you can see that someone is doing it and, if necessary, can forward the offer to the right person in the organization for approval before sending it to the customer. Similarly, if I'm working on a computer preparing a report in Excel, which I will then send via email to a colleague, the right kind of task here would be a manual task, not a user task.

If our process isn't automated, we can either not use task types at all or use manual tasks. If the process has been partially automated but contains steps that happen outside the system, then it may make sense to add user task steps where an employee can mark that they've performed some manual tasks. In the case of an automated process with manual tasks, the assumption is that the performers know what they're supposed to do and when, and the system automating the process will simply skip the manual tasks because it will treat them as invisible.

These three basic types of tasks allow us to analyze our processes very easily. For example, if we can see that all process steps are manual, then we can expect human error and delays. Most likely, adding support for employees through a process engine, using software robots, or more advanced process automation could greatly improve efficiency. However, even if our process can't be automated, we can expect that documenting it will help reduce the number of errors, while increased visibility of the process steps and the logic of a process may bring valuable ideas for improvement.

If we're dealing with a process, where most of the steps are user tasks and service tasks, we can expect better process performance. Of course, even in such a process, there may be situations where the user manually transfers data between two systems that coordinate two separate steps of the process. In such a case, the use of either the RPA tool or some other method of system integration will enable further improvement of the overall process.

Send and Receive tasks

The next two types of tasks we'll discuss are useful for more advanced modeling because they're used to describe the automated exchange of messages – one is used to send messages and the other to receive them. I'm introducing them at this point as a "foretaste" of what we'll be exploring in *Chapter 9*, which is devoted to more advanced elements of BPMN. However, it will also help me explain one of the most important concepts in BPMN – sending and receiving messages.

At this point, it's worth mentioning a few principles of BPMN regarding messages and icons. First, as we already know, by definition, messages are sent and received between different process participants (pools) and can be associated with a message flow arrow.

Second, as you may recall from the introduction to this chapter, the BPMN icon that denotes a message is always an envelope. This knowledge will come in handy in a moment when we discuss different types of events.

Third, in BPMN, active (throwing) elements always have dark icons, and passive (catching) elements have light icons. We'll expand on that soon.

Figure 8.26 – Tasks sending and receiving messages

Now that we know all this, it won't surprise us that a send task, which sends messages to other pools, will have a dark envelope icon in the top-left corner, while a receive task, which waits for a message from the outside for the process to continue, will have a light envelope icon in the top-left corner.

When using tasks that send and receive messages, it can be helpful to show the pools with which message exchanges take place, and to present the message exchanges with a message flows. However, this isn't mandatory, so you can present the sending and receiving tasks without showing message flows and other pools. This will help you save some space and avoid drawing many lines, although at the cost of losing some of the context.

Figure 8.27 shows the practical use of send-and-receive tasks in conjunction with message flows. Again, we're using the familiar complaint handling process – however, to represent the occurrence of sending and receiving tasks in tandem (as is very often the case), I've modified the process fragment slightly to describe the following logic: the process starts with the receipt of a complaint, which is submitted by the customer (again, here, we can see the start event, which is triggered by a message, as indicated by the envelope icon).

Then, the employee must analyze the complaint and inform the customer that the complaint has been rejected (if it isn't valid) or that the complaint has been accepted (if it's valid). In either case, we're sending a message outside our pool – in this case, to the customer.

The rest of the process has been changed slightly to make the example clearer. On the one hand, we assume that we always replace the goods (that is, we don't support refunds), while on the other hand, our acceptance also includes a request to the customer for shipping data.

At this point, it's worth noting the logic of the process: once we've informed the customer that the complaint is valid, our token immediately goes to the **Receive shipping details** task. However, since this is a receive task, we start waiting for a message from the customer. Only when the customer gives us the shipping data can we move on to the **Order shipping of a replacement product** task.

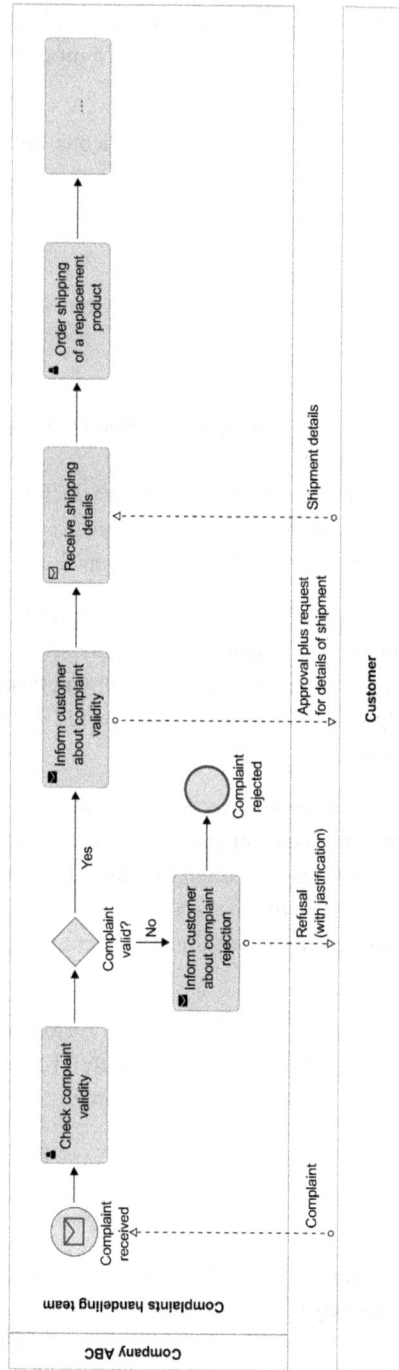

Figure 8.27 – Part of the example process – sending and receiving messages in practice

If the customer didn't respond to us, our process would never move on. Of course, this isn't something we're happy about because as part of the processes in which we communicate with others, we should be able to respond to the lack of response to our message. Fortunately, BPMN has several solutions to this problem, something we'll cover in *Chapter 9*.

In the case of sending and receiving tasks, it's worth remembering that the specification treats them as automatic process steps, so they shouldn't be used for steps in which an employee prepares and then sends an email. In such a situation, we could use, for example, a manual task or a user task, which can also send messages (this is denoted by an outgoing message flow arrow).

It's also worth noting that our **Inform customer about complaint validity** task is connected by a sequence flow with the **Receive shipping details** task. Some people assume that since we're sending a message out and waiting for a return message, we can skip the sequence flow, as shown in *Figure 8.28*. However, this isn't allowed as the two tasks must be connected by a sequence flow.

Those who find the concept of a token helpful can imagine that a token that doesn't have a sequence flow has no way to *jump* to the next task within the process as it isn't allowed to travel along the message flow.

Here, once again, the rule of reading BPMN diagrams comes in handy – we start from the start event and follow the sequence flow step by step, without breaks, always within a single pool, until the end event. As you can see, we would violate the *no-breaks* rule here.

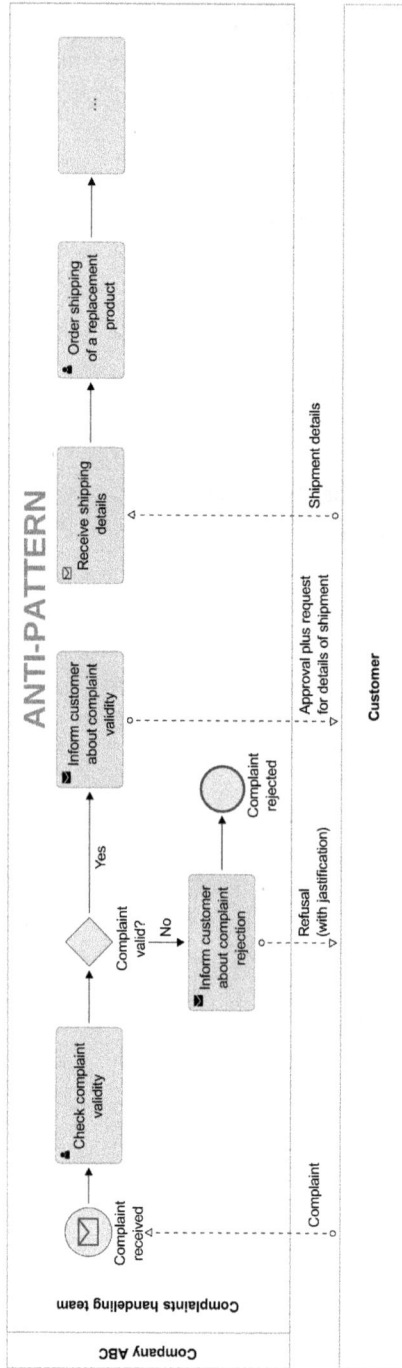

Figure 8.28 – Anti-pattern – a gap in a process between a send and a receive task

When discussing send and receive tasks, it's also worth mentioning another common mistake associated with these tasks, as shown in *Figure 8.29*. Many people who start working with BPMN associate the envelope symbol with the mail client icon and use send and receive tasks to show the exchange of emails between different teams (represented by lanes) within the same organization.

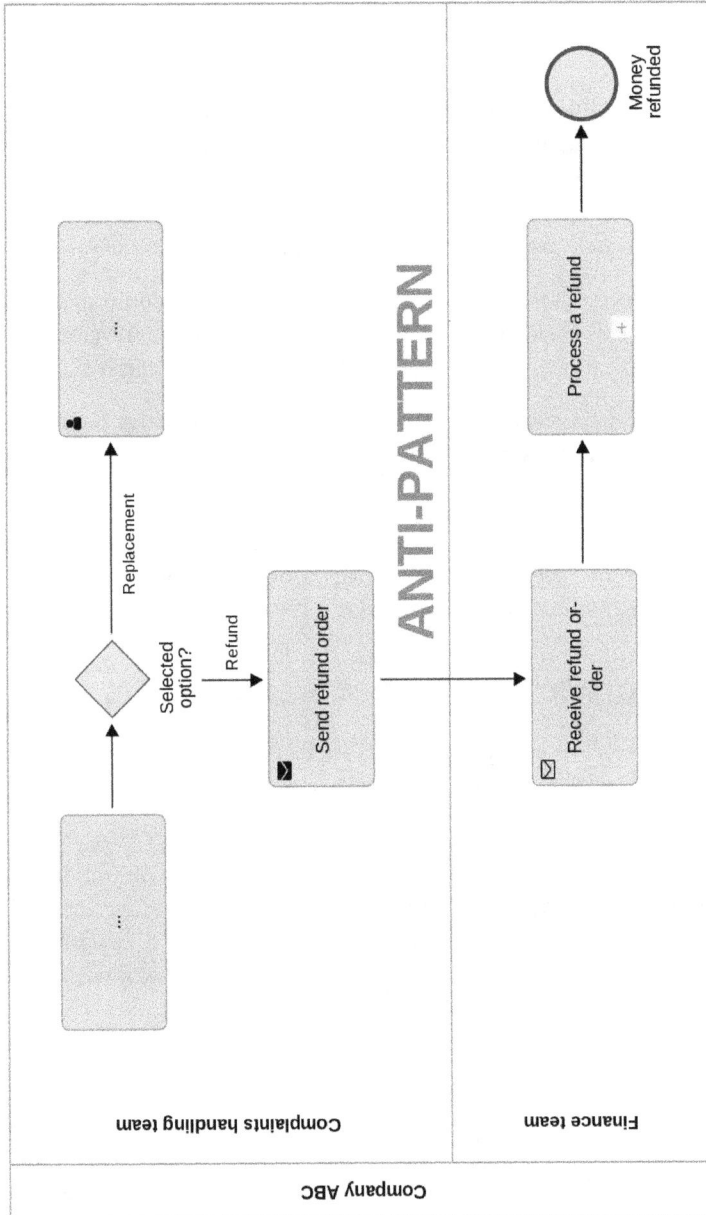

Figure 8.29 – Anti-pattern—sending and receiving messages within one pool

This approach is tempting, but unfortunately wrong. Since, by definition, a message is transferred only between pools and we aren't allowed to send messages within a single pool, we can't use send and receive tasks in this way either.

So, what can we do in a situation where we want to show that we're sending an email between one team and another? We can use a pair of manual or user (or no type) tasks – that is, **Send refund order** and **Receive refund order**.

This kind of modeling could make sense when, for our description or analysis, it's important to show clearly how we communicate with others using more classical methods. An example could be a process where paper documents are still used – someone must physically carry an envelope with documents and leave it at the secretary's office, and someone else must go and pick it up from there. By documenting those two tasks, we could show how much time this kind of work takes.

However, if it's a digital process, it may be enough for us to indicate that someone from team A sends something to someone from team B. This is because since the next task in the process will be in team B's lane, the very logic of the process shows us that the work has been transferred.

The task types that have been described so far are those most used in practice, but this isn't a complete list. In *Chapter 9*, we'll learn about some additional, slightly more advanced task types and discuss their use.

What we've learned here about send and receive tasks will come in very handy in a moment when we discuss the most important types of events in BPMN. Later in this book, we'll learn about special types of events that can replace send and receive tasks.

The scope of a process – start and end events

We already know how tasks allow us to present the work that needs to be done in a process. But how do we show what causes our process to start, and what results it can end with? As we already know, events are used for this purpose.

Events are an extremely useful element of the BPMN specification. They allow us to show what starts our process (start events) and what results our process may end up with (end events). In addition – and this distinguishes BPMN from other notations – we can use them to describe what important things may happen during the process (intermediate events) and how we'll react to these events in handling errors, exceptions, and special situations.

There are many different types of events in BPMN, some of which are useful for more advanced modeling scenarios (for example, process specification/automation), and some of which are used occasionally in practice. Therefore, in this chapter, we'll only focus on a few of the most common types of events, without which it's impossible to model in BPMN. This will help us understand the basics of how events work.

Simple start event

Start events are always shown as circles with a single thin line. The following is a start event with no trigger defined.

Start event

Figure 8.30 – Start event (no trigger)

Let's start with a simple start event. The start event is always represented as a circle with a single thin border. It represents what must happen for the process to start (technically speaking – what needs to happen so that a process instance or execution of a specific "case" can begin). In this case, the start event doesn't have a specific trigger defined (which is easily visible because there's no icon inside).

All start events are catching, which means that they passively *listen* to what's going on, and only when something happens that triggers them will they create a token that flows further and makes the process begin. Before the start event, there's nothing (at least from the perspective of the diagram of the process), so there can be no sequence flow arrows incoming to the start event.

Naming start events

The BPMN specification doesn't impose a specific way of naming start events. I like to name events so that their name clearly describes a certain state of reality that must exist for the process to start.

Various other approaches are also encountered in practice (shown in *Figure 8.31*), some of which may, for example, be inspired by flowcharts (**START**). While none of the examples shown are wrong from a BPMN point of view, they differ in their informational value. I like to use the passive side, which avoids confusion with the work that's done in the process. So, I could give the start event without a type a name such as **Summary of reasons of complaints needed** (for a process related to our complaint handling process) or **New employee needed** (for a process in which new employees are recruited).

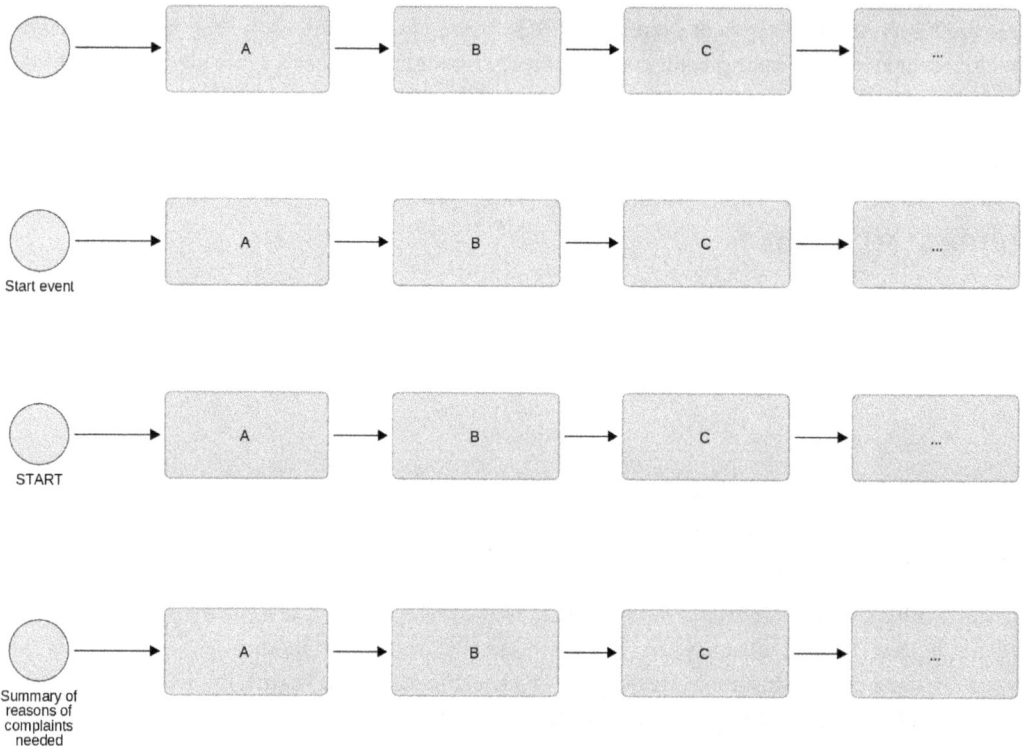

Figure 8.31 – Possible approaches to naming start events

A start event without a type is used often. It's particularly useful in processes when the decision of the employee involved in the process causes the process to begin, that is, it doesn't depend on external requests or isn't executed at specific times. Another possibility is a situation where some other process triggers our process through the mechanism of sub-processes. We'll discuss this case in more detail in the next section.

Simple end event

End events are also shown as circles. However, they have a border drawn with a single thick line. The following is an end event without any trigger.

End event

Figure 8.32 – End event (no trigger)

Now that we know how to use start events to show what starts our process, it's a good time to look at the other end of the spectrum and think about how our process might end. End events are the second element of the process scope. They illustrate what result our process might end with. Start events are, by definition, passive elements. End events are their opposite – they're always active, which in the BPMN specification is referred to as throwing.

As we know, there can't be anything before the start event in a process flow, so a sequence flow arrow can't enter it; only outgoing flows are allowed. On the other hand, in the case of an end event, we can't place any flow objects after them, such as events, gateways, or activities. Therefore, a sequence flow arrow can enter the end event, but there can be no outgoing sequence flow from it.

Each end event will have a border drawn with a distinctive single thick line, which allows us to easily distinguish it from the start event (which always has a single thin line).

Naming end events

As in the case of start events, the BPMN specification doesn't impose special ways of naming end events, so we have quite a bit of freedom. My preference is to name end events so that it's clear what result the process ends up with – that is, what we achieved. Ideally, this name should emphasize what *happened* in this process path and not something we *do*. This way, we can see *how* the process ended, not just that it's finished, as shown here.

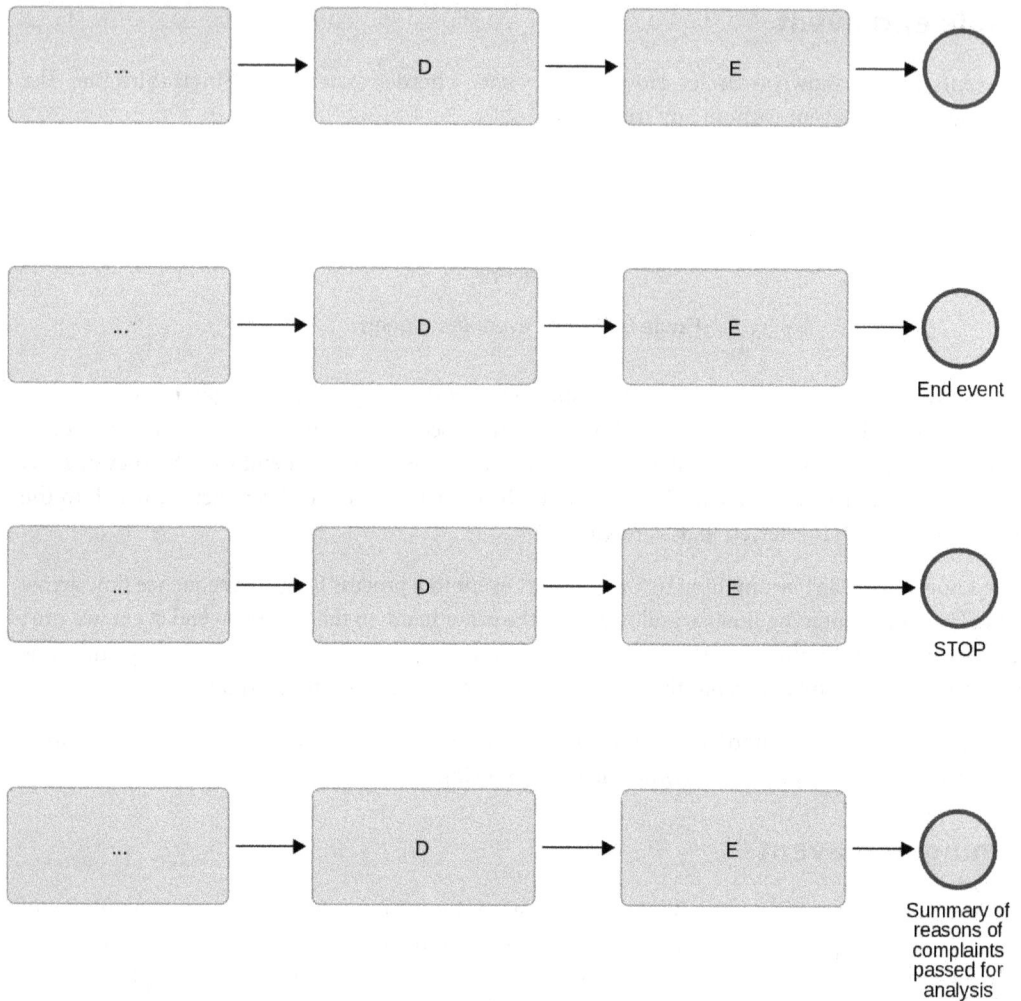

Figure 8.33 – Possible approaches to naming end events

One or more end events?

It's also worth noting that BPMN allows us to put multiple end events in a diagram, and this is a very useful option. As we saw in *Figure 8.4*, a glance was enough to determine what result our process could have, without us having to read the entirety of the diagram.

This is especially helpful when there are exclusive gateways in the diagram. Our process may finish in various other ways besides the "happy end," and we want to show them clearly for process analysis and improvement.

So, while it's possible to connect multiple sequence flow arrows to a single end event to show that multiple paths of the process share a common end (for example, in our process, the **Money refunded** end event is sufficient for analytical purposes; we don't need to emphasize how we make the refund), I'm not in favor of using only one end event where all paths – the happy one and the others – meet.

The standard end event behaves as follows: when a token reaches it, this token is *consumed* and disappears. If there are no more active tokens within that process instance, the process instance ends, and we can consider that the process has come to an end.

If, on the other hand, there are more tokens in the process, then the entire instance "lives," so long as at least one token is active. Let's look at the process example shown in *Figure 8.34*. If we assume that each of the tasks (A through E) lasts for 1 day, how long will the entire process instance live, assuming there are no delays?

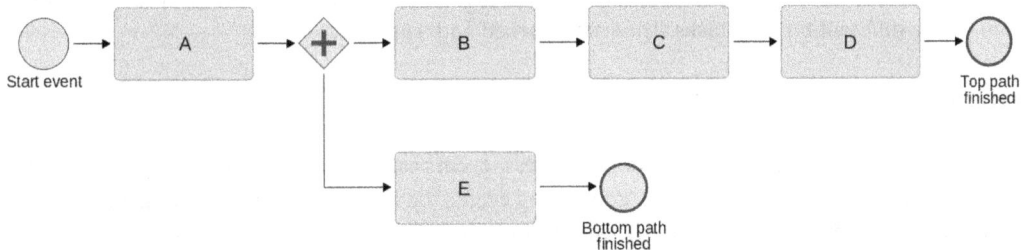

Figure 8.34 – Example of a process with many paths (process instance life cycle)

As you can easily calculate, even though the **bottom** token (that is, the one going to task E) will reach the **Bottom path finished** end event after just 2 days, we still have the **top** token within our instance. So, for the entire process to complete the longest of the paths (ABCD), we need 4 days. Only when task D is completed and the token reaches the **Top path finished** end event can we say that the process instance was completed.

Before we discuss start and end events with triggers, there's one more interesting thing to say about start and end events without types. From a formal point of view, the BPMN specification doesn't force us to insert start and end events without types. We can omit them from our diagrams because they're assumed to be there as **invisible and default** elements.

The only limitation is that we must be consistent in this approach – that is, we can't skip the start event without a type and must show the end events without a type. However, I don't recommend such an approach because with properly named events, it only takes one glance to determine when the process starts and what it might end with. *Figure 8.35* compares these two approaches:

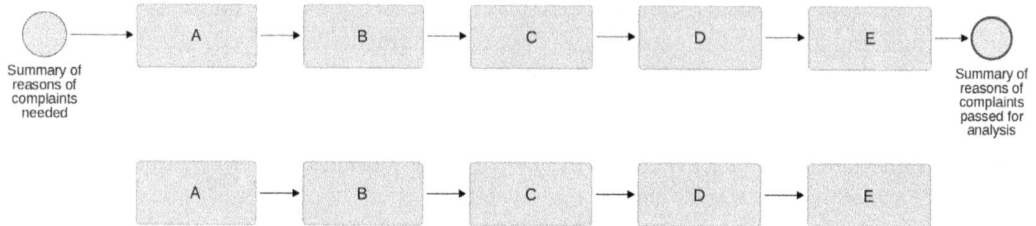

Figure 8.35 – Using start and end events versus skipping them

Now that we've learned the general rules for dealing with start and end events, we can move on to something a little more complex. As we know from the previous section, which was dedicated to tasks, we can define different types of tasks. These are marked with special icons.

Message events

As we learned from our complaint handling process, events can also contain additional icons that represent possible triggers. Let's begin by comparing events for which a message is a trigger since we already know a bit about messages. This will allow us to understand how different types of events behave.

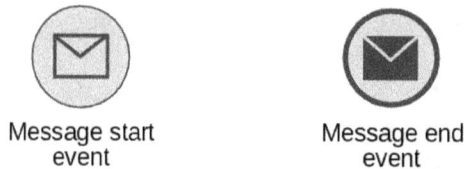

Figure 8.36 – Message start and end events

In addition to the rather obvious difference due to the type of events (a start event has a thin border, while an end event has a thick border), we can also see that the envelope icons differ in fill color. Using this example, we can observe a very important principle of BPMN: catching (passive) event icons are always light, while throwing (active) event icons are always dark.

Message start events indicate that a process is triggered by receiving some information from the outside – from some external entity, another organization, or perhaps a customer or partner. This information can be transmitted in a variety of ways – by letter, email, SMS, telephone, and so on.

For each message, we must always have a specific sender and a specific recipient, and that message exchange is always done between different participants (pools). Messages can't be sent or received within the same pool. As we've seen, the message icon is always an envelope, so the start event that's triggered by the message must have a light envelope icon.

If we want to show the readers of the diagram where the message comes from, we can draw an incoming message flow arrow, but this isn't mandatory. A message flow is always drawn with a dashed line, with an open arrowhead at the end and an open circle at the beginning. *Figure 8.37* shows the use of a message flow named **Complaint**, which flows from the **Customer** pool to the **Complaint received** start event.

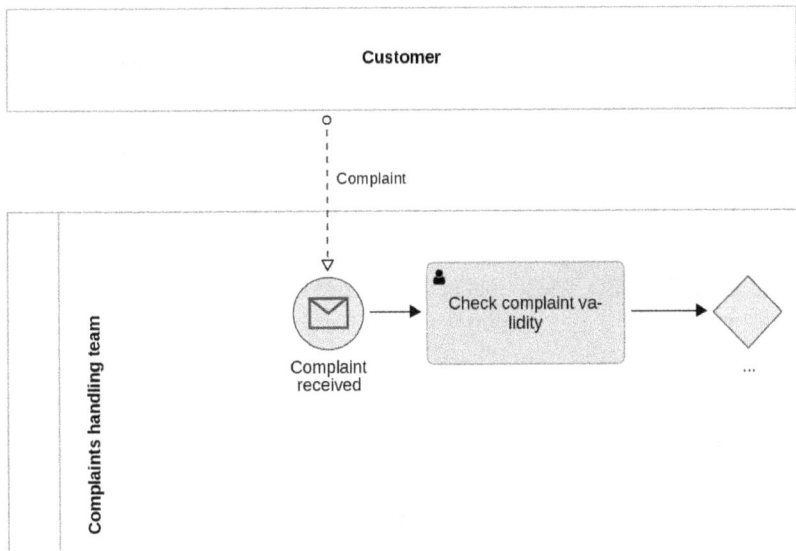

Figure 8.37 – Example of a message flow between a black-box (collapsed) pool and a start event

While this is often helpful, there's no obligation to show other participants or message flows, so we might as well start our process more easily, as shown in *Figure 8.38*.

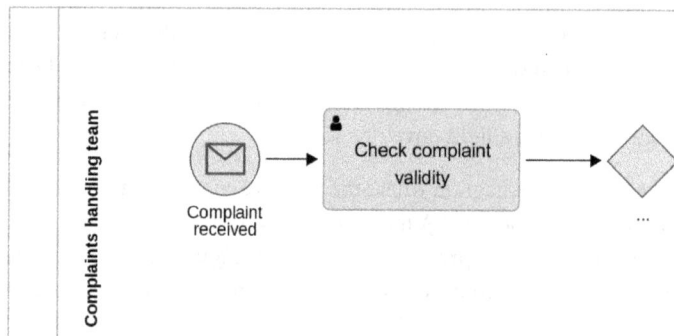

Figure 8.38 – A simplified process without an external participant and message flow

As for naming message start events, as in the case of plain start events, I would suggest using the passive side while referring to the message that starts the process. Possible examples include **Order received**, **Inquiry received**, **Invoice received**, and, as in our example of the complaint handling process, **Complaint received**.

I don't recommend using the active side so that you don't confuse the audience by implying that some work is being done within the event (for example, **Receive order**).

Now that we know how the message start event and regular end event behave, let's consider how the message end event works.

As you can easily guess, this type of end event is marked with a dark envelope icon. Like any end event, it consumes incoming tokens, but since it has a trigger defined, it also does something extra.

Since nothing else happens in the process after the end event, this *something extra* can be considered a *swan song* – the last breath of our process, so to speak. For a message end event, this something extra is the action of sending a message.

An example of this behavior might be sending an email to a customer regarding a record of a chat with a consultant or sending a request to evaluate an interaction – for example, a **Net Promoter Score (NPS)** satisfaction survey after the shipment was delivered.

At this point, it's worth noting that sending messages by end events makes sense in the case of highly automated processes, where such sending doesn't require human intervention. That's why we usually send messages with tasks, and the end event is only used to summarize what's already happened. This can be seen in *Figure 8.39*.

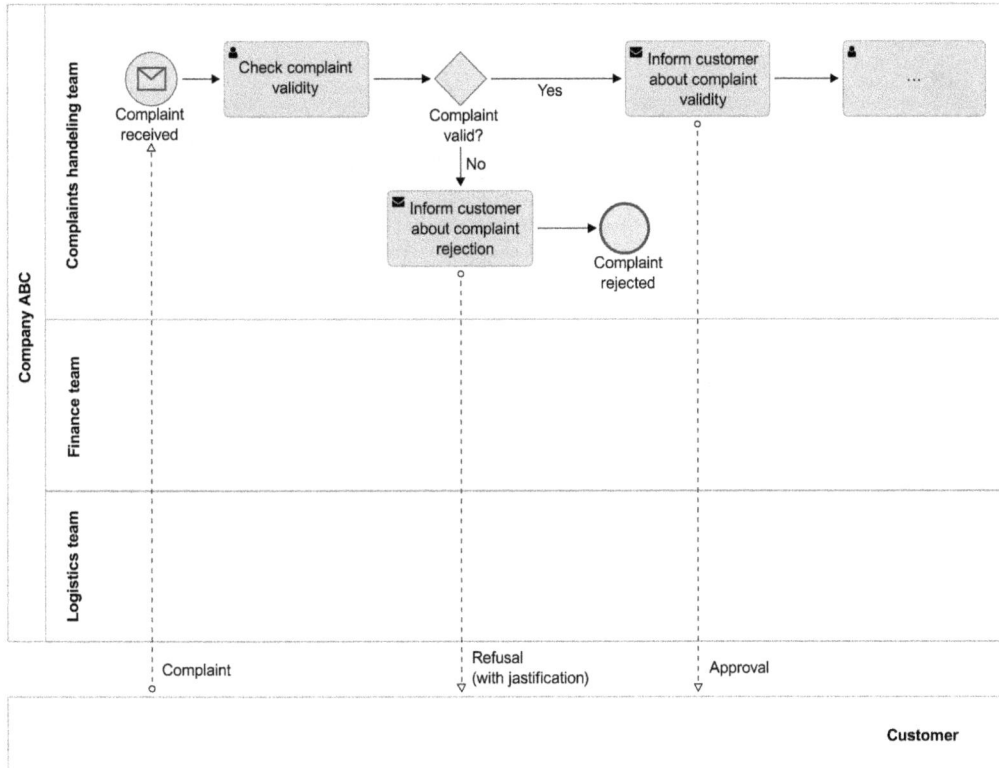

Figure 8.39 – Part of the example process – sending messages with tasks and proper naming of events

However, if we wanted to (and our process was properly automated), we could send a message from the end event, as shown in *Figure 8.40*:

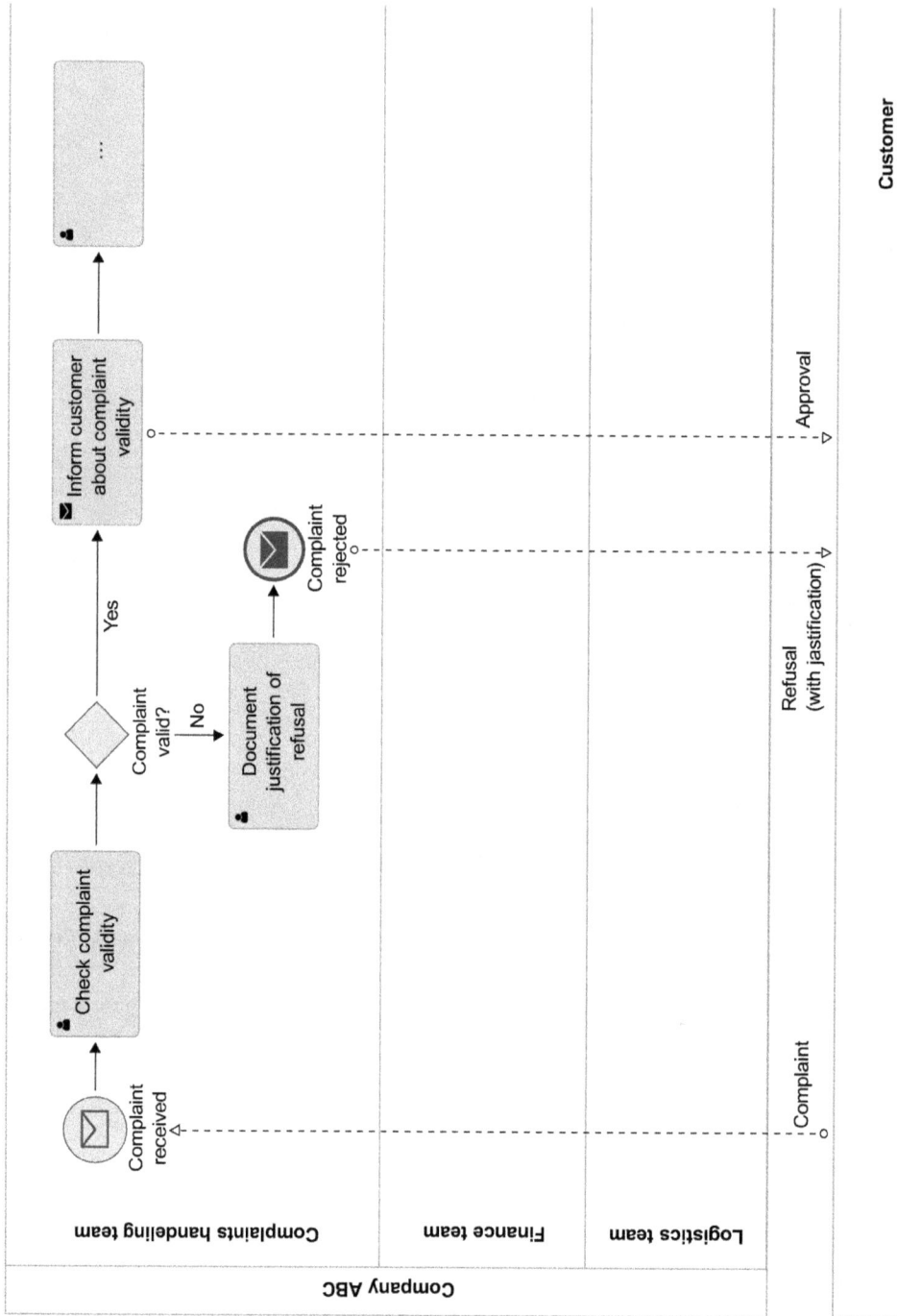

Figure 8.40 – Part of the example process – sending a message with the end event

Figures 8.39 and *8.40* are similar in meaning but there are still some differences. In the former figure, message flows are connected to the send task and the end event only states the result that refers to work that happened within the previous task.

In the latter figure, the task only *prepares the ground* for sending the message because the user enters the reason for rejection. This will be sent to the customer in the next step (in case you're curious, for *Figure 8.39*, this preparation should happen in the **Check complaint validity** task because the send task shouldn't be used for writing and sending emails, only for sending). The message is sent by the **Complaint rejected** end event.

If you use end events that send a message, it's worth taking care not to mistakenly suggest that messages are sent twice – once by a task and additionally by an end event, as seen in the anti-pattern shown in *Figure 8.41*. This kind of confusion is particularly dangerous when you don't use message flows, which clarify the communication with external participants:

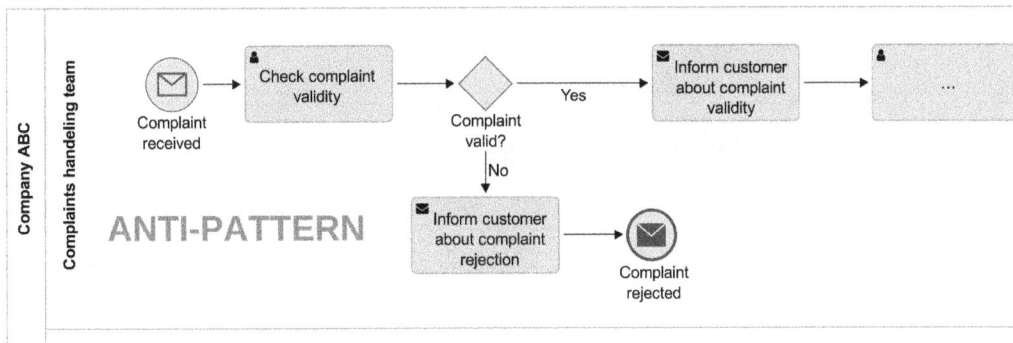

Figure 8.41 – Anti-pattern – sending a message twice with a task and an end event

Timer events

Now that we've learned about more advanced rules for modeling start and end events while using messages as examples, it's time to become familiar with an additional type of trigger – time. Since humans can't control time, this type of trigger only exists in a catching form, so there's no such thing as a timer end event.

Let's learn more about the timer start event. These events have a very distinctive appearance since their icon is a clock face. They're used to show that the process starts at a specific moment. This can be a specific moment (for example "The first business day of the quarter," "6 P.M. on weekdays," or "December 31, 11:59 P.M.") or a period (for example, "Every 8 hours"). With these types of events, we can easily represent time in our processes.

Timer start
event

Figure 8.42 – Timer start event

Let's return to our complaint handling example. When discussing *Figure 8.31*, we said that for the related process where we analyze reasons for complaints to improve our processes, we could use the **Summary of reasons of complaints needed** start event.

This would show that the process of analyzing the reasons for complaints is done on an irregular basis, depending on the expert decision of those involved in the process. However, if we wanted to ensure some regularity as part of organizational improvement, we could decide that this process is performed regularly every month, and we always perform it on the first working day of the month. *Figure 8.43* shows what this could look like.

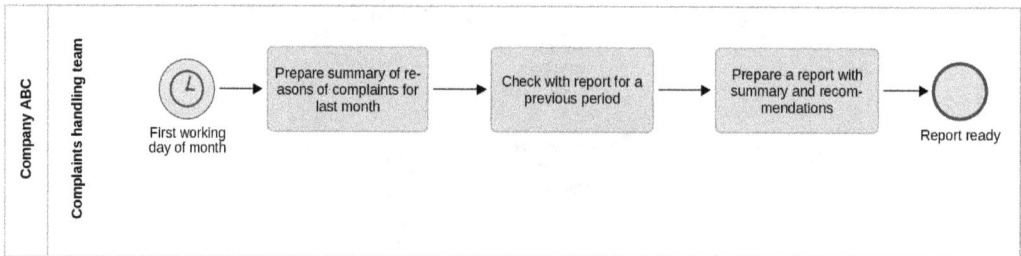

Figure 8.43 – Example – timer start event in practice

Similarly, a timer start event could be used within the shipment of goods to group a batch of packages and send them together once a day, for example, or within the process of refunding customers who have paid by wire transfer so that our employees from the finance team don't have to log in to e-banking every time a refund is needed. Instead, they gather a batch of transfers to be made and send them together at the right time.

In this section, we learned how start and end events allow us to convey very important information about what can start our process and how it can end. Thus, they define the scope of our process. But what can we do if, while modeling, we notice that there are so many process steps that our diagram is no longer readable? We'll talk about this in the next section.

Improving diagram readability with sub-processes

As we already know, a very important issue in creating models is to ensure that they can communicate with others. For this to happen, our models must be readable by the audience. Readability depends on many aspects, but some of the most important are the size of the model (how much space it takes up and how many objects it contains) and how easy it is to read.

At this point, it's worth noting that it's often difficult to convey good modeling practices in a book due to the nature of the medium. That's why some of the diagrams in this book are only available on its GitHub repository.

In practice, we usually create models on a computer and read them either electronically or as a hard copy. A paper book is much smaller than a standard printout, so larger diagrams need to be rotated and placed on separate pages; if they're placed in the text, there are suggestions to *squeeze* everything to make it look better. This often leads to *snake* diagrams, which is an anti-pattern.

While the BPMN specification itself doesn't place restrictions on us – a diagram containing one start event, one task, and one end event is just as correct as a diagram consisting of several hundred tasks and dozens of gateways – the size of the diagram is very important to its readers.

There's no consensus among modeling experts on how large a diagram can be to maintain readability. It's often argued that the ideal diagram should fit into a single sheet of paper.

I recommend creating diagrams that have no more than 20 to 30 elements. But what if we have a very complex process that needs 40, 50, or more elements to cover everything with a proper level of detail? This is when sub-processes come in handy.

Sub-processes allow modeling to occur hierarchically. While the BPMN doesn't support the high-level process architecture, it does allow us to move between different diagrams, from general to specific, in a very convenient way.

Let's look at *Figure 8.44*, which shows our example process for handling a complaint. To be more precise, we're looking at the part that documents what happens when the chosen complaint handling option is a refund.

We can see that an employee from the claims handling team needs to order a refund. Afterward, this refund is processed by the finance team.

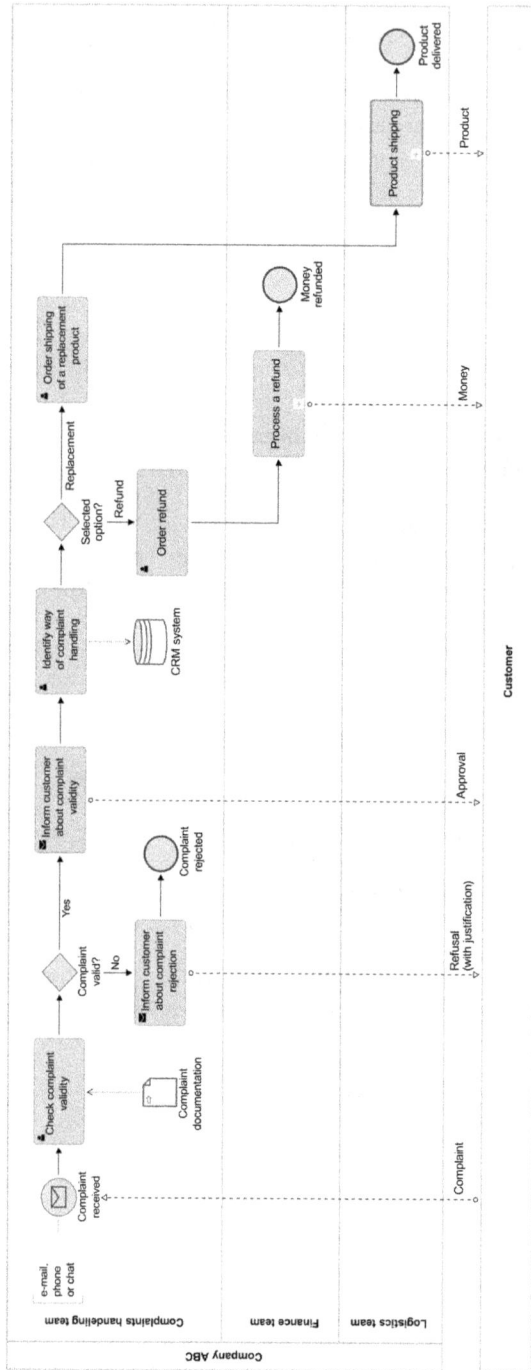

Figure 8.44 – Example process with visible sub-processes allowing us to navigate to lower-level diagrams

Embedded sub-process

The element we can see here is a standard type of sub-process known as the **embedded sub-process**. This often comes in a collapsed form and is shown as a rectangle with rounded corners, with a plus marker at the bottom.

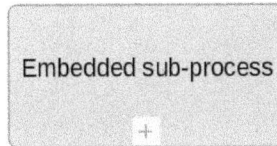

Figure 8.45 – Embedded sub-process

Of course processing refunds is quite a complex matter. Local regulations may differ just like company policies, but we can assume that if a payment needs to be refunded, the refund should be made using the same method that the customer picked.

Therefore, we should support not only card payments, but also e-wallets/payment systems, bank transfers, and possibly something more.

Are those details relevant to someone interested in the complaint handling process? Should we add them to the complaint handling process diagram? For most audiences, this would probably be too many details. So, instead of helping our readers, it would hinder communication. Therefore, according to the Goldilocks principle, it's better to show only as much as necessary.

How we could do this in practice? Instead of adding everything to the main diagram of the complaint handling process, we can create a new diagram showing how we process a refund and link it with the corresponding sub-process object in our main diagram. This hierarchical modeling makes it easy to move to a lower level with a single click, facilitating work with connected diagrams.

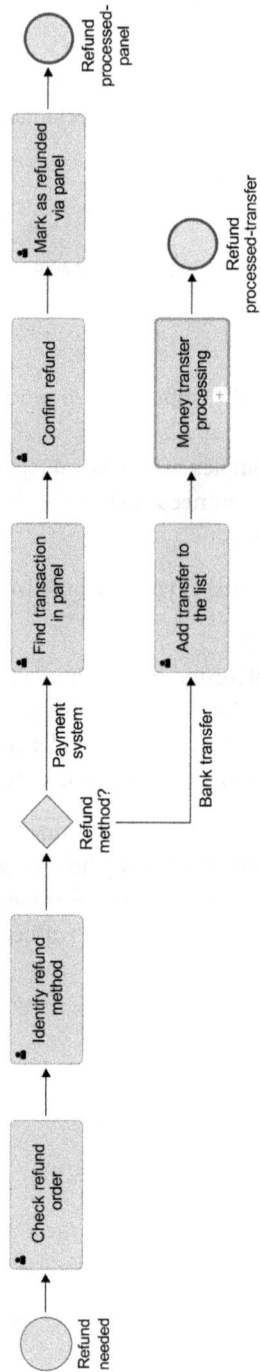

Figure 8.46 – Example diagram of processing a refund

Now, let's compare this hierarchical modeling with an option where we try to show everything in one diagram. (As already mentioned, it is hard to show bigger diagrams in a book. That's why I put the diagram showing everything on Github page for this chapter: `https://github.com/PacktPublishing/Practical-Business-Process-Modeling-and-Analysis/tree/main/Chapter08`. Take a look and compare it with a hierarchical approach and a variant of presentation where elements have been rearranged to make the diagram even smaller and easier to print. *Figure 8.47* shows an example of such a snake diagram.

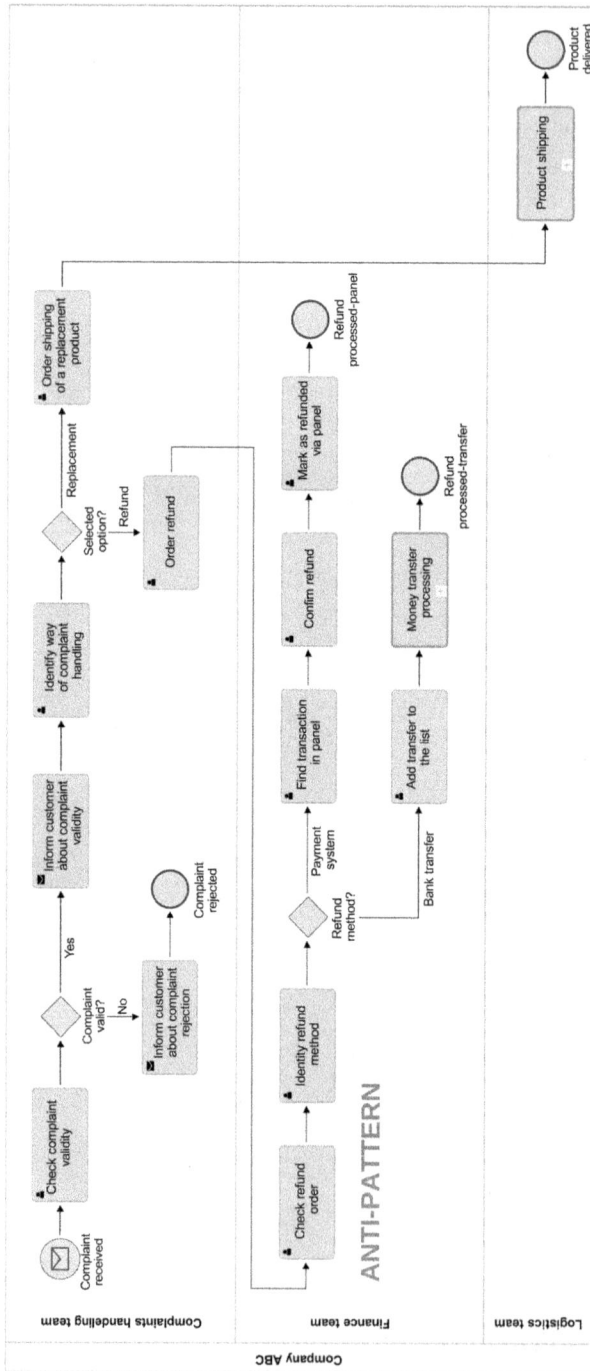

Figure 8.47 – Anti-pattern – saving space with "snake" diagrams

Sub-processes aren't only useful when we want to document our process with several hierarchically connected diagrams split for better readability. They also support the very important concept of reusing some standard service that's available in the organization.

Call activity

We saw an example of this approach in our complaint handling process, where there's a sub-process called **Product shipping**. An additional example was visible in *Figure 8.46*, where we had a sub-process for money transfer processing that has some (standard) way of executing defined bank transfers.

Cases like this – that is, situations where we don't refer to a separate part of our process, but to some standard way of doing things – require a different kind of sub-process: a **call activity**. A call activity can be recognized very easily as it has a characteristically thick border, drawn with a single continuous line.

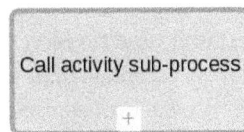

Figure 8.48 – Call activity sub-process

However, the differences between ordinary embedded sub-processes and call activities go much deeper. The contents of an ordinary embedded sub-process should be executed within the same lane as the sub-process linked with it (this is why, in the diagram describing the refunds, I didn't use a pool or lane).

Since we have a situation where a **child** diagram is called by its **parent**, the lower-level diagram must have a plain start event (without a trigger). This shows that this process doesn't start by itself but is called by the higher-level process.

In our case, this is quite intuitive because we wouldn't want a situation where someone from the finance team starts making refunds on their own, without a request from the complaint handling team.

On the other hand, when we use a call activity, the fact that this sub-process is placed in a particular lane of a higher-level diagram doesn't determine where the work will be done within the lower-level diagram. Since the process can be called by many other processes, we also need a plain start event, as well as additional start events with some triggers apart from the required one.

An additional element that distinguishes those two types of sub-processes is the approach to data. Simply put, we can say that for an embedded sub-process, we have a rather convenient situation because all the data of the "parent" is available within the "child."

In the case of call activity, however, we have a more complex situation as our processes must exchange data with each other in a more formalized way. This exchange requires interfaces to be established that guarantee that all required data will be passed to the called process, but also that results will be passed back for further processing.

A good example would be sending correspondence in the form of letters. If we do this ourselves, then we know what to send, how to send it, and to whom. However, if we need to send correspondence to hundreds of clients and we use the help of office clerks, it isn't enough to ask them casually to send mailings.

We need to clearly communicate what is to be sent (a letter template or all the required data), specify the method of sending (an ordinary letter, an express letter, or maybe a letter with proof of delivery), and provide addresses. We can also expect to receive a summary containing information regarding letters that were delivered successfully and those with invalid addresses.

In *Figure 8.46*, we had two end events showing how our refund could be processed. However, we didn't cover the case of a failed refund. In practice, however, our sub-process may have several possible outcomes, and not all of them are equally good for us. In such a situation, we often insert an exclusive gateway after the sub-process to show how to deal with the different outcomes of our sub-process.

It's worth knowing that sub-processes aren't only used for hierarchical modeling. It may also happen that the entire content of a lower-level process is contained in a sub-process object, which is a kind of container within which its content is shown. Such an approach is called *inline modeling*. This way of modeling sub-processes in an expanded form isn't usually recommended and generally makes sense when we use more advanced ways of modeling, allowing us to describe exception handling by boundary intermediate events (something we'll talk about in *Chapter 9*).

The following illustrations (*Figures 8.49, 8.50*, and *8.51*) show an example of hierarchical modeling contrasted with inline modeling:

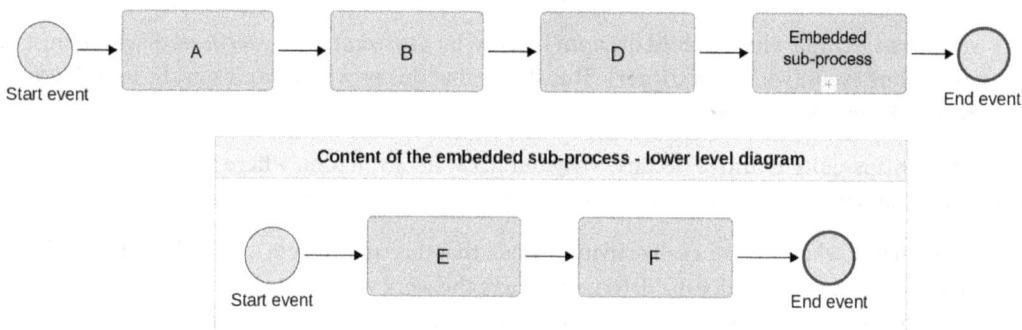

Figure 8.49 – Example of hierarchical modeling – moving to a lower-
level diagram through an embedded sub-process

It's worth noting that the expanded sub-process has no plus marker at the bottom and looks confusingly similar to the task, but most importantly, the sequence flow arrow coming out of task D reaches the edge of the embedded sub-process but doesn't cross it.

This is a very important rule – the sequence flow arrow can neither cross the boundary of the pool nor go from the outside to the center of the expanded sub-process. This reads as follows: when a token coming out of task D reaches an embedded sub-process, it activates it. In the start event located in the sub-process, another token is born and flows, triggering tasks E and F in turn. When it reaches the end event, it's consumed and the embedded sub-process is considered to be finished, which causes our main token, which has been patiently waiting, to move on (in this case, to the end event).

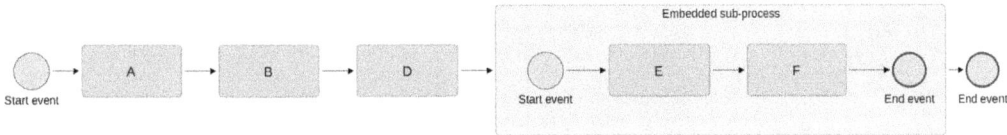

Figure 8.50 – Using an embedded sub-process for inline modeling

Such a way of modeling takes up even more space than if we didn't separate the elements into sub-processes but drew them within the main process. That's why you can sometimes see diagrams whose authors have taken the opportunity to omit start and end events, as mentioned previously. This is a perfectly allowed way of modeling, but I try to avoid it because it can be a bit confusing for people who aren't familiar with BPMN.

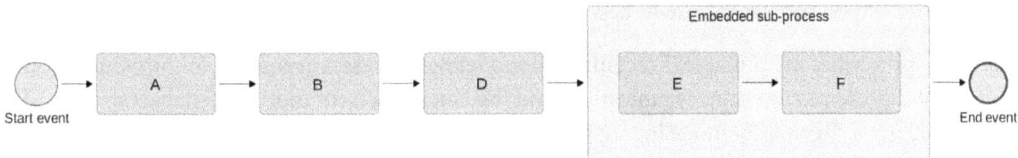

Figure 8.51 – An inline sub-process without start and end events

While sub-processes are very helpful for making diagrams easier to read by hiding some complexity, there are also times when we'll decide that it makes sense to add some elements to the diagram because they provide valuable information that offsets the increased diagram size. One of the most important aspects is the topic of responsibilities in a process. We'll cover this next.

Responsibilities in a process – pools and lanes

As we already know, BPMN lets us describe not only what happens within a process of our organization, but also how we interact with other entities. For this purpose, we use pools and lanes.

A pool represents a participant in a process, whereas a lane represents a logical division of that pool. Both the pool and the lane are always represented as rectangles, but the name of the pool is usually separated from its contents by a line, while the lane has no such line.

Figure 8.52 – A pool with two lanes

Interestingly, in BPMN, a pool can represent both the organization that performs the process and a department of that organization or another business role. The key issue is perspective as we assume that within the pool, the process is controlled in some way. This could be control resulting from the fact that the process has been automated and its steps are governed by a workflow application. Of course control can also be exercised by the owner of the process, who makes sure that the process is done properly, and no problems arise in it.

While both approaches are possible, I recommend modeling processes according to the assumption that the pool represents the entire organization, and the lanes represent individual departments and organizational units. This way of modeling supports the thinking of process management as a *team sport*.

Let's go back to the lanes – they always represent some kind of sub-partition of the pool, but we have a lot of freedom here as well. In theory, lanes could order tasks as, for example, value-adding or value-enabling, but in practice, lanes are often used to show responsibility for individual process steps. In this case, lanes correspond to organizational units or roles

The alternative approach, in which each unit has *its own* process and messages are exchanged with other pools, may seem tempting if the scope of our optimization project is about a single department or team because we can ignore what others need to do in a process. However, it tends to reinforce silo thinking, so it isn't a recommended modeling method.

These two approaches translate into different ways of naming pools. Often, a pool bears the name of a participant it represents. However, it's quite common – especially for models created for process automation on platforms that have this requirement – that the pool has the same name as the process that flows in it. A similar approach can also be found in simple modeling tools that have no other place to enter the name of the process being described.

As we have already seen in our example diagram, BPMN allows us to describe a pool with content, but also to show that there's a process participant with whom we exchange messages, without showing the detailed process of this participant.

In this case, we use a collapsed (black-box) pool, whose contents are not shown. Such a pool has no line separating the name from the content (because there is none), and its name is usually shown in the middle. Please note that you could also add a normal pool and leave it empty.

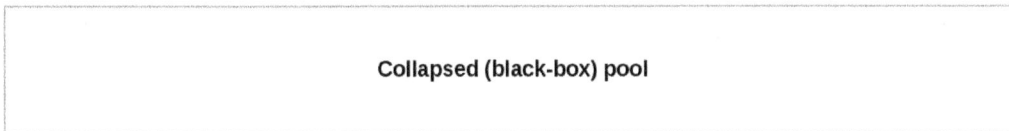

Collapsed (black-box) pool

Figure 8.53 – Collapsed (black-box) pool

One of BPMN's unique features is its support for showing how the process of one participant interacts with other participants. While other process modeling notations allow us to show who's responsible for what with different kinds of lanes, BPMN allows much more.

Private processes

The first interesting difference is that in BPMN, processes can be defined as private or public. A **private process** describes, at the appropriate level of detail, what's going on in the organization being analyzed. They can be used for documentation and analysis purposes (**non-executable** private process model) or process automation purposes (**executable** private process model).

By design, an executable diagram should contain much more technical information to automate the process, such as user forms, technical expressions to control the flow of the process through different paths (depending on the data that's received), and more.

A diagram that's used for documentation, on the other hand, can contain only as much detail as what's needed for the purpose for which it was created. *Figure 8.54*, which shows a simplified version of our process, shows what a diagram that's been created as process documentation may look like (it would also likely have descriptions of the process steps, but they've been hidden here).

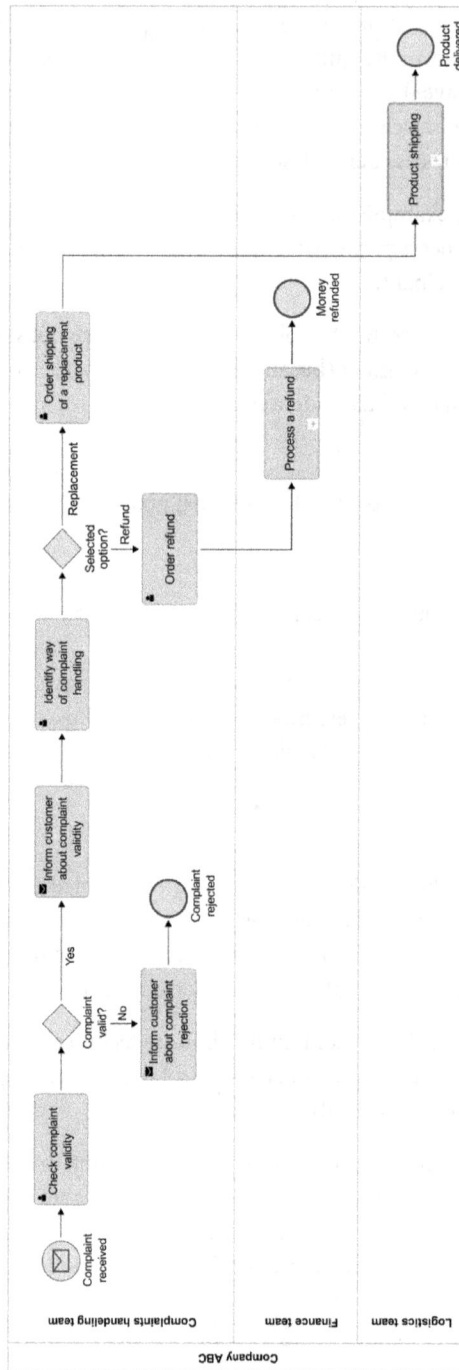

Figure 8.54 – Example process shown as a private process for documentation purposes

Interestingly, from a formal point of view, we don't always have to insert the pool into our diagram. The specification allows us to omit it for one selected process. So, once again, it invokes the concept of invisible default elements.

I don't recommend this way of saving space because for many audiences, the view of lanes dividing the invisible pool is highly confusing, and additionally, by getting rid of the lanes, we make it more difficult to see who's responsible for which steps within the process.

Public processes

A **public process**, on the other hand, is used to show only those elements of the process that are relevant to the communication between the participants (basically, elements related to sending and receiving messages). A public process is a abridged version of a private process that allows us to quickly show business partners what they need to know about our way of doing business, without burdening them with unnecessary information about process steps that don't interest them.

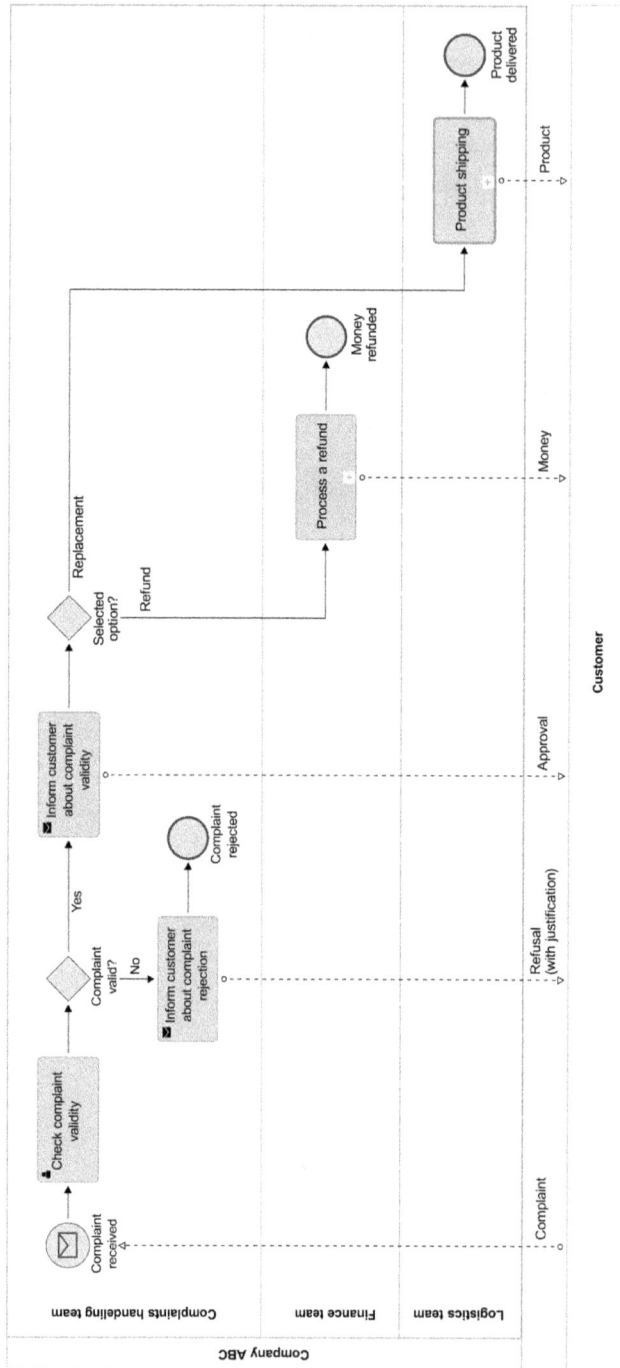

Figure 8.55 – Example process shown as a public process

Collaboration diagrams

Let's go a little further and show how different participants work together using **collaboration diagrams**. These contain two or more pools (expanded or collapsed) between which messages are exchanged.

Often, collaboration looks like the example we know from *Figure 8.1* – within the main pool, we have all the necessary process steps, not only those needed for message exchanges. Additional pools can be collapsed or contain their processes inside.

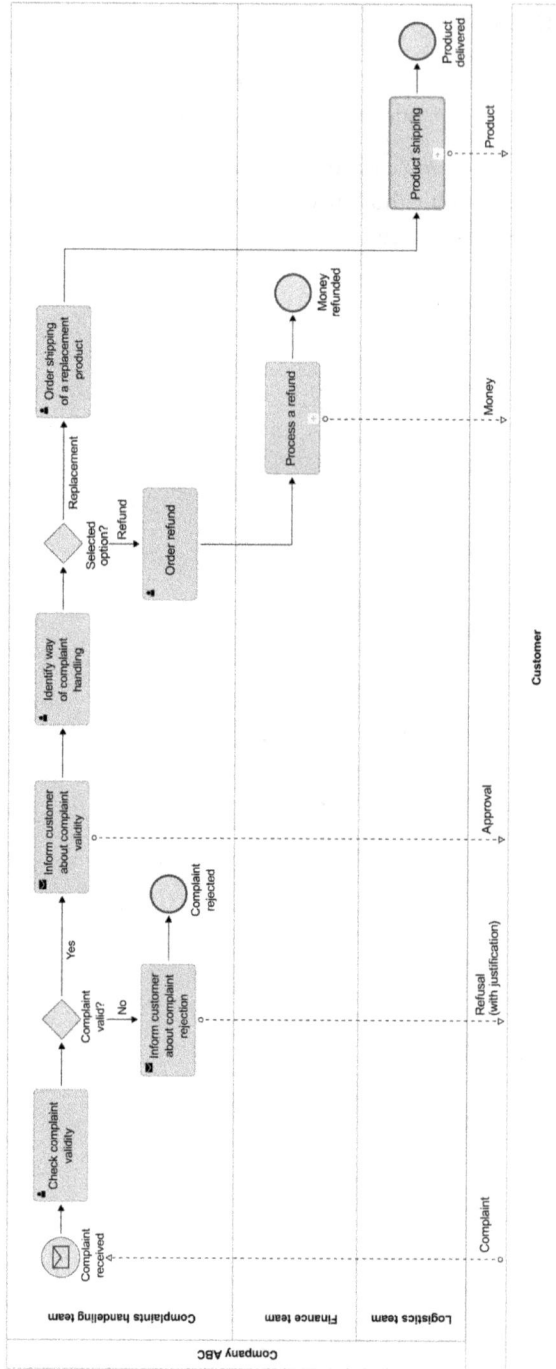

Figure 8.56 – Example process shown as collaboration

If we wanted to show only the communication between pools, we could use a collaboration diagram with all pools collapsed, but this isn't common.

Good practices and errors to avoid

Speaking of pools and lanes, it's also worth remembering three BPMN modeling principles that can help us avoid many common mistakes (examples of which I've included in *Figure 8.57*):

- The process flows within a specific pool and can move between different lanes, from the start event through various activities and gateways to the end event. It always flows along the sequence flow arrow (without "gaps" or "jumps").

- The sequence flow can only occur within the pool; it can't cross the border of the pool.

- The message flow can only occur between pools; it can't take place within a single pool. This also applies to sending and receiving messages between lanes in the same pool.

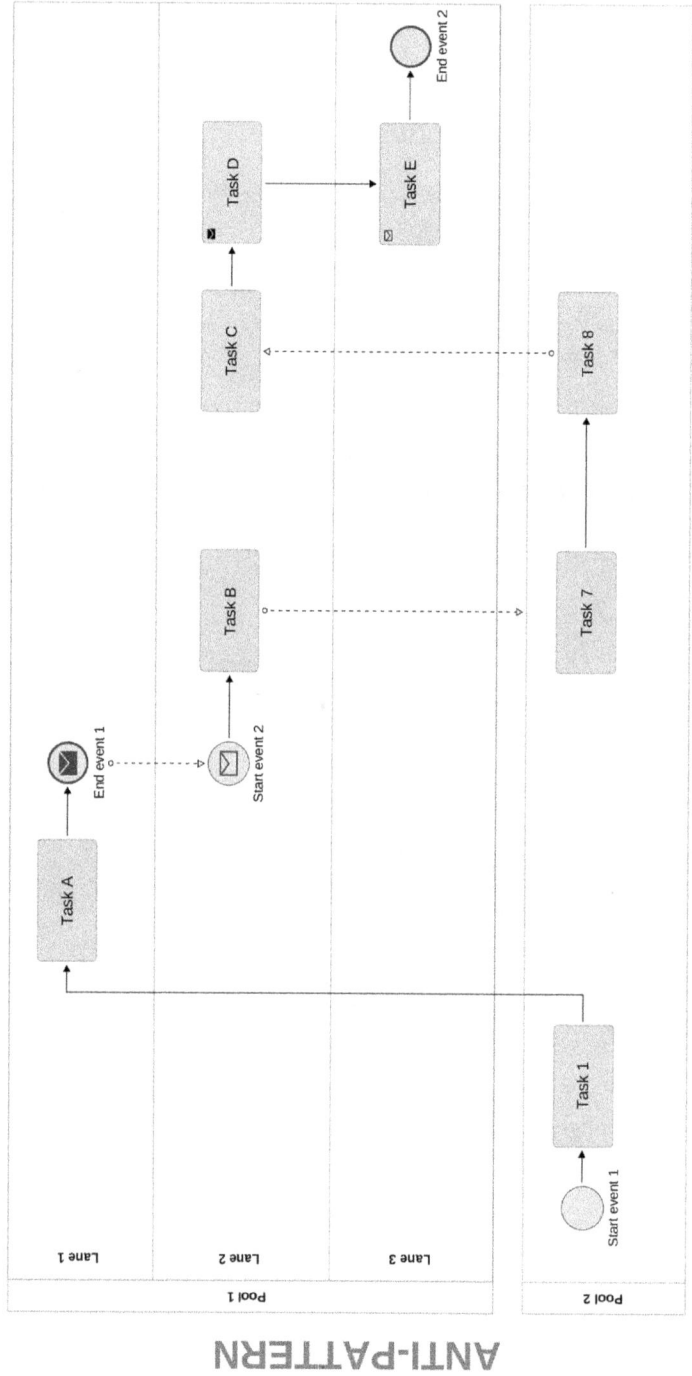

Figure 8.57 – Anti-pattern – a summary of the most common errors related to pools and lanes

The first thing that strikes us is the sequence flow between **Task 1** and **Task A,** which are in two different pools. This is not in accordance with the rules of notation because the sequence flow can't pass between different pools – it's always related to a specific pool.

If we take a closer look, we can also see a more subtle error – the process starts with **Start event 1** in **Pool 2** and then continues in **Pool 1**. This is also wrong because **Pool 1** should have its own start event, which would most likely have an incoming message flow coming out of **Task 1.**

The next mistake is that **Lane 1** and **Lane 2** are too independent as they have their own start and end events, while the process should flow through the entirety of **Pool 1**. This would emphasize that the lanes are just divisions of the pool and the process is associated with the pool, not assigned to a specific lane.

Another error that isn't so easy to catch is that the message flow coming out of **Task B** doesn't enter **Task 7** in **Pool 2** but is attached to the pool edge. Admittedly, BPMN allows us to start and end message flows at the edge of the pool, but this only makes sense for pools that don't contain content (usually collapsed pools). If the pool does have content, then we should show precisely where our message flow is leading to or from.

Errors occur in two more places: in **Pool 1**, we can see that **Task B** and **Task C** aren't connected by the sequence flow. In **Pool 2**, on the other hand, we have a gap in the sequence flow between **Task 1** and **Task 7**. Both cases violate the rule that says that there can be no "gaps" or "jumps" in a sequence flow.

In the case of **Pool 2**, we can also see that the process is incomplete. It has a start event and **Task 1,** but then there's a break. Later, we can see that **Task 7** and **Task 8** exchange messages with the process contained in **Pool 1**, but we don't know what comes after **Task 8** because there's no end event at the end.

This kind of modeling, in which we describe some but not all elements of a process and don't even bother to connect them properly, isn't appropriate.

If we don't need details, then representing the participant with a collapsed pool is enough. If we're only interested in the elements that are important for communication, we use the public process, which may not contain all the elements (as in our example, where we have **Tasks 1, Task 7,** and **Task 8**), but it still needs to be valid. Of course, we could also model the process contained in **Pool 2** in detail.

The last major error – sending messages within a single pool – also occurs in several places. The first time we saw it was between **End event 1** and **Start event 2**. This is a consequence of "slicing" the process into mini processes for each lane: not from the perspective of the whole organization (represented by the pool) but from the perspective of its organizational unit (represented by lanes).

Of course, messages can't be exchanged between **End event 1** and **Start event 2** because we aren't allowed to have message flows (or message exchanges) within a single pool.

A second, slightly less drastic occurrence of the error related to message exchanges is seen at the end of **Pool 1**, where **Task D** and **Task E**, both of which are connected with a sequence flow, are marked as send and receive, respectively.

This would only make sense if we were sending something to **Pool 2** and receiving from it, but we see nothing to indicate such use. Therefore, this isn't correct – we aren't allowed to send messages within a single pool, even if the reasoning goes: "But after all, I'm sending an email to colleagues in another department, and they receive it and get acquainted with its content."

The pools and lanes that we've become better acquainted with in this section can sometimes be extremely useful for conveying very important information about a process – that is, who's involved in the process and who's responsible for each step of the process. However, we might want to include some more information in our diagram.

Adding more information to your diagram with artifacts

As we already know, artifacts are used to convey more information about our diagram without affecting the way it's interpreted and executed. In this section, we'll learn more about **text annotations** and **groups**.

Text annotations

The most used type of artifact is text annotation, which allows you to insert text into your diagram.

This annotation is quite simple – it always has the shape of an opening square bracket, followed by text. Depending on our needs, we can only change the size of the object so that the text takes up more or less space.

Figure 8.58 – Text annotation

Despite this simplicity, annotations can be very useful. First, the text they contain is always visible within the diagram (unless, of course, we shrink the object so that the text no longer fits in the available space), making it easy to spot on the printout and accessible to viewers who aren't BPMN experts and don't realize that many objects may have additional, invisible information (descriptions, but not only). Thus, annotations allow us to convey relevant information relating to the context of the process.

Second, because annotations are easy to see, we can use them to document problems in the process and ideas for improvement. Of course, such use mainly makes sense if the tool we're using doesn't offer a better change management mechanism.

Third, text annotations can be used in a wide variety of scenarios. The BPMN specification defines quite a lot of different attributes, but – as we mentioned earlier – the authors decided that its goal isn't to support all possible business modeling scenarios. So, if we're using a tool that doesn't provide support for time-cost analysis of a process, and we'd like to show how much time it takes on average to execute individual process steps or classify process steps in terms of value-creation for documentation and improvement purposes, we can use annotations.

In the same way, we could use a text annotation to record who is the process owner, or to document the purpose of a process or other attributes that are important to us.

When using annotations, it's worth remembering that anything we write in them is treated as text only – it doesn't affect the behavior of the process being described, isn't the basis for automating it, nor does it allow for more advanced analysis. We can jokingly say that annotations are the equivalent of colored sticky notes that we attach to important documents with information for recipients on what they should pay attention to, where to sign, and so on.

Annotations can be linked to a selected element of the diagram, or they can refer to the diagram as a whole. In the first case, the annotation connects to another element (for example, a task) using an **association** arrow, which is indicated by a dotted line.

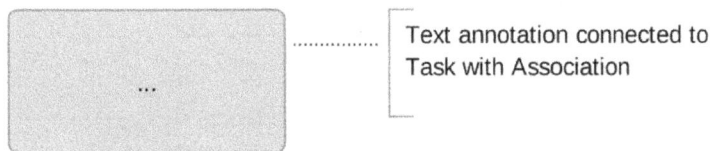

Figure 8.59 – Text annotation and an association arrow

In the second case, we can simply place the annotation *freely floating*, without connecting it to other elements of the diagram. We can see examples of both approaches in the following diagram fragment (*Figure 8.60*). The text annotation, which uses association, is linked to the start event, while the annotation that's been placed *freely* shows how the process owner and its goal can be visualized.

This diagram also illustrates some of the risks of using artifacts: they're very useful for showing something important on a diagram, but the more you add, the worse the readability of the whole diagram gets, so it's a good idea to exercise moderation.

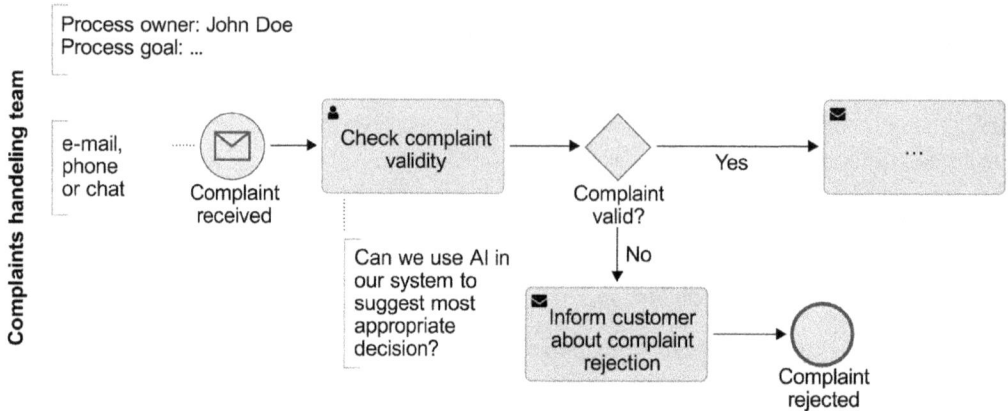

Figure 8.60 – Example of using annotations to provide additional information about a process

Groups

Another type of artifact is a **group**. A group, like a text annotation, is always presented in one way. It's shown as a rectangle with rounded corners, but it's very difficult to confuse it with tasks and sub-processes because it has a very distinctive line composed of alternating dashes and dots (like in the Morse alphabet) and doesn't connect to other elements of the diagram via an arrow.

Figure 8.61 – Group

A group is used when we want to draw the recipient's attention to the fact that the selected diagram elements have something in common – they belong to a certain common category. If we wanted to use a similar analogy as in the case of a text annotation, we would say that the use of a group is like marking certain elements of a document with a highlighter.

In practice, adding a group involves adjusting its size to cover all the elements we want to have, and giving it a proper name that suggests what those elements have in common. This allows us to highlight diagram elements that represent a happy path or elements that will be handled in a similar way (for example, "To be eliminated after the implementation of XYZ system").

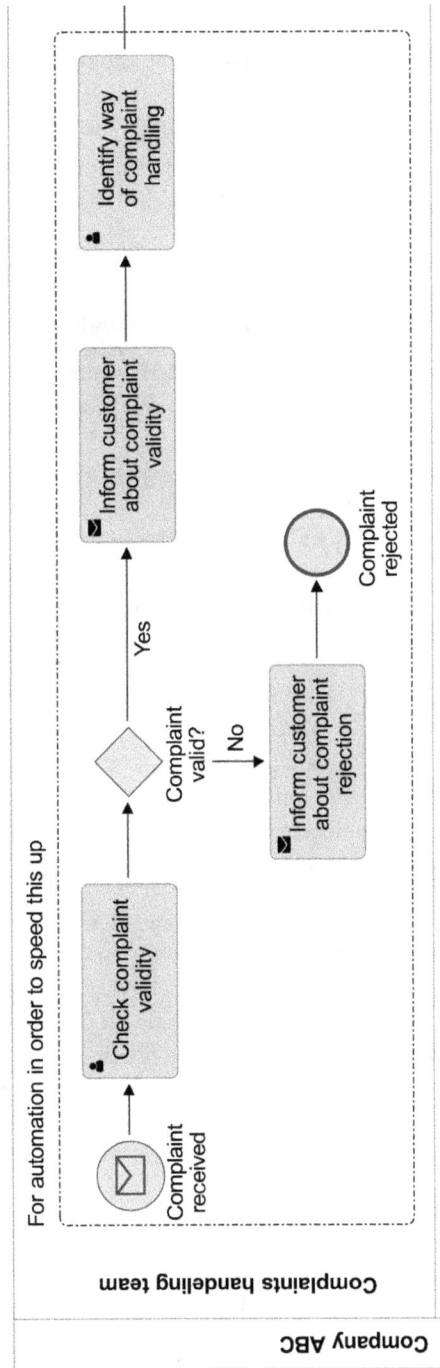

Figure 8.62 – Example of using a group to highlight part of a process

The BPMN specification also allows other types of artifacts to be added to diagrams. However, this is more of a theoretical possibility as they would have to be supported by a process modeling tool, something we don't encounter very often in practice. It's worth remembering that according to the rules of the BPMN specification, they would have to look different from the objects that have already been defined – that is, you can't create a new type of artifact, which would be a circle with a single thin border (because such a symbol is already reserved for the start event), but the shape of the polygon would be allowed.

The artifacts that were covered in this section make it possible to expand the BPMN diagram with additional information, but in a way that doesn't translate to how the process is interpreted and executed.

Now, it's time to discover the last category of BPMN objects. These objects allow us to add more context about a process to the diagram but in a way that can be (at least in theory) more than purely informational.

Showing data flows in a diagram with data objects

Data usage is another area where BPMN goes beyond its core focus of describing a process. It's worth noting that the elements we'll discuss in this section make it possible to show how data flows within a process, but that's not all that IT professionals may need to model the data adequately – for example, they don't provide support to ensure that data structures and their dependencies are represented.

It's also worth noting that the data layer in BPMN often has a weaker level of support in IT tools – especially those for process automation – than other elements of the notation. Many process automation tools use their methods for describing the data in a process, so the data modeling concepts included in the BPMN specification are often treated only as documentation and have no impact on how the process is executed. There are even situations where automation tools remove data objects when importing diagrams from other modeling tools!

As we know, the basic object for representing data is the data object. Its symbol looks like a piece of paper with a folded top-right corner. However, it's worth noting that a data object may or may not correspond to a physical document (the specification emphasizes that data can refer to physical or informational elements). Often, we use it to describe a certain set of data that's processed as part of a process. Examples of such data may be "Complaint documentation," "Transfer data," and "Waybill"

Data object   Data object
                     [Status]

Figure 8.63 – Data object

In addition to the name, data objects frequently have a status presented in square brackets after the name. Thanks to this status, we can immediately see what changes our data undergoes due to actions within the process. For example, in our process for the **complaint documentation** data object, we could define the following states: for analysis, rejected, accepted, and closed. Of course, such a way of modeling takes up more space, but it allows us to describe what happens in our diagram in terms of data in more detail.

To show how data flows between activities within a process, we use **data association** arrows. Because they have arrowheads at the end, you can immediately see where the data is flowing from and to. Importantly, the data flow doesn't have to coincide with the process flow, so we can have a sequence of ABCD tasks and a data flow where data comes out of task A and is the input for task D (assuming that it isn't processed in steps B and C).

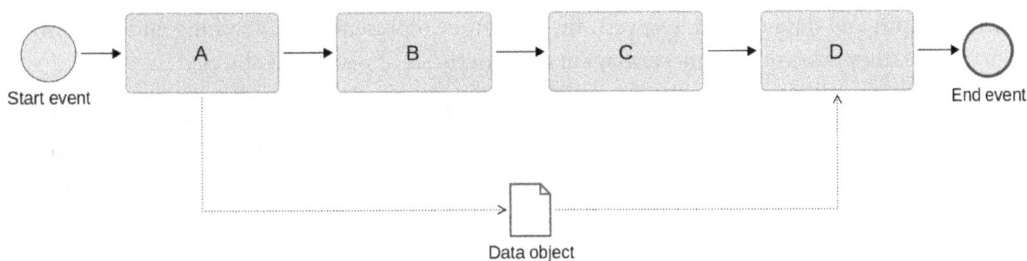

Figure 8.64 – Using data associations to show the data flow

It's also worth mentioning that neither data objects nor data stores (which we'll deal with in a moment) can be connected with tasks via a sequence flow. This kind of mistake is especially dangerous for people with long flowcharting experience who started using BPMN with simple diagramming tools, which often don't have built-in rules for correct notation.

Speaking of the data layer in BPMN, it's good to be aware that a standard type of data object is something that's processed as part of a given process – a kind of variable held in the computer's RAM that's "cleaned up" when the computer is turned off. This means that after a particular process instance is terminated, we have no way to reach this data as it isn't permanent!

If we want to show that the data in our process is stored permanently, we should use another type of object – a **data store**. A data store is represented by a database icon (cylinder). Here, you should be aware of another surprise – although its appearance suggests that the data is stored in electronic form, data stores can be used in physical form, such as filing cabinets.

Data store

Figure 8.65 – Data store

Data stores can also connect to other diagram elements via data association arrows to show how the data flows. If the diagram is quite large, we may want to avoid too many connectors coming to and from the data store. In this case, it's possible to insert the data store with the same name several times into different parts of the diagram to increase its readability. If you're interested in the technical aspects, in this situation, our diagram has one data store definition and several references to this common definition, but this can only be noticed by analyzing the BPMN diagram export file.

Since data stores look like stylized databases and because BPMN doesn't have anything better to visually represent IT systems used in a process, it's common to see data stores that represent applications used in a process. Of course, this is usually the case for simple modeling tools that don't have shared repository mechanisms and dictionary definitions.

The last two types of data objects are used to show data entering and leaving the process. These are called **data input** and **data output**, respectively. Since they represent data incoming and outgoing from a process, they don't share non-permanent characteristics of plain data objects.

The symbols for data input and data output are very similar to those for normal data objects, but they have an additional arrow icon in the top-left corner. As you may expect, the rules of marking activity and passivity in BPMN are kept, so the data input icon (data that enters a process, such as from a preceding process) has a light fill, while the data output icon (data leaving a process, perhaps to another process) has a dark fill.

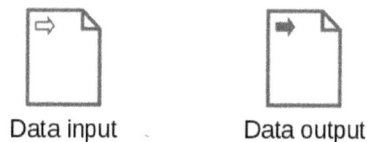

Data input   Data output

Figure 8.66 – Data input and data output

In addition to the icons symbolizing types of data objects, there may be another marker – three vertical dashes. This is called a **collection**. In practice, such a marker can occur when we want to show that we're working with not one invoice, but a whole bunch of invoices, or that we're entering multiple items into the CRM system to be included in the offer we want to generate. Often, if we use this marker with data objects, we should consider whether the tasks and sub-processes in our diagram have been described in a way that indicates that more items are being processed. We'll learn more about this topic in *Chapter 9*:

Collection

Figure 8.67 – Collection

A final interesting aspect related to data objects in BPMN is the accessibility of this data within multi-level process diagram structures. Within a single diagram, the behavior is quite logical as the data object contained in that diagram can be accessed by all activities from that diagram.

But what happens if we insert a sub-process into our diagram that leads to another diagram, which also contains another data object? The data object located in the higher-level diagram will be accessible to all activities in its diagram and the lower-level diagram, but (and this is worth noting) the data object located in the lower-level diagram will only be accessible to the sub-process in the higher-level diagram, activities from its diagram, and possible activities from even lower-level diagrams.

This may have sounded a bit technical, and for good reason – data modeling is a slightly more advanced element of BPMN that's more useful in diagrams that are created with more sophisticated process analysis in mind. Before using the data objects and stores in diagrams intended to serve as process documentation for a wide audience, we should think carefully about whether it will help us achieve our communication goal.

The same will be true for further elements of notation, something we'll discuss in the next chapter. They offer many interesting possibilities, but they may not always be intuitive for everyone, so they should be used with caution.

Summary

In this chapter, you learned about the most important elements of BPMN. With the help of BPMN, you can create diagrams that not only serve as process documentation and process analysis but also create the foundation for future process automation programs. The elements we learned about are very popular and most of them should be intuitive for people who read the diagrams, even if they're not BPMN experts. Usually, it is a good idea to start with a diagram using such easy shapes and iteratively work on it by adding descriptions to the process steps or (when needed) providing more information using additional elements of BPMN.

In the next chapter, we'll cover more advanced concepts and shapes from BPMN based on what we've learned so far.

Further reading

If you would like to learn more about the concepts covered in this chapter I would suggest checking BPMN Quick and Easy Using Method and Style: Process Mapping Guidelines and Examples Using the Business Process Modeling Standard from Bruce Silver – well known expert.

In addition to the resources for this chapter available on `https://github.com/PacktPublishing/Practical-Business-Process-Modeling-and-Analysis/tree/main/Chapter08`. I would also recommend checking the official webpage of the standard: `https://www.bpmn.org/`.

Unlock this book's exclusive benefits now

Scan this QR code or go to `packtpub.com/unlock`, then search this book by name.

Note: Keep your purchase invoice ready before you start.

9

Advanced BPMN

In *Chapter 8*, we learned about the key elements of BPMN. With this knowledge, you can easily understand most real-life diagrams. However, BPMN also allows you to create more sophisticated diagrams for process analysis and automation. To help you benefit from those additional possibilities, we will cover more advanced elements of BPMN.

We will also discuss how BPMN can be extended to support concepts such as decision management, knowledge-intensive processes implemented through case management, simulation, risk management, showing responsibilities with RACI, and more.

In this chapter, we're going to cover the following main topics:

- How to handle special cases in BPMN with events

- When and how to use additional types of tasks, sub-processes, and gateways

- How to extend BPMN with additional notations and attributes

> **Note**
>
> This chapter is authored by Zbigniew Misiak.
>
> Additional resources for this chapter have been uploaded here: `https://github.com/`
> `PacktPublishing/Practical-Business-Process-Modeling-and-Analysis/`
> `tree/main/Chapter09`.

Additional types of events

In *Chapter 8*, we learned about the most important types of start and end events that define the scope of a process. However, it's worth knowing that BPMN also allows you to model intermediate events, which, as the name implies, occur during the process: after the process begins and before the process ends.

BPMN also allows the use of more complicated types of start and end events—we will deal with them in this chapter too. We'll begin our discussion of the more advanced elements of BPMN with events because they are a big part of all BPMN objects. In addition, without events, it is difficult to understand the use of many other advanced elements of the notation.

Intermediate events—basics

Intermediate events are represented as circles with an icon in the center, indicating their trigger, just like all other events. However, you can easily distinguish them from start and end events by looking at their border. While start events always have a single thin line as a border and end events have a single thick line, intermediate events always have a double thin line.

Start Event   Intermediate
                Event   End Event

Figure 9.1 – Comparison: start, intermediate, and end events

Intermediate events come in different variants. Most commonly, they are a part of a process flow, where they show that the process has reached some special state, or that the process must wait for some event to happen before it can continue. As you may expect, we can apply a familiar concept here: **throwing (active)** and **catching (passive) events**.

As in the case of start and end events, there can also be intermediate events without a defined trigger. This type of event does not have an icon inside, so it is a simple circle with a double thin line as a border. An intermediate event without a trigger always behaves actively; it is a throwing event (although visually it is impossible to guess since there is no icon). It is rather uncommon, but it can be used to show that the process has reached some important stage (**milestone**).

Intermediate events can also be used to mark exceptions, errors, and special situations in the process. For this purpose, **boundary intermediate events** are used. They are always attached to the borders of tasks or sub-processes for which they provide exception handling. Boundary intermediate events are always catching (passive) elements that behave like sentries. They are used to "listen" for things that may affect the execution of the activity to which they are attached and specify how to handle those cases.

Generally speaking, there are two possible options: something can happen that forces us to interrupt the work we are doing (this is described by **interrupting intermediate events**), or without interrupting the activity we are currently performing, it can cause us to do something additional "on the side" (this is what **non-interrupting intermediate events** are for).

Message events—recap

Let's start learning with **message events**—that is events for which the message is a trigger. To help you learn about this more easily, we will use a slightly modified version of our complaint handling process, in which we use intermediate events (instead of tasks) to communicate with the customer.

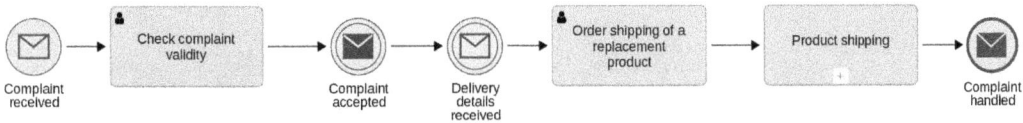

Figure 9.2 – Usage example: start, intermediate, and end events in a complaint handling process

The start event triggered by the message is identical to the one we discussed earlier—it simply means that the process starts when a message from a customer about a complaint arrives at our company.

The end event that sends the message should also look familiar. It informs us that when our **Product shipping** sub-process ends, the main process of handling the complaint also ends, but in addition, we send a message (e.g., an email) to the customer with information that a complaint has been closed and most likely a link to a survey, so that we can find out the customer's satisfaction with the complaint handling process.

Catching and throwing intermediate events

The new items worth noting in *Figure 9.2* are two intermediate events: **Complaint accepted** and **Delivery details received**. For both, a message is a trigger, as shown by the envelope icons inside the objects. As you can see in our example, the active (throwing) event has a dark envelope icon, and the passive (catching) event has a light one. All intermediate events behave in this way, making it easy to interpret the meaning of the diagrams.

Let's complicate our example a bit and add two boundary intermediate events, both of which will be attached to the **Order shipping of a replacement product** task. As the bright icon shows, both events are passive, since their role is to "listen" whether something particular occurs during the execution of the activity to which they are attached and specify what our reaction will be.

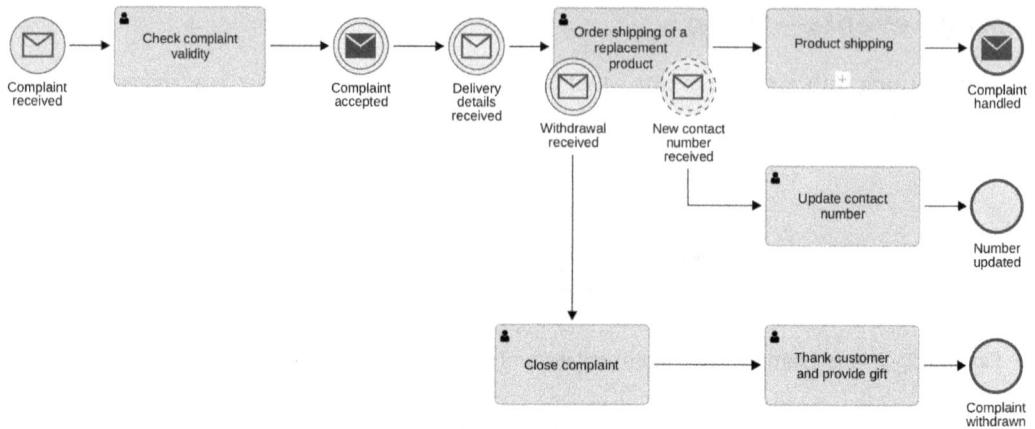

Figure 9.3 – Usage example: boundary intermediate events in a complaint handling process

Interrupting and non-interrupting boundary events

Let's imagine that we need to handle a (hypothetical) situation in which the customer withdraws their claim because they have determined that the problem was not the fault of our company or courier, but that it was a child who hit the package while playing and caused damage to its contents. In this case, it does not make sense to finish the **Order shipping of a replacement product** task because we do not need to send a replacement product. After we close the complaint (perhaps marking it in the CRM system), we may want to thank the customer for their honesty and, as a small gift, give them a discount on their next order.

The second situation we may want to respond to is a change of contact phone from the customer's side. If our customer accidentally provided the wrong number (e.g., a business phone) when making a complaint, they may want to change to a different number (e.g., a private phone) so that the courier calls the correct number. This change can be made at any time while we are still ordering the shipping, but it must occur before we proceed to the product shipping sub-process (it will be too late to make the change).

As you can see, in both cases, the boundary events contain an identical icon as they wait for a message. Also, both have outgoing sequence flows leading to activities needed to handle those special cases. Different types of lines used for borders suggest that those events may have different meanings when it comes to interrupting the activity to which they are attached.

Non-interrupting boundary events have a dashed double thin line, and interrupting boundary events have a solid double thin line for the border. How can you remember this? This trick may be helpful for you: a solid line means a "confident and assertive" event. When it occurs, it takes the token away from its "parent" (the activity to which it is attached), thereby interrupting that activity, and uses the token for its purposes. The dashed line, on the other hand, means that the event is "shy" and in order not to disturb its "parent," it produces its token and executes some additional process steps without bothering the "parent."

Interestingly, there is no visual difference between the intermediate catching event and the boundary catching interrupting event—both have a double solid line and an icon with a light fill. However, they differ in their attributes (of course, this depends on the tool you are using) and in the fact that the catching intermediate event, which is part of the process flow, has an inbound and outbound sequence flow, while the boundary event, attached to the activity boundary, can only have an outgoing sequence flow.

It is worth noting that boundary events are not always ready to do their job. Boundary events (with one exception, which we'll cover later in this chapter) "listen" only when the task or sub-process to which they are attached is active.

How does it work in practice? If the message that our boundary event is waiting for arrived before we started the task or just after we finished it, it would be ignored. The same would happen for the other types of boundary events.

Sometimes, this is good because it allows us to accurately show exception handling for a specific process step. However, if we would like to show that exception handling is the same in two tasks, we should add one boundary event to each task, or put both tasks in a sub-process and add a boundary event to it.

What if we wanted to show that we could handle a certain situation within a whole process? Fortunately, the BPMN specification makes this possible with a special type of sub-process and associated special start events.

Event sub-processes

These special sub-processes are called **event sub-processes**. When it comes to their usage, they are rather unusual elements of BPMN, since we do not insert them as part of the normal process flow (no sequence flow can enter or exit them) but simply place them somewhere in a pool. This is enough to show that they are responsible for handling exceptions for this process.

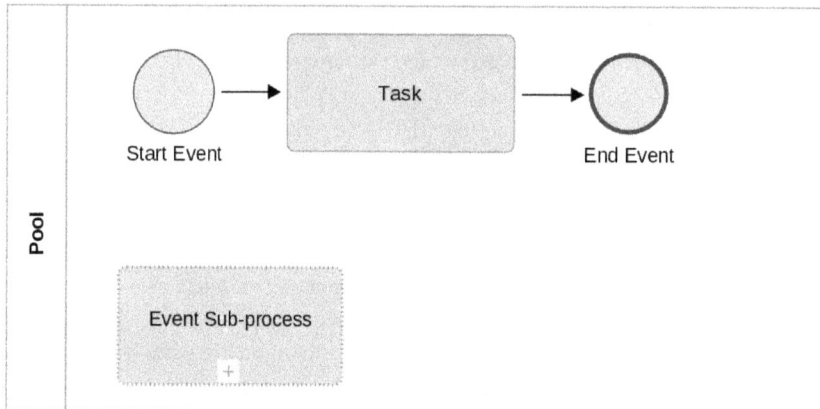

Figure 9.4 – Visualization and usage of an event sub-process

Another unusual aspect is their visualization—like all sub-processes, they have a rectangular shape with rounded corners, but they have an uncommon, dotted border.

Like other sub-processes, they can be used for hierarchical modeling (indicated by a + icon). Slightly more often, however, they are used in expanded form—with the contents immediately visible and without the + icon.

This second case can sometimes lead to confusion, especially if you use a tool in which all the elements of the notation are black and white, since it is easy to confuse such a sub-process with a group, especially if a diagram is zoomed out and it is hard to distinguish a line drawn with dots from a line drawn with dashes and dots.

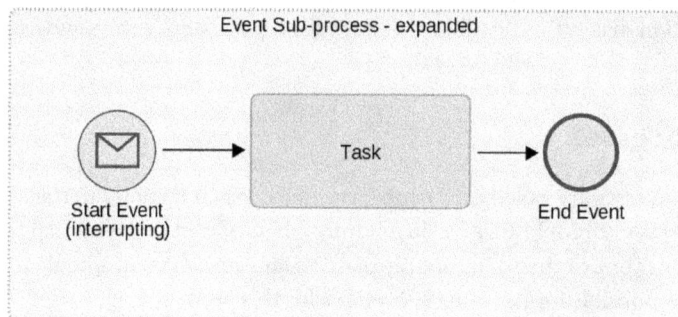

Figure 9.5 – Expanded event sub-process

Event sub-processes are more challenging, but they are worth learning about because they enable exception handling for the entire process, which can sometimes be extremely useful. I find it helpful to think about event sub-processes as older siblings of boundary events. They can either interrupt the entire process or be executed without interrupting the process. However, there are also more similarities. You will discover these next.

Start events in event sub-processes

Each event sub-process always has one start event with a defined trigger. Here, too, there is a strong similarity to boundary events, because the vast majority of trigger combinations are identical for boundary events and start events for these sub-processes.

Let's see this in practice with the example of messages. The boundary events triggered by a message can be interrupting or non-interrupting. To distinguish between them, all you have to do is look at their border. Interrupting events are marked with a solid line, while non-interrupting events are marked with a dashed line.

The start event triggered by a message in an interrupting event sub-process has an envelope icon with a light fill. Since the event sub-process behaves in an interrupting way, the start event has a border drawn with a solid line. This means that the start events for interrupting event sub-processes are visually identical to "normal" start events. In contrast, the start event in a non-interrupting event sub-process has a border drawn with a dashed line. Both variants are shown in *Figure 9.6*.

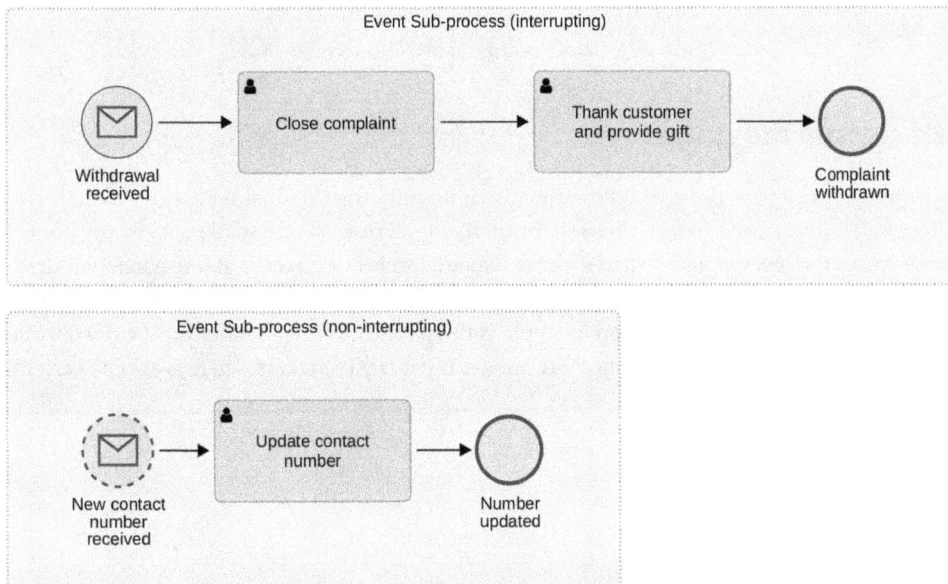

Figure 9.6 – Event sub-processes: interrupting and non-interrupting (triggered by a message)

Now that we've learned how different types of intermediate events work using the example of messages, it's time to discuss the rest of the possible triggers. To help you learn, we'll begin with a trigger that behaves in a pretty similar way to a message.

Signal events

From the previous section, we know that messages are very useful when we want to show the exchange of information between different pools, with always one sender and one recipient. But what if there is an exchange of information in our process, but it does not meet those conditions?

Here, a **signal event** comes in handy. You can think of it as a twin brother of the message, since this type of trigger occurs in all types of events where you could use the message as a trigger. However, it allows us to bypass the limitations of message events.

While the message icon is always an envelope, the signal icon is an equilateral (regular) triangle with the tip pointing upward. As always, for catching signal events, the triangle has a light fill, while for throwing signal events, it has a dark fill.

Start event
(signal)

End event
(signal)

Figure 9.7 – Signal events: active and passive

Signals versus messages

Before discussing examples of signal types, it is worth mentioning the dual nature of a signal. First, the creators of BPMN wanted to describe a situation in which there is one sender, but many possible recipients—hence the name *signal*. Just as an ambulance siren is not directed at one particular driver, but to every driver in the area, a signal informs all potentially interested parties of a certain situation, but how they react is up to them. A good example is the publication of a tender on the portal. Such information is published by one entity, but there are usually many recipients. There is also no certainty as to who will react to the signal.

Secondly, the signal has additional usage derived from a desire to overcome the message limitations. For many people, the concept of sending and receiving a message is extremely useful, but they find it difficult to come to terms with the limitation that the sender and recipient of a message are two different participants who have their own pools. Since it is not always possible, signals have a second use case: they can be used to transmit information both between different pools and within one pool. In this way, you can show that you are receiving an information from colleagues in the same organization. An example of such a signal start event could be **Payroll transfers confirmed**.

As we discussed earlier, a signal behaves quite similarly to a message, so intermediate events whose trigger is a signal can be both catching and throwing, and in the case of boundary events, they can be interrupting as well as non-interrupting. The same goes for start events (including those associated with event sub-processes) and end events.

Figure 9.8 shows examples of various signal events. Let's assume that the signals 1, 3, 4, 5, 7, and 8 are different, and we react to them in different ways. For example, **Signal 4** will cause us to interrupt **Task 2**, and **Signal 7** will cause us to interrupt the entire process.

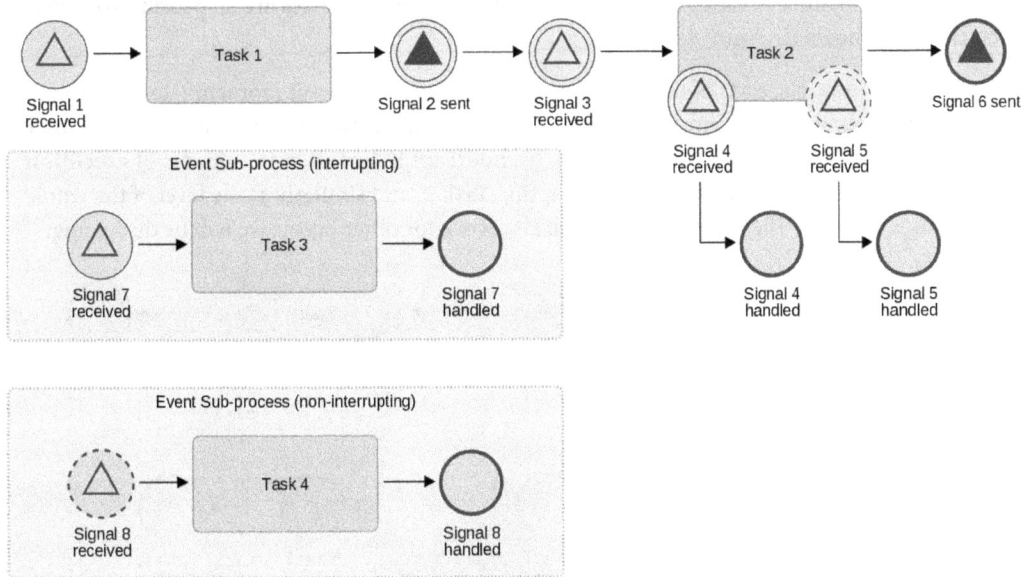

Figure 9.8 – Signal events

Timer events

Now that we've discussed message and signal triggers, it's time for another pair of twin triggers: **timer** and **conditional**. Let's start with a trigger we already know from *Chapter 8*: timer. Events for which time is a trigger are called **timer events**. They are always marked with a clock icon.

When it comes to time, we are always passive (we can only wait for a specific moment; we cannot influence the time), so the icon occurs only in a variant with light fill.

Start event
(timer)

Figure 9.9 – Timer event: passive

Start events, intermediate events within the process flow (obviously, only catching), interrupting and non-interrupting boundary events, and start events of event sub-processes are all possible for timer events. These are shown in *Figure 9.10*.

Of course, in this example, each of the timer events can signify a different moment—for example, a process may start every Monday morning (**Timer 1**); after executing **Task 1** we wait until noon (**Timer 2**); if **Task 2** takes more than 1 hour (**Timer 3**), we interrupt it, but after 45 minutes of execution (**Timer 4**), we can do something without interrupting **Task 2**, and similarly at the level of the whole process (**Timer 5** and **6**). The same approach will also work for other events we will be discussing.

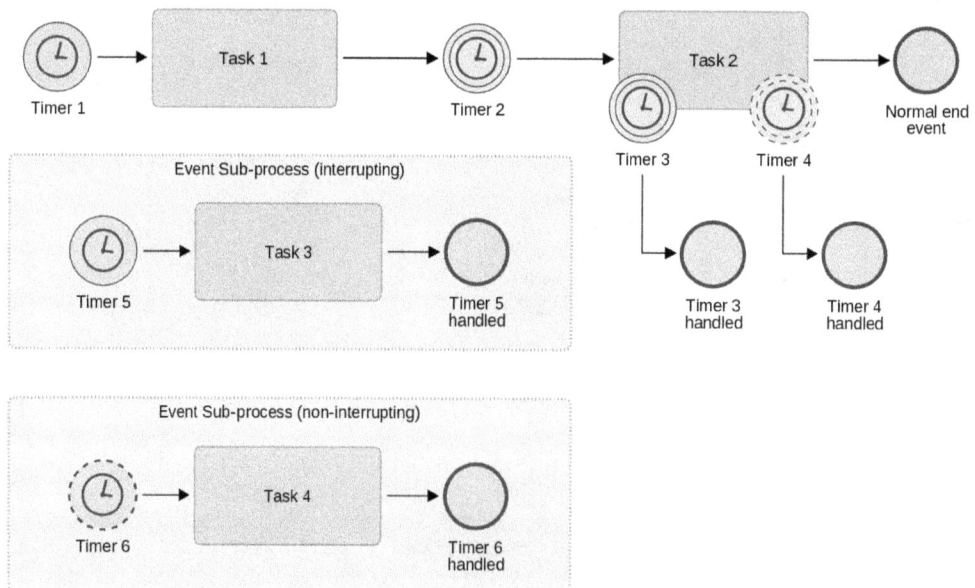

Figure 9.10 – Timer events

Conditional events

Now, let's see how what we've learned about timer events applies to events that are triggered by conditions. **Conditional events**, such as those triggered by time, come only in a catching (passive) form. Their icon is always a lined paper.

Start event
(conditional)

Figure 9.11 – Conditional event: passive

With conditional events, we can show that our processes respond to what happens in their environment. There are many cases where conditions could be used. Even for the rather humorous example from the specification, which refers to the temperature (most likely for cooking), we could find a business-oriented case, such as the process of suspending classes in a school, that begins with a start event of **Temperature in the rooms where classes are held below 18 degrees Celsius/64 degrees Fahrenheit**.

Conditions can also refer to inventory (**Number of items in stock below the defined minimum**—if we were to create a replenishment process for key goods offered by the company), stock prices (**Stock price in market A lower than...** for automatic arbitrage transactions under so-called high-frequency trading), and many other aspects.

In general, if there is something we can measure, a condition can be added to handle it. This allows processes to respond to a broad spectrum of events, from the classic examples we cited to more technically advanced cases, such as sensor data collected by the **Internet of Things (IoT)**.

Just like timer events, start events, intermediate events within the process flow (catching), interrupting and non-interrupting boundary events, and start events of event sub-processes can be conditional. They are all shown in *Figure 9.12*.

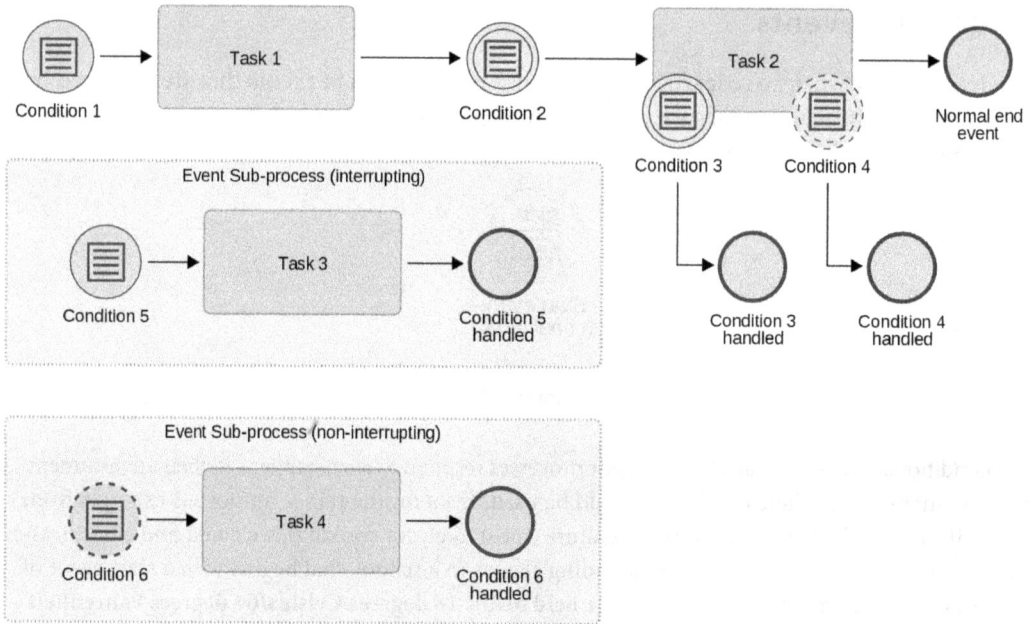

Figure 9.12 – Conditional events

The two pairs of twins we covered so far (message and signal, as well as timer and conditional) allowed us to discuss the most important uses of events in BPMN. However, there are more trigger types available, as well as some other ways of using events that we have not covered so far. In the remainder of this chapter, we will briefly discuss the more technical and slightly more complicated uses of events. We'll start with another pair of triggers, but this time, they are not as closely related as the ones we've already learned about.

Escalation events

The ability to describe error and exception handling is extremely important when modeling processes for automation. This allows us to specify what should happen if something undesirable occurs in the process so that we can handle it properly.

Importantly, BPMN distinguishes two types of problems of different severity: less serious escalations and very serious errors (which we will cover shortly). An **escalation** is always indicated by an upward-facing arrowhead icon (which reminds me a bit of the *Star Trek* insignia).

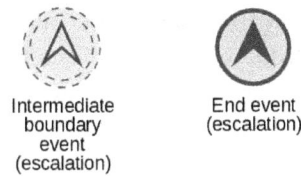

Figure 9.13 – Escalation events: passive and active

Events whose trigger is escalation can be both throwing and catching, but they have far fewer allowed options compared to the events we've covered so far. This is due to the nature of the trigger used to handle exceptions, such as a delay in a process that we need to inform someone about, the unavailability of a product, and so on.

Therefore, escalation cannot be used for normal start events, but for intermediate events within the process flow, where it only occurs as a throwing event (it shows that the process is continuing, but something has gone wrong, and we need to handle this situation somehow). We can also throw an escalation in the end event and use escalation for interrupting and non-interrupting boundary events, as well as for both variants of event sub-processes. We can see all these options in *Figure 9.14*.

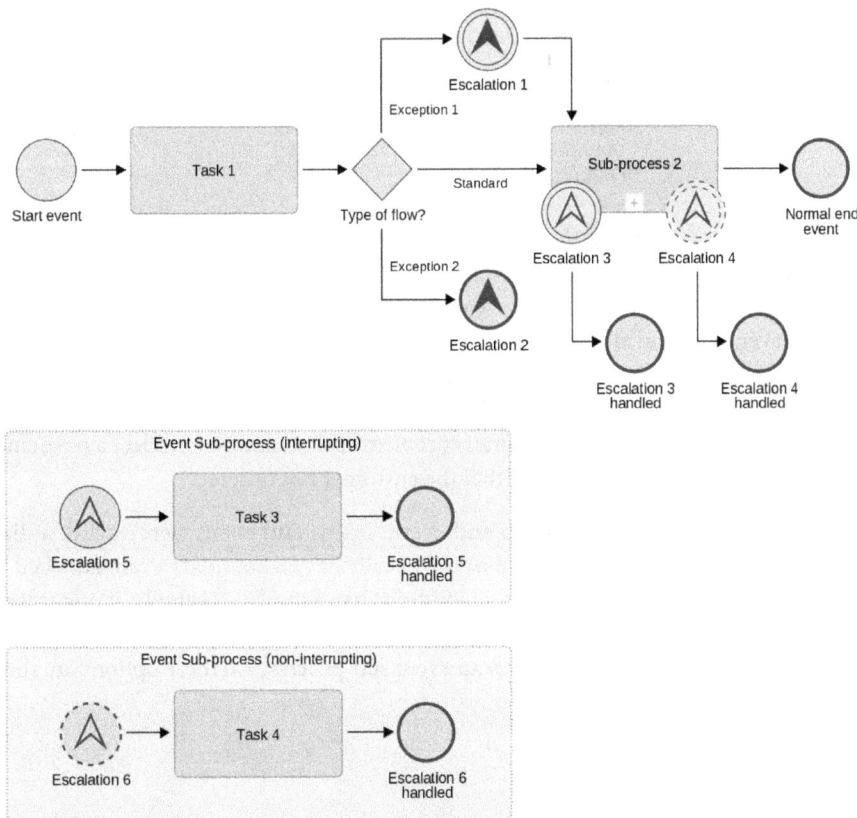

Figure 9.14 – Escalation events

It is worth noting a slight change in *Figure 9.14* from the previous examples. Why do we have **Sub-process 2** instead of **Task 2**? This is due to the nature of escalation, which is often used to inform a higher-level process that it needs to respond to something that happened (for example, a delay in a process, or an unusual process result that may require special handling).

The example shown in *Figure 9.14* could be extended by an additional diagram showing the content of **Sub-process 2**. Escalations 3 and 4 would be thrown (similar to how, in our example, escalations 1 and 2 are being thrown) so that we could catch them by boundary events attached to the border of **Sub-process 2**. This is because escalations should occur in "teams"—they must be thrown somewhere so that they can be caught and handled in a higher-level process.

Error events

As we know, escalations are used to describe situations when not all is lost, and the process can continue. However, there can be cases of severe problems in our process that do not allow the process to finish successfully. **Error events** are meant to provide handling for such situations. Error events have an easy-to-recognize and remember lightning bolt icon.

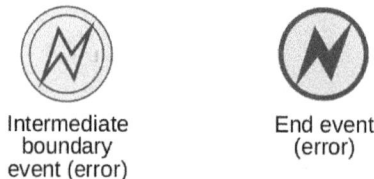

Intermediate
boundary
event (error)

End event
(error)

Figure 9.15 – Error event: passive and active

As you can see, just like it was the case for escalations, both throwing and catching error events are possible. However, error events have fewer options than escalations. This is because an error is something extremely serious, preventing the process from normal completion. That's why there are no non-interrupting error events. Examples of situations where we could use error events are a critical IT failure that we cannot overcome, a big business problem such as failure to collect a payment from a customer's credit card, or a lack of the item that the customer has ordered.

The only type of throwing error event is an end event. If this end event were part of a diagram documenting the content of a sub-process, we would usually have a boundary event attached to this sub-process that would catch this error and provide some handling. For example, if our error was a failed payment, we could contact the customer and use an alternative payment method. We can also handle the error within the same diagram with an event sub-process. All these options are shown in *Figure 9.16*.

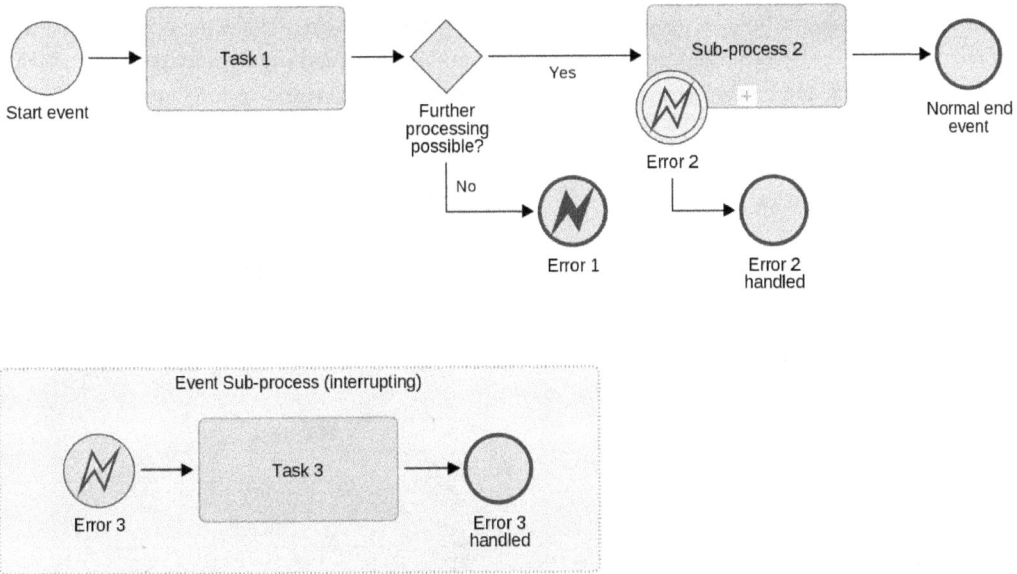

Figure 9.16 – Error events

Errors and escalations allow us to handle various problems with our processes. However, there are also additional options for handling emergencies.

Compensation events

Many people happen to do something in life that they regret and wish they could undo. While this is not always possible in relationships, there is a way to do it in business processes with **compensation events** and **compensation activities**. Compensation is symbolized by an icon commonly used in music players for rewinding.

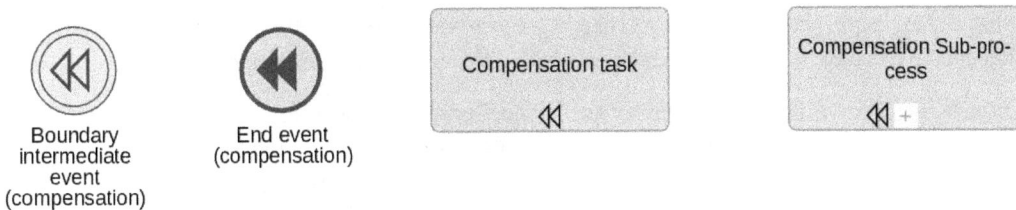

Figure 9.17 – Compensation icons: passive and active events and activities

As you can see, compensation events can be both catching and throwing. Throwing occurs either as an intermediate event within the process flow or as an end event. Catching compensation can be a boundary event, or it can be the start event for an event sub-process, as shown in *Figure 9.18*.

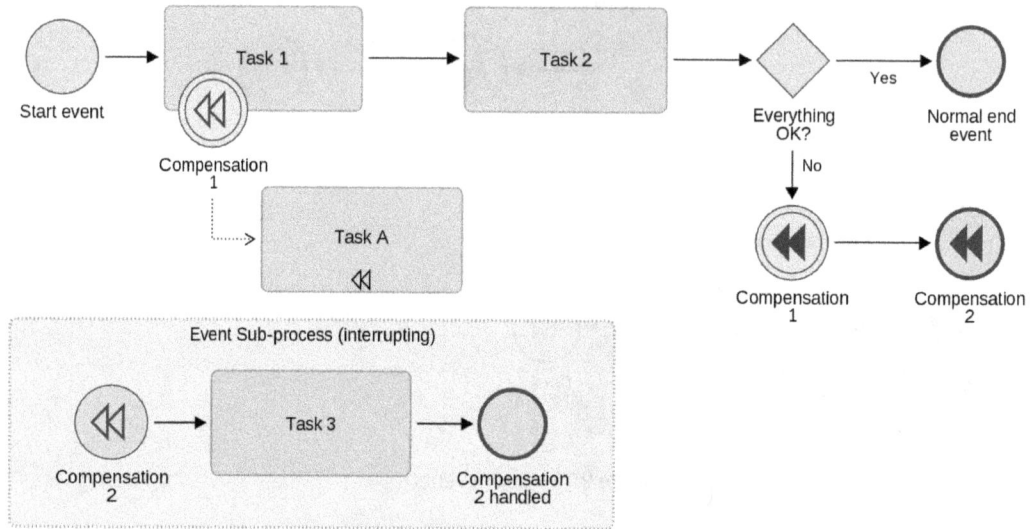

Figure 9.18 – Compensation events

Compensation events have several unique features. These are visible in *Figure 9.18* and will be discussed here. First, since compensation is used to undo something that has already happened, we model it in a rather unusual way, so reading diagrams with compensations requires some preparation.

For the so-called "sunny day scenario," where everything is OK with our process, after performing **Task 1** and **Task 2**, we would reach an end event, **Normal end event**. However, if we have determined that something is not right, we cannot finish the process normally, so we need to roll back something that has already happened in **Task 1** (e.g., charging a customer account, setting a status in the system, saving data to a database, etc.), after which we need to throw appropriate compensation(s).

Let's start with a throwing intermediate event named **Compensation 1**. From the pure logic of the process, you can see that after this event, we go to the end event, where the token of our process instance will be consumed. However, since **Compensation 2** is also a compensation event, it will throw additional compensation, which will provide additional handling for this situation.

Now, let's look at a **Compensation 1** boundary event, which is attached to the border of **Task 1**. This will help us understand the concept of undoing/reverting to a previous state. As you can see, next to **Compensation 1**, we have **Task A**, with a compensation marker. However, this does not look like the diagrams that we've covered so far.

We can read it as follows: if we throw a specific compensation, it must be caught somewhere. Here, there is an exception to the rule, which states that boundary events can only "listen" so long as the element to which they are attached is active. This is completely different from compensation boundary events—they only start "listening" when the task or sub-process to which they are attached is completed.

However, a compensation that is not a part of a normal flow does not follow the standard rules we've learned about so far. As you can see, there is nothing more after **Task A**. There is no outgoing sequence flow because it only shows what needs to be done to undo **Task 1**.

Interestingly, **Task A** also has no incoming sequence flow! This is because it connects to the boundary event through an association relation—the same one that is used for attaching text annotations to elements of a process flow. However, this relation also has an arrowhead, indicating the direction of the flow.

An important rule related to compensation events is that to undo specific process steps, you usually need to "call by name" their specific compensations. In our case, this was quite simple, but there may also be process diagrams in which we want to roll back many different steps. Does this mean we always need to throw many compensations in such situations?

Cancel events

Many people try to use cancel as a marker for an end event to signify, for example, the end of a process that occurred prematurely, such as a customer's decision to cancel an order. **Cancel events**, however, are meant as a workaround for the problem of calling each of the many compensations separately. There are only two types of cancel events: the end event and the intermediate boundary event. Both have the icon of a rotated cross with dark and light fill, respectively.

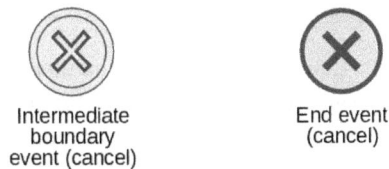

Intermediate
boundary
event (cancel)

End event
(cancel)

Figure 9.19 – Cancel events: passive and active

However, cancel events always occur in tandem with a special type of sub-process: transaction. It can easily be recognized by its characteristic double-lined boundary.

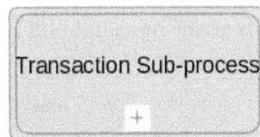

Transaction Sub-process

+

Figure 9.20 – Transaction sub-process

A **transaction sub-process** is used to mark parts of a process that either must be performed correctly or must be undone. As the name suggests, we may use it for banking transactions or IT (e.g., database transactions), but these are just two of many examples. The important thing is that if a cancel boundary event attached to the boundary of a transaction sub-process is triggered, all the elements in it for which we have defined the ability to undo using compensation will be triggered collectively, without the need to call each of them by name.

Terminate events

Like cancel events, terminate events can also be a bit tricky, because their name seems to imply something different than what is in the BPMN specification. **Terminate end event** is the only event with this trigger type. The marker for this event is a black dot.

End event
(terminate)

Figure 9.21 – Terminate end event: active

Typically, this type of event is used by new adepts of BPMN to emphasize that the process ends. However, terminate end event has some other meaning. As we know, a standard end event "consumes" the token entering it, but so long as there are other active tokens for this process instance, the instance lives. This behavior corresponds to our most common business need: to be able to divide a process into independent paths that flow separately, and only when each of them ends can we consider the entire process done.

Sometimes, however, we may reach a state in our process where there is no point in continuing with other activities. This is when a terminate event comes in handy. When a token reaches such an event, all other tokens within the process instance are found and removed.

Link events

It's now time to look at the next (unusual) type of event. While the other types of events we've covered so far had clear connections with real-life scenarios, **link events** only serve navigational purposes. They can only be used as intermediate events within the process flow. The link icon is always an arrow pointing to the right. Not surprisingly, this arrow has a light fill for catching events and a dark fill for throwing events.

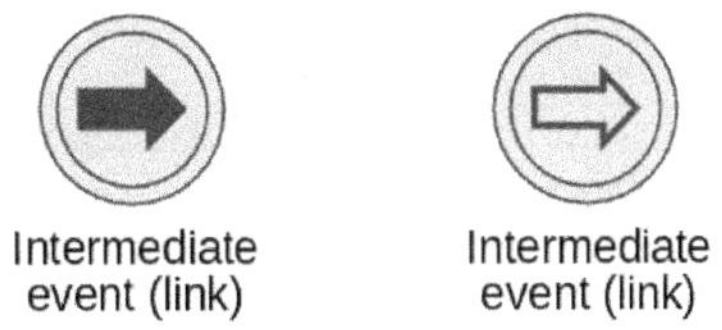

Figure 9.22 – Link events: active and passive

The idea behind link events is quite simple: when dealing with large diagrams, readability is an important issue. In the early 2000s, when process modeling tools were not yet as developed as they are today, it could be a problem to work with diagrams that needed more than one sheet of paper. Even today, in the case of large diagrams with many elements and arrows, there is a risk that the sequence flows will intersect, which may confuse the process readers because they will not be able to tell where a particular arrow leads.

Link events allow us to deal with such situations. They allow a process model to be split into several parts (each easy to print) and facilitate navigation between them, both in digital and printed form. Luckily for us, currently, decent process modeling tools rarely have problems with big models, so we do not need link events as much. However, an additional reason remains: link events allow us to avoid intersecting sequence flows. Instead of drawing a long line that will be crossing other sequence flows (which looks a bit messy), we can use link events.

Figure 9.23 shows two equivalent diagrams. In the first one, the flow elements are connected by a normal sequence flow (the bridges where the lines intersect are not part of BPMN; this is a feature available in ADONIS). In the second one, we have a pair of intermediate events: **A** (throwing) and **A** (catching).

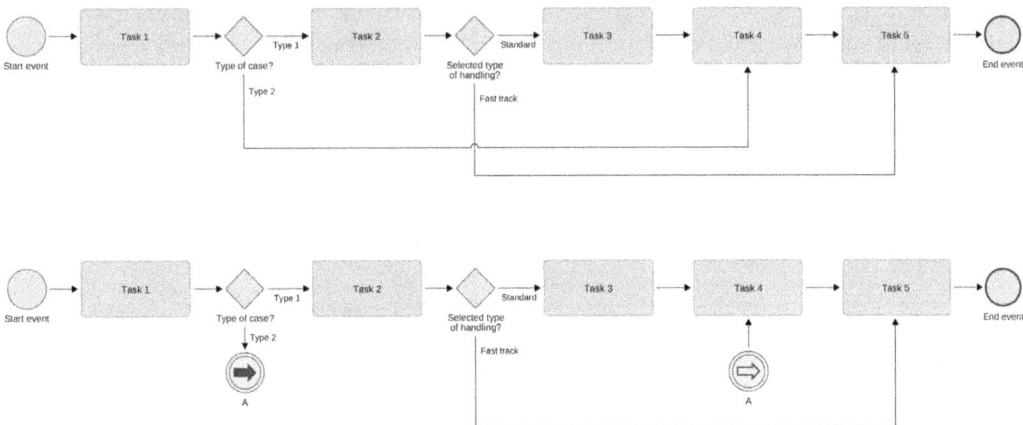

Figure 9.23 – Using link events to improve the readability of big diagrams

🔍**Quick tip**: Need to see a high-resolution version of this image? Open this book in the next-gen Packt Reader or view it in the PDF/ePub copy.

🔖**The next-gen Packt Reader** and a **free PDF/ePub copy** of this book are included with your purchase. Scan the QR code OR go to `packtpub.com/unlock`, then use the search bar to find this book by name. Double-check the edition shown to make sure you get the right one.

Even though you can't see the sequence flow line between them, you should interpret the diagram as if that line were there. This is important because sometimes, people learning BPMN try to use link events to circumvent the notation's rules that do not allow a sequence flow to cross the boundary of a pool (or sub-process). They hope that link events can work as teleports that transfer the token from one pool to another. As you probably expect, this is not a recommended way of modeling, because even if the user manages to cheat the tool validation mechanism, the diagram itself will still be incorrect.

Multiple and parallel events

We have already learned about many types of events and triggers. So far, however, one event has always had one trigger. This is by far the most common situation, but there are also possible exceptions to this rule. The specification allows us to use events that have multiple triggers, in two types, something we will discuss in this section.

Start event	End event	Start event
(multiple)	(multiple)	(parallel
		multiple)

Figure 9.24 – Multiple and parallel events

The first type is the **multiple event**. As you can see, it can be catching or throwing. Its icon is a regular pentagon. The second type is the **parallel multiple event**, whose icon is a plus sign. This event can only be catching.

Let's start with a simple introduction to understand the idea behind these events; we will learn more about them later.

How to start a process

Often, while modeling a process diagram, we use a single start event so that it's easy for readers to see where they should start reading the diagram. However, there are times when we need to show that our process can start in response to several events.

BPMN allows us to add many start events to our diagram. For example, if our process starts at a specific point in time or in response to a customer request, we can insert two start events, triggered by time and message, respectively.

It is also possible that a diagram has several start events leading to various parts of the process. A simple example would be the process of ordering new computer equipment. If a request for a new laptop is made by an ordinary employee, it will most likely take some time, and several verification steps will be needed. Only after a few people accept this purchase can IT provide the equipment to the employee. However, if the new laptop is needed by a director or CEO (or there is another case of higher urgency), we can expect that the verification part of the process will be skipped, or at least severely reduced, and the person ordering will quickly get the equipment he or she needs.

However, the situation in which a process has many start events is the exception rather than the rule. Although it is allowed by the rules of BPMN, the more start events there are, the more difficult it is for the audience to read the diagram correctly. In addition, many start events are often a problem if we intend to perform process optimization using simulation mechanisms, since many simulation engines require that there is only one start event in a process diagram.

For authors of the BPMN specification, multiple start events are the solution to the dilemma of whether to keep the diagram easy to read (and allow only one start event) or rather allow the diagram to document more complex situations too (by allowing many start events). Multiple start events allow us to have our cake and eat it too because we can have a single start event with many triggers. How does it work? For example, in the situation described previously, in which our process starts either at a certain time or when an order from a customer arrives, we could use only one multiple start event and mark that it can be triggered by time or a message.

Interestingly, in the case of multiple events, one glance is not enough to determine what triggers the process: regardless of whether our trigger is a message and a timer, or a timer and a signal, or perhaps a condition and a message, the icon will always be the same, and it will be a pentagon. Therefore, to be able to communicate to the recipients what triggers the process, we have to give the start event a meaningful name, such as **Order received OR deadline reached**.

The BPMN authors did not stop there—a **parallel multiple start event** is also possible. While for a multiple start event, *any of the triggers* is enough for the process to start, for a parallel multiple event, *all of them* must occur.

As you can see, for catching events, the principle of using multiple and parallel events is simple. The multiple event (the one with the pentagon) shows that any of the triggers is enough to go forward, while the parallel event (the one with the plus) shows that all are required. Unfortunately, things become more complicated in the case of throwing events, as shown in *Figure 9.25*.

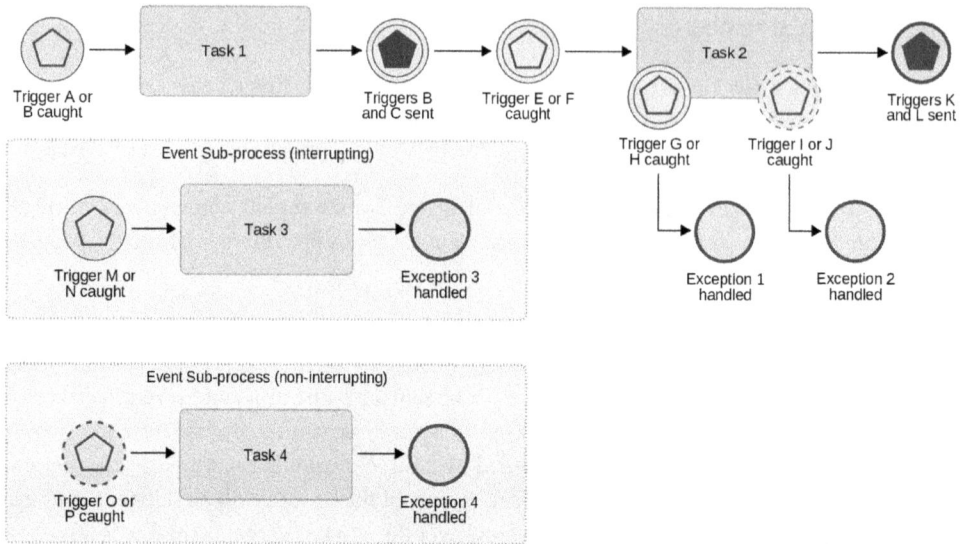

Figure 9.25 – Multiple events

As you can see, in the case of multiple throwing events, we are dealing with logic that we would rather expect from parallel multiple events. This is because *multiple throwing events throw all defined triggers* (e.g., they send a message and a signal). Therefore, it should not come as a surprise that there are no multiple parallel throwing events, as shown in *Figure 9.26*.

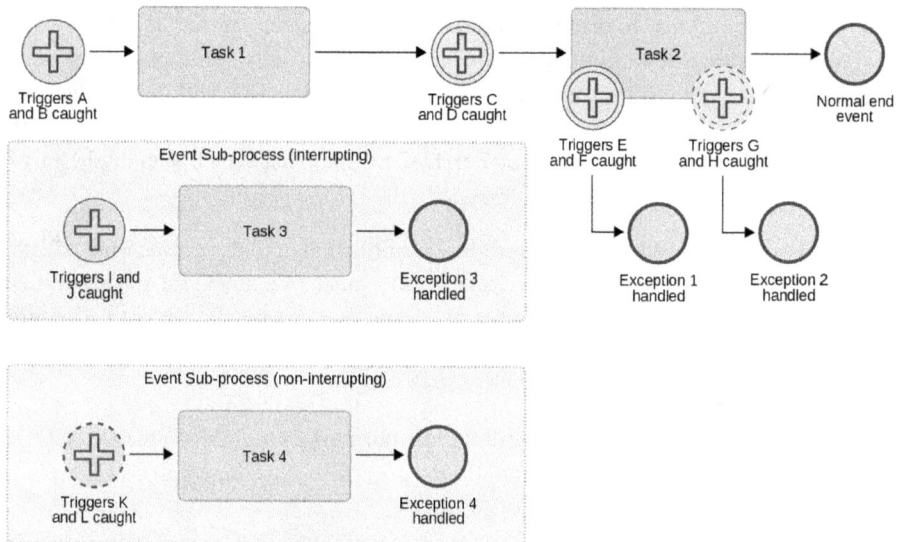

Figure 9.26 – Parallel multiple events

In practice, neither multiple events nor parallel multiple events are used often, but it is worth remembering the pentagon icon. That's because—as we will see in a while—it is used in a very interesting element of BPMN, for which understanding the mechanism of multiple events will prove very useful to us.

Additional types of gateways

The gateway types we've covered so far (XOR, AND, OR) are the most popular ones. However, BPMN also offers more advanced (and less frequently used) types of gateways. We will cover them in this section.

Event-based gateways

All the gateways we have learned about so far are data-based. In practice, this means that when a token arrives at a gateway, we can instantly (by checking the type of gateway and, where necessary, the conditions on the sequence flows) determine which path or paths will get a token.

Sometimes, however, we can't tell that right away, because we have to wait for something to happen. In this case, **event-based gateways** come in handy. If you take a closer look at such a gateway, the marker shown inside will suggest to you that it is different from other gateways we've covered so far. Like all gateways, event-based gateways are diamonds (rhombuses), but they contain a distinctive icon that looks like an intermediate multiple (catching) event. Take a look at *Figure 9.27* and compare it with the catching intermediate event from *Figure 9.25*.

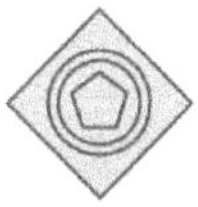

Event-based
gateway

Figure 9.27 – Event-based gateway

How should these gateways be used? Event-based gateways are like exclusive gateways—after the gateway, there can be two or more outgoing sequence flows, but only one of them can be selected (i.e., get a token) at a time.

The difference is that we do not select on the basis of conditions defined for the sequence flows, but by examining the intermediate catching events. The principle is simple: after the gateway, we can have several intermediate events, and each of them represents a certain option that we expect. The first event to occur determines the path we will take. If a moment after the first event occurs, something else happens too, then the other event is ignored.

The message, signal, conditional, timer, and multiple intermediate events can be used after an event-based gateway (but only with triggers we already mentioned).

Interestingly, the specification allows not only intermediate events after this gateway, but also receive tasks. The only requirement is that we need to be consistent and not use receive tasks and intermediate catching message events at the same time. In practice, however, this kind of modeling is neither frequent nor recommended.

How could we use an event-based gateway in practice? Let's go back to our complaint handling process. Let's assume that a customer makes a complaint via chat. Our consultant asks for a choice of options, and we usually get one of two possible answers: to refund or replace the goods. However, it may happen that the customer does not give us an answer. Previous versions of our diagram couldn't handle this (of course, we could add an additional sequence flow with a condition stating *No answer within 15 minutes* and for people interested in process documentation it would probably be fine, but such a diagram would not be 100% correct), but by using an event-based gateway, we can show that if a response doesn't arrive within a predefined time (e.g., 15 minutes), a reminder email and a link to a web form will be sent.

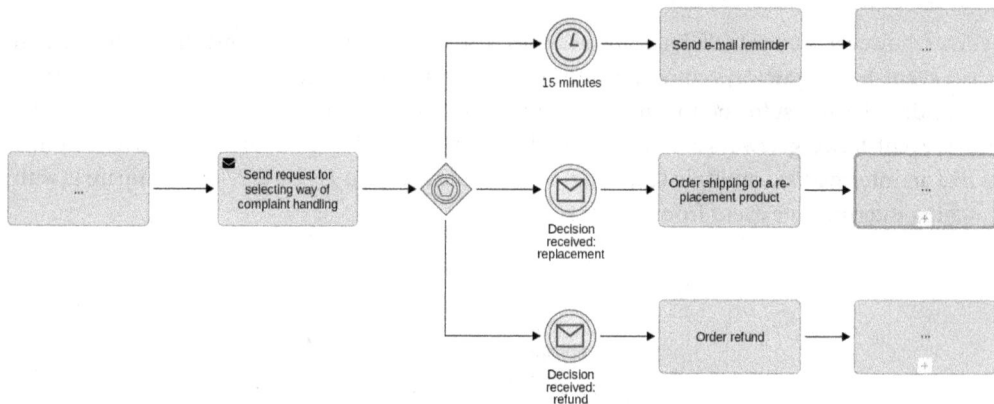

Figure 9.28 – Event-based gateway in practice

An event-based gateway is very useful, especially when our processes communicate with other participants (pools), and we want to show how we will respond to messages from them and what to do in case no response is received. It can also be used in any process where certain events must happen within a certain time, such as quick payments for online orders (if the payment is not made within a certain time, the order will be canceled).

(Partial) Alternative to event-based gateways

While being useful, event-based gateways are also a somewhat more complex BPMN concept. Not every recipient may know how to interpret them correctly. Therefore, I want to present a method that allows you to handle the most common scenario—handling different messages when there is a time limit—without using event-based gateways. I learned this brilliant trick (which is allowed by the BPMN specification and not tool-specific) from my two colleagues from BPMN MIWG: Denis Gagné and Falko Menge.

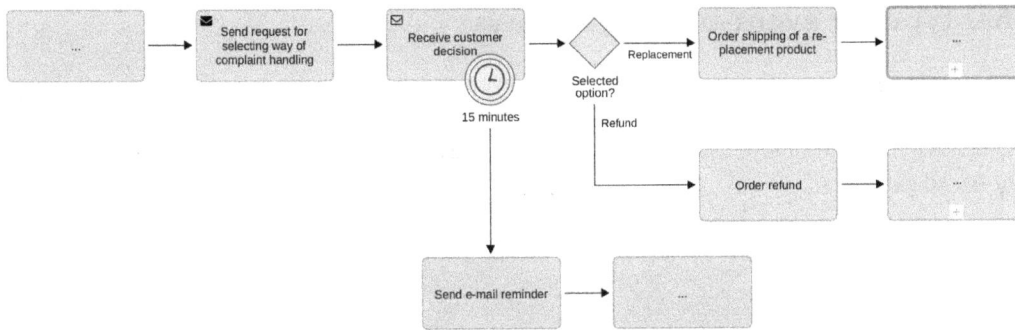

Figure 9.29 – Alternative to event-based gateways

As you can see, the beginning of our diagram is identical to what we had in *Figure 9.28*. The difference appears at the stage of handling messages with customer decisions. Instead of using two separate intermediate events to catch each of the messages, we insert a single receive task, where we get the information from the customer. After receiving the message, we have the data required to pick the correct sequence flow, so we can use an easy-to-understand exclusive gateway.

But how do we deal with the time limit? We can't just add a third path to the exclusive gateway and call it *Time elapsed*, because it's clear from the diagram that we enter the gateway only after receiving a message, so without a message, we will never move on.

Luckily, at this point, we know about the concept of exception handling with boundary events. Since our expected behavior is to stop waiting for a decision from the customer after 15 minutes and send an email, we can simply use an interrupting boundary timer event, which will make sure we don't wait forever for an answer.

Other types of event-based gateways

Event-based gateways occurring within process flows represent a more advanced—but useful in certain situations—element of the notation. However, it is worth mentioning that the specification also describes two more variants of these gateways that can start a process. They are called **instantiating event-based gateways**.

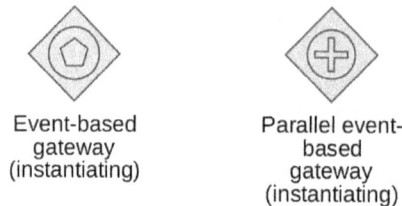

Event-based
gateway
(instantiating)

Parallel event-
based
gateway
(instantiating)

Figure 9.30 – Instantiating event-based gateways

As the icon inside suggests, those gateways are meant to replace start events in some way (that's why they have a circle drawn with a single thin line), where several triggers are possible (a pentagon or plus icon with light fill as they need to be catching). Depending on the type, either any or all of these events must occur to start the process. This way of modeling is neither popular nor recommended; I just wanted to show them to you to help you avoid any misunderstandings.

Complex gateways

In addition to the event-based gateways that we have just discussed, there is another type of data-based gateway in BPMN. This is the **complex gateway**. It has a distinctive asterisk icon in the center and quite specific behavior.

Complex
gateway

Figure 9.31 – Complex gateway

The behavior of the XOR and AND gateways we started with was clear immediately (with XOR, only one path gets a token, while with AND, every path gets a token). For the OR gateway, this was a little more difficult, but it was also clear that by reading the conditions on the sequence flows (to determine which paths get a token), we would know what happens in a process. However, the complex gateway behaves in a more complex way (pun intended).

This gateway can, in principle, behave like any other (or have super sophisticated behavior that we could not get with any other gateways)—its behavior depends on a special condition defined not for the sequence flows, but for the gateway itself. Unfortunately, this condition is one of the invisible attributes of BPMN, so a person seeing only the graphic of the BPMN diagram has no way to determine how this gateway will behave, unless the model creator decides to show the condition through a text annotation, for example.

For some users, the possibility of a gateway that can behave so flexibly is very appealing. In my opinion, however, despite its apparent versatility, the complex gateway is of little use in practice as it has little informational value, but it has great potential to mislead less experienced diagram readers.

The specification allows the use of complex gateways for both opening and closing flows, but in my experience, if the gateway is used at all, it is to merge paths and only for more advanced cases of modeling (e.g., for automation purposes). In general, I would not recommend its use unless your automation project really needs it.

Additional types of sub-processes

In *Chapter 8*, we learned about the two most common types of sub-processes: embedded and call activity. In this chapter, while discovering additional types of events, we also learned about two more: event sub-processes and transactions. We also know that sub-processes can be used in two variants: a **collapsed** variant, which can lead to lower-level models, or an **expanded** variant (the contents of the sub-process are visible).

Now, it's time to cover the last type of sub-process, known as the **ad hoc sub-process**, which is denoted by a tilde (wave).

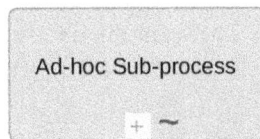

Figure 9.32 – Ad hoc sub-process

This sub-process allows us to document processes that are less structured and require much more knowledge from their performers. It does not contain the complete set of elements that we usually see in a process—for example, there are no start or end events, and the tasks or sub-processes we put inside do not have to be connected by a sequence flow.

We can think of the entire contents of an ad-hoc sub-process as a buffet with lots of options to select from. This gives people performing a process lots of flexibility to choose the elements that they find useful, without being forced to execute all of them or perform them in any specific order.

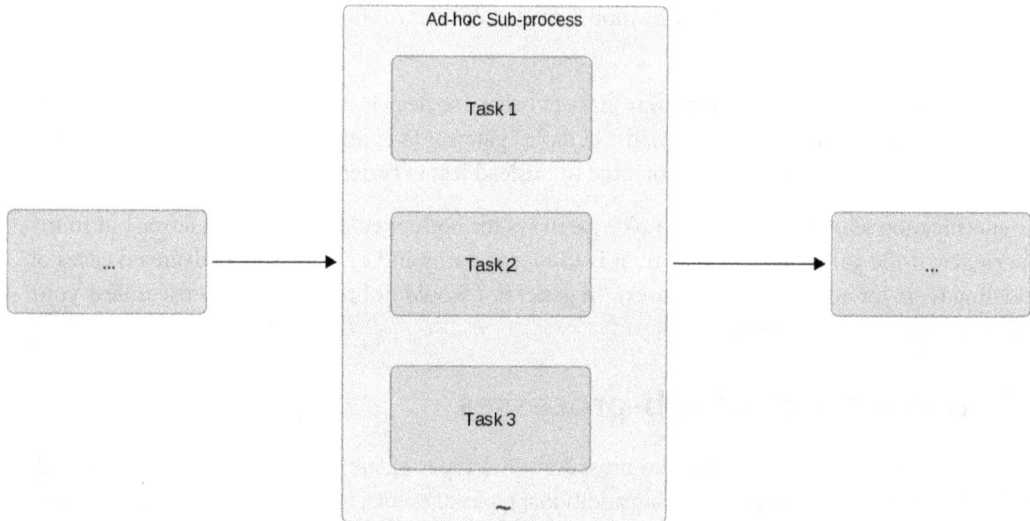

Figure 9.33 – Ad hoc sub-process in practice

While the concept of providing more flexibility for a process is very valuable, ad-hoc sub-processes are not very popular in practice. One of the reasons may be that these elements are not supported by process automation solutions. There's also an additional one—there are several other approaches for knowledge-intensive processes. They may be as simple (but powerful) as checklists or as formal as an additional specification provided by OMG, known as **Case Management Model and Notation** (**CMMN**). This is something we will briefly cover in the last part of this chapter.

Additional types of tasks

Earlier in this book, we learned about the most important types of tasks: those without a type and user, service, manual, send, and receive tasks. In this section, we will briefly discuss other types of tasks found in the BPMN specification.

Business rule tasks

We will start with a **business rule task**. It is a bit more advanced than the other tasks we've covered so far, but it is very useful for complex processes, where many aspects impact the execution of the process, especially the processes we want to automate. This task type icon is a stylized table.

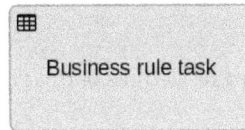

Figure 9.34 – Business rule task

A business rule task allows us to simplify our diagrams significantly by eliminating many unnecessary decision gateways and sequence flows, but most importantly, it makes our automated processes more flexible.

Imagine a company that sells its products in different markets to different customer segments. Some order more, some order less. Some are regular, long-time customers. Some are new customers we don't know yet. We can offer goods to the public sector through tenders or to private entities. Add to that different countries, legal systems, and currencies and, as you can see, the situation gets quite complicated. Will we offer the same price to everyone? Or will we vary the levels of discounts?

If we were to model the sales process, we would have to decide how we would approach the discount calculation. Shall we try to describe everything in the form of a single diagram? Such a diagram would be large and complicated to read. Moreover, based on such a model, it is extremely difficult to determine whether our rules are consistent, free of internal contradiction, or whether we have forgotten some important combination of conditions relevant to a certain customer segment. Modifying rules described in such a way is difficult and risky.

Such problems occur not only in processes related to discounts but also in determining insurance premiums, pricing complex services, sophisticated purchasing processes, or those related to accepting invoices or other documents, where there are multiple levels of acceptance, depending on the type and amount.

As you can see, using business process diagrams to show such aspects of **decision management** may not always be an acceptable choice. Luckily, there is a better way, popularized by **The Business Rules Manifesto**, which suggests that business process models should not contain detailed written rules, but that rules should be described and managed differently.

These rules are not only used for documentation purposes. A special type of software, known as a business rules engine, also allows those rules to be automated, and a BPMN business rule task assumes that a process can use this approach. By using a business rule task, we can greatly simplify our diagram by presenting a piece of the process where we refer to business rules, and then showing how this can affect our process.

As you will learn in the last part of this chapter, we can extend this even further thanks to the additional specification provided by OMG: **Decision Model and Notation (DMN)**.

If you would like to learn more about the concept of business rules, I would suggest reading The Business Rule Manifesto at `https://www.businessrulesgroup.org/brmanifesto.htm`.

Script task

Another type of task in BPMN is the **script task**. Tasks of this type have an icon of a written scroll of paper, or simply a script.

Figure 9.35 – Script task

Like a service, it is a process element that is executed automatically, but in a slightly different way. As intended by the authors of the specification, a service is a step in which the process automation engine calls out external applications that provide certain services. A script, on the other hand, is a step in which certain simple actions are performed directly by the process execution engine.

Examples of such elements include simple validation of user-entered data and running simple calculations. These are only theoretical recommendations; however, as in many models, these principles are not followed. In some tools, service tasks are used to call specific classes of Java code. In general, service tasks are much more common in BPMN diagrams than script tasks.

Call activity

The last type of task is the **call activity task**. It is unique in many respects. First, it does not have an icon specific to its type and instead features a thick border, identical to that of a call activity sub-process.

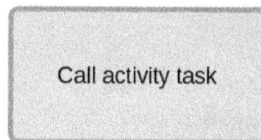

Figure 9.36 – Call activity task

BPMN allows us to have call activities that are tasks or sub-processes. In both cases, it refers to reusing a certain standard, but in a different way.

The sub-process call activity, which allows us to call other process diagrams, is an extremely useful and popular element of BPMN. On the other hand, task call activity is neither very helpful nor popular.

What is the reason for this? The authors of the BPMN specification wanted to make it possible to show that certain standardized activities occur in processes. Their idea makes it possible to define certain types of tasks (e.g., user, manual, script, and business rule tasks) as so-called **global tasks**, serving as a kind of definition of how things should be done.

Global tasks can be referenced by a task call activity. The concept is quite interesting, but in my opinion, it doesn't quite meet actual business needs. There is also no well-defined way in which modeling tools are supposed to support this, which means that the implementation of this piece of the specification can vary greatly. Thus, this is an element of notation that is unlikely to be used in practice in a standardized way across tools.

Multi-instances

The last element of the BPMN specification that I want to mention in this chapter is the mechanism for marking activities as being performed many times.

Usually, when we think of a process and its steps, what comes to our mind is that once a step is finished, we can move on. Sometimes, however, the situation is a bit more complex. It may be that after completing a step, a check is needed to see whether the desired result has been achieved—if so, we can move on, and if not, the step must be repeated. It is also possible that we can tell in advance that a certain process step will need to be performed several times for us to move on.

For situations like this, BPMN provides special markers that can be applied to both tasks and sub-processes.

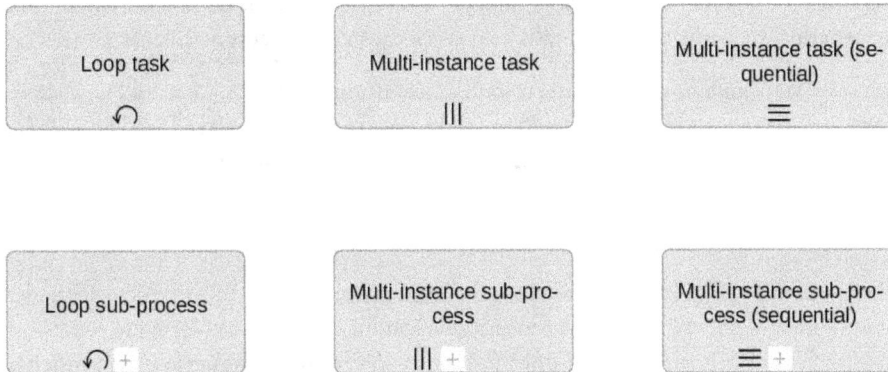

Figure 9.37 – Loop, multi-instance, and sequential multi-instance tasks and sub-processes

A **loop**, whose marker is an arrow in a circle, means that a given step must be performed several times, but we cannot tell how many times in advance. We can only say it will be done as many times as needed (until some condition is met). A classic example is negotiation—going into a meeting, we are not sure whether an agreement will be reached the first time, or whether further meetings will be necessary.

Multi-instance, often shortened to **MI**, tasks have the familiar symbol of three vertical lines, which in BPMN indicates that there is more of something.

Such elements also execute more than once, but this time, we know how many times it will be in advance. A perfect example is processing batch/group of invoices that need to be paid. While performing this activity, we know that all the transfers must be executed, and we cannot leave any invoice unpaid.

A multi-instance marker can also have a **sequential** variant, indicated by three horizontal lines. This means that the work cannot be divided among different people who do it in parallel (which is what the standard MI version assumes), but that it must be done sequentially. If you are not sure how to remember which marker version is for parallel and which for sequential, there's a great trick that I learned from Filip Stachecki from EduMAX: the parallel variant has three vertical lines in its name (three **l**s).

Extending BPMN

As you've seen, BPMN offers you many possibilities. It is an easy-to-use standard notation that can be used by both business and IT users. There are hundreds of tools that support it, and lots of learning materials that can help you deepen your knowledge.

However, even a 500+ page specification of BPMN could not cover all business modeling scenarios (especially when you take into account that the BPMN 2.0 specification also covers so-called **choreography diagrams** and **conversation diagrams**—two additional types of diagrams that are not very popular). The authors clearly state that the scope of BPMN is about the processes and not about concepts such as organizational modeling, data and information modeling, and strategy modeling, as well as modeling business rules, process simulation, and monitoring. They do not even mention other important scenarios, such as risk and compliance management or process architecture.

Luckily for us, BPMN contains the brilliant concept of extensions. It is possible to add new attributes, markers, or artifact shapes, so long as the changes do not conflict with already existing elements. Extensions are also saved in a special way in XML BPMN Diagram Interchange files.

BPMN extensions in practice

BPMN extensions allows tool vendors to store their extensions inside BPMN files (such as form definitions and other elements needed for process automation), but they also provide some add-ons for standards such as BPMN in Color and BPMN i18n (as you've probably guessed, the former allows colors to be exchanged in BPMN diagrams, while the latter provides support for internationalization, which involves storing diagram translations that are in several languages in a single file).

I want to share a simple example taken from the reference files provided by BPMN MIWG at `https://github.com/bpmn-miwg/bpmn-miwg-test-suite/tree/master/Reference`. If you would like to explore more than a small snippet of the BPMN XML taken from a full file, please check out the `C.8.0.bpmn` file:

```
<semantic:sendTask id="_a97c1a48-faba-447b-bfa6-7aa81a6fe0a0"
name="Notify Employee of Approval" triso:readOnly="false"
implementation="##WebService">
<semantic:extensionElements>
<adonis:MailTo>${email}</adonis:MailTo>
<adonis:MailSubject>Your Vacation Request ${SYS.PROCESSINSTANCE_ID}
was approved manually</adonis:MailSubject>
```

```
<adonis:MailBody>Dear ${first-name},
your Vacation Request ${SYS.PROCESSINSTANCE_ID}
from ${fromdatepicker}
to ${todatepicker}
was approved manually.
Comment: ${comment}
Best regards,
Your BOC Adonis Process Automation</adonis:MailBody>
<zeebe:taskDefinition type="emailService"/>
<zeebe:ioMapping>
<zeebe:input source="= &quot;&lt;html&gt;&lt;p&gt;Hi  &quot; +
Current Vacation Status.name + &quot;,&lt;/p&gt; &lt;p&gt; &lt;/
p&gt; &lt;p&gt;Your vacation request from &quot; + From + &quot; to
&quot; + To + &quot; was approved.&lt;/p&gt; &lt;p&gt; &lt;/p&gt;
&lt;p&gt;Best regards&lt;/p&gt; &lt;p&gt; &lt;/p&gt; &lt;p&gt;This is
an automated message generated by the vacation system.&lt;/p&gt;&lt;/
html&gt;&quot;" target="mailBody"/>
<zeebe:input source="= &quot;Vacation Approved&quot;"
target="mailSubject"/>
<zeebe:input source="= Current Vacation Status.email"
target="mailAddress"/>
</zeebe:ioMapping>
<kp:field name="to" stringValue="info@knowprocess.com"/>
<kp:field name="htmlVar" stringValue="vacationApproved"/>
<i18n:translation xml:lang="de">Mitarbeiter über die Genehmigung
informieren</i18n:translation>
<i18n:translation xml:lang="es">Notificar al empleado de la
aprobación</i18n:translation>
<i18n:translation xml:lang="fr">Aviser l'employé de l'approbation</
i18n:translation>
</semantic:extensionElements>
<semantic:incoming>_f2b0da63-d841-4457-ad85-7d86c8b5c1d2</
semantic:incoming>
<semantic:outgoing>_a5441c65-06f8-4972-8158-e6f61f904841</
semantic:outgoing>
</semantic:sendTask>
```

As you can see, apart from standard elements for the task, such as the type (in this case, send), name, ID, information about incoming and outgoing sequence flows, and more, there is also a block where all the extensions can be stored.

For simplicity, I removed some elements, so this is not a complete fragment of an XML file, but it gives you a nice overview of how different tools (in this case, **Trisotech**, **ADONIS**, **Camunda/Zeebe**, and **KnowProcess**) can add their technical extensions to automate the process (in this case, send an email about the acceptance of holiday request) and how translations could also be stored. Of course, this is an example file used by BPMN MIWG to showcase how different BPMN tools can work together, so in a real-life scenario, you would not have extensions from that many tools.

This example only contained BPMN extended with additional technical attributes, but it is also possible to extend BPMN with additional notations. For example, full case C.8.0 uses DMN and decision services to make some decisions about holiday requests fully automatic.

BPM+ (BPMN, DMN, and CMMN)

We've already mentioned several times that OMG also created other standards that can be used together with BPMN. The trio of BPMN, DMN, and CMMN is called **BPM+**. This set of standards can be very useful in healthcare, but also in other areas.

The **DMN** specification is a notation that allows business rules to be described in the form of decision requirements diagrams and an organization's decisions to be automated.

The **CMMN** specification deals with Adaptive Case Management, an area where it is not possible to specify exactly what needs to be done step by step since human decisions are needed. CMMN provides a graphical notation and interchange format for those purposes.

While BPMN is mature, stable, and increasingly popular, DMN is not as popular yet, but is developing rapidly (as of June 2025, work on DMN 1.7 is in progress), while CMMN is not subject to such frequent updates (version 1.1 was published in 2016) and is the least popular of the three.

Why DMN?

I find DMN a very interesting standard. It is gaining popularity rapidly and is very valuable for organizations with lots of complex rules that are frequently changing. Keeping those rules outside BPMN diagrams allows them to be easier to read and much easier to maintain.

That's because attempting to keep all the rules inside process diagrams would usually require a lot of gateways and additional tasks. This would not only make diagrams bigger but would often lead to other problems. Let's see it in practice using our complaint-handling process.

The process we've used so far (shown in *Figure 8.1*) assumed that the complaint documentation needs to be checked by an employee in some kind of IT system, automating the whole process. Based on a decision of an employee about complaint validity, two options were possible: a complaint could be rejected or found valid and accepted for further processing.

Even though this process has IT support, this process would not be very fast since an employee needs to check all the documentation before the process can continue. How could we speed it up?

While for some cases it may be necessary to involve the employee, perhaps we could identify cases where fully automated fast-track handling could be possible.

For this example, I will assume that we can automatically reject cases where the complaint documentation does not confirm that the product was bought from our company. For cases that are not automatically rejected, we will have two types of handling. Some cases where it is obvious that the complaint should be accepted are accepted automatically to speed up the process, while cases that are not obvious are routed to employees so that they can be checked. This way, employees would only need to check complex cases while the rest could be done automatically.

How should we decide whether a case is obvious or not? Perhaps if there were several valid complaints regarding the same product and delivery method within a short period of time, this means there is a common root cause of problems, so similar complaints should also be accepted. It would also be a valuable input for continuous improvement specialists, who could figure out what should be changed to avoid problems like this in the future.

Maybe an additional rule could be suggested: for low-value complaints from long-term customers, we could automatically accept them too. This would probably trigger a suggestion to check whether those customers did not have too many complaints in the past year or too many rejections (to avoid fraud).

Of course, real-life complaint-handling is much more sophisticated. We should consider more robust fraud protections (for example, not only covering cases of our long-term customers), ensuring that our process creates a good customer experience while gathering all the data needed for decision-making, plus ensuring legal compliance.

This last point could be especially tricky if our company were serving customers in various countries with different legal systems because it would impact the way we handle customer data (e.g.,GDPR for customers from the European Union), how returns are processed, and whether the customer gets all the necessary information about their rights regarding the complaint (e.g., that customers from the UK are informed that escalation to the Legal Ombudsman is possible and that vulnerable customers are treated fairly).

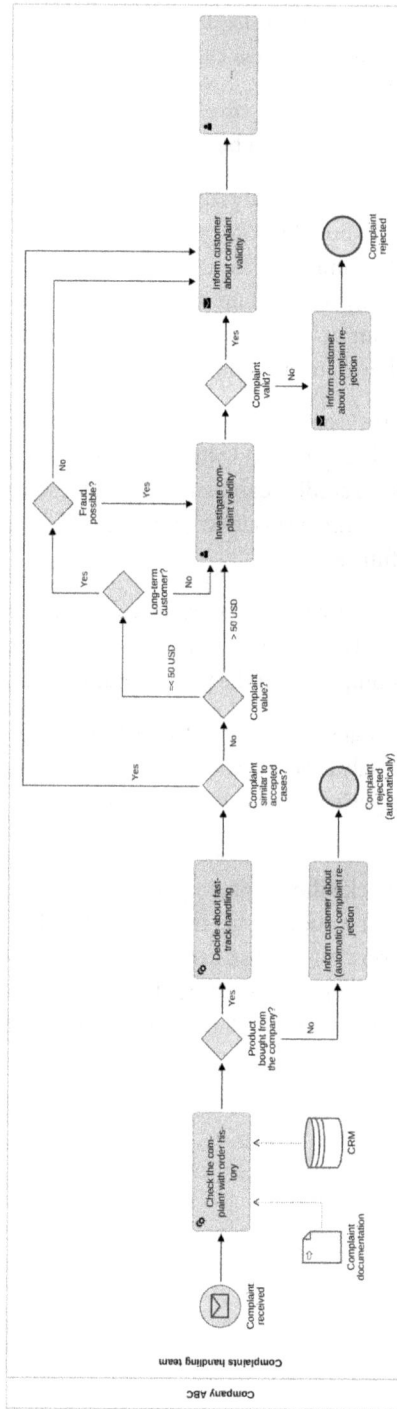

Figure 9.38 – Attempt to document rules with gateways and tasks

Figure 9.38 shows a possible diagram of a process where all the mentioned rules are handled with tasks and gateways. As you can see, it is not very easy to read. If we need to change some values (e.g., 50 USD to 100 USD), this will take some time. If we need to add more rules or change their combinations, the situation becomes difficult. Spotting places where something is wrong with our rules is nearly impossible. Now, let's see how this could be simplified with DMN.

Basics of DMN

While DMN itself is a relatively new standard (DMN 1.0 was officially published in 2015), it is based on many best practices of business rules management experts. Just like BPMN, it can be used for documentation purposes, but also for automation.

A graphical model that allows decisions to be documented in DMN is called **Decision Requirement Diagram (DRD)**. *Figure 9.39* shows a very simple example DRD that could help us document our customer complaint process.

As you can see, there are a few elements of DMN here, such as **Decision**, **Input Data**, and **Knowledge Source**. Other, more advanced ones, such as **Business Knowledge Model**, plus two types of **Decision Service**, are not shown.

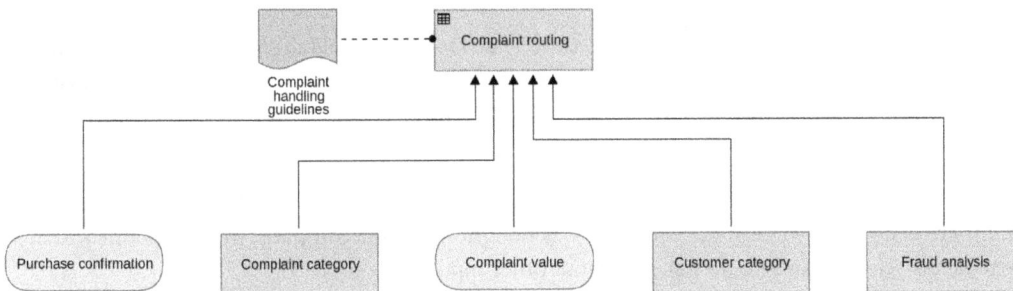

Figure 9.39 – Simple DRD

The rectangles (**Complaint routing**, **Complaint category**, **Customer category**, and **Fraud analysis**) are **decisions**. In DMN, they show places where some input data needs to be analyzed to come up with some results (outputs).

The oval shapes (**Purchase confirmation** and **Complaint value**) are **input data**. They represent data needed as input for the decisions.

The element with three straight lines and one wavy (**Complaint handling guidelines**) is a **Knowledge Source**. It represents elements that influence decisions, such as regulations or pieces of legislation.

DMN also offers several types of lines that connect objects. The solid line is called **Information Requirement**. The dashed line with a black dot is called **Authority Requirement**. There are also several other types of arrows not used in our example.

While the graphical model showing the connections between decisions, input data, and other elements can be useful for a better understanding, it does not help us solve our problems with the complexity of decisions. For this purpose, we need another DMN element: **decision tables.**

A decision table allows us to show, clearly and unambiguously, which combinations of input data lead to which outputs (i.e., the results of our decision). This is very useful as documentation, but even more powerful when used for automation.

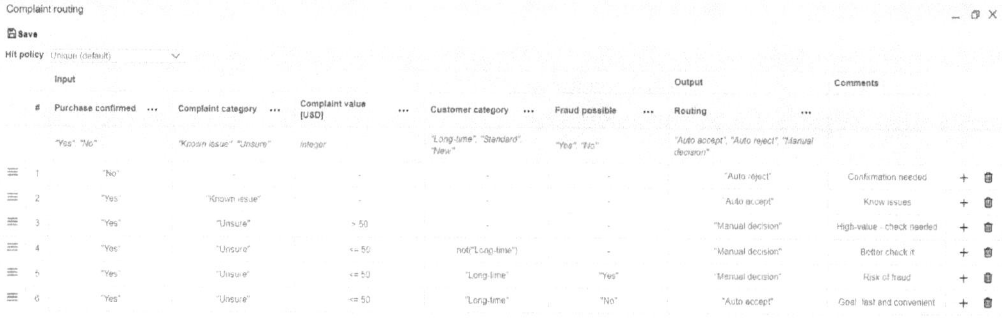

Complaint routing

Save

Hit policy Unique (default)

	Input					Output	Comments
#	Purchase confirmed	Complaint category	Complaint value [USD]	Customer category	Fraud possible	Routing	
	"Yes", "No"	"Known issue", "Unsure"	integer	"Long-time", "Standard", "New"	"Yes", "No"	"Auto accept", "Auto reject", "Manual decision"	
1	"No"	-	-	-	-	"Auto reject"	Confirmation needed
2	"Yes"	"Known issue"	-	-	-	"Auto accept"	Know issues
3	"Yes"	"Unsure"	> 50	-	-	"Manual decision"	High-value - check needed
4	"Yes"	"Unsure"	<= 50	not("Long-time")	-	"Manual decision"	Better check it
5	"Yes"	"Unsure"	<= 50	"Long-time"	"Yes"	"Manual decision"	Risk of fraud
6	"Yes"	"Unsure"	<= 50	"Long-time"	"No"	"Auto accept"	Goal: fast and convenient

Figure 9.40 – Decision table

Figure 9.40 shows a simple example of a decision table. Each row represents a rule. Columns 2 (**Purchase confirmed**) to 6 (**Fraud possible**) represent inputs needed to make a decision. Column 7 (**Routing**) shows the output, which is the result of our decision. Column 8 (**Comments**) allows us to add some background information to those rules.

As you can see, decision tables are meant to be easy to read and use. For example, the first row shows that if there is no confirmation that the item was bought from our company, the complaint will be automatically rejected, and we do not care about other inputs.

The second row is also easy to read. If we know that the customer bought from us and that the item could be faulty due to our error (either in production, packaging, or shipping), we want to save time for the customer and the company, and we accept the case of known issues automatically.

In rows 3 to 5, things start to get more interesting. Purchase is confirmed, but this time, we are not sure why the problem occurred. That's why we will need to ask our employee to investigate the case.

Those three rows are needed because we achieve the same results, but based on different inputs. Row 3 shows that if the value of the complaint is over 50 USD, we want a manual check due to the high value. Rows 4 and 5 cover cases when the value is up to 50 USD, but we have different categories of customers, while for long-time customers, we are concerned about possible fraud.

To understand those rules better, we need to learn about an additional important concept covered by DMN: **Friendly Enough Expression Language** (FEEL). Let's take a look at the values in the **Complaint value** column. In row 3, we have **> 50**, while in rows 4 and 5, we have **<= 50**. As you may expect, this shows for which complaint amounts which rule will be applied.

FEEL offers many types of operators. For numbers, we could use comparisons (less than, greater than, or equal to) or ranges. For example,]**30..50**] would mean a range from over 30 (but without it) to 50. There are also operators for texts. For example, row 5 shows that for customers of the "Long-time" type with a risk of fraud, we will trigger a manual check. Row 4 applies to all customers who are not of the "Long-time" category.

DMN allows many interesting possibilities for process professionals. It can make automation much easier and reduce the risk of misunderstandings because the diagrams and decision tables make it abundantly clear what should be done in which situation. This is a very valuable extension to BPMN. However, as you will see next, there are other ways to extend BPMN to make it more valuable for both business and technical users.

BPMN fit for business

Apart from extending BPMN with technical attributes for the purpose of automating processes or combining it with other OMG standards, it is also possible to link it with other attributes, objects, and models to support other business scenarios.

Many vendors of EBPA tools add special attributes to BPMN diagrams so that they can be used for different purposes. I will show an example ADONIS from BOC Group where the so-called fit for business BPMN is available. You can learn more about this topic at `https://docs.boc-group.com/adonis/en/docs/17.0/sample-models`.

Let's go back to our complaint-handling process. How could we extend it? Apart from providing meaningful descriptions that could serve as documentation for people responsible for performing this process, most probably, we would like to specify roles in the organization that are responsible for executing tasks, along with people accountable for approving results and keeping them consulted and informed (**RACI**). We would also probably like to give process performers documents containing best practices and how-tos, mention which applications are used, how this step can be improved, and how we measure **KPIs**, what the risks are (e.g., fraud), how long it takes to perform this process step, and how much it costs.

In the GitHub repository that contains the resources for this chapter (`https://github.com/PacktPublishing/Practical-Business-Process-Modeling-and-Analysis/tree/main/Chapter09`), you can find more information about extending BPMN, as well as examples showing elements such as risk management, simulations, and more.

The key thing is that the elements of BPMN that you've learned about in this book are universal and the same from tool to tool. If your tool supports BPMN Diagram Interchange, you can move diagrams between tools so that you can work with business users in one tool, and when you have a vision of a future state process, you can move the diagram to the automation tool, where it can be extended by IT specialists with technical details. Therefore, you can use your BPMN skills not only to document processes, but also to analyze and improve them, as well as plan digital transformation and process automations.

Of course, as was already hinted, diagrams used for process automation often contain many more technical details needed to make everything run smoothly. However, those details are tool-specific, so I will not cover them here. If you would like to learn more, check out the aforementioned GitHub repository.

Summary

In this chapter, you learned about the more advanced concepts of BPMN. We covered events and their various uses, especially the support for handling errors, exceptions, and special situations in processes (which is one of BPMN's unique features). You learned how events help us create sophisticated models that can be used not only for documentation purposes, but also for analysis and automation. We also covered other types of elements, such as tasks, sub-processes, and gateways, so that you know which ones could be beneficial in your projects. Finally, we had a chance to see how BPMN can be extended to support scenarios that are not covered by BPMN out of the box.

Further reading

- If you would like to learn more about DMN, CMMN, and how they work together with BPMN, I suggest looking at a great document, *Field Guide to Shareable Clinical Pathways*. Since the group responsible for it recently moved from OMG to Health Level Seven International, check out the download link provided in this book's GitHub repository: `https://github.com/PacktPublishing/Practical-Business-Process-Modeling-and-Analysis/tree/main/Chapter09`.

- If you would like to learn more about CMMN, there's a great book, *CMMN Method and Style: A Practical Guide to Case Management Modeling for Documentation and Execution*, written by Bruce Silver. Bruce also wrote *DMN Method and Style: 3rd edition, with DMN Cookbook*. You need to learn about his "Method and Style" approach!

- I also want to recommend *Real-Life BPMN (5th edition): Includes an introduction to DMN*, written by Bernd Ruecker and Jakob Freund. My five-star reviews of their books are a good indicator of how much I like what they write.

- Finally, if you want to explore the topic of decision management, the best location I know of is `https://dmcommunity.org`, run by Jacob Feldman. Apart from DMN-related content, you will find many thought-provoking posts about decision management and AI.

Unlock this book's exclusive benefits now

Scan this QR code or go to `packtpub.com/unlock`, then search this book by name.

Note: Keep your purchase invoice ready before you start.

10

Measuring the Business Value of Process Transformation

As we've progressed through the book, you may have noticed our emphasis on the significance of business processes in the context of digital transformation and how this impacts your career.

Engaging in process transformations, digital automation programs, and comprehensive overhauls of business operations can help you develop new skills that enhance your expertise in business technology. We aim to inspire you to explore the world of business processes and view them as essential components of your professional skill set.

How can you convey the importance of embracing process management within your business group or company, especially when some colleagues are skeptical?

In today's fast-paced business environment, companies continually seek ways to improve, automate, and enhance the strategic adaptability of their operational processes to remain competitive and navigate a world that can change from one day to the next.

Digital initiatives fail for one simple reason: nobody can see how work gets done. Sometimes, understanding what work is on a global scale can present significant challenges. Invisibility breeds waste and delays, and AI projects often fail to pass compliance checks. Without a robust process architecture, discussions about digital transformation or AI automation programs lack a solid foundation.

In an AI-driven future, a well-structured process architecture will be crucial for governance, ensuring that AI solutions perform tasks according to the responsible standards set by the organization. By requiring documentation for every step of business operations, process architecture enforces traceability, making it easier to audit AI decisions and AI-driven processes—an essential requirement for regulatory and ethical compliance.

While the prospect of acquiring new skills and participating in innovative projects can energize us at work, our business sponsors must justify and recognize these transformations as successful. Digital initiatives succeed or fail based on one key question: Can we prove the business payoff? Optimizing workflows, launching automation projects, or even re-architecting an entire process landscape sounds compelling. However, at the end of the day, your sponsors will still ask, "Show me the money" or "What's the **Return on Investment (ROI)**?" This necessitates accurately forecasting and measuring the business value or benefits of such initiatives, and this chapter equips you to answer these questions with confidence.

This chapter addresses the following key questions:

- What is business value?

- Why is it necessary to measure business value?

- What are the key metrics for measuring business value?

- What recognized methodologies are available for business value analysis?

- What tools and techniques can be used to measure business value?

- What are some common challenges in measuring business value?

- What does a case study of a **business value assessment (BVA)** look like?

- How can we measure the business value of AI transformations?

What is business value?

Business value, in terms of business and process transformation, refers to the tangible and intangible benefits that an organization gains by discovering and improving its processes.

When our Citizen Developer Automation program at Nordstrom started to grow in size and costs, requiring additional resources, the VP didn't ask for a prettier dashboard—he asked for a demonstration of how many dollars were saved each day.

When UnitedHealthcare started applying process automation to new use cases, enabling business users to control the authoring and deployment of business rules in a highly controlled environment supporting millions of Medicare users, the first step involved creating a BVA.

When the Microsoft Operations team started applying RPA automation to its manual purchase order process, the sponsor wanted to evaluate this investment with a scenario-based analysis, reliably projecting the business value over three years. Then, to gain higher confidence and predictability of results, the team wanted to standardize the way of capturing and forecasting business value for all automation projects.

Questions like these force practitioners to measure business value instead of measuring the improvement of process steps, and they are usually asked at the very beginning of initiatives, making it somewhat challenging to forecast such numbers very early into the project for several reasons.

Business value, in terms of business and process transformation, refers to the tangible and intangible benefits that an organization gains by discovering and improving its processes. **Business value analysis (BVA)** is a structured method for identifying pain points with measurable upside, connecting solution options with technical feasibility, applying organization-specific scaling factors, quantifying tangible (capital, hours) and intangible (**net promoter score (NPS)**, risk) benefits, and tracking the realization of benefits over time to continuously improve the framework and keep sponsors engaged.

The following business benefits can be measured with the help of BVA:

- Increased revenue
- Reduced operational costs
- Reduction of process errors
- Improved productivity due to added process efficiency
- Improved employee engagement and efficiency
- Decreased employee turnover
- Improved customer satisfaction and reduced churn
- A stronger competitive position in the market
- Increased customer loyalty
- Avoidance or reduction of out-of-compliance fines
- Reduction in solution development costs
- Risk mitigation

In workflow automation, businesses achieve value by optimizing processes, minimizing manual intervention, and accelerating decision-making. These types of initiatives lead to a more agile and responsive business environment, a characteristic referred to as **strategic adaptability**.

Measuring business value enables organizations to validate their investments, align with strategic goals, and foster continuous improvement.

Here are some examples of tangible benefits:

- Increased revenue through higher sales by providing an exceptional partner experience on the sales channel (sales, finance)
- Reduced operational costs by optimizing resource utilization (contact centers, operations)

- Improved **service-level agreements** (**SLAs**) for end-to-end business processes, with the possibility of changes as impressive as decreasing the timeline from 20 days to 12 hours (for example, in domains such as insurance, finance, and so on)

- Enhanced efficiency by automating repetitive tasks such as reconciliation and accounting ledger updates (finance)

- Shortened time to market for new products, allowing for a broader product selection to address seasonality (product design)

- Lowered inventory costs through better demand forecasting, shipment tracking, and route optimization (supply chain)

- Reduced shrinkage by implementing security processes that address theft, loss, and fraud (retail)

- Fewer cases of non-compliance issues, leading to a reduction in penalties and improved patient trust (healthcare claims and prior authorizations)

The concrete results can be easily measured and have a direct impact on the bottom line, which is typically expressed as numerical data or a percentage. On the other hand, there are intangible benefits that are more difficult to quantify but still offer significant value to the organization while not being immediately reflected in financial statements. While these benefits are easy to recognize, measuring them effectively poses a greater challenge. Assessing their value requires more nuanced evaluation methods, such as customer feedback surveys, employee engagement scores, or brand perception analyses.

Here are the intangible benefits:

- Enhanced customer satisfaction due to faster and more accurate service delivery

- Improved employee morale, resulting from a more streamlined work environment and a reduction of mundane, repetitive, energy-draining tasks

- A stronger competitive position through innovation and agility

- Increase in brand loyalty and a better overall reputation

- Greater adaptability to market changes and evolving customer needs

- Shorter deployment cycles

- Shorter time to market

- Business empowerment

While these benefits may be harder to quantify, they are crucial to the organization's overall success and sustainability and should be included in your BVA as influencing factors.

Recognizing the importance of quantifying business value

Transformation initiatives are crucial for maintaining a competitive edge in a rapidly changing business environment. For professionals driving digital change within organizations, articulating and quantifying business value is essential. This skill justifies future investments, ensures alignment with strategic priorities, and facilitates data-driven decision-making. While the initial ROI may not be significant, approaching process transformations with a focus on business value right from the start will set you on the right long-term path as your projects pursue the target ROI. Thinking about business value also compels you to seek answers to critical questions. The following few scenarios explain why assessing and validating benefits is essential.

Building the business case for justifying investments

Large-scale transformations often require significant investments in technology (such as software, platforms, tools, and infrastructure), talent (labor costs), new skills (for training), and change management (which encompasses time and experience). Financial justification is crucial for stakeholders and must be included in the project charter as a requirement.

A clearly defined framework for measuring business value provides concrete evidence of expected returns, allowing leaders to gain support from boards, steering committees, decision-makers, and operational leaders. Metrics such as ROI, **net present value (NPV)**, payback periods, and qualitative strategic benefits create a strong business case for transformation initiatives involving multiple projects.

This same approach can be applied to smaller projects that have the potential to become larger transformations. Citizen developers and business professionals often face challenges because they lack access to consultants and their analytical resources. However, starting small does not mean the journey cannot lead to significant transformational savings.

While working on a transformation at Nordstrom, our program was driven entirely by business users who recognized the value of solving their problems with low-code **digital process automation (DPA)**. The following diagram illustrates some key wins that were identified, designed, and launched, generating significant business value through several initiatives. These initiatives often began small but sometimes expanded into larger implementations.

Our business savings were categorized into three groups: less than $15,000, $50,000, and over $100,000 annually. Notably, some projects delivered benefits exceeding $1,200,000 in annual value. It's important to understand that even the smallest project could be part of a much larger initiative, and a process identified by a citizen developer might have the potential to significantly impact the bottom line. Therefore, we should not underestimate projects that may initially seem minor.

When these savings are compounded, the story of process transformation reveals its true potential, as shown in *Figure 10.1*.

Featured Wins

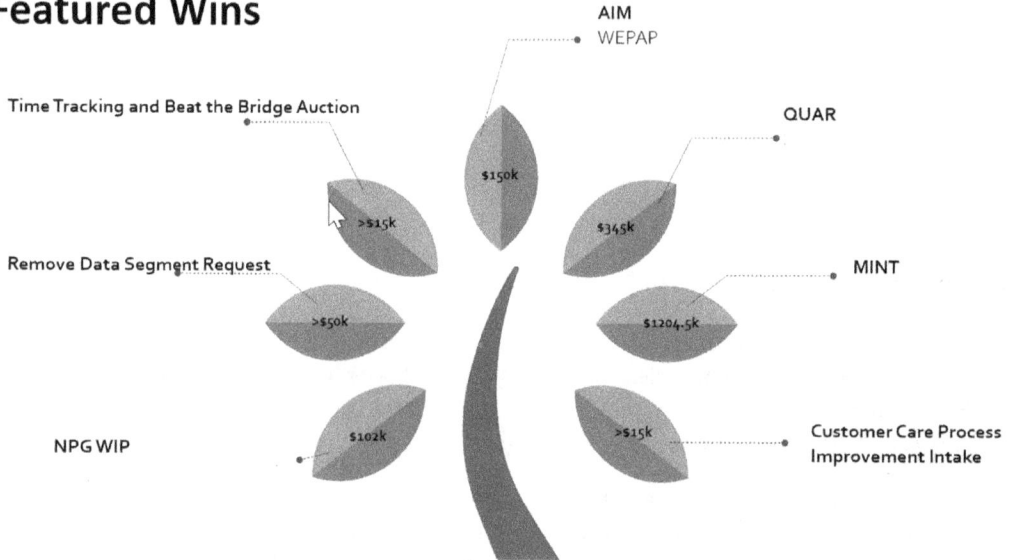

Figure 10.1 – Tracking the benefits of citizen developer process applications

Over time, realized business savings can accumulate quickly, especially with each passing quarter. When even the smallest successes in your program get recognized, the overall value created can multiply rapidly, potentially leading to larger initiatives as well. This is why the value proposition of a well-executed process transformation program is so attractive to businesses—it's as if the savings grow on a tree. However, it's important to emphasize the phrase "well-executed," as poorly managed programs can negatively impact both budgets and reputations.

Ensuring strategic alignment across the enterprise

Business professionals recognize the importance of aligning initiatives with overarching corporate strategies, often articulated through **objectives and key results (OKRs)**. Measuring business value is essential to ensure that transformation projects contribute directly to long-term goals, such as market expansion, operational excellence, and customer-centric innovation. This alignment maximizes the impact of resources and investments while fostering cross-functional collaboration, ensuring that all departments work toward a unified vision.

As projects are launched and progress, the visibility of OKRs and overall business value often diminishes. Daily workloads can take precedence, and discussions about future funding may exclude input from those directly involved. In large, matrixed organizations, business professionals might lack the opportunity for one-on-one interactions with leaders to showcase the success of their initiatives, making it challenging to connect their work to strategic objectives.

Wise leaders understand that consistently generating small-scale business value can lead to significant impact without the complications of managing large-scale programs involving vendors and external consultants. These consultants often shift between projects, which require substantial oversight and incur the cost of acquiring institutional knowledge, adding additional expenses that may only be justified across larger transformations.

Moreover, smaller transformations can propel much larger programs forward, as their direct impact tends to snowball over time when actual business challenges are identified, addressed, and operationalized. It is crucial to emphasize that democratizing digital change tools requires a similarly democratized approach to evaluating and measuring business value, even if that value appears small. Traditional project delivery mechanisms involving implementation teams present more challenges in a citizen developer scenario.

Data-driven continuous improvement

The mantra "what gets measured gets managed" is particularly relevant in continuous improvement. By tracking **key performance indicators (KPIs)** linked to business value, organizations can identify inefficiencies, prioritize areas for optimization, and develop actionable roadmaps for digitization. Regular assessments of business value provide essential feedback, enabling companies to quickly adapt to reorganizations or changing market conditions, thereby confirming the benefits of technology-driven process improvement initiatives.

The initial phase of this process can be challenging, as data collection involves gathering numerous data points and establishing baselines. While most leaders agree that data collection is crucial—echoing W. Edwards Deming's saying, "In God we trust; all others must bring data"—disagreements can arise regarding which types of data to collect and when to collect it, as well as the formulas used to calculate business value.

Calculating business savings for process transformation begins with understanding the various work types represented through process fragment examples, which are expressed via automation patterns. This understanding leads to being able to identify impacts and determine the ROI range. If you can support your analysis with existing case studies and provide recommendations on the technical footprint, your data collection efforts will be more effective:

Work Type	Process Example	Automation Pattern	Time Savings Impact	Dollar Savings Impact	Employee Satisfaction Impact	ROI Range	Case Studies	Tech Stack
A personal productivity, task-oriented routine process involving humans	Automated workflows between favorite apps and services, causing notifications to be received, files to be copied, and data to be collected	Personal process automation	X	X	X			Power Automate
A task-oriented routine process involving humans		Process automation		X	X			K2, Power Automate, Azure Services
A task-oriented routine process involving humans, characterized by a high number of exceptions	HR, clinical negligence, land plot conveyancing	A blend of case management and process automation		X	X	*800 people hours saved weekly *Reduction of yearly operating expenses by $205k/ years *20% development hours saved	European Law Firm	K2, SharePoint, SAP
Knowledge work involving multiple processes, decisions, and research-intensive work	HR investigation	HR investigation	X	X	X			K2, Power Automate, Azure Services
Labor-intensive, routine, and predictable tasks	HR investigation	Attended and unattended RPA		X	X			Power Platform
Citizen developer initiatives	Customer care intake requests, time tracking, employee auction, and network operations center support	Personal and process automation		X	X	$15k-$1,500k/ year, average yearly expenses of $150k/year	US-based retailer	K2, Azure

Table 10.1 – Breaking down work types into specific process patterns enhances the quality of the BVA

Driving employee engagement and customer loyalty

Successful process transformations happen when both employees and customers can perceive clear benefits. Engaged employees, equipped with better tools, streamlined workflows, and well-defined objectives, become strong advocates for digital change. Their involvement accelerates adoption and drives business success, allowing the organization to progress in the direction outlined by process architects. Additionally, enhancements in measurable service delivery, speed, and quality directly improve customer experience, fostering loyalty and advocacy.

Establishing a foundation for future digital innovation

Measuring the business value of current initiatives is essential for setting the foundation for future transformations, program expansions, and the development of citizen developer applications. Even initial metrics from small-scale citizen developer projects can provide critical benchmarks for scaling digital innovation, allowing organizations to justify future investments more effectively. Over time, this improved ability to measure value enhances an organization's resilience, agility, and competitiveness in a process-driven environment.

As we transition toward a world increasingly influenced by AI workflows, adopting a strategy of informed experimentation will be crucial, recognizing that the path may not always be straightforward. By systematically documenting your business benefits and comparing them to initial business assumptions, you can effectively navigate from one business challenge to another while minimizing risks.

The following screenshots illustrate the BVA management life cycle flow for a portfolio of citizen developer applications, from ideation to launch. This system moves concepts through several stage gates: intake, risk assessment, technical fit, design review, test deployment, and production deployment. This approach ensures that the appropriate technology is chosen to address the relevant business problem while capturing and tracking BVAs across the portfolio:

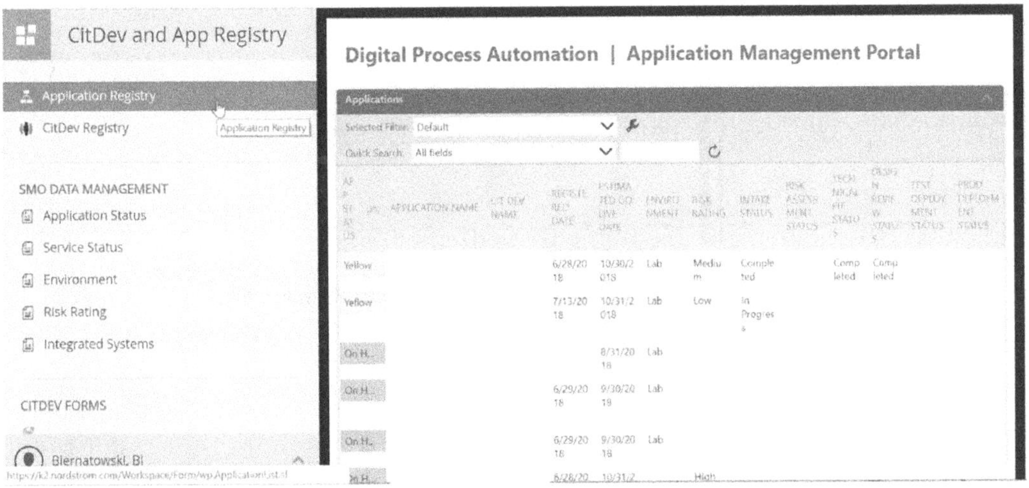

Figure 10.2 – Citizen Developer app registry (portfolio view)

The following view describes a single application, an automated process called *Decision Registry*, that is fully deployed to production, operationalized, and carries a low-risk rating without having to handle any sensitive data:

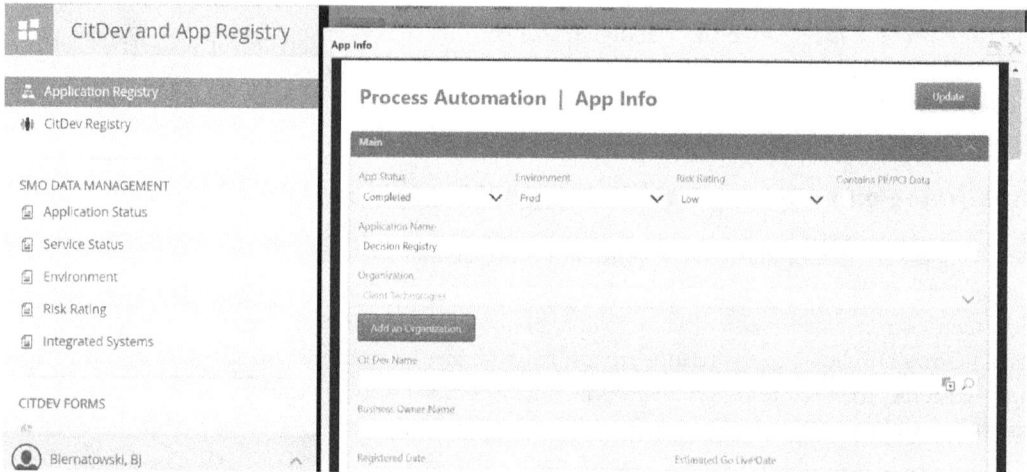

Figure 10.3 – Citizen Developer app registry (application view)

The following view displays the application's audit trail, highlighting all expert services that have been applied to the process, including their go-live dates:

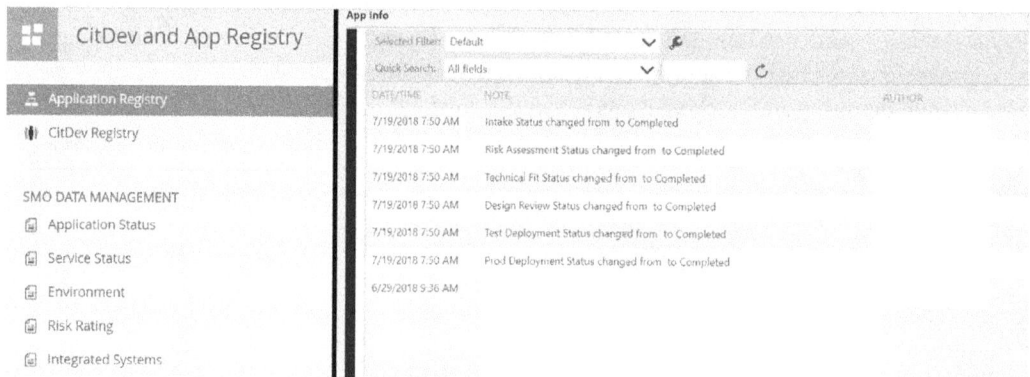

Figure 10.4 – Citizen developer app registry (service life cycle view)

The following view outlines the data used to describe the business problem and highlights the pain points that align with the proposed solution. It also enumerates both the tangible and intangible drivers of business value. For the application to be considered effective, the automated process must meet the specified success criteria:

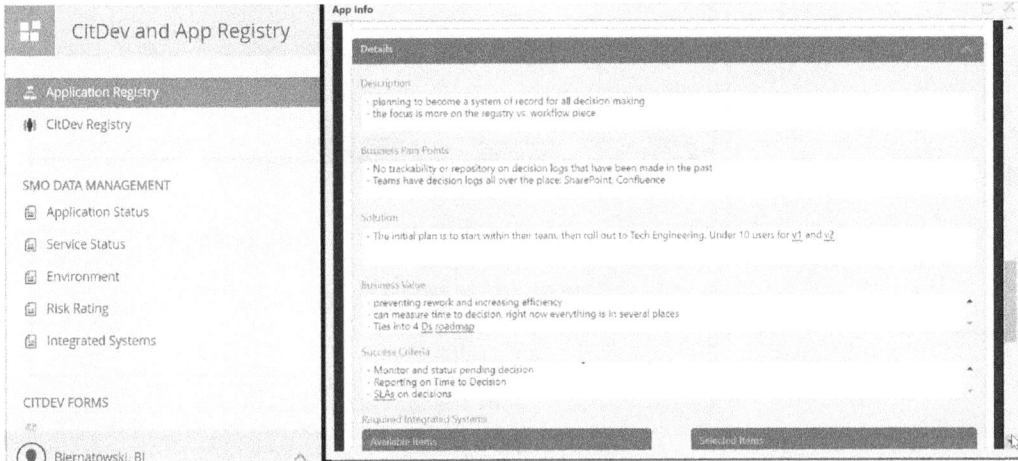

Figure 10.5 – Citizen developer app registry (BVA view)

This view identifies potential automation platforms and gathers initial data elements necessary for forecasting BVA. Additionally, the process is assessed for risks, and various types of solution components are highlighted to ensure technical alignment:

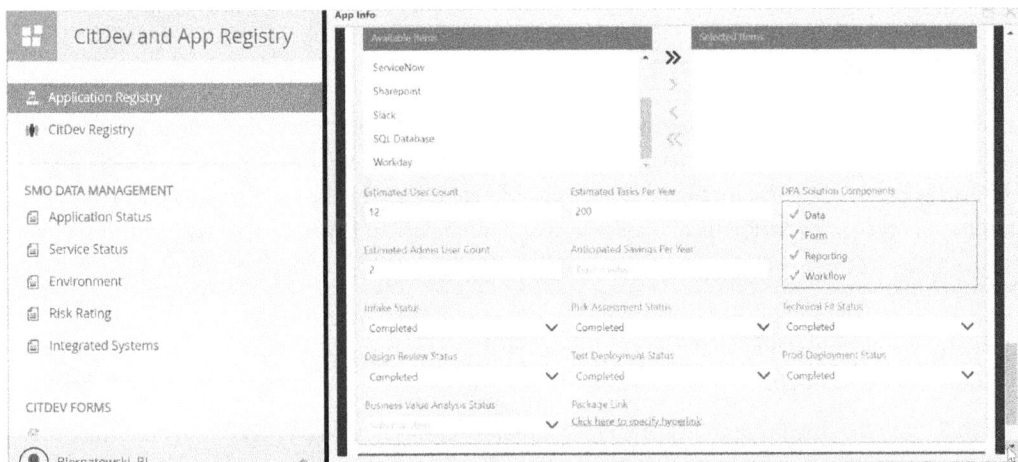

Figure 10.6 – Citizen developer app registry (expert service status)

After the intake process, the application allows us to collect supporting documentation and links to user stories, test cases, and Jira or Azure DevOps repositories, thereby enhancing the quality of the documentation and providing additional context:

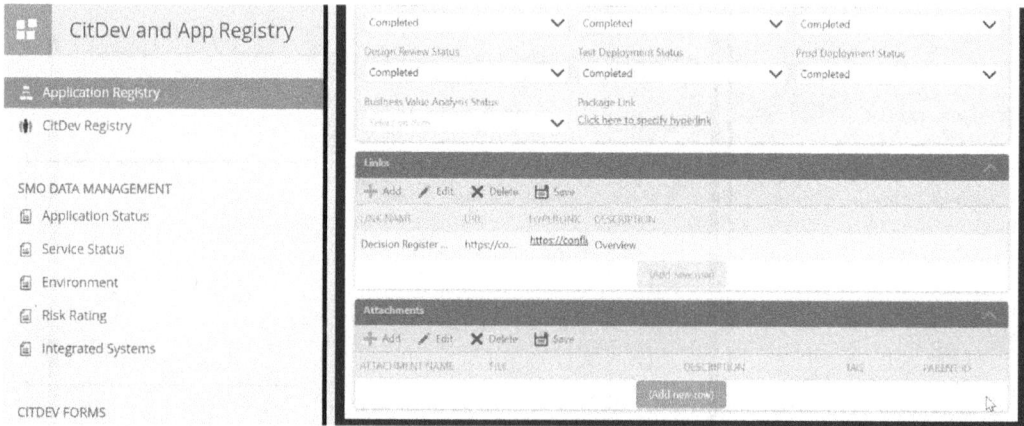

Figure 10.7 – Citizen developer app registry (app documentation)

Work and process applications go through a life cycle that mirrors the business processes they support. Similar to groceries, some applications have an expiration date. New applications can be quickly developed and added to the portfolio to address immediate process challenges, while others may only serve specific purposes and can be phased out in just a few weeks. This approach is in line with the **business process management** (**BPM**) life cycle. What's crucial is creating a system that measures the value these applications deliver to the organization.

Key metrics for measuring business value

In the dynamic landscape of process transformations, various metrics play a key role in driving successful initiatives. Such metrics include financial, operational, customer, and employee-focused metrics. These can be used to create a baseline for digital change experimentation, which is recommended as a strategy to introduce process digitization technologies at scale incrementally. Let's explore each in more detail.

Financial metrics

- **ROI**: Measures the financial gains or losses resulting from process transformation relative to the initial investment.

- **NPV**: Assesses the profitability of an investment or project. A positive NPV signifies that the expected earnings surpass the estimated costs, thereby deeming the investment feasible.

- **Payback period**: Determines the time it takes for an investment to generate enough cash flow to recover the initial cost.

- **Cost savings**: Evaluates the reduction in costs due to improved efficiency and elimination of waste.

- **Revenue growth**: Assesses the increase in revenue as a result of improved processes that enhance productivity and market reach.

The business benefits of individual transformations, including your citizen developer initiatives, should roll under the financial metrics umbrella. In other words, if you expect the ROI of your three-year investments to be 320%, the collective ROI of all individual projects that are executed as part of your programs should amount to 320%. ROI, cost savings, and revenue growth will be monitored throughout the execution of your program, while NPV will be used at the beginning to help you make an investment decision.

Operational metrics

- **Cycle time reduction**: Measures the decrease in the time taken to complete a process from start to finish

- **Error rates**: Tracks the reduction in errors and defects, leading to higher-quality outputs

- **Productivity improvement**: Evaluates the increase in output per unit of input (e.g., labor hours, machine usage)

These metrics will roll under your company's OKRs. They can also be included in your individual performance goals.

Let's consider some examples:

- Reduce the rate of late payment errors by 10% over the next six months (quality improvement scenario)

- Due to increasing business volumes and budgetary freeze, your goal is to improve the productivity of your team by 20% within the next 6–9 months (do more with less scenario)

Customer-focused metrics

- **Customer satisfaction**: Gauges improvements in customer satisfaction through surveys and feedback mechanisms. **Customer satisfaction score** (**CSAT**) is measured by customers through a rating on a scale.

- **NPS**: Measures the likelihood of customers recommending the company's products or services to others. This is measured on a scale of 0 to 10, measuring customers as Promoters (9-10), Passives (7-8), or Detractors (0-6).

- **Customer retention**: Assesses the impact of process improvements on customer loyalty and retention rates. It's expressed as a percentage of customers who continue to do business over a specific period.

- **Customer churn**: Also known as customer attrition, this refers to the percentage of customers who discontinue using a company's products or services over a certain period. It is a crucial metric for businesses, especially those with subscription-based models or long-term customer relationships, such as in the telecom, **Software-as-a-Service (SaaS)**, and retail industries.

Employee-focused metrics

- **Employee satisfaction**: Measures increased employee morale and job satisfaction due to streamlined processes. It's expressed through surveys and **employee net promoter score (eNPS)**.

- **Training time**: Evaluates the reduction in training time required for new processes, leading to quicker employee onboarding.

- **Employee turnover**: Assesses the impact of process transformation on employee retention and turnover rates.

Working with poorly designed or manually executed processes can cause all types of challenges for your team or business. Employee-focused metrics tend to be evaluated a bit on the sidelines, while core business metrics get immediate visibility. There is a clear connection between the quality of your processes' execution and team thriving scores. Happy and high-performing teams are not bugged by missing operating procedures, broken processes, or the need to search for clarifications while performing work. Considering employee-focused metrics in the scope of process design is a smart business strategy that directly contributes to operational metrics. If you want to drive successful operations, don't neglect to include employee-focused metrics in the scope of your transformation. Your leaders and your teams will thank you for it.

In addition to the reasons mentioned here, defining and measuring metrics can serve as a compass that's used to evaluate the maturity of your DTX program. Let's take a closer look:

- **Establishing a baseline for digital change experimentation**: The measured benefits of the early stages of digital change programs will evolve as the program progresses, and the organization becomes more comfortable adopting new skills, frameworks, and technologies. This process will continually enhance the cycle of BPM and continuous improvement. By establishing a baseline for your program's value, you will be able to immediately notice shifts in performance as your processes launch and mature over time. Time spent transforming operations flies quickly and, sooner rather than later, you will have to explain or contribute to a business justification as your initiatives require additional funding or program extensions. Coming to these discussions prepared with data collected over time will elevate these conversations to a different level. The alternative is to scramble for data and models while attending your day-to-day job, trying to piece together data to demonstrate the work that's been completed over the last few months. It's harder to do than it seems, as in this case, a methodical, forward-looking approach to data collection and business value evaluation will be key. It is the most frustrating feeling in the world trying to piece together the BVA story by chasing your project stakeholders, refreshing assumptions and calculations from over 1-2 years ago, and working with teams when people move and priorities shift. You may find yourself in a tough spot, having to explain to others what you did and did not accomplish with your time and resources. Leaders can suffer from short-term memory when it comes to overcoming challenges if the numbers they present do not reflect well on their historical decisions. Protect yourself from this type of self-preservation and scapegoating by embedding fair and transparent methodologies for BVA and benefits verification.

- **Challenging assumptions**: Projects that promise significant ROI but take much longer to deliver than initially planned require a reality check through a thorough retrospective. Launching AI automation or process transformation programs without using the critical BVA methodology, especially by individuals lacking experience in this area, can lead to prolonged implementations, failure to achieve the intended vision, or damage to the reputation of otherwise promising initiatives. There is nothing wrong with an organization encouraging learning and experimentation, so long as fundamental principles are firmly established upfront. Your BVA framework should act as an anchor amid the uncertainty and chaos that can arise when business professionals experiment with digital change. Capturing and aligning people around assumptions will provide everyone with a unified starting point, allowing learning through experimentation to take place. Unspoken assumptions should be treated as cracks in the foundation of your initiative; it's always safer to bring them into the open.

In the following section, we will describe the most commonly encountered techniques for measuring business value.

Models and techniques for measuring business value

Accurately measuring value is critical to ensuring that investments provide tangible benefits. Different models and techniques have been developed to drive companies in this endeavor, each offering unique perspectives and advantages. Adopting different methodologies allows businesses to modify their approach to specific needs or phases of the program, whether it's optimizing processes, evaluating financial implications, or assessing potential program ROI. Leveraging a diverse set of methodologies allows us to make informed decisions. Among these methodologies, the following six deserve a mention:

- **Six Sigma**: A data-driven methodology that focuses on improving processes and reducing variation to enhance overall performance. An example of this is provided in the *Case study 3* section of this chapter.

- **Cost-benefit analysis (CBA)**: A systematic approach that's used to evaluate the financial and non-financial impacts of a project or decision. By comparing the total expected costs against the total expected benefits, CBA helps organizations determine the feasibility and profitability of an initiative. This method involves identifying and quantifying all relevant costs, such as technology, implementation, training, and maintenance, as well as the anticipated benefits, including cost savings, revenue increases, productivity gains, and quality improvements. For an example, see *Case study 1*.

- **Analyst methodologies—Forrester TEI**: This comprehensive methodology combines four key components: cost, benefits, flexibility, and risk. By assessing these elements, organizations can gain a holistic view of the financial impact of their initiatives. The TEI methodology involves detailed data collection and analysis to quantify the costs associated with technology investments, implementation, and ongoing operations. It also identifies and measures the benefits, such as cost savings, productivity gains, and revenue growth. Additionally, the TEI technique considers a solution's flexibility to adapt to future changes and the risks that may affect the expected outcomes. An example of this can be found at `https://tools.totaleconomicimpact.com/go/forrester/teioftei/index.html`.

- **Digitization platform vendor ROI calculators**: These serve as a structured framework to quantify and articulate the business value generated from a process transformation. By leveraging this toolkit, organizations can systematically assess key value drivers such as cost savings, efficiency gains, risk reduction, and enhanced user experience resulting from automation or optimization initiatives led by citizen developers. The toolkit enables teams to capture tangible and intangible benefits through standardized metrics, helping build a clear business case for transformation efforts. Additionally, it supports continuous improvement by offering insights into value realization and alignment with broader organizational goals, ensuring that process transformations deliver measurable impact and strategic advantage. Examples include UiPath Automation Hub, Microsoft Power Platform COE Starter Kit, and Pega Solution Finder.

- **Citizen developer COE business value toolkit**: This is a powerful resource for measuring the business value of process transformations led by citizen developers. This toolkit provides a structured framework for evaluating initiatives' financial and non-financial impacts, ensuring that even small-scale projects can demonstrate their value effectively. By leveraging this toolkit, organizations can quantify costs such as technology investments, implementation expenses, and training while identifying benefits such as cost savings, productivity gains, and revenue growth. The toolkit includes data collection and analysis methodologies, enabling citizen developers to present clear and compelling evidence of their projects' ROI. Additionally, it offers guidance on assessing flexibility and risk, ensuring that the solutions are adaptable to future changes and resilient to potential challenges. An example of this can be found at `https://learn.microsoft.com/en-us/power-platform/guidance/coe/business-value-toolkit#the-business-value-toolkit`.

- **Service-play-based BVA**: This methodology employs expert services to systematically evaluate the various stages of a new initiative. It integrates elements of process management, solution architecture, estimation, and risk management. The analysis draws on historical use cases, industry benchmarks, and scaling factors such as utilization, self-enablement levels, and experience. These factors are adjusted dynamically to suit the specific scenario being assessed. Staying updated on the latest technology and software options that are proposed as solutions is essential. Additionally, this service provides valuable insights for financial models that calculate values for CBA, ROI, and Net NPV. For an example, see *Case study 2*. The method for assessing business value depends on your preference, the type of project, the technology being utilized to solve the business problem, and the organization's maturity level. Moreover, the individual's experience in measuring the benefits is critical. This role demands strong analytical skills, effective data collection, and prior experience in process improvement and work automation. It's essential not to underestimate the expertise required to conduct this type of analysis, as it necessitates a diverse range of skills. According to Wayne Padcayan, senior enterprise business and process architect, "It is helpful to conduct BVA in partnership with other teams such as Finance to put together a pro forma as supporting documentation." A **pro forma** is a financial document or projection that outlines expected results based on certain assumptions. It's often used to forecast future performance, evaluate potential investments or projects, and support business cases during initiatives such as DTX or work automation.

While these methodologies provide robust frameworks for evaluating business value, practitioners must remain vigilant to avoid common pitfalls that can undermine the effectiveness of their analysis.

Common challenges in conducting BVA

Although analyzing business value may appear simple at first glance, numerous pitfalls can unexpectedly hinder practitioners. To help you steer clear of these mistakes and enhance your confidence in your analysis, I'm sharing the following list of common errors to avoid:

- Reinventing the wheel by developing multiple internal Excel-based models that do not leverage the organization's past experiences.

- Not sharing financial data with others and wanting to make your analysis perfect.

- Building financial models without adequate practical experience in transforming and automating processes.

- Failing to connect financial analysis with process and solution architecture.

- Not evaluating benefits across a range of scenarios.

- Neglecting to fully document and revise assumptions.

- Not prioritizing improvements to the BVA model.

- Failing to treat business value analysis and benefits validation as a mandatory, ongoing activity to support the goals of company transformation.

- Calculating the ROI of your projects at the wrong point in time. This is usually caused by rushing to the financial part of the analysis without stepping through and collecting inputs for the requirements review, process landscape, and technical fit services.

- Not validating BVAs after project implementation.

- Overlooking institutional learning as a scaling factor.

- Underestimating the impact of a missed BVA on the success of the program.

Measuring the business value of agentic AI systems (experimental)

Several robust methodologies and approaches are employed to measure the effectiveness of AI-driven workflow automation and transformation programs. The **Balanced Scorecard (BSC)** framework, Six Sigma, and Lean Metrics stand out here. BSC provides a comprehensive view by evaluating financial, customer, and internal processes, as well as learning and growth perspectives.

For instance, a global insurance firm applied this methodology to measure the impact of AI on their claims processing, achieving a 30% reduction in processing time and a significant increase in customer satisfaction. With its focus on reducing errors and improving quality, Six Sigma has been utilized by manufacturing giants such as General Electric to optimize AI-driven predictive maintenance, resulting in substantial cost savings and uptime improvements. Lean Metrics, emphasizing waste reduction and efficiency, was instrumental for an e-commerce leader in streamlining their AI-powered supply chain operations, leading to faster deliveries and reduced operational costs. These methodologies provide quantifiable metrics and align AI transformations with strategic objectives, supporting data-driven decision-making and fostering a culture of continuous improvement.

BVA case studies

To provide a comprehensive understanding of how BVA can be applied in various scenarios, I will explore three distinct case studies. Each case study will focus on a different type of analysis, highlighting its unique approach and impact on business decision-making:

- **Case study 1: Retail industry**: This study examines how a company optimized and automated its core processes by implementing a low-code DPA platform across the enterprise.

- **Case study 2: Financial services**: This analysis looks at how a global finance business unit improved its core processes, reduced cycle times, and achieved significant cost savings through process transformation and **robotic process automation (RPA)**.

- **Case study 3: Adaptive logistics and fulfillment**: This hypothetical use case focuses on workflow automation driven by agentic AI through the use of autonomous agents, with a focus on dynamic workflows and intelligent systems that optimize supply chains, delivery networks, and customer satisfaction through continuous adaptation and high-level autonomy.

- **Case study 4: Agentic AI and the modern ranch**: AgSights is transforming Canada's ranching sector by enabling smaller producers to access real-time insights, optimize processes such as feed costs and grazing schedules, and compete more effectively with larger operations. This technology, combined with strategic frameworks such as BSC and BPA, empowers ranchers to align AI-driven actions with measurable growth objectives and operational efficiency.

Let's take a look at each case study in greater detail.

Case study 1: Calculating the BVA of enterprise adoption of a low-code DPA platform

A national retailer has transformed its core and supporting processes by shifting from a brick-and-mortar model to a digital business approach. To expedite this transformation, the company's leadership is considering investing in a DPA platform to enhance the automation of the existing process architecture.

Preferring in-house development, the company aims to launch, manage, and support the initiative internally to minimize consulting costs. However, this initiative carries significant risks due to past negative experiences with scaling automation technologies. It requires careful planning, a non-standard grassroots and bottom-up approach to project delivery, and multiple checkpoints throughout the program.

The analysis is based on various inputs that need to be collected in advance, resulting in several outputs that outline comprehensive benefits over three years. You will need to invest time in collecting data used for inputs.

The following are inputs:

- Process discovery and repository licensing costs

- Process architect training costs

- Investment in the internal team

- Citizen developer training costs (effort and certification)

- DPA platform licensing costs:

    - Cloud infrastructure spend forecast, including connectivity costs (varied by scenario)

- Evangelism and community-building costs

- 6-9 months' worth of consulting costs in the staff augmentation model:

    - Platform launch

    - COE operating model

    - Support of the first quick-win project

    - Support of the second quick-win project

    - Monitor and grow

This analysis results in several data points and outputs being calculated that help describe the scope of the anticipated investment.

The following are outputs:

- CBA:

  - Gather the benefits that have been calculated over the past three years:

    - Reduction in the risk of manual process errors, including driver value, driver growth, improvement factor, financial factor, percentage of benefit accrued, and total

    - Reduced time to market for revenue-generating applications

    - Reduction of customer churn through improved customer experience

    - Reduction of monitoring hours for new business applications

    - Improved business productivity through added process efficiencies

    - Reduction of labor costs through reduced reliance on senior-level developers

    - Reduction of BPA development costs

- Calculate for worst, optimal, and best-case scenarios

- Express the ROI as follows:

  - Three-year total cost

  - Three-year total benefit

  - Net benefits

  - Net present value

  - Payback period

  - ROI

Calculating outputs over three years allows us to chart the benefits-to-costs ratio, clearly demonstrating the positive impact of the investment from year 1 to year 3. See *Figure 10.8*:

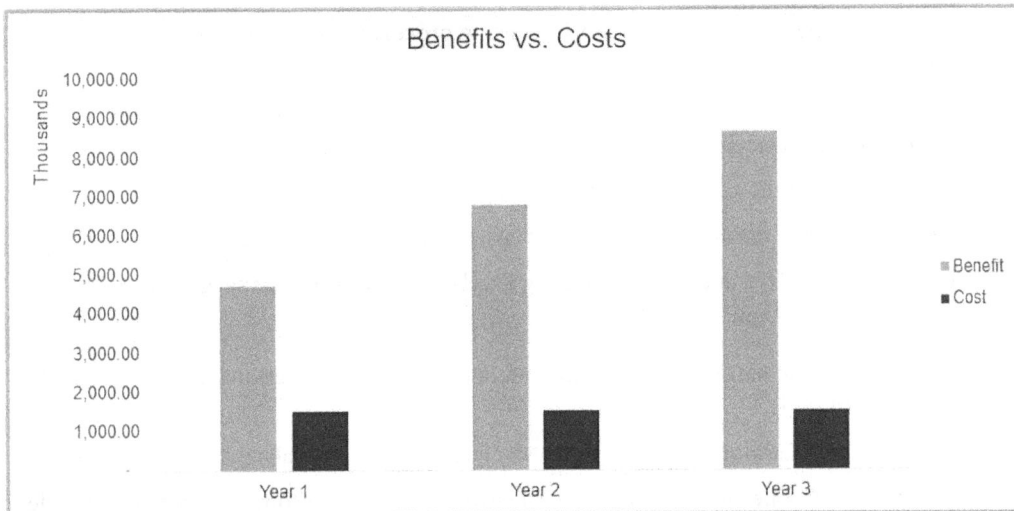

Figure 10.8 – CBA of a process transformation over three years

Outcome: The company made a strategic investment in licensing the DPA platform, which included consulting and cloud services, and funding for the internal process automation support team. Subsequently, this investment resulted in the incubation of 60 projects over two years, comprising 3 large-scale projects, 10 medium-sized projects, 25 small-sized projects, and 22 prototypes.

Case study 2: Calculating the ROI of RPA-based process automation

A global tech company was looking to enhance its core fund investment process. Project leadership aimed to leverage RPA to improve this business process. Previous efforts by the product management team involved creating Excel spreadsheets that contained custom calculations, which ended up exceeding initial estimates and diminishing the credibility of the automation program. To address this situation, the following steps were taken:

1. They gained support from leadership to recalculate business value while utilizing a field-tested methodology.

2. They created a working deck to educate and level-set stakeholders and leadership on the approach and timelines that were being implemented.

3. They designed the service play to address the medium-sized process based on readily available information.

4. They created realistic timelines describing the duration of the BVA effort.

5. They shared the timelines, explaining anticipated outcomes for each phase of the BVA. The results were surprising.

6. They collected and analyzed requirements.

7. They assessed the process landscape by reviewing process maps of the core and supporting processes to identify known gaps.

8. They performed a fit assessment for two technical alternatives, after which they highlighted and learned from their differences.

9. They produced T-shirt and ROM effort estimates.

10. They grouped benefits into hard and soft groups, connecting project drivers with benefits.

11. They calculated the ROI and NPV by utilizing Excel or professional tools such as Shark Finesse, Forrester TEI, and so on:

    i. For ROI calculation models, Excel offers the following functions: `NPV()`, `IRR()`, and `XNPV()`.

    ii. For Monte Carlo simulations, use `RAND()` and `@RISK` to analyze risk and uncertainty.

    iii. Prompt: Create an ROI analysis for a citizen developer automation project. Include ROI, NPV, IRR, payback period, TCO, as well as inputs regarding initial investment costs and operational costs.

    iv. Provide details regarding savings, revenue impact, development savings, and risk and sensitivity analysis. Include scenario analysis and a dashboard.

12. They reflected on lessons learned and incorporated them into their BVA process.

13. They launched the project and validated the benefits 3-6 months post-go-live.

Outcome: The final presentation was accepted by the group leader, whose direction was to streamline and standardize the BVA based on this methodology. The project was approved:

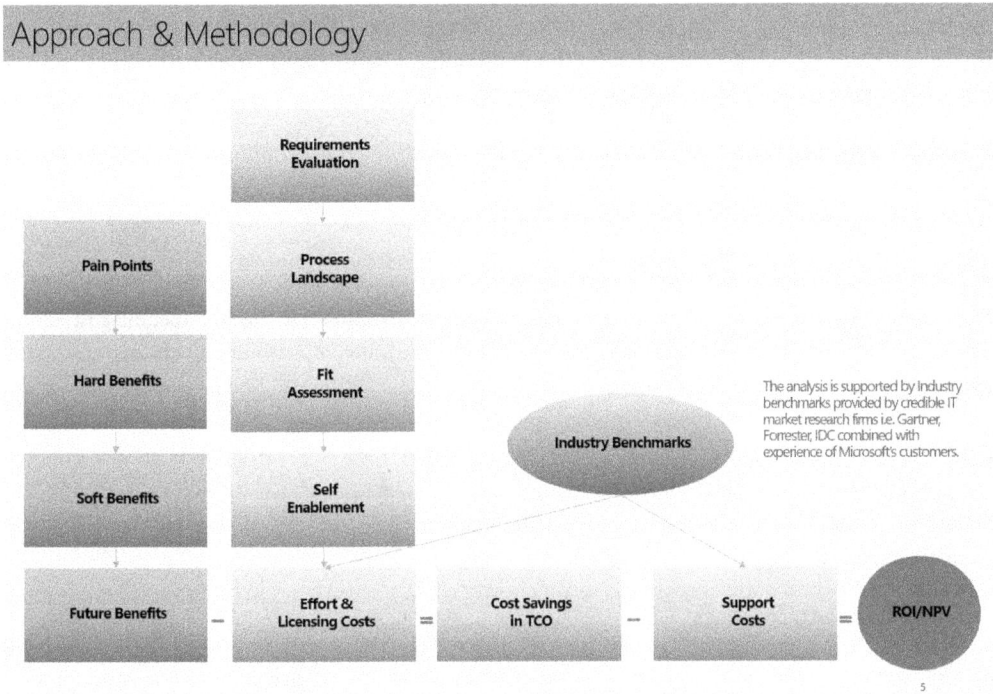

Figure 10.9 – BVA approach for a medium-sized process transformation

Case study 3: Adaptive Logistics and Fulfillment: BVA process transformation involving AI and agents

Adaptive Logistics and Fulfillment, a hypothetical company, harnesses the transformative power of agent-based AI to revolutionize supply chain operations. This approach involves utilizing AI agents capable of dynamic decision-making, real-time analysis, and predictive modeling. As a result, organizations can optimize fulfillment processes, reduce lead times, and enhance customer satisfaction.

The incorporation of agent-based AI enables a more responsive logistics system that can adapt to unpredictable factors such as demand fluctuations, resource constraints, and external disruptions. By automating processes, these intelligent agents can streamline complex workflows and facilitate seamless coordination between suppliers, warehouses, and distributors.

The outcome is a logistics framework that is not only efficient but also scalable, driving tangible business value and operational excellence.

This hypothetical case study provides a detailed model for evaluating the business value of this project. It includes methodologies, metrics, and sample calculations to demonstrate the assessment process based on a hypothetical medium-sized US-based global organization.

Our model assumes yearly revenues of $90 million ($75-$100 million range), showing a 2.22% increase in revenue due to AI-driven agent-based automation ($2 million).

Components of the BVA model

In this scenario, we calculate BVA from four different perspectives, each tailored to a specific audience. One of the most time-consuming aspects of any BVA is the accurate collection and validation of data throughout the project, especially as new information or more reliable data becomes available. Treat your BVA as a mini-project, complete with a timeline, milestones, and clear objectives. Depending on your audience, you can utilize the BVA, BSC, Lean methodology, Six Sigma, or a combination of these approaches to achieve your targets. For high-stakes projects, such as supply chain, it may be beneficial to conduct multiple types of analyses to engage with different stakeholders within your organization effectively.

Identify and quantify costs

To begin, accurately identify and quantify all costs associated with the AI-driven workflow automation project. These costs include the following:

- **Technology costs**: Expenses for new software, hardware, and infrastructure
- **Implementation costs**: The costs of consulting services, project management, and deployment
- **Training costs**: Expenses for training employees to use the new digital tools and processes
- **Maintenance and support costs**: Ongoing expenses for maintaining and supporting the AI systems

Cost Category	Details	Amount (USD)
Technology costs	AI platform licensing, cloud computing, data infrastructure, and cybersecurity enhancements. These are one-time and annual costs.	$2,500,000
Implementation costs	System integration, process redesign, AI model training, and deployment. One-time costs.	$1,200,000
Training costs	Employee training, change management, and AI literacy training programs. One-time plus ongoing.	$350,000
Maintenance and support costs	Ongoing AI model tuning, infrastructure monitoring, compliance updates, and customer support. Annual.	$400,000

Cost Category	Details	Amount (USD)
Total costs		$4,050,000
Recurring annual		$400,000

Table 10.2 – Example calculation (identified costs)

Identify and quantify benefits

Next, identify and quantify the benefits of the AI-driven workflow automation project.

These benefits are as follows:

- **Cost savings**: Reduction in operational costs due to increased efficiency
- **Productivity gains**: Enhanced productivity due to automated workflows
- **Resource efficiency**: Ensuring that AI-driven agents and systems use resources optimally
- **Real-time feedback and iteration speed**: Processes rely on real-time decision-making to iterate and improve quickly
- **Revenue increases**: Additional revenue generated from improved service delivery
- **Quality improvements**: Reduction in errors and enhanced service quality
- **Customer satisfaction**: Improved customer satisfaction scores due to faster and more accurate services

Benefit Category	Description	Value Metric	Estimated Impact (Hypothetical)	Amount (USD)
Cost savings	Reduction in manual effort, operational costs, and overhead through AI automation	% reduction in labor costs, system maintenance costs	21% cost reduction in back-office operations	$1,500,000
Productivity gains	Autonomous agents reduce process cycle time and allow employees to focus on high-value tasks	% increase in tasks completed per hour	17% faster task completion	$1,200,000

Benefit Category	Description	Value Metric	Estimated Impact (Hypothetical)	Amount (USD)
Resource efficiency	AI optimizes the allocation of computing power, the workforce, and process execution	% reduction in wasted resources	11% reduction in redundant workflows	$750,000
Real-time feedback and iteration speed	AI agents adjust dynamically based on real-time data, improving agility	% reduction in decision cycle time	7% faster decision making	$500,000
Revenue increases	Faster processes and automation enable increased transaction volume and service offerings	% increase revenue from new opportunities, such as improvements, product innovation, and market expansion	29% growth in revenue streams	$2,000,000
Quality improvements	Reduction in errors and rework	% reduction in process errors	6% fewer processing errors	$400,000
Customer satisfaction	Improved customer satisfaction scores	% increase in NPS or CSAT	9% improvement in CSAT	$600,000
Total Benefits				$6,950,000

Table 10.3 – Example calculation (quantified benefits)

Calculate the ROI

Calculate the ROI by comparing the total benefits to the total costs. The ROI formula is as follows:

ROI (%) = [(Total Benefits - Total Costs) / Total Costs] x 100

There are some assumptions to consider here. The 8% discount rate for NPV reflects the **weighted average cost of capital (WACC)** for a medium-sized US-based company. 8% is on the conservative side and used in business cases where the project has medium risk, and the company is stable and diversified across regions.

Benefits	$6,950,000
Annual Net Benefits	$6.550,000
Costs	$4,050,000
Total Investment (year 0 + ongoing support costs over three years)	$4,050,000 + ($400,000 x3) = $5,250,000
Total Net Benefits (years 1-3)	$19,650,000 = (3 x $6,550,000)
Three-Year ROI	[($19,650,000 – ($4,050,000 + $1,200,000)) / $5,250,000] x 100 = 274%
NPV (using 8% discount rate)	$-4,050,000 + [$6,550,000/(1.08)] + [$6,550,000/(1.08)^2] + [$6,550,000/(1.08)^3] = $12,829,140
Payback	~8 months into year 1

Table 10.4 – Example calculation—ROI

The ROI of 274% indicates that the AI-driven workflow automation project is going to deliver rapid payback, strong results, and significant benefits compared to the costs incurred.

The BSC approach

Implement the BSC approach to provide a comprehensive view of the project's impact. This involves evaluating the project across four perspectives:

- **Financial**: Assess financial performance metrics, such as cost savings and ROI
- **Customer**: Evaluate customer satisfaction, retention, and loyalty
- **Internal processes**: Measure improvements in operational efficiency and process quality
- **Learning and growth**: Monitor employee engagement, skill development, and innovation

The following tables demonstrate an example calculation using the BSC metrics method:

Area	Impact	Metric/Value
Cost savings	Reduction in infrastructure and legacy system maintenance	$1,500,000 annually
Revenue increase	Additional revenue driven by AI-enabled automation	$2,000,000 annually (2.2% revenue uplift)
Operational cost reduction	Resource efficiency and reduced manual work	$750,000 annually
Payback period	Rapid return on initial investment	~8 months
3-year ROI	High return over the investment horizon	274% ROI over 3 years
NPV	Future value of project benefits	$12.83M over 3 years (8% discount rate)

Table 10.5 – Financial perspective

Area	Impact	Metric/Value
Customer satisfaction	Improved NPS/CSAT due to faster service and fewer errors	$600,000 value from reduced churn/loyalty
Faster service delivery	Enhanced speed to fulfill customer requests and resolve issues	~20% reduction in service resolution time
Product/service quality	AI improves quality, reducing errors and rework	$400,000 annual value from quality improvements
Customer retention	Increased lifetime value and decreased churn	+5% customer retention improvement

Table 10.6 – Customer perspective

Area	Impact	Metric/Value
Process automation	AI automates manual, repetitive tasks	~35% automation of current manual processes
Efficiency gains	Reduced cycle times and streamlined workflows	$1,200,000 in productivity gains annually
Real-time insights	Faster iteration, decision-making, and feedback loops	$500,000 annual value from faster iterations
Risk mitigation	Reduced operational risks (errors, compliance gaps)	Qualitative and $400K saved via fewer incidents

Table 10.7 – Internal process perspective

Area	Impact	Metric/Value
Employee upskilling	AI implementation requires upskilling for the workforce	$350,000 in training investments
Cultural shift	Transition to a data-driven, agile culture	Improved employee engagement scores
Talent retention	Higher satisfaction and reduced burnout due to AI handling repetitive tasks	Qualitative benefit
Innovation enablement	Teams are empowered to innovate with faster feedback loops	+15% faster time to market on initiatives

Table 10.8 – Learning and growth perspective

Perspective	Metric	Value
Financial	$5.25M total costs versus $19.65M benefits	Short payback, high ROI
Customer	$600K + CSAT-driven value	Higher retention, faster service
Internal processes	$2.45M in process-driven savings annually	Streamlined operations, risk reduction
Learning and growth	$350K investment	Upskilled workforce, cultural improvement

Table 10.9 – Summary view

Based on this BSC-based analysis, the project is expected to deliver significant financial benefits, improved customer outcomes, enhanced operational efficiency, and foster growth and learning.

Case study 4: Agentic AI and the modern ranch—democratizing process insights in a data-concentrated supply chain

In the Canadian ranching sector, smaller producers have long been disadvantaged by fragmented data, dependence on legacy systems (such as the Red Books), and inflexible pricing structures dictated by upstream buyers. The emergence of agentic AI is changing this.

At its core, agentic AI transforms traditional AI from a passive data repository into an active decision-making partner, enabling ranchers to query insights, receive personalized recommendations, and operate with a degree of autonomy previously reserved for large-scale operations.

Challenge

Traditional value chains in agriculture are tightly controlled by large aggregators and processors. Smaller producers, often data-poor and resource-constrained, operate at a disadvantage, forced into price-taking positions with little leverage to optimize their operations or negotiate contracts.

Transformation with agentic AI

Agentic AI empowers ranchers to bridge this gap through accessible, real-time data analysis. Partnering with firms such as AgSights, Canadian ranchers are leveraging tools that integrate biometric sensors, environmental data, and supply chain forecasts to generate insights they can act on immediately.

Let's consider an example:

- A rancher can ask, "How did feed costs correlate with weight gain across breeding groups last season?" and receive AI-generated insights that adjust feed purchasing

- By connecting herd dynamics and pasture data, they can rebalance grazing schedules to improve carbon efficiency and reduce overgrazing risk

Strategic alignment through BSC

Agentic AI is not deployed in isolation—it is framed within a performance-driven architecture. By anchoring key initiatives to a BSC, ranchers can align AI-enabled actions to tangible outcomes across four strategic pillars:

Perspective	Objective	KPI	Target	Initiative
Financial	Increase revenue	Sales revenue ($)	+30% over three years	Market Expansion: Farm to Fork
Customer	Improve satisfaction	NPS	40% ≥ 8+	Product Redesign: Direct Sales
Internal processes	Streamline data capture	New content sourced	+20% in one year	Partner with Local Processors
Learning and growth	Upskill workforce	Competency scores	95% in six months	Training Launch: Feed Optimization

Table 10.10 – BSC view (agentic AI and the modern ranch)

Through this lens, AI becomes a measurable contributor to strategic growth, not just a technological experiment.

The role of BPA and automation

To ensure successful AI adoption, ranchers utilize BPA to visualize and optimize existing workflows. This includes the following aspects:

- Discovering and mapping "as-is" operations such as breeding schedules, calving checks, or pasture rotation
- Identifying process inefficiencies such as manual water tank checks, grazing misalignment, and feed planning to better assign team resources
- Integrating data flows between GPS sensors, IoT devices, and herd management software
- Training ranchers to collaborate with AI agents—blending local knowledge with intelligent systems, focusing on keeping the rancher in the loop

With this, BPA becomes the bridge from data availability to decision autonomy.

Outcome and broader implications

This shift creates a compounding advantage: small producers gain the power to self-optimize, forecast market trends, and even form cooperative alliances with other data-enabled ranchers to compete on new terms. They're no longer invisible nodes in a global supply chain, but active, agile participants.

As Betty-Jo Almond, General Manager of AgSights, puts it, *"AI is giving ranchers access to insights from their own data. Simply asking questions using their phone… is unlocking tremendous potential."*

For organizations invested in continuous improvement methodologies and to further refine operational excellence and translate insights into actionable metrics, methodologies such as Six Sigma and Lean Metrics offer a framework for assessing AI-driven solutions.

Six Sigma and Lean Metrics

Six Sigma and Lean Metrics can be used as a framework for assessing the business value of solutions that incorporate AI and agents. By concentrating on reducing defects and eliminating inefficiencies, these methodologies help quantify improvements in quality and operational effectiveness. This dual approach enables organizations to align innovations with strategic goals while promoting continuous improvement across their processes. The following Six Sigma metrics-based BVA example focuses on reducing errors and improving quality:

Six Sigma Metric	Impact of AI Automation	Quantified Outcome
Defects per million opportunities (DPMO)	AI reduces manual errors in key processes (e.g., data entry, approvals)	30% reduction in defects, moving from 4σ (6,210 DPMO) to nearly 5σ (~233 DPMO)
First pass yield (FPY)	AI automates routine processes and reduces rework	FPY improves from 85% to 95% due to fewer human errors
Cost of poor quality (COPQ)	Lower rework and scrap due to AI decision-making accuracy	$400,000 annual savings (as previously quantified under quality improvements)
Process sigma level	Shift from ~4σ to ~4.8σ-5σ across key processes	Improved process capability index (Cpk) > 1.67
Cycle time reduction	Automation decreases manual processing steps	~25-30% cycle time reduction across automated workflows

Table 10.11 – Example calculation (Six Sigma metrics)

The Lean Metrics view of BVA emphasizes waste reduction and efficiency:

Lean Metric	Impact of AI Automation	Quantified Outcome
Value-added versus non-value-added time	AI eliminates non-value-added tasks (e.g., data gathering, routine validations)	Reduction in non-value-added activities by ~35%
Lead time reduction	AI enables faster process completion end to end	20-25% reduction in lead time per process
Takt time alignment	Improved ability to meet customer demand rhythms	Increased capacity utilization and throughput by 15-20%
Inventory/WIP reduction	Less WIP and backlog due to automation speed	~20% WIP reduction in targeted departments
Employee utilization	Employees reallocated to high-value tasks	Improved utilization from 65% to 80% for knowledge workers

Table 10.12 – Example calculation (Lean Metrics)

Here is a comparison of BVA, BSC, Lean, and Six Sigma concerning business analysis and value realization:

Framework	Best For	Key Weakness
BVA	Business cases and financial justifications	Limited view on non-financial value
BSC	Holistic view of performance across all dimensions	May be too strategic and not always action-oriented
Lean	Waste reduction, faster processes, and better agility	May sacrifice depth of quality focus if overused
Six Sigma	Quality improvement, defect reduction, and process control	Can be rigid or overly detailed for fast-moving organizations

Table 10.13 – A comparison of business analysis frameworks and their suitability

Many successful organizations integrate BVA with BSC to make investment decisions guided by balanced key performance indicators, and combine Lean and Six Sigma methodologies (**Lean Six Sigma**) to enhance operations while maintaining quality control.

The hidden costs of mismanaged AI

As companies increasingly deploy AI as part of their process transformation initiatives, one crucial element must be closely monitored to ensure that BVA remains on track. AI innovation has a hidden downside—one that is costly, silent, and often overlooked. Not all failures are evident during the project's execution; some gradually undermine the process over time. This can be seen in teams starting to second-guess outputs, diminishing confidence in automation, and eroding trust in automated programs, all of which make it harder to achieve the anticipated business benefits.

Additional rework may need to be incorporated into the project scope to achieve the efficiency gains initially expected. Even the most advanced tools, including AI, can be implemented without proper governance and safeguards, or they might be trained on inappropriate data and launched out of enthusiasm or to showcase AI capabilities to the company board.

Joy Mookerji, director of consulting and sales, warns: "*The most dangerous AI isn't the one that fails rapidly. It's the one that performs well enough to obscure its misalignment. Until it quietly starts altering decisions, leaking value, and confidently hallucinating, that's not transformation.*" Joy further cautions about AI, stating that it is "*a liability disguised as innovation. What you don't see can cost you the most.*"

To ensure successful AI governance and promote responsible AI practices, these will need to be foundational assumptions for all transformations and BVAs measuring the future benefits of programs that involve such technologies.

Understanding these hidden risks and implementing robust safeguards ensures that the process transformation initiatives deliver measurable business value and remain aligned with organizational goals.

Summary

Measuring the business value of process transformation is essential for demonstrating the impact of these initiatives and ensuring their long-term success. This task becomes even more critical when the transformation is led by citizen developers or technologists who may lack the tools or experience to capture the results of their work effectively. By combining financial, operational, customer, and employee-focused metrics, organizations can gain a comprehensive understanding of the benefits of process transformations.

Utilizing tools and techniques such as BSC, Six Sigma, Lean Metrics, Forrester TEI, CBA, and ROI calculations provides valuable insights that support data-driven decision-making. Effectively measuring business value helps organizations justify investments, align with strategic objectives, and cultivate a culture of continuous improvement.

Typically, these types of measurements are utilized only at the beginning or end of programs, when teams or leaders seek additional funding. However, this approach is a strategic mistake. While technologists involved in process automation initiatives may undervalue financial analysis, BVA should be a critical activity guiding the direction of your organization's efforts over the long term. Using a consistent BVA framework not only educates stakeholders but also protects against unnecessary scrutiny, especially when the future of your initiative may be at risk.

It is a red flag if your leaders do not invest resources or time in measuring business value. Raising awareness about the importance of this topic and addressing any gaps is essential. Unlike many other technical initiatives, process transformations can impact the bottom line quickly, placing greater responsibility on practitioners to articulate the value of their contributions. Reliable BVA assessments require a blend of process expertise, solution architecture, and financial analysis skills. While it may be challenging to arrive at high-confidence values from the outset, adopting a mindset of continuous improvement, gathering necessary information, and properly validating business benefits will enhance the credibility of your model and experiences.

The next chapter provides a comprehensive summary of the most essential ideas from this book. It emphasizes the significance of well-managed business processes in achieving operational excellence, better financial results, and exceptional customer experience. It also encourages you to reflect on turning your newly acquired knowledge into new career paths as you turn your attention to additional learning opportunities.

Unlock this book's exclusive benefits now

Scan this QR code or go to `packtpub.com/unlock`, then search this book by name.

Note: Keep your purchase invoice ready before you start.

11

A Few Final Thoughts

In this book, you have had a chance to learn how modeling and analysis of business processes can support digital transformation. This chapter provides a summary of the most important ideas from the whole book. You will also find further ideas that will help you improve and practice your process modeling skills, but also, more importantly, create value for your organization.

In this chapter, we're going to cover the following main topics:

- Recap of the key ideas
- Your next steps

Recap of the key ideas

We started by discussing how process modeling supports successful digital transformation in *Chapter 1, Winning at Digital Transformation with Process Modeling*. Processes are the key to operational excellence (which leads directly to better financial results), effectiveness, and the building of an exceptional customer experience. Good processes are efficient, effective (often thanks to process automation), transparent, flexible, and compliant.

Well-managed business processes can give an organization a competitive advantage because, while competitors can acquire the same technology, replicating effective business processes is a challenging task.

That's because business processes require collaboration among many people from different teams, who perform various tasks throughout the process. Without process models, even people in the same organization would not grasp the overall design of a process with all its dependencies. Good process models facilitate communication but also allow process analysis and improvement.

While process automation has been a very popular concept for several years, there are still many areas where digital transformation is needed, because many high-volume processes still do not operate optimally. There are several reasons for that. Among others, knowledge work can be challenging to automate (even with the support of AI). Many people don't understand process theory, apply the wrong tools for the job, or there are too many processes in the company to pursue, eliminating the ability to track and automate all of them using the top-down approach with a small group of specialists. While searching for digital transformation drivers for your organization, consider which topics are most relevant. The more mature your process management is, the easier it is to both improve the customer experience and make processes more efficient (more transparent, faster, and cheaper to run and change).

Process models illustrate the connections between processes' activities and resources providing a shared understanding of the current situation and helping build a consensus regarding the future solution. However, we need to consider aspects beyond processes in our modeling to better understand how organizations operate and to enable smart processes to utilize AI. It is important to note that different modeling approaches can benefit varying needs. Various styles (e.g., structured processes, case collaboration, and IoT/bot collaboration) offer modeling guidelines based on complexity and purpose. The adoption of GenAI tools already helps to jump-start process models for team members by creating models from verbose descriptions through prompting, or through AI-supported modeling tools such as **ADONIS** (with AI Assistant), Camunda's **Copilot**, or **Lucidchart**. For example, Camunda Copilot's intuitive suggestions become actionable advice, enhancing quality and accelerating the development of process maps. These AI-powered suggestions improve the accuracy and efficiency of BPMN processes , ultimately accelerating overall development. Using these suggestions speeds up the creation of process models and saves time and resources while educating users about the art of the possible.

The other new area of opportunity for process modeling involves modeling the interactions of AI agents, thereby augmenting both human and machine resources. In the very near future, autonomous agents will become the primary controllers of processes, managing dynamic interactions and monitoring outcomes in real time. Being able to grasp and visualize these process interactions may determine whether AI-driven actions meet the standards of responsible AI policies or emerging legislations. The value AI brings to process modeling will depend on how AI affects the actual processes modeled and whether the process models represent future designs or representations of exact execution, in-flight, or after the fact, when combined with process and data mining. Ultimately, as AI becomes the controlling manager of processes, from the dynamic assembly of process components and the execution of processes to monitoring process outcomes and adjusting and compensating in real time, your process architecture will offer a set of boundaries, ensuring humans are still in control of their end-to-end processes.

Your key takeaway from *Chapter 1*, is to start by identifying the business goal behind your digital transformation initiative so that it is clear what you want to achieve and how it impacts your processes.

In *Chapter 2, Pillars of a Successful Digital Transformation*, we explored digital transformation. It is a complex topic, and there is no single source of truth or commonly agreed-upon definition of it. However, many definitions emphasize that it is not about using technology for its own sake sake; instead, digital technologies are are intended to transform the way an organization operates, create value for customers, and enhance or introduce new business processes. What we find especially important is the strategic adaptability aspect of digital transformation.

It is challenging to describe modern organizations, as they are constantly evolving, multi-dimensional systems with various dimensions, including business, process, and data architecture, customer journeys, value creation, and more. One of the challenges faced by many organizations is the lack of properly defined processes or up-to-date designs, which often leads to suboptimal results.

There are several scenarios for digital change: top-down, grassroots, legacy modernization, triggered by **mergers and acquisitions (M&A)**, and accidental. Creating a good vision of digital change helps a lot with planning. Ensure that employees are involved so they feel that they helped define the vision, not that it was pushed from the top.

The planning of digital transformation initiatives should cover aspects such as continuous adaptability, disruption of the workforce supported by a strong focus on self-learning, generating and managing intellectual property, planning for the long term while delivering short-term goals, regular plan updates, managing size and scope, and keeping growth in mind.

Your key takeaway from *Chapter 2* is to consistently deliver on the short-term goals of your digital transformation initiative to build credibility and maintain the momentum needed for long-term success.

Chapter 3, The Wheel of BPM Driving Your Competitive Advantage, helped you understand the relationship between digital transformation and process management. Starting a digital transformation initiative without focusing on business processes will create partial results, with minimal possibility to scale your success and transform the entire value chain.

Business process management not only helps reduce costs and increase productivity and quality but also boosts customer satisfaction and aligns processes with an organization's strategy. It is not about running a one-off initiative but rather building a culture of continuous improvement and process thinking.

It takes time to increase an organization's process maturity. It is helpful to remember that you need time to deliver results from projects focusing on digital change and build knowledge and skills in your organization (e.g., citizen developers for people who will be automating processes, but also general BPM knowledge for all employees so that they understand the basic BPM concepts). It helps to build momentum by starting with smaller successes, followed by more complex and challenging projects that can create large-scale results.

There are many theoretical frameworks for launching a BPM program. In *Chapter 3*, we highlighted the following framework: define the scope and objectives (it helps a lot to figure out what past process-related initiatives were and what artifacts they created; also, it is a good idea to invest in training your team before buying software licenses), identify the gaps and opportunities for improvement (process architecture is instrumental here for identifying areas for improvement as well as pain points and benefits; picking the right business area to start with is also very important), develop the business case and roadmap, communicate and align the vision and strategy (you can start small and later add more sophisticated methods to make sure there are many possible ways to communicate what you are doing; support for the BPM from the top management would be very helpful), and establish the governance and roles for the transformation (process owners, BPM team, and the proper tooling, playbooks, and frameworks).

Even when the BPM initiative takes off, it still needs the support and buy-in of senior management to survive. When pitching BPM, ensure that what you propose is relevant and compelling to others, compatible with the company culture, aligned with the strategy, and easy enough to understand (without being too technical). Quick wins showcasing the value of the practice are very helpful.

It helps a lot to convince not only management (sponsors, business leaders, and process owners) but also other people involved in the initiative, such as citizen developers. Consider what motivates the people you want to be involved in your initiative, what worries them, and what they need to know to participate effectively.

You should also invest in your BPM expertise in process design and discovery, implementation (this includes automation), monitoring, and improvement, as well as consulting skills such as presentation, storytelling, and public speaking.

Your BPM initiative needs to deliver measurable results and outcomes. Tracking KPIs that are aligned with the organization's strategy (and communicating them to the proper people!) will help you prove the benefits of your BPM transformation.

Since one BPM initiative is just a start, it is helpful to consider building a BPM community of practice that can evolve into a BPM **Center of Excellence (COE)** that can help facilitate and accelerate BPM transformation through expert services spanning business, process, and technology. This team will spend a lot of time collaborating with other groups of BPM practitioners, such as the citizen developer COE.

It may also be helpful to create a BPM playbook, i.e., a reference guide for implementing BPM that will help you avoid many common errors by educating business teams and providing a set of best practices. This should reduce the risk of pitfalls, such as a BPM initiative not linked with the organization's strategy, failing to deliver measurable results/benefits, or lacking initial quick wins.

Just as we needed KPIs to show the results of the BPM initiative, KPIs can also help measure the success of BPM (or citizen developer automation) and secure funding.

While "one platform to rule them all" may be compelling, you may need to work with several different digital process automation tools and platforms. Each tool may differ its support for BPM standards such as BPMN, DMN, and CMMN; however for now, BPMN is the best option for process analysis and serves as a universal language for describing process work. Also, using BPMN allows easier governance of your processes (ideally with a centralized and standardized repository) and orchestration of the processes powered by various technologies.

When selecting tools for process automation, you need to look not only at the technical capabilities but also at aspects such as scalability, understanding of work predictability, ability to realize and track ROI, cultural fit between the vendor and company, and availability of talent.

For many of those topics, we need enterprise process architecture to make an informed decision, ideally supported by insights provided by process mining.

The best way to avoid common mistakes in launching a BPM program is to follow a methodology that ensures we are not skipping needed steps and. Additionally, learning from the mistakes of aspiring practitioners, such as focusing on technology alone or failing to adapt the approach to the organization's culture is crucial.

Your key takeaway from *Chapter 3* is that BPM as a management discipline not only helps you improve the performance, efficiency, and agility of your business processes but also creates a solid foundation for digital change programs, which ultimately lead to your organization's digital transformation.

Chapter 4, Long-Term Trends and the Impact on Your Job, covered a very important topic: how do all those things impact your career? Digital transformation impacts not only your organization but also your job. Since you cannot always count on the training provided by your employer, it makes a lot of sense to invest in your skills.

Digital transformation and BPM are vast areas, but fortunately, you do not need to know everything to get started. It is sufficient to get a basic understanding of the key concepts so that you know just enough to avoid costly errors often caused by weak spots in knowledge.

While software vendors provide many functional learning materials, having a broader and more business-oriented perspective that comes from learning from several sources instead of relying solely on one software product or vendor is helpful. No company owns BPM as a science or business practice. Business orientation is also fundamental. Often, in digital change programs, it turns out that people lack a shared vision because everyone has a different understanding of the foundational building blocks of the organization (i.e., business processes). That's partly because business processes are in tangible and are constantly evolving.

Business processes are critical because they help improve operational efficiency, create value, translate strategy into action, are adaptable, and allow for continuous organizational improvement. BPM also introduces a process-centric view of organizations, providing a holistic perspective that considers interactions between processes, people, technology, culture, and strategy. It is beneficial to model processes to properly understand those inter-dependencies and organization in some formal way using standards.

Apart from gaining an understanding of digital transformation and BPM, you should also be aware of other significant trends that affect DTX and BPM, such as agentic AI, cloud computing, robotic process automation, process mining, and many others. Their impact is substantial and non-linear, so you should expect that changes may occur faster than we expect and that the future will be very different from the present. Those trends also interact with and influence one another, creating new possibilities for more advanced process management. In addition, they create fundamental shifts and transformations in the market. This can pose a risk to your career and present a great opportunity if you know how to create value in this new environment.

Some skills you need to learn (such as BPM and change management) can be treated as the core foundation of your skillset. They will not change radically very often (even though there have been several significant changes in BPM in the past, such as the transition from paper-based processes to digital ones, and the democratization of automation technologies). On top of them, you can add more technical skills, which will likely require constant learning to stay relevant. Therefore, you should also learn how to update your skills along with changes in the market. Finally, remember to keep up with the latest trends to identify relevant skills you should acquire or update.

Your key takeaway from *Chapter 4* is that BPM concepts are a solid foundation for your other skills and will help you stay relevant in the market.

Chapter 5, Business Process 101, provided you with the necessary theory of BPM. What are the most important things about the processes you need to remember? Business processes are vital for creating value, which is relevant for every organization. Modeling (documenting) processes allows for a common understanding of the process steps and how they interact with other processes and resources to create the desired outcomes, which help the organization achieve its goals.

By managing processes, an organization can increase performance, bring order to chaos, improve operational excellence (as well as the bottom line!), and build a continuous improvement culture. Managing processes also supports changes in business models. Through cross-functional collaboration, BPM facilitates company transformation, and that is not all! Organizations that manage their processes effectively can also enhance compliance, increase customer experience, and boost workplace satisfaction.

The concept of cross-functional processes is very important for professional BPM. To be able to manage and improve processeseffectively, it is essential to have a broader view of the process ecosystem, taking into account connections with other processes, inputs, outputs, and elements that support and guide the process. A good process model should answer the key questions we may have about the process and facilitate communication and knowledge transfer for the purposes relevant to the organization (e.g., process improvement or process automation). It is crucial for processes that span outside the organization. In such a scenario, when people do not have the whole picture, they may create point solutions with limited scope. This creates multiple issues outside that bring chaos inside.

Your key takeaway from *Chapter 5* is that processes are the backbone of organizations. When core processes change, they impact every aspect of the organization.

In *Chapter 6, Establishing Process Architecture*, we continued with the topic of process management, this time, focusing on process architecture. Since processes are very complex entities with many interdependencies, it is very helpful to use something more than a flat list with names, a simple text document, or a spreadsheet to manage them. Process architecture is a perfect tool to facilitate the end-to-end view of processes, understanding the dependencies, and avoiding the problems caused by silo thinking or lack of a broader view.

Process architecture categorizes processes into groups that help understand their role in value creation (i.e., do they create value or provide guidance or resources needed for building value). It also provides a hierarchical view of the processes, allowing for drill-down from the top-level overview process landscapes to the detailed diagrams showing all the steps of each process. Process architecture can also store many process attributes that aid in their management, such as owner assignments or information that supports analysis, including which processes are best suited for automation. Depending on the organization's experience and expectations, process architecture can be built using tried-and-tested standards such as the APQC Process Classification Framework or can be created internally.

Your key takeaway from *Chapter 6* is that building process architecture will help you with other process management activities, both related to detailed process modeling (as it shows you which processes need to be documented in more depth) and to implementing and running organization-wide transformation (because it helps understand the impacts and plan the scope and order of required work).

Chapter 7, Process Modeling Notations, provided an overview of methods for process modeling. There are several approaches to creating detailed process diagrams, each utilizing different notations to visually represent process steps, various flows, and other crucial information. In addition to well-known flowcharts, the **Business Process Model and Notation** (**BPMN**) can be employed to document processes effectively. This method not only enhances a common understanding and collaboration between business and IT users but also supports more advanced documentation, analysis, improvement, and automation of processes. Your key takeaway from *Chapter 7* is that the BPMN standard remains the preferred approach for those just starting their process management journey. But remember that you can start with a reduced set of the most popular and useful shapes instead of learning and using all elements from this notation.

Chapter 8, BPMN – What You Need to Know, and *Chapter 9, Advanced BPMN*, were all about various aspects of BPMN. BPMN allows the creation of both simple diagrams for process documentation and more advanced ones for process analysis and automation. For those interested in creating simple diagrams, learning BPMN can be as easy as learning a handful of intuitive shapes.

For those needing more, BPMN also allows additional object types and attributes that add more precision to process diagrams and enable the automation of such diagrams. Additionally, BPMN is a standard with defined rules of what is allowed and what is not, so if you are using a tool with full support for the standard, you can not only share your diagrams with other tools using common XML-based standards but also check the validity (i.e., whether all the rules of BPMN are maintained) and ideally well-formedness of your diagram with one click.

Your key takeaways from *Chapters 9* and *10* are that BPMN is a compelling method of documenting processes, but learning it does not have to be tough. Start with the basics and only use elements that are helpful and easy for your colleagues to understand.

Chapter 10, Measuring the Business Value of Process Transformation, helped you understand how to approach process management initiatives to make sure they provide value to the organization. Modeling, improving, and managing processes can benefit the organization by enhancing the bottom line, improving customer and employee satisfaction, and many other key metrics. The best way to start with BPM is to build a solid business case focused on value, ensure strategic alignment, use measurements in continuous improvement, ensure that BPM benefits are also visible to customers and employees, and establish a foundation for future digital innovation.

You can use several metrics for measuring business value: financial, operational, customer-focused, and employee-focused.

These are your key takeaways from *Chapter 10*: BPM can bring many benefits to your organization, but if you want BPM to thrive as a new way of working, your responsibility is to deliver results and demonstrate how those results bring value to the organization.

In this book, we have explored many ideas for implementing changes within your organization. As we conclude this chapter section, we want to share some final thoughts on processes and their value.

Processes are one of the most commonly discussed concepts in business; however, many people still do not fully understand their true meaning or role within the scope of enterprise architecture. Terms such as capabilities, process optimization, and improvement are used loosely without aligning teams on their meaning. While process management may not seem as attractive, viral, or exciting as other current topics discussed within the enterprise, it is crucial. Process management forms the foundation for effectively transforming the organization and achieving its strategic vision. While the business strategy defines goals, competitive positioning, and value proposition, process architecture translates these into operational workflows. Well-developed process architectures provide the structure required to deliver strategic programs (including AI-enabled automation initiatives) and drive successful execution.

Changes to core processes are significant because nearly every aspect of the company must adapt when these processes change. Moreover, process management is essential for operational excellence, driving continuous improvement, and harnessing innovation. It enhances performance and quickly brings order to chaos. By viewing operations through the lens of the business process lifecycle, we can accurately identify errors, exceptions, and process gaps rather than perceiving the operational world as an unruly Wild West.

In modern organizations, **artificial intelligence** (**AI**) and automation significantly improve process capabilities. Leadership should make technological investment decisions based on a clear understanding of process architecture, ensuring that the right areas of operations are targets for automationand that business is ready to change how the work gets performed.

Moreover, process models provide a blueprint for work that everyone can easily understand, making daily tasks simpler and changes more manageable. BPMN diagrams can serve as practical communication tools and can be integrated directly into process automation platforms, such as **Pegasystems' GenAI**

Blueprint. This integration allows for the automatic generation of enterprise case applications. Other vendors, such as **Camunda**, **Bonitasoft**, **Microsoft Power Automate**, **Appian**, and **Bizagi**, support direct modeling or importing of BPMN models, which helps accelerate development and shorten deployment times.

So, why should people care about processes? When business processes run smoothly, they enhance the client's experience and improve employees' quality of work life, enabling us to focus on higher-level and more enjoyable tasks. By adequately describing your process layer, you open better opportunities for both life and work.

Your next steps

Through this book, you had a chance to learn a lot about the fundamental concepts of BPM, as well as about process modeling with BPMN. However, you should always remember that models are a great communication tool and a wonderful enabler, but they need to be complemented by other things to create real value. In this chapter, we will share with you a few suggestions for further areas closely linked with BPM and process modeling.

Pick those that look interesting and relevant for you and your organization and combine them with the knowledge and skills from this book for even better results.

If the concept of processes as vehicles for value creation resonates with you, lean management could be a valuable area for further study to help you minimize waste. Additionally, some individuals find that Six Sigma offers useful methodologies aimed at reducing errors and variability.

To ensure the success of your organization's Business Process Management initiatives, consider exploring topics such as **Change Management**, **Center of Excellence (CoE) Playbooks**, and **Evangelism**. Following a certification path, such as the **OMG Certified Expert in BPM (OCEB)**, can also be beneficial. Engaging with peers in professional organizations for practitioners, such as the **Association of Business Process Management Professionals (ABPMP)**, may also provide valuable insights.

As highlighted in this book, process automation is a critical topic. Depending on your organization's needs and maturity, you might want to investigate traditional process automation using **Business Process Management Systems (BPMS)** tools or explore more advanced options such as **Robotic Process Automation (RPA)**, low-code platforms that support citizen developer initiatives, process and task mining, or tools that unify various automation solutions to orchestrate end-to-end processes. At the time of writing this chapter, a term introduced by Gartner, **Business Orchestration and Automation Technologies (BOAT)**, is widely recognized as a key concept in for this rapidly evolving category of technologies. These tools facilitate autonomous automation and integrate elements such as human tasks, AI agents, RPA bots, API integrations, AI platforms, and more.

As you might expect, this area is subject to frequent changes and breakthroughs, unlike the previous topics discussed, which tend to change more slowly over time. Therefore, while the earlier chapters included a section for further reading with recommended books, we suggest checking this book's GitHub repository for the most current set of books and authors' recommended materials: `https://github.com/PacktPublishing/Practical-Business-Process-Modeling-and-Analysis/tree/main/Chapter11`.

If you want to have an overview of the hot topics in BPM, you may also enjoy the series of blog posts about BPM skills published on Zbigniew's blog since 2016: `https://bpmtips.com/category/bpm-skills/`.

Final thoughts

In this book, we aimed to introduce you to a world that might have seemed familiar yet remained largely unexplored. We hope to have broadened your understanding of this area, which, in our experience, is often overemphasized, misunderstood, or overly theorized. There are individuals and companies deeply passionate about the practical application of process science and BPM, and their financial results reflect this commitment. Unfortunately, these voices are often overlooked and hidden within the realms of IT or business operations. They work tirelessly to drive results until they reach a critical scale that can no longer be ignored. Their efforts create tipping points for digital transformation, but these voices often take years rather than months to gain visibility and recognition.

As the world of AI and business come together, knowing how to lay the foundation for AI automation practices will be even more critical than in the past, requiring the foundational knowledge described in this book. The predicted density of AI automation in large companies is expected to increase significantly in the coming years. According to a McKinsey report, 92% of companies plan to increase their AI investments over the next three years. However, only 1% of companies consider themselves "mature" in AI deployment, meaning fully integrated into workflows and driving substantial business outcomes (`https://www.mckinsey.com/capabilities/mckinsey-digital/our-insights/superagency-in-the-workplace-empowering-people-to-unlock-ais-full-potential-at-work?form=MG0AV3`).

A World Economic Forum study also indicates that 41% of companies plan to reduce their workforce due to AI automation by 2030. These trends suggest a high density of AI automation as companies strive to streamline operations and enhance efficiency.

The economic impact of AI is also substantial, with enterprises worldwide expected to spend $632 billion on AI solutions by 2028, accounting for 3.5% of global GDP by 2030 (`https://moneycheck.com/wef-study-41-of-companies-plan-ai-related-job-cuts-by-2030/?form=MG0AV3`).

AI automation will become increasingly prevalent in large companies, transforming how they operate and manage their workforce and processes. Would you want to be ready and equipped for this wave of innovation, which is reshaping the job market by incorporating the universal skills mentioned in our book to your arsenal? We hope so.

We would like to express our gratitude for your attention and wish you success in your AI-driven, process-led transformations. We hope that the knowledge shared in this book helps you avoid unsuccessful initiatives and bruised egos. May it accelerate your career growth, and creates value for your organization while fostering positive changes for your customers, society, and the world.

With gratitude,

BPM practitioners and authors: Jim, Zbigniew, and BJ.

Unlock this book's exclusive benefits now

Scan this QR code or go to `packtpub.com/unlock`, then search this book by name.

Note: Keep your purchase invoice ready before you start.

Index

‹packt›

`packtpub.com`

Subscribe to our online digital library for full access to over 7,000 books and videos, as well as industry leading tools to help you plan your personal development and advance your career. For more information, please visit our website.

Why subscribe?

- Spend less time learning and more time coding with practical eBooks and Videos from over 4,000 industry professionals
- Improve your learning with Skill Plans built especially for you
- Get a free eBook or video every month
- Fully searchable for easy access to vital information
- Copy and paste, print, and bookmark content

Did you know that Packt offers eBook versions of every book published, with PDF and ePub files available? You can upgrade to the eBook version at `packtpub.com` and as a print book customer, you are entitled to a discount on the eBook copy. Get in touch with us at `customercare@packtpub.com` for more details.

At `www.packtpub.com`, you can also read a collection of free technical articles, sign up for a range of free newsletters, and receive exclusive discounts and offers on Packt books and eBooks.

Other Books You May Enjoy

If you enjoyed this book, you may be interested in these other books by Packt:

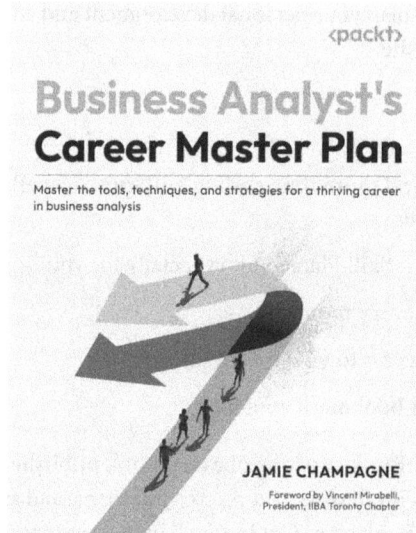

Business Analyst's Career Master Plan

Jamie Champagne

ISBN: 978-1-83620-684-2

- Master foundational skills and apply them to real-world scenarios
- Explore techniques for effective requirements elicitation and modeling
- Improve stakeholder communication, ethics, and leadership skills
- Plan career progression by setting goals and creating a roadmap
- Explore business analysis specializations and find your path
- Stay updated on emerging technologies' impact on analysis work
- Build and grow your career with best practices in a dynamic field

Packt is searching for authors like you

If you're interested in becoming an author for Packt, please visit `authors.packtpub.com` and apply today. We have worked with thousands of developers and tech professionals, just like you, to help them share their insight with the global tech community. You can make a general application, apply for a specific hot topic that we are recruiting an author for, or submit your own idea.

Share Your Thoughts

Now you've finished *Practical Business Process Modeling and Analysis*, we'd love to hear your thoughts! Scan the QR code below to go straight to the Amazon review page for this book and share your feedback or leave a review on the site that you purchased it from.

`https://packt.link/r/1805126741`

Your review is important to us and the tech community and will help us make sure we're delivering excellent quality content.

www.ingramcontent.com/pod-product-compliance
Lightning Source LLC
Chambersburg PA
CBHW061745210326
41599CB00034B/6792